The Voice of the Lord

The Voice of the Lord

Messianic Jewish Daily Devotional

Edited by David J. Rudolph

Messianic Jewish Publishers
a division of
The Lederer Foundation
Baltimore, Maryland

Unless otherwise noted, all Scripture quotations are taken from the *Complete Jewish Bible.* Copyright by David H. Stern, Jewish New Testament Publications, Inc., 1998.

Unless otherwise noted, all quotations from the Talmud are taken from *The Babylonian Talmud* (English Edition). Copyright by The Soncino Press, 1961.

Unless otherwise noted, all quotations from the *Midrash Rabbah* are taken from *The Midrash Rabbah.* Copyright by The Soncino Press, 1977.

All Yiddish quotations are taken from *Book of Yiddish Proverbs and Slang.* Copyright by Kogos Publications Co., 1966.

Printed in the United States of America
Cover design by Now You See it! graphics

04 03 02 01 00 99 98 7 6 5 4 3 2 1

ISBN 1-880226-70-7

Messianic Jewish Publishers
a division of
The Lederer Foundation
6204 Park Heights Avenue
Baltimore, Maryland 21215
(410) 358-6471

Distributed by
Messianic Jewish Resources International
order line: (800) 410-7367
e-mail: MessJewCom@aol.com
Internet: http://www.MessianicJewish.net

Endorsements

The Voice of the Lord

I believe you have done an excellent and very worthwhile piece of work in gathering these daily readings for Jewish believers. I pray that they may be widely used among Jewish believers, but also among Christians who need a different perspective in their daily readings from Scripture and in their devotions.

Edith Schaeffer
Author and Lecturer

David Rudolph has done a masterful job of bringing together the devotional thoughts of some of the top leaders and scholars in the Messianic Jewish movement. A practical, insightful, and even inspirational work!

Dr. Michael L. Brown
President
Brownsville Revival School of Ministry

The Messianic devotional will serve as a useful tool for building the spiritual lives of both Jewish and Gentile believers alike. The Word of the Lord is communicated by the authors with great personal warmth and integrity—it is clear that each one is writing out of personal experience with the living God. I recommend it highly.

Mitch Glaser
President
Chosen People Ministries

You will find yourself moving into vital contact with the "Believing Remnant" among the Jewish people today. Listen as you are addressed from the heart. Then, turn to the Lord in prayer, praise, worship and adoration. I highly recommend it!

Dr. Arthur F. Glasser
Dean Emeritus
Fuller Theological Seminary

As the Messianic movement matures we are seeing the development of those things that make it legitimately distinct within the Body of the Messiah. One of those things that lead to personal maturity is devotional thought.

All legitimate movements develop their own literature which accomplishes the spiritual purposes. We see in this volume a devotional book with different Messianic leaders sharing their reflections on God, Y'shua, what it means to move in a Messianic milieu. The authors of the devotional articles are the virtual Who's Who of the modern Messianic Movement.

The book is well written, extremely well edited and anyone will be drawn to the God of Abraham, Isaac and Jacob by this unique devotional breviary.

Moishe Rosen
Founder
Jews for Jesus

Twenty-two distinguished leaders in the Messianic Jewish movement share their hearts' response to Scripture, reminding us to practice the presence of Yeshua the Messiah daily.

Dr. David H. Stern
Author and Translator

אשת-חיל מי ימצא

"A wife of noble character who can find?" (NIV)
I did, and her name is Harumi

This book is dedicated to my wife Harumi,
who came from the Land of the Rising Sun
to be my lifelong companion.
Thank you, my darling, for ten wonderful years!

Contents

[1] The above western months are approximate midpoints (i.e., Tishri may also occur in September or November).

Introduction

> The voice of *Adonai* [the Lord] causes deer to give birth
> and strips the forests bare —
> while in his temple, all cry, "Glory!"
>
> *Adonai* sits enthroned above the flood!
> *Adonai* sits enthroned as king forever! (Ps. 29:9–10)

Psalm 29 is special. It is a beloved psalm among the Jewish people. Every Friday evening as the traditional Jew prays in the synagogue and prepares to enter into the Sabbath, he meditates on Psalm 29, a text chosen by the rabbis because of its emphasis on the the voice of the Lord and the majesty of God. Seven times in this psalm, David repeats the expression *kol Adonai* (voice of the Lord). He cries out, "The voice of *Adonai* is over the waters . . . the voice of *Adonai* in power, the voice of *Adonai* in splendor. The voice of *Adonai* cracks the cedars. . . . The voice of *Adonai* flashes fiery flames; the voice of *Adonai* rocks the desert. . . . and strips the forests bare." Those who read this psalm are humbled, inspired, and filled to overflowing faith as they hear of the *kol Adonai* and of the King who reigns forever. The words, "the voice of the Lord," serve as a powerful exhortation to give adoration, worship, and daily devotion to the Ruler of the Universe. Such is also the high purpose of this book.

Why a "Messianic Jewish" devotional? A number of years ago I was given a devotional in booklet form. It was Bible-based and easy to read. Millions of people subscribed to it. Nevertheless, I had difficulty using it because it was not written for Jewish people. The language, stories, pictures, even the theology, reflected a Gentile Christian way of thinking that was foreign to my Jewish mindset. Several American ethnic groups had their own "culturally sensitive" editions in English but there wasn't one for a Messianic Jew. The booklet had also been translated into more than forty languages, but the language of the Land of Israel—Hebrew—was not included. "How could this be?" I thought to myself. Here was a Christian devotional that seemed to be designed for every people-group in the world except the Messiah's own people—the Jewish people.

Since that time, I have held a vision for a Messianic Jewish daily devotional—one that would be tailored to meet the needs of the remnant of Israel, but also able to bless the larger body of Gentile believers. I imagined a devotional that would reflect a distinctly Messianic Jewish way of thinking—one that would mine the riches of *Ruach HaKodesh* (the Holy Spirit) and the *Torah* (God's instruction), in addition to the Jewish cultural heritage. I dreamed of a devotional that would be based on the Jewish calendar, with its many seasonal themes, festivals and days of commemoration. Truly, in the Kingdom of God, dreams do come true! It is my hope that this volume will be the first of many such devotionals.

Why are daily devotionals in such demand among God's people? There are many aspects of devotional life: *tefillah* (prayer), *teshuvah* (repentance), *derashah* (searching the Scriptures), and *gamilut chasadim* (deeds of lovingkindness). A daily devotional helps the believer organize and apply these various spiritual disciplines. Like the *kol ADONAI*, it reminds the reader to return to his first love and spend intimate daily fellowship with his Creator. The result is a fruitful spiritual life. Yeshua (Jesus) said, "I am the vine and you are the branches. Those who stay united with me, and I with them, are the ones who bear much fruit" (John 15:5). A good devotional helps Messianic Jews, and all believers, abide in the Vine daily to bear spiritual fruit.

The devotions contained in this book are written by twenty-two servant leaders. Like the twenty-two letters of the Hebrew alphabet—all different—these authors represent a broad spectrum of the Messianic Jewish community. They are Jews and Gentiles, Israelis and Americans, Messianic congregational leaders and organizational heads, scholars and emissaries. Although diverse in background and lifestyle, these authors are united in a common commitment to strengthen the Messianic Jewish movement and the worldwide body of believers in Yeshua. From their intimate knowledge of the Jewish roots of Christianity, the Hebrew language, the Land of Israel, and from their unique perspective of being part of the Messianic remnant of Israel, each writer has sought to lift Yeshua to his full glory. The result is a work that encourages the reader daily to draw living water from the depths of God's Spirit and Word.

Guide to Using the Devotional

You may choose to skip this section and use the daily devotional without referring to the side columns. However, if you are interested in following the biblical calendar, this key will help you understand the symbols used in this book. These symbols—located immediately following the Gregorian date—indicate the Scriptures to be read on this day. A date followed by mutliple symbols indicates that multiple passages are to be read. The side columns also provide information in the following catagories: Biblical—God-inspired festivals and anniversaries of important events noted in the Scriptures, see Appendix A; and Traditional—Man-inspired Jewish cultural celebrations, commemorations, festival names and datings, see Appendix B.

In addition, it is important to note that each day on the biblical calendar begins and ends at sunset (e.g., in 1996, Tishri 10—*Yom Kippur*—began at sunset on Sunday night, September 22, and ended at sunset on Monday night, September 23). Therefore, all Hebrew calendar days noted in this devotional should be thought of as beginning on the previous evening (e.g., if Tishri 10—*Yom Kippur*—is on a Monday, then it began at sunset on the previous evening—Sunday).

Throughout the devotional, Hebrew words are both transliterated and translated. Some of the Hebrew words use the "ch" letter combination, a gutteral sound, as in the name "Bach." Regarding translation, the Hebrew words Yeshua (Jesus), *Torah* (the Five Books of Moses; Pentateuch), *Tanakh* (Old Testament), and *Talmud* (the codified commentary on the Oral Law) are used so frequently that English translation is not provided.

Key to Using the Symbols

NUMBERS (1, 2, 3, . . .) Weekly Scripture readings. See Appendix C, Chart 1.

LETTERS (A, B, C, . . .) Additional or replacement readings. See Appendix C, Chart 2.

מ Festival and fast day readings. See Appendix C, Chart 3.

* Additional readings for New Moon proclamation on the Sabbath. See Appendices A and C.

Abbreviations

Gen.	Genesis
Exod.	Exodus
Lev.	Leviticus
Num.	Numbers
Deut.	Deuteronomy
Josh.	Joshua
Judg.	Judges
Ruth	Ruth
1 Sam.	First Samuel
2 Sam.	Second Samuel
1 Kings	First Kings
2 Kings	Second Kings
1 Chron.	First Chronicles
2 Chron.	Second Chronicles
Ezra	Ezra
Neh.	Nehemiah
Esther	Esther
Job	Job
Ps. (Pss.)	Psalm (Psalms)
Prov.	Proverbs
Eccles.	Ecclesiastes
Song of Sol.	Song of Solomon
Isa.	Isaiah
Jer.	Jeremiah
Lam.	Lamentations
Ezek.	Ezekiel
Dan.	Daniel
Hos.	Hosea
Joel	Joel
Amos	Amos
Obad.	Obadiah
Jon.	Jonah
Mic.	Micah
Nah.	Nahum
Hab.	Habakkuk
Zeph.	Zephaniah
Hag.	Haggai
Zech.	Zechariah
Mal.	Malachi
Matt.	Matthew
Mark	Mark
Luke	Luke
John	John
Acts	Acts of the Apostles
Rom.	Romans
1 Cor.	First Corinthians
2 Cor.	Second Corinthians
Gal.	Galatians
Eph.	Ephesians
Phil.	Philippians
Col.	Colossians
1 Thess.	First Thessalonians
2 Thess.	Second Thessalonians
1 Tim.	First Timothy
2 Tim.	Second Timothy
Titus	Titus
Philem.	Philemon
Heb.	Hebrews
James	James
1 Pet.	First Peter
2 Pet.	Second Peter
1 John	First John
2 John	Second John
3 John	Third John
Jude	Jude
Rev.	Revelation
B.C.E.	Before the Common Era
C.E.	Common Era

Contributors

The following initials are used—at the bottom of each page—to indicate the author of the devotion.

JB Jonathan Bernis

Executive director of Hear O Israel Ministries, a Messianic outreach and congregational planting ministry. Since 1993 he has been organizing Messianic Jewish music festivals in concert halls and stadiums throughout the former Soviet Union to present the good news of Yeshua "to the Jew first and also to the Gentile." He is also an author and conference speaker.

DB David Brickner

Executive director of Jews for Jesus (JFJ). He is a graduate of Moody Bible Institute, Northeastern Illinois University and the Fuller School of World Mission. David has produced many of JFJ's Liberated Wailing Wall albums and written numerous articles.

JC Jonathan Cahn

Congregational leader of Beth Israel Messianic Center, in Garfield, New Jersey. His daily teachings and meditations are broadcast over 300 radio stations throughout the United States and over short-wave. Jonathan also hosts a live, two-hour, weekly radio broadcast ("Two Nice Jewish Boys") heard in the New York metropolitan area. Jonathan is president of Hope of the World, an international ministry to Jew and Gentile.

DC David Chernoff

Messianic leader of Congregation Beth Yeshua, in Philadelphia, Pennsylvania. He is also executive director of Kesher Ministries International and author of *Yeshua the Messiah.* In addition, David serves on the Executive Committee of the Messianic Jewish Alliance of America (MJAA) and its counterpart, the International Alliance of Messianic Congregations and Synagogues (IAMCS).

BC Bruce Cohen

Messianic leader of Congregation Beth El of Manhattan. He has served as principal and teacher at the Chalutzim Academy, a Messianic Jewish day-school;

development chairman and international outreach envoy to Israel, Russia and South Africa for the Messianic Jewish Alliance of America (MJAA); and songwriter, arranger, instrumentalist and producer for the Messianic vocal ensemble "Kol Simcha" and for "Cohen & Rose."

JEF Jeff Enoch Feinberg, Ph.D.
Messianic leader of Congregation Etz Chaim in Buffalo Grove, Illinois. He chairs the education committee for the Union of Messianic Jewish Congregations (UMJC) and has written extensive curriculum materials that are being used worldwide in Messianic *Shabbat* (Sabbath) school settings. Jeff has studied at the University of California at Berkeley, the University of Chicago, Stanford University, Trinity International University, and the UMJC Yeshiva.

JF John Fischer, Ph.D., Th.D.
Messianic leader of Congregation Ohr Chadash, in Clearwater, Florida. He has been active in the Messianic Jewish movement since 1973 and is one of the founders of the Union of Messianic Jewish Congregations (UMJC). He is also head of the UMJC Yeshiva Institute, vice president of academic affairs at St. Petersburg Theological Seminary, and is the executive director of Menorah Ministries.

ZG Zhava Glaser
Chosen People Ministries director of publications. She holds a B.S. degree in Hebrew and Judaic Studies from the University of Southern California in conjunction with Hebrew Union College. She also holds an M.A. degree from Fuller Theological Seminary School of World Mission. A popular conference speaker, Zhava co-authored a book on the fall feasts with her husband, Mitch, president of Chosen People Ministries.

DJ Daniel Juster, Th.D.
Senior congregational leader of Beth Messiah Congregation in Rockville, Maryland, and director of Tikkun Ministries. He has served as president and general secretary of the Union of Messianic Jewish Congregations (UMJC). Dan has done graduate work in Philosophy of Religion at Trinity Evangelical Divinity School and Spertus College of Judaica. He is the author of many works on Messianic Judaism.

BK Barney Kasdan

Congregational leader of Kehilat Ariel Messianic Synagogue in San Diego, California. He has degrees from Biola University (B.A.), Talbot School of Theology (M.Div.) and did a year of graduate studies at the University of Judaism. He is currently serving on the Executive Committee of the Union of Messianic Jewish Congregations (UMJC) and is author of the popular books *God's Appointed Times* and *God's Appointed Customs* by Messianic Jewish Publishers (a division of The Lederer Foundation).

CK Craig Keener, Ph.D.

Visiting professor of biblical studies at Eastern Seminary. He received his doctorate from Duke University and is the author of eight books, including: *The IVP Bible Background Commentary, Matthew* (from the IVP New Testament Commentary Series), and *Spirit in the Gospels and Acts.* Craig is a biblical scholar specializing in the early Jewish context of the New Covenant Scriptures.

KK Kai Kjær-Hansen, Ph.D.

Chairman of the Danish Israel Mission; international coordinator of the Lausanne Consultation on Jewish Evangelism (LCJE), editor of the LCJE Bulletin; and general editor of *Mishkan.* He has also served as a congregational leader in Jerusalem. Kai received his Ph.D. from the Lund University in Sweden.

EK Elliot Klayman, J.D.

Associate congregational leader of Beth Messiah Congregation in Columbus, Ohio. and past president of the Union of Messianic Jewish Congregations (UMJC). He presently serves on a Judicial Chair of the UMJC and is the editor of *The Messianic Outreach.* Elliot has been an associate professor of legal environment of business at Ohio State University and has authored three business law textbooks.

MM Moshe (Marvin) Morrison

Serves on the leadership team of Ohalei Rachamim Messianic Congregation in the Haifa area of Israel. He founded Rosh Pina Messianic Congregation in Baltimore, Maryland, and led it for 13 years. In 1994, Moshe and his family moved to Israel.

RN Rich Nichol

Messianic leader of Congregation Ruach Israel in Needham, Massachusetts. He is the past president of the Union of Messianic Jewish Congregations (UMJC) and is the current vice president of the International Messianic Jewish Alliance (IMJA). Rich has an M.Div. degree from Biblical Theological Seminary, and has studied at the Spertus College of Judaica. He is presently a doctoral candidate at Gordon Conwell Theological Seminary.

RP Ray Pritz, Ph.D.

Director of Hebrew language programs at the Caspari Center for Jewish and Biblical Studies in Jerusalem. He also works half time for the translations department of the United Bible Society. Ray served for seven years as director of the Bible Society in Israel. He received his M.A. and Ph.D. from the Hebrew University in Jerusalem. Ray has lived in Jerusalem since 1973.

RR Russ Resnik

Congregational leader of Adat Yeshua Messianic Synagogue in Albuquerque, New Mexico. He also serves as vice president of the Union of Messianic Jewish Congregations (UMJC) and is an editor of *Kesher: A Journal of Messianic Judaism.*

JR Joseph Rosenfarb, Ph.D.

Congregational leader of Beth Messiah Synagogue in Virginia Beach, Virginia. He has also served in various positions in the Messianic Jewish Alliance of America (MJAA), the International Alliance of Messianic Jewish Congregations and Synagogues (IAMCS), the Union of Messianic Jewish Congregations (UMJC) and the International Messianic Jewish Alliance (IMJA).

DR David J. Rudolph

Associate dean and professor at Messiah Biblical Institute & The Joseph Rabinowitz Graduate School, a Messianic Jewish Bible school. He is also the assistant principal of Ets Chaiyim Messianic Day School. David served as the congregational leader of Shulchan Adonai Messianic Synagogue in Annapolis, Maryland for seven years.

ES Eitan (Andrew) Shishkoff

Congregational leader of Ohalei Rachamim, a Hebrew-speaking Messianic Jewish congregation in Israel. Eitan is one of the founding directors of Tikkun Ministries. He has also served as the congregational leader of Beth Messiah Congregation; principal of Ets Chaiyim Messianic Day School; radio talk show host for "The Gates of Zion"; and faculty member of Messiah Biblical Institute & Graduate School of Theology.

JS Joseph Shulam

Director of Netivyah Bible Instruction Ministry and serves as director of the Messianic Midrasha, a Messianic Jewish Bible School in Jerusalem, and as elder of Congregation Roeh Israel, a Hebrew-speaking Messianic Jewish congregation in Jerusalem. He was educated at Hebrew University in Jerusalem where he received a B.A. in Bible and Bible Archeology and an M.A. in the History of Jewish Thought in the Second Temple Period. He is presently a Ph.D. candidate.

MW Michael Wolf

Congregational leader of Beth Messiah Messianic Congregation in Cincinnati, Ohio since 1977. Michael is also presently an executive member and midwest regional director of the Messianic Jewish Alliance of America (MJAA), as well as head of the International Alliance of Messianic Congregations and Synagogues (IAMCS) Yeshiva committee.

When you seek me, you will find me, provided you seek for me wholeheartedly (Jer. 29:13).

Every year as we celebrate R*osh HaShanah* (the traditional New Year), we are reminded of many important spiritual truths. Perhaps the most graphic teaching tool of this season is the *shofar* (ram's horn) which is sounded in our services. We are told that the sounding of the ram's horn is a call for Israel to wake up and return to God. This holy day is a picture of the future regathering of believers, signaled by the sounding of the *shofar* (see 1 Thess. 4:16–18). Thus, the sound of the *shofar* contains spiritual truth applicable to believers today.

Our tradition calls attention to the shape of the *shofar* itself. Because the *shofar* is curved in appearance, we are reminded that this is the preferred posture of God's people. We are not to arrogantly rely on our own wisdom or to think we can correct our spirit to align with our Father. Instead, we are to take the humble stance of the *shofar*; that is, to be curved or bowed in submission to what God would tell us.

When we rely on our own ways, we so often create our own *tzores* (troubles)! King Shlomo (Solomon) noted that there is a way which seems right to man but it actually leads to death (Prov. 14:12). However, Scripture promises that God has "plans for well-being, not for bad things; so that you can have hope and a future" (Jer. 29:11).

Rosh HaShanah is a time to take an honest look into our spirits to make sure we are aligned with our Father's plan for us. The curve of the *shofar* tells us that the only way to find God's best is to bend our will to his will. May we enjoy a sweet New Year as we give heed to the lesson of the *shofar*!

Today I Will

. . . not rely on my own wisdom but will listen carefully to God's Word that I may be in line with his will.

Sept. 21,1998 (מ)
Sept. 11, 1999 (מ)
Sept. 30, 2000 (מ)
Sept. 18, 2001 (מ)
Sept. 7, 2002 (מ)
Sept. 27, 2003 (מ)

Biblical
Rosh Chodesh
(the New Moon)

Yom Teru'ah
(the Day of Blowing [the *Shofar*])
Annual Sabbath

On this day, the returning exiles offered sacrifices on a rebuilt altar (Ezra 3:6); Ezra read the Book of the Law aloud (Neh. 8:2).

Traditional
Rosh HaShanah
(the New Year)
Day 1
See Appendix B, endnote 5

Yamim Nora'im
(Days of Awe)
Day 1

BK

TISHRI

2

תשרי

Sept. 22, 1998 (מ)
Sept. 12, 1999 (מ)
Oct.1, 2000 (מ)
Sept.19, 2001 (מ)
Sept 8, 2002 (מ)
Sept. 28, 2003 (מ)

Biblical
On this day, the heads of families in Israel studied the Law (Neh. 8:13).

Traditional
Rosh HaShanah (the New Year) Day 2

Yamim Nora'im (Days of Awe) Day 2

Prayer Focus

BK

Blessed are the people who know the joyful sound! (Ps. 89:15[16] NKJV)

The *shofar* (ram's horn) elicits many different thoughts during the High Holy Day season. Its shrill sound beckons us to consider our ways and to turn back to *HaShem* (God; literally, "the Name"). The blast called "*teru'ah,*" sounded in our synagogue services, is the "alarm" sound meant to wake us up! Such is the important theme of *Rosh HaShanah* (the traditional New Year). We must wake up, evaluate our spiritual condition, and turn back to our Father through repentance. For this reason, we tend to think of *Rosh HaShanah* as a serious, even somber, time as we examine our spiritual state.

However, there is always a hopeful note when we look to God. The above Scripture may seem like a contradiction, for we are said to be blessed by hearing the joyful alarm! The sound of the *shofar*, for believers in Yeshua the Messiah, is a mixture of seriousness and rejoicing. We too must evaluate our lives at this season; yet as believers we do not merely hope that our sins are forgiven. Indeed, this is the very reason our Father sent the Messiah to us—that we might have the confidence of the forgiveness of our sins by receiving his love gift.

During this High Holy Day season, let us turn from anything that would hinder our walk with Messiah. Then the *shofar* will truly be the joyful sound to our ears that it is meant to be!

Today I Will

...walk in joy as I reflect on the sound of the *shofar*.

He will bring to light what is now hidden in darkness; he will expose the motives of people's hearts (1 Cor. 4:5).

The sounding of the *shofar* (ram's horn) on *Rosh HaShanah* ushers in ten sacred days that end on *Yom Kippur* (the Day of Atonement). This ten day period is known as the *Yamim Nora'im* (Days of Awe).

Traditional Jews believe that during this sacred time, one's final destiny in the Age to Come is sealed in the Book of Life. Consequently, our people have approached the *Yamim Nora'im* with great reverence—getting right with God and man, forgiving and asking forgiveness, tying up the loose ends of life.

After this life is over, we will all stand before God. Once we breathe our last breath, we will never again be able to prepare for eternity. Therefore, this present life is a sacred time. These are our Days of Awe, given for us to prepare for eternity. We should use them wisely, tying up the loose ends of our lives. We must get right with God and man, forgiving those who have wronged us, so that we can be forgiven. We should also express our love to the ones who need it, for eternity stands just around the corner, and we will never again have these days to ready ourselves for it. These are our *Yamim Nora'im*, our Days of Awe!

Today I Will

. . . live as though it is my last and only day to get things right with God and man.

TISHRI

3

תשרי

Sept. 23, 1998 (מ)
Sept. 13, 1999(מ)
Oct. 2, 2000 (מ)
Sept. 20, 2001 (מ)
Sept. 9, 2002 (מ)
Sept. 29, 2003 (מ)

Traditional
Tzom Gedaliah
(the Fast of Gedaliah)
See Zech. 7:3–5; 8:19

Yamim Nora'im
(Days of Awe)
Day 3

Prayer Focus

JC

Sept. 24, 1998
Sept. 14, 1999
Oct. 3, 2000
Sept. 21, 2001
Sept. 10, 2002
Sept. 30, 2003

Traditional
Yamim Nora'im
(Days of Awe)
Day 4

Prayer Focus

RR

Return, Isra'el, to *ADONAI* your God, for your guilt has made you stumble (Hos. 14:1[2]).

The prophets called Israel to turn away from sin and make *teshuvah* (repentance) unto God. No matter how far Israel had wandered, return was always possible. *Teshuvah* was also Yeshua's opening message: "Turn from your sins to God [do *teshuvah*], for the Kingdom of Heaven is near" (Matt. 4:17). Yeshua, however, shifted the emphasis in his proclamation of *teshuvah.* He came not only to call the lost to *teshuvah*, but to "seek and save what was lost" (Luke 19:10).

When a shepherd finds his lost sheep, he returns with it, rejoicing. Likewise, there is joy in heaven when one sinner returns to God. *Teshuvah* is not so much a religious requirement as it is a restoration of relationship. Our Father has great joy when a child is restored to him, but the "99 righteous people who have no need to repent" (Luke 15:7) never seem to share this joy. The joy of *teshuvah* is for those sheep who know they have wandered and who have been found by their loving shepherd.

Today I Will

. . . look for any trace of self-righteousness in my life that keeps me at a distance from God and unable to experience his joy.

Let those who are suffering according to God's will entrust themselves to a faithful Creator (1 Pet. 4:19).

The *Talmud* (Menachot 29b) preserves a legend about one of the great teachers of Israel, Rabbi Akiva. When Moshe (Moses) heard what a great teacher Rabbi Akiva would be, he asked God why he (Moshe) had been chosen to give the *Torah*, instead of Rabbi Akiva. God's reply was enigmatic but unequivocal: "Be silent, for such is My decree."

Moshe then asked that he might be permitted to see what reward Rabbi Akiva would receive. With God's permission he was able to see that Rabbi Akiva would be martyred, dying a most painful death. Moshe was shocked. "Lord of the Universe," he protested, "Such a great *Torah* teacher and such a reward?" "Be silent," God replied, "For such is My decree."

Yirmeyahu (Jeremiah) put it succinctly, "Don't both bad things and good proceed from the mouth of the Most High? Why should anyone alive complain . . . about the punishment for his sins?" (Lam. 3:38–39)

None of us deserves good from God. If he would pardon the sins of only one person, we would have to say that his grace is infinite. And yet he has provided pardon through the death of his Son to all who believe. God is not confused; he has the very best reasons for what he does and allows to happen. "Are we to receive the good at God's hands but reject the bad?" (Job 2:10)

Today I Will

. . . acknowledge that God's wisdom and his definition of goodness are far above my own, and I will entrust myself totally into his faithful hands.

Sept. 25, 1998
Sept. 15, 1999
Oct. 4, 2000
Sept. 22, 2001 (52/K)
Sept. 11, 2002
Oct. 1, 2003

Traditional
Yamim Nora'im
(Days of Awe)
Day 5

Prayer Focus

RP

TISHRI

6

תשרי

Sept. 26, 1998 (52/K)
Sept. 16, 1999
Oct. 5, 2000
Sept. 23, 2001
Sept. 12, 2002
Oct. 2, 2003

Traditional
Yamim Nora'im
(Days of Awe)
Day 6

Prayer Focus

RR

His grace continues forever (Ps. 136:1).

The Lord is a God of both mercy and justice. He is like a king who had several empty goblets and said, "'If I pour hot water into them they will burst; if cold [water] they will contract [and snap].' He [the king] mixed hot and cold water [together] and poured it into them [the goblets], and so they remained [unbroken]. Even so, said the Holy One, blessed be He: 'If I create the world on the basis of mercy alone, its sins will be great; on the basis of judgment alone, the world cannot exist. Hence, I will create it on the basis of judgment and of mercy, and may it then stand!'" (Genesis Rabbah 12:15)

God must exercise judgment to sustain the moral universe he created, but he delights in showing mercy. When Moshe (Moses) asks the Lord to show him his glory, the Lord responds, "I will cause all my goodness to pass before you, and in your presence I will pronounce the name of *ADONAI*" (Exod. 33:18–19). The Lord then appears and proclaims what the rabbis came to call the Thirteen Attributes of Mercy. Only then does he mention the attribute of justice.

God must exercise judgment, but he delights in showing mercy. He demonstrated this priority once for all by sending the Messiah, his own Son, to take the righteous judgment of God upon himself, and to provide mercy for all who would receive it.

Today I Will

. . . seek to practice justice in my actions, and I will delight to show mercy to those around me.

Shim'on [Simeon] and Levi are brothers. . . . I will divide them in Ya'akov [Jacob] and scatter them in Isra'el (Gen. 49:5–7).

Considering human weakness, it's no wonder that we are vulnerable to discouragement, especially when we fail the Lord. Shim'on and Levi had seriously jeopardized the future of their descendants by their act of violence and cruelty, as recorded in Genesis 34. They avenged the rape of their sister Dinah by killing all the males in the city where the rapist lived. In fact, their father Ya'akov had prophesied that they would be dispersed throughout Israel, thus missing their own unique inheritances.

The prophecy came true for both of the tribes. The sons of Shim'on, rather than having their own territory, were settled in cities within the boundaries of Judah, where they were eventually swallowed up by that tribe. However, for Levi, the prophecy was fulfilled for good and not for evil. Their dispersal throughout the nation facilitated their role as ministers and priests in Israel.

The difference in outcome was due to the faithfulness of the Levites when the majority of the nation sacrificed and bowed down to the golden calf (see Exod. 32). In spite of the overwhelming pressure to compromise in the face of mass defections, the tribe of Levi chose to do what was right. The temptation to submit to idolatry would have been reinforced by the knowledge that, as the above Scripture says, they already had a curse pronounced against them for a past transgression. That could have easily led to despondency since it seemed their fate had already been sealed. However, the sons of Levi stayed faithful to God and changed the curse that was on them to a blessing.

Today I Will

. . . cast off all discouragement and despair over my past sins and failures. Instead, I will remain faithful to my God, knowing that he remains faithful to me.

Sept. 27, 1998
Sept. 17, 1999
Oct. 6, 2000
Sept. 24, 2001
Sept. 13, 2002
Oct. 3, 2003

Traditional
Yamim Nora'im
(Days of Awe)
Day 7

Prayer Focus

MM

TISHRI

8

תשרי

Sept. 28, 1998
Sept. 18, 1999 (53/K)
Oct. 7, 2000 (53/K)
Sept. 25, 2001
Sept. 14, 2002 (53/K)
Oct. 4, 2003 (53/K)

Traditional
Yamim Nora'im
(Days of Awe)
Day 8

Prayer Focus

I am doing something new; it's springing up—can't you see it? (Isa. 43:19)

It was a sea of people in the nation's capital. One million men gathered from every city and state of this country to humble themselves before the Lord God. After wading through the packed crowd, my brother and I finally came to a small place in the center where we could stand with our friends. The assembly was beginning and a mass of men stood to their feet in unison. Suddenly, I could see a giant *kippah* (head covering) and *tallit* (prayer shawl) appear on the fifty foot high projection screens that lined the mall area. "Who is that?" I wondered. Was I dreaming? No, it truly was a Messianic Jew. He was opening the event.

Before a million men, from every stream in the body of Messiah, this Messianic leader declared the occasion a sacred assembly and explained that it was *Shabbat Shuvah*, the Sabbath in the middle of the *Yamim Nora'im* (Days of Awe). Then, making a sound that I'm sure was heard in heaven, several Messianic Jewish men lifted triple twisted *shofars* (rams horns) and blew them. The blasts resonated throughout the mall area and the streets of Washington, D.C. The men loved it! All one million of them shouted, raised their hands and clapped. I kept wondering, "Am I dreaming?"

In the afternoon, I went home and saw two Messianic Jewish leaders on network television. We live in extraordinary times; God is doing something new. Can you see it?

Today I Will

. . . ask the Lord to bless those throughout the world who hear the sound of the *shofar* on *Shabbat Shuvah*. "Lord, may they be used by you."

DR

If he has wronged you in any way or owes you anything, charge it to me (Philem. 18).

Yom Kippur (the Day of Atonement) is a time when we seek reconciliation with God. Yet this reconciliation should occur not only between us and our heavenly Father. The theme of this important holy day should have a direct impact on our earthly relationships as well. Our verse today is directed toward a godly man named Philemon, who had received great blessings from our Father through the Messiah Yeshua. Rabbi Sha'ul (Saul; i.e., Paul) was thankful for such a friend whose faith was evident to all.

However, Philemon was faced with a tremendous test of his faith regarding the estranged servant who once worked for him. Onesimus, whose name means "useful," had proven to be "useless" to his former master (v. 11). In prison, Sha'ul had met Onesimus and led this useless slave to new life in the Messiah. This short, yet moving, letter is Sha'ul's appeal to his friend to forgive this newborn spiritual brother and to receive him for *his* sake. The *shaliach* (apostle) even offered to make restitution of any debts by saying "charge it to me."

This is truly a classic story of what *Yom Kippur* should be all about. As believers in Messiah, we have been reconciled to our Father. "Charge it to me" is what Yeshua was saying as he paid the price for our sins. If we have been forgiven such a debt, do we dare withhold forgiveness from those around us? *Yom Kippur* is the perfect time for believers to share the blessings we have received through our relationships with Yeshua *HaMashiach* (the Messiah).

Today I Will

. . . forgive others just as I have been forgiven through Messiah.

TISHRI

9

תשרי

Sept. 29, 1998
Sept. 19, 1999
Oct. 8, 2000
Sept. 26, 2001
Sept. 15, 2002
Oct. 5, 2003

Biblical
Erev Yom Kippur (Eve of the Day of Atonement)

Traditional
Yamim Nora'im (Days of Awe)
Day 9

Prayer Focus

BK

Sept. 30, 1998 (מ)
Sept. 20, 1999 (מ)

Oct. 9, 2000 (מ)
Sabbatical Year

Sept. 27, 2001 (מ)
Sept.16, 2002 (מ)
Oct. 6, 2003 (מ)

Biblical
Yom Kippur
(the Day of Atonement)
Annual Sabbath

On this day, a new fiscal year cycle begins (Lev. 25:9–54).

Traditional
Yamim Nora'im
(Days of Awe)
Day 10

Prayer Focus

BK

Even if your sins are like scarlet, they will be white as snow (Isa. 1:18).

Since the days of Moses, *Yom Kippur* (the Day of Atonement) has been the most holy day on the Jewish calendar. The focus of this day is the most important issue facing humanity. We are told that this is the day when we are to find atonement and forgiveness for our sins.

In Temple times, *Yom Kippur* centered around the sacrifice of the two goats described in Leviticus 16. The *chatat* (sin goat) was to be killed after the priest had confessed the sins of the nation over it. The second goat, the *azazel* (scapegoat), was also to have the sins of the people confessed over it. But instead of being slain as a sacrifice, this goat was to be set free in the wilderness. By so doing, the people of Israel were to realize that their sins were taken away from them as they trusted in God's way of atonement.

The *Talmud* (Yoma 39b) tells us about an unusal part of the goat ceremony. A crimson thread was attached to the scapegoat and, every year, the thread would miraculously turn white. For the rabbis, this illustrated the truth of Isa. 1:18, that God had cleansed the people of their sin. Strangely, the thread stopped turning white about forty years before the destruction of the Second Temple, around the year 30 C.E. Something had changed! Believers in Yeshua know what happened. The Messiah came at that time and fulfilled what those two goats had foreshadowed. The thread, no longer turning white, was a sign to the world that God sent his Son to be the propitiation and atonement for our sins (Rom. 3:23–25). Have you given heed to the sign of *Yom Kippur*?

Today I Will

. . . let the love of Messiah show through me, knowing my sins are as white as snow.

Only the *cohen hagadol* enters the inner one; and he goes in only once a year (Heb. 9:7).

Oct. 1, 1998
Sept. 21, 1999
Oct. 10, 2000
Sept. 28, 2001
Sept. 17, 2002
Oct. 7, 2003

Y*om Kippur* (the Day of Atonement) is the day when men stand before God, and the sins of God's people are forgiven. Unlike the other festivals of the Lord, the most important practice of *Yom Kippur* was performed in secret. No one saw the atonement that was made on the altar! The central event took place in secret behind the veil of the Holy of Holies, a place where only the *Cohen HaGadol* (High Priest) entered.

The Hebrew word for "holy" is *kadosh*. It literally means "set apart." As children of God, we need to have a secret place—a place set apart from our jobs, our day-to-day lives, and even from our congregation or ministry. Each of these has a place. But the problem is that we easily get lost in them. It's easy, even doing the things of God, to lose God himself! But the secret place is only big enough for us and God.

We need to put aside all those other things and make time to be alone with our beloved. If we dwell in the secret place, then everything else will be in its proper priority. The most holy secret of the most holy day is to come back to our first love and be filled to overflowing in the radiance of his presence, hidden away in our secret place.

Prayer Focus

Today I Will

. . . think of the fact that Yeshua gave his life for me—a priceless gift to make my life a priceless treasure. I won't waste it.

JC

TISHRI 12 תשרי

Oct. 2, 1998
Sept. 22, 1999
Oct. 11, 2000
Sept. 29, 2001 (53)
Sept. 18, 2002
Oct. 8, 2003

The period from Tishri 11–14 is a time to make preparations for *Sukkot* (the Feast of Tabernacles), which begins on Tishri 15. Activities during this period include building a *sukkah* (booth) and purchasing the four species.

The Word became a human being and lived with us, and we saw his *Sh'khinah* [Glory of God] (John 1:14).

When I was young, my family would go to my *bubbe* and *zeyde*'s (grandmother and grandfather's) house to celebrate *Sukkot* (the Feast of Tabernacles). *Zeyde* rigged up an ingenious device to fulfill the biblical command to dwell in *sukkot* (tabernacles). He hinged the roof of the enclosed back porch and attached a pulley. When the holiday arrived, he cranked up the roof, tied it out of the way, and then covered the open space with branches and greenery. The end product, decorated with hanging fruit, kept out the glare of the sun, but allowed us to see the stars peeking through at night.

For almost all of my adult life, I have also built a *sukkah* (tabernacle) for my family to celebrate this holiday. Although mine have been bigger and more elaborate than *Zeyde*'s, they have all shared the same transience and vulnerability. If it rained, we got wet. If it was cold, we sat bundled up in our coats. Whatever the weather may have been, the joy and blessing of this *mitzvah* (divine obligation) far outweighed any discomfort.

Similarly, the body prepared for Yeshua was like a *sukkah.* It was susceptible to cold, pain, and even death. Yet he embraced it gladly for our own sake, knowing that the way would be opened for us to inherit a permanent dwelling place with him in the heavens.

Prayer Focus

Today I Will

. . . enjoy the physical symbols that God gives us to deepen our understanding of spiritual truth.

MM

Yah, if you kept a record of sins, who, _Adonai_, could stand? (Ps. 130:3)

Nordau Mall is an outside shopping area bordering the ultra-Orthodox neighborhood in downtown Haifa, Israel. Several days before *Sukkot* (the Feast of Tabernacles), it is packed with dozens of vendors selling ready-made booths (*sukkot*; i.e., tabernacles), branches to cover them, and decorations with which to beautify them. However, the most prominent items for sale are the *lulav* (palm fronds bound together with myrtle and willow branches) and *etrog* (lemon-like fruit) which are used in worship during the holiday according to Lev. 23:40.

While visiting the mall, I noticed an old rabbi I knew sitting under the shade of a tree. He was intensely scrutinizing the tips of a *lulav* in order to be completely confident that the *lulav* was without flaws. It occurred to me that though the *lulav* might hold up under that type of examination, we human beings could not. Self-examination has value, even though a tendency toward perfectionism can turn it into an unhealthy process (not to mention the human propensity to judge everyone *else's* lack of perfection). The miracle is that, although God can clearly see every blemish in our lives, in his great mercy through Yeshua *HaMashiach* (the Messiah), he chooses to extend to us grace and forgiveness. He uses us even with all our flaws.

Today I Will

. . . be appreciative of God's scrutiny in my life, knowing that it is not for judgment, but for leading me in the everlasting way.

Oct. 3, 1998 (53)
Sept. 23, 1999
Oct. 12, 2000
Sept. 30, 2001
Sept. 19, 2002
Oct. 9, 2003

Prayer Focus

MM

TISHRI

14

תשרי

Oct. 4, 1998
Sept. 24, 1999
Oct. 13, 2000
Oct. 1, 2001
Sept. 20, 2002
Oct. 10, 2003

Biblical
Erev Sukkot
(Eve of the Feast of Tabernacles)

Prayer Focus

Take choice fruit, palm fronds, thick branches and river-willows. . . . You are to live in *sukkot* for seven days (Lev. 23:40, 42).

The *Torah* mandates two visual symbols for *Sukkot* (the Feast of Tabernacles): the *lulav* (the fruit and boughs of leafy trees) and the *sukkah* (tabernacle). These speak of opposite poles of our spiritual experience.

The *lulav* is the symbol that celebrates our entry into the Land of Promise. The Feast of Tabernacles is the season of our rejoicing, the Festival of Ingathering, the culmination of our year, of our labors, and of God's redemption.

The *sukkah*, in contrast, is a simple hut, the dwelling of the desert, of the barren wilderness. As the *lulav* signals abundance and completion, the *sukkah* evokes simplicity and transition. The *lulav* is the emblem of the Promised Land; the *sukkah*, the reminder of wilderness wanderings.

Even as we celebrate our finished redemption, we remember what we were before being redeemed. The God of Israel rescued us out of bondage and aimlessness to serve him; yet, we still have not arrived at the final redemption. Indeed, the presumption that Israel had arrived was one of the great pitfalls encountered in the Land of Promise. Further, our arrival is not complete as long as multitudes remain in bondage. So we "celebrate in the presence of ADONAI" our God (Lev. 23:40) as *Torah* requires, but we also await the final ingathering when all nations will go up to worship the king, and keep the festival of *Sukkot* (see Zech. 14:16).

Today I Will

. . . tell someone who is lost the good news of the *Malchut HaShem* (Kingdom of God) in Messiah.

RR

Celebrate in the presence of *ADONAI* your God for seven days (Lev. 23:40).

As one considers *Sukkot* (the Feast of Tabernacles), it becomes clear why God commanded this time as a central celebration for Israel. The last of the fall High Holy Days, *Sukkot* contains a practical, yet vital, lesson—to reflect on our blessings with a spirit of thankfulness. Since *Sukkot* takes place during the time of the final harvest of the year, this festival was a perfect time to celebrate God's goodness. The four species of fruit and vegetation mentioned in the *Torah* (Lev. 23:40) symbolize the fruitfulness of the land which God brought our forefathers into. It was fitting that our people were exhorted during the days of *Sukkot* to take their eyes off the troubles of the world and enter into a time of thanksgiving.

It should be noted that the early pilgrims to "the new world" also experienced the loving faithfulness of the Lord. They had survived the long journey from Europe and the harsh conditions that surrounded them. Since the pilgrims read their Hebrew Bible, these believers knew there was a holy day of the Jews, designated for giving thanks. The result was the feast of Thanksgiving, which could actually be called the American version of *Sukkot*!

The Feast of Tabernacles is still a great reminder to us today: "In everything give thanks, for this is what God wants from you who are united with the Messiah Yeshua" (1 Thess. 5:18). What joy should fill our hearts as we see our loving heavenly Father providing for our every need! Take a look around . . . the blessings of God will become evident.

Today I Will

. . . ask God to give me a thankful spirit as I see his blessings in my life.

Oct. 5, 1998 (מ)
Sept. 25, 1999 (מ)
Oct. 14, 2000 (מ)
Oct. 2, 2001 (מ)
Sept. 21, 2002 (מ)
Oct. 11, 2003 (מ)

Biblical
Sukkot
(the Feast of Tabernacles)
Day 1
Annual Sabbath

Prayer Focus

BK

TISHRI

16

תשרי

Oct. 6, 1998 (מ)
Sept. 26, 1999 (מ)
Oct. 15, 2000 (מ)
Oct. 3, 2001 (מ)
Sept. 22, 2002 (מ)
Oct. 12, 2003 (מ)

Biblical
Sukkot
(the Feast of Tabernacles)
Day 2

Prayer Focus

Everyone left from all the nations that came to attack Yerushalayim will go up every year to worship the king, *Adonai-Tzva'ot,* and to keep the festival of Sukkot. (Zech. 14:16).

We know that all of God's appointed times have a prophetic significance for believers in Yeshua. *Sukkot* (the Feast of Tabernacles), the last feast mentioned in Leviticus 23, receives special emphasis in the Scriptures. All the other feasts will have already been fulfilled when Tabernacles takes its rightful place in God's timetable.

Distinctive to *Sukkot* is the fact that seventy oxen were sacrificed in Temple days (Num. 29:13–34). According to the rabbis, these were to be offered for the proverbial seventy Gentile nations of the world. Hence, in contrast to the other holy days, *Sukkot* is the one feast that is international in nature.

Why the extended boundaries for this particular festival? As the last celebration on the Jewish calendar, *Sukkot* is seen as representative of the Kingdom of God coming to earth. God will finally complete his plan of dwelling in the midst of his people through the person of Messiah Yeshua.

Because of the prophetic meaning of *Sukkot,* it seems logical that this would be the preeminent celebration of the Kingdom for both Jewish and Gentile believers in Yeshua *HaMashiach* (the Messiah). Messiah is coming soon to dwell with us. Are we ready for the celebration?

Today I Will

. . . give thanks for fellow believers in Yeshua who are from every tribe and nation.

BK

We have a permanent building from God . . . to house us in heaven (2 Cor. 5:1).

Perhaps the most obvious symbol of the feast of *Sukkot* (Tabernacles) is the flimsy hut called the *sukkah* (tabernacle). For seven days out of the year, our people are commanded to dwell in the *sukkah* to contemplate certain spiritual lessons. The very nature of the hut is a graphic reminder about life itself. The structure is purposely designed to be frail, with substandard walls and a roof that one can see through!

The spiritual lessons learned during *Sukkot* serve as a yearly reminder of the frailty of life and our absolute need for God himself to be our dwelling place. Indeed, Rabbi Sha'ul (Saul; i.e., Paul) notes that our earthly bodies are a type of temporary *sukkah*. Despite some short-term delusions from our youth, our outward person is often weak and deteriorating. Our culture, for the most part, is in a battle to build up this *sukkah* with hopes that it will show limited wear.

While it is commendable to keep ourselves in good physical shape, the Scriptures often remind us that the physical world is temporal and passing away. The believer in Yeshua looks with a tempered realism at this life and with an optimistic hope towards the things that are eternal.

As we consider the tabernacle during *Sukkot*, may we reflect on the permanent building of God which is coming—the Kingdom of Messiah.

Today I Will

. . . place greater value on the things of God's Kingdom than on the things that will pass away with this world.

TISHRI

17

תשרי

Oct. 7, 1998 (מ)
Sept. 27, 1999 (מ)
Oct. 16, 2000 (מ)
Oct. 4, 2001 (מ)
Sept. 23, 2002 (מ)
Oct. 13, 2003 (מ)

Biblical
Sukkot
(the Feast of Tabernacles)
Day 3

On this day, Noah's ark rested on the mountains of Ararat (Gen. 8:4).

Traditional
The period from Tishri 17–21 is called *Chol Hamo'ed* (Intermediate Days). In Israel, this period begins on Tishri 16.

Prayer Focus

BK

TISHRI

18

תשרי

Oct. 8, 1998 (מ)
Sept. 28, 1999 (מ)
Oct. 17, 2000 (מ)
Oct. 5, 2001 (מ)
Sept. 24, 2002 (מ)
Oct. 14, 2003 (מ)

Biblical
Sukkot
(the Feast of Tabernacles)
Day 4

On this day, Yeshua went to the Feast of Tabernacles (John 7:14).

Prayer Focus

The Word became a human being and lived with us (John 1:14).

During the days of *Sukkot* (the Feast of Tabernacles), we are to dwell in the *sukkah* (hut) as a reminder of our camping trip in the wilderness (Lev. 23:43). By so doing, we remember that God was faithful to provide for our people on the arduous journey to the Promised Land. The temporary quality of the *sukkah* teaches us that, though our earthly life is frail, all will be well because God is dwelling with us. As believers in Yeshua, we rejoice that God has sent forth his Son, the Messiah, into our midst.

It is natural that followers of Yeshua would celebrate Messiah's birth. Interestingly, people acknowledge different dates, looking at God's appointed times for clues. As Yochanan (John) was describing the first coming of the Messiah to our people, he used terminology which is simple, yet profound: "The Word became a human being and lived [literally, "tabernacled"] with us."

Could the message of Messiah's coming to tabernacle with us be connected to *Sukkot*? Yeshua's birth, probably in the late fall, is perfectly pictured in the Feast of Tabernacles. *Sukkot* seems to be the ideal time to celebrate that God, in the Messiah, was born to tabernacle among his people!

Today I Will

. . . seek to dwell in God's presence, even as he has already come to dwell in me.

BK

For to God we are the aroma of the Messiah (2 Cor. 2:15).

Part of the biblical tradition of *Sukkot* (the Feast of Tabernacles) is the use of the four species. According to Lev. 23:40, these include the palm, leafy myrtle, willow, and *etrog* (citron), a lemon-like fruit with some important distinctions. Similar to the lemon, the *etrog* has a pleasant fragrance, yet it is known to be sweeter to taste.

While the *etrog* is used to symbolize some of the harvest aspects of *Sukkot*, the rabbis note that there is another important lesson associated with this fruit of Israel. The sweet taste of the *etrog* is symbolic of a Jew who has a knowledge of *Torah*. We are to be people who love the good taste of God's Word, as did King David (Ps. 119:103–104).

Yet, there is more to the *etrog* than sweet taste. The rabbis equate the pleasant fragrance of the fruit with a person who lives out the Scripture in his or her everyday life. The believer in Yeshua is challenged by this calling every day. We have come into the good taste of the Word of God. We desire to let our lives of obedience be a fragrance of the Messiah to those around us. Indeed, the *etrog* is a vivid reminder that God desires to be evident in all that we say and do. The *etrog* reminds us of the question, "What perfume or fragrance have we been wearing lately?"

Today I Will

. . . seek to perform a *mitzvah* (good deed) that will give off the fragrance of Messiah.

Oct. 9, 1998 (מ)
Sept. 29, 1999 (מ)
Oct. 18, 2000 (מ)
Oct. 6, 2001 (מ)
Sept. 25, 2002 (מ)
Oct. 15, 2003 (מ)

Biblical
Sukkot
(the Feast of Tabernacles)
Day 5

Prayer Focus

BK

Oct. 10, 1998 (מ)
Sept. 30, 1999 (מ)
Oct. 19, 2000 (מ)
Oct. 7, 2001 (מ)
Sept. 26, 2002 (מ)
Oct. 16, 2003 (מ)

Biblical
Sukkot
(the Feast of Tabernacles)
Day 6

Prayer Focus

The crowds ahead of him and behind shouted "Blessed is he who comes in the name of *Adonai*!" (Matt. 21:9)

One of the beautiful symbols reminding us of the lesson of *Sukkot* (the Feast of Tabernacles) is the *lulav* (palm branch). Part of our tradition is to march in processionals in the synagogue, waving the *lulav* in every direction while we chant from the *Hallel* (Psalms 113–118). By doing so, we acknowledge that God dwells among us. We therefore understand why the Feast of Tabernacles is considered a messianic holiday. It perfectly foreshadows the time when the *Mashiach* (Messiah) will come and dwell in the midst of Israel.

In light of these traditions, a rather astounding thing happened one year in Jerusalem. As Yeshua entered the holy city just prior to Passover, multitudes of our people welcomed him in a peculiar way. "Crowds of people carpeted the road with their clothing, while others cut branches from trees. . . . " (Matt. 21:8) We might think this is a strange way to celebrate Passover. But since the crowds believed Yeshua was the Messiah, it was a perfectly appropriate way to welcome him into their midst! With the chanting of the Hallel, they embraced Yeshua, "Blessed is he who comes in the name of *Adonai* [the Lord]!"

The full meaning of the *lulav* is seen as we welcome King Messiah to dwell in our midst, as many did in his own day. There is a growing number of people embracing Yeshua in our own generation as well. *Hoshi'ana*! (Lord, save us!)

Today I Will

. . . welcome Yeshua to dwell as King Messiah of my life.

BK

You will joyfully draw water from the springs of salvation (Isa. 12:3).

Sukkot (the Feast of Tabernacles) is the preeminent festival of joy. In Temple times, a special ceremony depicted a prophetic promise in the festival. The event was called *simchah beyt hasho'evah* (rejoicing in the place of water-drawing). During the celebration, a priest would take a golden pitcher down to the pool of *Shiloach* (Siloam) in Jerusalem. After dipping it into the water, he would lead a procession of praise back to the Temple, including dance, music and chanting the *Hallel* (Psalms 113–118).

The highlight of the ceremony came when the priest dramatically poured the water onto the altar. Why all this joy? Based upon the above verse from Isaiah, the rabbis taught that this ceremony foreshadowed the time when God would pour out the *Ruach HaKodesh* (Holy Spirit) in the days of the messianic redemption (Sukkot 55).

An amazing thing happened during a first-century *Sukkot* celebration in Jerusalem: "Now on the last day of the festival, *Hosha'na Rabbah* [the Great *Hosanna*] Yeshua stood and cried out, 'If anyone is thirsty, let him keep coming to me and drinking! Whoever puts his trust in me, as the Scripture says, rivers of living water will flow from his inmost being!'" (John 7:37–38) What a statement! By this proclamation, Yeshua was openly saying that he was the Messiah, the fulfillment of this ceremony.

What great joy Messianic believers have on *Sukkot* as we remember that we have found the one who quenches our spiritual thirst.

Today I Will

... drink from the living waters of Yeshua by allowing the *Ruach HaKodesh* to take control of my life.

Oct. 11, 1998 (מ)
Oct. 1, 1999 (מ)
Oct. 20, 2000 (מ)
Oct. 8, 2001 (מ)
Sept. 27, 2002 (מ)
Oct. 17, 2003 (מ)

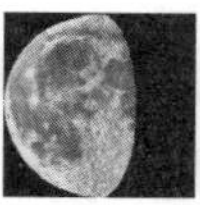

Biblical
Sukkot
(the Feast of Tabernacles)
Day 7

On this day, Haggai received a prophecy about the glory of the second Temple (Hag. 2:1); Yeshua called all who were thirsty for living water to come to him (John 7:37).

Traditional
Hosha'na Rabbah
(the Great *Hosanna*)

Prayer Focus

BK

Oct. 12, 1998 (מ)
Oct. 2, 1999 (מ)
Oct. 21, 2000 (מ)
Oct. 9, 2001 (מ)
Sept. 28, 2002 (מ)
Oct. 18, 2003 (מ)

Biblical
Shemini Atzeret
(the 8th Day
Assembly)
Annual Sabbath

On this day, Yeshua rebuked a self-righteous crowd and ministered to a woman caught in adultery (John 8:2; 7:37).

Traditional
Simchat Torah
(the Joy of
the Law)
in Israel only

Prayer Focus

Those who stay united with me, and I with them, are the ones who bear much fruit (John 15:5).

Every year, as we come to the end of the High Holy Days, we come to the intriguing feast called *Shemini Atzeret* (the Eighth Day Assembly). The *Torah* says that at the conclusion of the seven-day celebration of *Sukkot* (the Feast of Tabernacles) we are to add an extra day (Lev. 23:39). While this eighth day is designated as an "assembly," it may also be translated as "abiding or waiting."

Rashi, the medieval rabbinic commentator, likens the celebration to a king who held a banquet for his friends. It was so wonderful that when it came time to depart, the king pleaded with his friends not to leave but to abide just one more day in his presence. Such is the purpose of *Shemini Atzeret.* It is as if, even after all the wonderful fall Holy Days, God himself is pleading with his people to stay in his presence just a little longer.

The Messiah used this concept to teach his disciples of their need to stay connected to him. The only hope of a victorious messianic life is for Yeshua's followers to stay connected to him in a dynamic way. We must abide in his precepts (John 15:7), in his power (John 15:5), and in his presence (John 15:9) if we are to experience all that God intends for us. The Messiah does not want us to leave him. Have we learned the lesson of *Shemini Atzeret* by abiding in Yeshua in our daily walk?

Today I Will

. . . abide with Yeshua by putting aside my own ways and letting *Ruach HaKodesh* (the Holy Spirit) guide me in the ways of the King.

BK

Pay attention to the public reading of the Scriptures (1 Tim. 4:13).

A fitting close to the fall Holy Days is the joyful celebration called *Simchat Torah* (the Joy of the Law). Although it is not part of the Leviticus 23 list of feasts, *Simchat Torah* was designated as a time to celebrate the completion of the annual cycle of Scripture readings chanted each week in our synagogues. While some believers may find it curious to rejoice in the Law, our people have always found joy in knowing that we have been entrusted with the words of *HaShem* (God; literally, "the Name"). In fact, the word *Torah* is properly translated as "teaching" or "instruction" (from the Hebrew root *horah*), which tells us the precise purpose of the Scroll.

When properly understood, the *Torah* should be viewed not as some negative legal system, but as God's instructions for living a life blessed by him. For this reason, the Lord commanded Moshe (Moses), at the end of his ministry, to teach a portion of the *Torah* to Israel in its chanted form (Deut. 31:19), a tradition which continues to this day.

From the above passage, we are also reminded that public reading of Scripture was a part of worship in the Messianic synagogues of the first century. Timothy, a young congregational leader, is exhorted to give attention to the public reading of the Scriptures.

The Word of God must always be before us if we are to know God's will and how to accomplish it. Certainly, we can rejoice that we have the instruction of God in his Word!

Today I Will

. . . apply the Word of God to my life, that I may experience the blessings of the Father.

Oct. 13, 1998 (מ/54)
Oct. 3, 1999 (מ/54)
Oct. 22, 2000 (מ/54)
Oct. 10, 2001 (מ/54)
Sept. 29, 2002 (מ/54)
Oct. 19, 2003 (מ/54)

Biblical
On this day, Solomon sent the Israelites home after dedicating the Temple (2 Chron. 7:10).

Traditional
Simchat Torah (the Joy of the Law) in diaspora only

Prayer Focus

BK

Oct. 14, 1998
Oct. 4, 1999
Oct. 23, 2000
Oct. 11, 2001
Sept. 30, 2002
Oct. 20, 2003

Biblical
On this day, Nehemiah and the Israelites confessed their sins to the Lord (Neh. 9:1).

Prayer Focus

The joy of *ADONAI* is your strength (Neh. 8:10).

The Jewish Sages teach about a righteous man who was thrown to the lions for an unrighteous reason. The lions did not eat him. A nearby heretic scoffed, "The reason they did not eat him is that they are not hungry." To test his theory, the guards threw the heretic to the lions, and he was promptly eaten (Sanhedrin 39a). This story sheds light on Neh. 8:10. Nehemiah was not saying that our strength is in a feeling of joy we get from the Lord. Rather, he was speaking of strength we obtain by pleasing God. The Hebrew says, *Chedvat Adonai hi ma'uzzekhem* (The Lord's pleasure is your strength).

When we have the favor of God, he will watch over us. The favor of God was on the minds of the people in the above passage from Nehemiah 8. The *Torah* had been rediscovered. When the people came to understand how far they had fallen from God's ways, and the terrible penalties involved, they fell into a panic. Their leaders comforted them with reminders of the promises of God, for they were beginning their return journey towards being a God-pleasing nation.

Today's passage from Nehemiah says that an increase in the degree to which God is pleased with us will increase our strength. It is for this loving purpose that God's Spirit summons us to learn God's ways.

Today I Will

. . . make it my ambition to be pleasing to God.

BC

At last Yosef could no longer control his feelings in front of his attendants and cried, "Get everybody away from me!" So no one else was with him when Yosef revealed to his brothers who he was (Gen. 45:1).

There are many parallels between the lives of Yosef (Joseph) and Yeshua. However, there is one area that many tend to overlook. It is the story of Yosef's relationship with his brothers, who symbolize the Jewish people.

In the above passage, Yosef becomes emotionally moved when his brothers—those who despised him and sold him into slavery—are brought before him. It is clear that Yosef still loves them.

Yeshua loves all the peoples of the earth. He has provided a way for every nation to come to him. Yet, we can see from the climax of Yosef's story a parallel in Yeshua, whose heart longs for his own brothers—the house of Israel. There will be no one else involved when Yeshua finally reveals himself to them. Zechariah says that when Israel sees Yeshua, they will "weep" and "grieve bitterly" because of their role in his death (12:10–11). But today's passage in Genesis shows us yet another parallel in Yeshua's life: Yeshua will gladly forgive Israel and weep for joy at their repentance.

Oct. 15, 1998
Oct. 5, 1999
Oct. 24, 2000
Oct. 12, 2001
Oct. 1, 2002
Oct. 21, 2003

Prayer Focus

Today I Will

. . . set my heart to long for that which Yeshua longs for—the day when he reveals himself to his own brothers.

MM

Oct. 16, 1998
Oct. 6, 1999
Oct. 25, 2000
Oct. 13, 2001 (1)*
Oct. 2, 2002
Oct. 22, 2003

Prayer Focus

He. . . went to the hill east of Beit-El and pitched his tent. . . he built an altar there and called on the name of *Adonai* (Gen. 12:8).

When God calls Abraham out of his homeland, he promises him land, offspring, and a blessing. Abraham arrives at Bethel in the heart of his new homeland, he responds to these promises by erecting two very different structures—a tent and an altar.

The tent is a symbol of transience. You don't really build a tent. When you reach your evening's destination, you pitch your tent; and when you leave, you pick up your tent; after you are gone, no sign remains.

In contrast, an altar is built to be solid and permanent. When Abraham returns to Bethel after his visit to Egypt, the tent is gone, but the altar remains. Abraham lives in the Land of Promise as a nomad, constantly moving, but the promise itself remains firm.

Outward circumstances may change, but the promises of God remain. As the tent reflects the impermanence of earthly things, so the altar represents the permanence of what is holy. A healthy spiritual life embraces both.

Today I Will

. . . maintain my original commitment to God, even though the circumstances of my earthly life may change.

RR

You are to name him Yeshua (which means '*Adonai* saves'), because he will save his people from their sins (Matt. 1:21).

Several years ago I was teaching through the Book of Matthew. When I came to the above passage, I explained to my congregation that the name "Yeshua" means "*Adonai* saves," and that he was given this name because his purpose on earth was to "save his people from their sins."

From the moment that Yeshua took on human form, everything he said and did was focused on that objective. It led him to lay down his life to atone for our sins. "As his representatives here on earth, we need to reflect this same attitude of servanthood," I told the people. "Everything we do needs to be carried out with one purpose in mind—'to save his people from their sins.'"

That message transformed our congregation! For months, our ushers would arrive at the building earlier than usual to prepare the sanctuary. Our *Shabbat* (Sabbath) school teachers served with extra enthusiasm. Our music ministry team spent extra hours in prayer and preparation. All of them declared, through word or deed, that they were performing their tasks for one purpose—"to save his people from their sins."

We need to look at our walks with the Lord in this light. We should begin seeing everything that we say and do with singleness of purpose—"to save his people from their sins."

Today I Will

. . . say and do everything with one thought in mind—"to save his people from their sins."

Oct. 17, 1998 (1)*
Oct. 7, 1999
Oct. 26, 2000
Oct. 14, 2001
Oct. 3, 2002
Oct. 23, 2003

Prayer Focus

Oct. 18, 1998
Oct. 8, 1999
Oct. 27, 2000
Oct. 15, 2001
Oct. 4, 2002
Oct. 24, 2003

Prayer Focus

Since I am going and preparing a place for you, I will return to take you with me (John 14:3).

The ancient Jewish marriage involved a betrothal, which was a commitment of the couple to wed. In preparation for the marriage, it was common for the man to return to his village and build an extension onto his father's house. This, of course, would take some time, depending upon the elements, the help, and the industriousness of the groom.

Meanwhile, the bride would await the return of her man. She would undoubtedly keep occupied in conversation with her girlfriends. The topic would gravitate toward the groom: "When do you think he will finish your house and return?"

Perhaps, when the bride would least expect it, the groom, with his family and friends, would begin the return journey to meet her. The bride, who would watch for the groom every night, would see the bright torches signaling their return and hear the shout, "The bridegroom is coming!" She would run to meet her betrothed.

After the wedding, the man would take his bride back to the house that he had worked so hard to complete. There they would remain for all the days of their life together.

In like manner, our Bridegroom is preparing a place for us. At the right time, he will return to bring us to his Father's house, where we will remain with him forever.

Today I Will

. . . think about Yeshua's return and about the house in heaven that he has prepared especially for me.

EK

Kefa, who had a sword, drew it and struck the slave of the *cohen hagadol*, cutting off his right ear (John 18:10).

Altz iz gut, nor in der tzait is Yiddish for "Everything is good, but only in its time." When Kefa (Peter) cut off the man's ear, he thought, "Aha, the time is right for the Romans to be vanquished." Yeshua set him straight and healed the man's ear. Kefa's timing was wrong.

Right timing is everything. I am always amazed when I speak the truth to someone, and he reacts as if I have attacked him or missed his real need. Many times it was the right thing to say, but the wrong time to say it.

The Scriptures teach that he who sings songs to a heavy heart is like one who takes off someone's garment on a cold day, or like one who pours vinegar on a wound (Prov. 25:20).

Speaking the truth at the right time is difficult if we have not prepared our hearts to understand what is needed. When truth is combined with the right timing and sensitive words, the result is a three-fold cord that cannot be easily broken.

Today I Will

. . . wait upon the Lord's timing and learn the right way to speak the truth.

Oct. 19, 1998
Oct. 9, 1999 (1/B)*
Oct. 28, 2000 (1/B)*
Oct. 16, 2001
Oct. 5, 2002 (1/B)*
Oct. 25, 2003 (1/B)*

Prayer Focus

JR

TISHRI

30

תשרי

Oct. 20, 1998
Oct. 10, 1999
Oct. 29, 2000
Oct. 17, 2001
Oct. 6, 2002
Oct. 26, 2003

Traditional
Rosh Chodesh
(the New Moon)
Day 1

Prayer Focus

To: All those in Rome . . . who have been called (Rom. 1:7)

The Greek word *klaytos* (called) is best translated "invited." As we examine the word *klaytos*, it becomes apparent that it is a call to an elegant banquet, a solemn and special event.

Rabbi Sha'ul (Saul; i.e., Paul) was telling the Messianic believers in Rome that they should treat one another respectfully, understanding that each of them was equally invited to the banquet of Yeshua.

It's quite a feeling to see someone's gold embossed invitation. We treat them with more respect. We honor them more. We have more concern for their feelings. Is this not the way in which we should treat one another?

The angel said to Yochanan, "Write: 'How blessed are those who have been invited to the wedding feast of the Lamb!'"(Rev. 19:9)

What a glorious invitation we, and all believers, have been given. We have been called to attend a first-class affair!

Today I Will

. . . remember that my fellow believer has also received an invitation to the banquet of Messiah.

JR

Teach us to count our days, so that we will become wise (Ps. 90:12).

God is concerned about time. This can be seen in the ancient observance known as *Rosh Chodesh* (the New Moon). Every month, at the appearance of the cresent of the new moon, the Lord commanded Israel to hold a festival with sacrifices and offerings (Num. 28:11–15). The entire biblical Jewish calendar was to be lunar based (as opposed to solar) to give an accurate estimation of the monthly cycle. Whereas the solar calendar focuses on the annual path of the sun, the lunar calendar gives heed to the monthly status of the moon and its various stages. *Rosh Chodesh*—the starting point of the lunar cycle—is symbolic of light being born into darkness. Similarly, the Jewish day starts at sundown, seemingly to express God's intention for the world to move from darkness to light and not vice-versa. "So there was evening, and there was morning, one day" (Gen. 1:5).

Leave it to mankind to change God's calendar to just the opposite! Still, no matter how one may calculate time, the festival of *Rosh Chodesh* has an important lesson for us. Time marches on, month by month. We should see *Rosh Chodesh* as an opportunity to reflect on God's blessings toward us, and to evaluate how we walk with him. By numbering our days, we will walk in wisdom in this present age. Then, in the day of Messiah, we will be confident that we fully sought to do our master's will.

Today I Will

. . . evaluate my schedule and my goals in light of Yeshua's plan for my life.

Oct. 21, 1998
Oct. 11, 1999
Oct. 30, 2000
Oct. 18, 2001
Oct. 7, 2002
Oct. 27, 2003

Biblical
Rosh Chodesh
(the New Moon)

Traditional
Rosh Chodesh
Day 2

Prayer Focus

BK

CHESHVAN

2

חשון

Oct. 22, 1998
Oct. 12, 1999
Oct. 31, 2000
Oct. 19, 2001
Oct. 8, 2002
Oct. 28, 2003

Prayer Focus

For what great nation is there that has God as close to them as *ADONAI* our God is, whenever we call on him? (Deut. 4:7).

Sometimes we feel far away from the Lord. We wonder if he's left us to fend for ourselves. If you're feeling that way today, it's not because God has left you. Perhaps you have moved away from him.

The *Midrash* (traditional commentary) on the above verse states, "Idols are near and yet distant, and the Holy One, blessed be He, is distant and yet near" (Deuteronomy Rabbah 2:10). The gods of the heathen nations are idols made of wood and stone. They are the things that people worship in place of the one true God. They are near because they are tangible, visible; you can reach out and touch them. They are near, yes, but they are also far. They are far because, when you call out to them in your time of need, they will not answer. On the other hand, the God of Israel is far but he is near. He is far because his throne is higher than the highest heaven. He is exalted above all creatures. He is far, but he is also near. He is as close to us as a word uttered in prayer. That is intimacy.

In Yeshua, we have been brought near to God's holy presence, and can lay our burdens at his feet.

Today I Will

. . . draw near to the Lord in prayer and seek to experience renewed intimacy through Messiah Yeshua.

DB

I have learned to be content regardless of circumstances (Phil. 4:11).

In Hebrew, you can't really "have" anything. You can't say, "I have this" or "I have that." At best you can say, "There is to me a house" or "There is to him a car," but you can't "have" anything. As Messianic Jews and Gentile believers, we need to learn this lesson.

What is our inheritance here on earth as children of Abraham? Nothing. We have nothing. But having nothing is a blessing. We are not children of this world who own things. We must teach our hearts this lesson. It is the blessing of our hearts to "have nothing" to worry about, to "have nothing" to be burdened down with, to "have nothing" to be chained in bondage to, and to "have nothing" to be upset about. It's so good to "have nothing"! It makes our burdens so much lighter.

So, as children of Abraham, we need to teach our hearts to think and speak Hebrew! We must unload and let go, taking the "my" out of our hearts and rejoicing in the wonderful freedom and blessing of "having nothing"! For to such belong the Kingdom of Heaven and the one real treasure we do possess—knowing God.

Today I Will

. . . teach my heart Hebrew and let go of my possessions and burdens.

Oct. 23, 1998
Oct. 13, 1999
Nov. 1, 2000
Oct. 20, 2001 (2)
Oct. 9, 2002
Oct. 29, 2003

Prayer Focus

JC

Oct. 24, 1998 (2)
Oct. 14, 1999
Nov. 2, 2000
Oct. 21, 2001
Oct. 10, 2002
Oct. 30, 2003

Prayer Focus

Although the doors were locked, Yeshua came, stood among them and said, "*Shalom Aleykhem!*" (John 20:26).

What did Yeshua say to his disciples after he rose from the dead? The King James translation tells us that he said, "Peace be unto thee." That's a fine translation, but we know that the Messiah didn't speak King James English. He spoke Hebrew. What we read in our Bibles is clearly a translation of the Hebrew greeting that is spoken in Israel to this day—*Shalom Aleykhem*!

The Hebrew word *shalom* means much more than the English word "peace." *Shalom* can mean completion, fulfillment, fullness, soundness, healthiness, wholeness, prosperity and well-being. Our people have greeted each other with the words "*shalom aleykhem*" throughout the ages and on all occasions. But it's very significant that the Scriptures specifically record the Messiah speaking these words after the resurrection, for it is only by the death and resurrection of Messiah that we truly can receive completion—*shalom*.

The Hebrew word *aleykhem* means, "to you," *and it's* plural. So when Messiah says *aleykhem*, he's giving the power and completion of *shalom* to every "you" who will receive it. The Lord is saying to us right now, "*Shalom aleykhem*!" Let us receive his beautiful greeting, and all the blessings of life, fullness and completion therein. *Shalom aleykhem*!

Today I Will

. . . receive the powerful blessing of the words of Messiah in my life. I will walk in his *shalom*—his life, fullness, wholeness, completion and joy.

JC

When Kefa came to Antioch, I opposed him publicly, because he was clearly in the wrong (Gal. 2:11).

If we have mistaken our eternal salvation in Yeshua for a quick ticket to Utopia, then life in the real world can undo us. The Scriptures tell us that there can be value in conflict, if it is handled correctly. The well-known "iron-on-iron" image (Prov. 27:17) teaches that undesirable areas can be sanded away by friction between companions. *Torah* and Yeshua both affirm this principle, saying that we must actively seek reconciliation with a brother, whether we have something against that person or he has something against us (Lev. 19:17; Matt. 5:23–24; 18:15–19). The skill of "fair-fighting" is one of the most precious items in the inventory of spiritual maturity, and disagreements can become vehicles of spiritual refinement that would be difficult for us to attain otherwise.

Eliezer ben Yehuda, who almost single-handedly brought back the Hebrew language into modern use, was viciously criticized by many of the very people to whom he was seeking to impart the blessing of a restored Jewish national language. He said simply, "Bread rises, wine ferments, and brothers are born to quarrel." The fellowship of Rabbi Sha'ul (Saul; i.e., Paul) and Kefa (Peter) was able to stand the test of sincere and even heated disagreement. May ours do so as well.

Oct. 25, 1998
Oct. 15, 1999
Nov. 3, 2000
Oct. 22, 2001
Oct. 11, 2002
Oct. 31, 2003

Prayer Focus

Today I Will

. . . take a sober look at my ability to confront others in a self-controlled manner, and ask God for the wisdom to discern between issues needing active resolution and those I should overlook.

BC

CHESHVAN

6

חשון

Oct. 26, 1998
Oct. 16, 1999 (2)
Nov. 4, 2000 (2)
Oct. 23, 2001
Oct. 12, 2002 (2)
Nov. 1, 2003 (2)

Prayer Focus

So there remains a *Shabbat*-keeping for God's people (Heb. 4:9).

Of all the festivals appointed by God, *Shabbat* (the Sabbath) stands out as the preeminent celebration. Some think that because it occurs every week, *Shabbat* is somehow common or mundane. However, our people have always felt the opposite; that is, because *Shabbat* is so special, it is to be observed every week.

Why is special emphasis put on this holy day? Of the many reasons put forth through the ages, the writer of the Letter to the Hebrews (i.e., Jewish believers in Yeshua) notes a central focus. The very name "*Shabbat*" means "rest," which is a calling upon all believers in Yeshua. God himself modeled the *Shabbat* principle; certainly we who are his children are also to rest from our labors in the world.

Too often we fall into the trap of relying on our own "creative power" and not resting in the Lord. *Shabbat* is God's practical reminder that we are to have a lifestyle of rest in our heavenly Father. He has promised to work all things for his glory, and for our good, as we trust in him (Rom. 8:28). Someday, all believers will enter the fulfillment of *Shabbat* in the eternal Kingdom of God. In the meantime, are we experiencing the weekly spiritual rest that God desires for his children?

Today I Will

. . . relinquish some of my power to create my own world and let the meaning of *Shabbat* bring rest to my spirit.

BK

He . . . put the mud on the man's eyes, and said to him, "Go, wash off in the Pool of Shiloach!" (John 9:6–7)

Oct. 27, 1998
Oct. 17, 1999
Nov. 5, 2000
Oct. 24, 2001
Oct. 13, 2002
Nov. 2, 2003

I love Scriptures that make us stop and think. Why didn't Yeshua simply say, "Be healed of your blindness"? Since there are many kinds of blindness, perhaps the reason Yeshua made clay and put it into the blind man's eyesockets was because the blind man had no eyes. For Yeshua to heal him, perhaps he actually had to make eyes, or a part of them. The Scriptures say that man is clay formed from the dust of the ground (Gen. 2:7). Yeshua said, at the time of this incident, that the reason for the man's sickness was that "God's power might be seen at work in him" (John 9:3). Many of our traditional Jewish blessings call God *Yotzer Adam* (the Former of Man). Here we see the Son of God doing what only God does, and by this he proved himself to be the greater Son of David (i.e., the Messiah) awaited by all Israel (Psalms 2 and 110).

Even as we rejoice to see Yeshua fulfill the Messianic promises, let us determine to remove all limits on what he might do in our lives, or through us. We are his body on earth right now.

Prayer Focus

Today I Will

. . . remember Yeshua's promise to us: "He [who believes in Yeshua] will do greater ones [works], because I am going to the Father" (John 14:12).

BC

Oct. 28, 1998
Oct. 18, 1999
Nov. 6, 2000
Oct. 25, 2001
Oct. 14, 2002
Nov. 3, 2003

Prayer Focus

Those whom he knew in advance, he also determined in advance would be conformed to the pattern of his Son (Rom. 8:29).

A king had twins. The older one was destined to the throne. However, the twins were mixed up at birth and no one knew for sure who was the eldest. To complicate matters, the king told each of his children not to worry, that in due time the rightful heir to the throne would be revealed. As the king got older and older, many—including his royal court—pressed him to make the selection. He would respond, "Be patient, time will tell." He told his wife that the real successor to the throne would become apparent to all. But his wife became frustrated, saying, "If you do not know the rightful heir, then how can others know?" The king refused to select one of his sons, instead saying, "Give it time."

Eventually, one child began to look more and more like his father, the king. That same son also began to act more and more like his father. Then everyone knew that this was the real prince, the successor to his father's throne.

Many profess the name of God, and purport to be co-heirs with Yeshua. However, the true heirs are the ones who look like their Father.

Today I Will

. . . seek to come closer to my Father so that I might look and act more like his Son.

EK

Surely your God is a God of gods and Lord of kings and a revealer of mysteries (Dan. 2:47 NASB).

Oct. 29, 1998
Oct. 19, 1999
Nov. 7, 2000
Oct. 26, 2001
Oct. 15, 2002
Nov. 4, 2003

Yoisher is the Yiddish word for "justice." It is something which every Jew longs for. Some long for it in the coming of Messiah and some in the evolution of mankind. *Yoisher* is essentially the righting of what was wrong.

The injustices that wound our *nafshim* (souls) are often very difficult to deal with. The wounds of life often exile us from other people, and even from God himself. Yeshua will indeed return to set things aright, but what of today's toil? Perhaps our wounds need to encounter the "God of gods and Lord of kings" who is a "revealer of mysteries." He will reveal the root of the wound, help us to understand it, and even heal our wound.

Scriptures show us how God took Daniel in the exile, and revealed to him the love of the God of Abraham, Isaac and Jacob. In the process, those around him were also blessed by God's revelation.

Prayer Focus

Today I Will

. . . not be brought into exile from God because of my woundedness, but I will allow God to heal me.

JR

CHESHVAN

10

חשון

Oct. 30, 1998
Oct. 20, 1999
Nov. 8, 2000
Oct. 27, 2001 (3)
Oct. 16, 2002
Nov. 5, 2003

Prayer Focus

Since the first day that you determined to understand . . . your words have been heard (Dan. 10:12).

Daniel is a good example of someone with a positive attitude. He lived in Babylon during the exile. He was taken from his home in Eretz Yisra'el (the Land of Israel) to be a servant in the court of a pagan Babylonian king. But Daniel never forgot his origin or identity as a Jew. He did not bow down to the idols of Babylon, even at the penalty of death. And Daniel never lost his positive attitude, which rested on his hope and faith in God.

How many of us could keep a positive attitude if we were cast into a lion's den? Keeping a positive attitude in times of trouble is a tremendous statement of one's relationship with God. In fact, such a positive attitude can only come from a very intimate knowledge of the Almighty himself. Similarly, if I knew my boss personally, there would be a trust between us because of our intimate communication. Maintaining intimate communication with God was Daniel's secret weapon against the power of the Babylonian king and against a negative attitude.

Today's Scripture passage tells us that in the midst of Daniel's trials, he became determined to understand and to humble himself before God. What an example of a positive attitude! And because of his faith and hope in God, the Lord heard Daniel's prayers.

Today I Will

. . . approach every situation, no matter how difficult, with a hope and faith in God.

JS

Sir, don't you care that my sister has been leaving me to do all the work by myself? (Luke 10:40).

Oct. 31, 1998 (3)
Oct. 21, 1999
Nov. 9, 2000
Oct. 28, 2001
Oct. 17, 2002
Nov. 6, 2003

Prayer Focus

Miryam (Mary) and Marta (Martha) were two Jewish sisters who were close friends of Yeshua. We all know their story, but as we read it carefully from a Jewish perspective, one interesting point stands out clearly: Marta was not a Jewish mother.

As much as Marta worried in this passage, you might actually think that she *was* a Jewish mother, but as a Jewish mother myself, with many years' experience, I can tell you that she definitely was *not*!

You see, a Jewish mother would never have approached Yeshua saying, "Sir, don't you care that my sister has been leaving me . . . " Rather, the text would read, "It's OK, Yeshua, don't you worry about me. You just go ahead and let Miryam enjoy herself while I slave here over this hot stove . . . don't worry, I don't mind working my fingers to the bone while she lounges there at your feet . . . I'm sure a little Ben Gay at the end of the day will make me feel much better . . . in a week or so . . . maybe."

But seriously, Marta showed deep insight in this passage, because she knew where to go for help. She was Jewish—she couldn't help *kvetching* (complaining)—but she took her troubles right to Yeshua. He's big enough to handle any complaints we might have.

Today I Will

. . . not complain about my problems, no matter how small or large. Instead, I will bring them to Yeshua, from whom comes my help.

CHESHVAN 12 חשון

Nov. 1, 1998
Oct. 22, 1999
Nov. 10, 2000
Oct. 29, 2001
Oct. 18, 2002
Nov. 7, 2003

Prayer Focus

With all kinds of people I have become all kinds of things (1 Cor. 9:22).

Rebbe Nachman told the story of the Turkey-Prince. The king's son went mad, and sat under the table nude, picking on food like a turkey. No one could cure him. Then a wise man was told about the situation and came to help. He took off his clothes, went under the table with the prince, and acted like a turkey. The wise man asked, "Who are you?" "I am a turkey," said the prince. "I am a turkey also," said the wise man.

Upon request, two shirts were thrown under the table. The wise man put on one and said, "Do you think a turkey can't wear a shirt, and still be a turkey?" The king's son put on a shirt. The wise man did the same with the rest of the clothing. The son followed.

Then the wise man said, "Do you think that if you eat good food, that you can't be a turkey?" They ate together.

Then the wise man said, "Do you think a turkey has to sit under a table? You can be a turkey and sit up at the table." In the end, the wise man cured the prince, to the king's delight.

Rabbi Sha'ul (Saul; i.e., Paul) became all things to all men to reach the lost. He empathized with them. This is what Yeshua did when he became a man to set us free from our sin-ridden natures.

Today I Will

. . . meet someone where he or she is, and introduce that person to Yeshua.

EK

All things come from you, so that we have given you what is already yours (1 Chron. 29:14).

One of the first words we learn, especially if we have older siblings, is "mine." And it seems to be one of the first words we are ready to fight for. We hold on to things and are very reluctant to give them up.

Beruryah was the wife of Rabbi Meir, a second century teacher. One Sabbath, both of their sons died while Rabbi Meir was praying and studying at the synagogue. In order not to grieve her husband on the Sabbath, Beruryah waited until after the final *havdalah* (closing of the Sabbath) prayer to break the news to him. She said to her husband, "Some time ago a certain man came and left something in my trust; now he has called for it. Shall I return it to him or not?"

Rabbi Meir replied that of course it was her obligation to return another's property on demand, and only then did she take him to the bedroom where his sons lay dead. As Rabbi Meir began to weep, she asked, "Didn't you tell me that we must give back what is given in trust? 'The Lord gave, and the Lord has taken away'" (*Midrash* [traditional commentary] on Prov. 31:1).

Nov. 2, 1998
Oct. 23, 1999 (3)
Nov. 11, 2000 (3)
Oct. 30, 2001
Oct. 19, 2002 (3)
Nov. 8, 2003 (3)

Prayer Focus

Today I Will

. . . thank the Lord for all that he has given me, and remember that all I have, and all I am, belong to him.

RP

Nov. 3, 1998
Oct. 24, 1999
Nov. 12, 2000
Oct. 31, 2001
Oct. 20, 2002
Nov. 9, 2003

Prayer Focus

Can any of you by worrying add a single hour to his life? (Matt. 6:27)

Yeshua speaks with great compassion on this issue. I can almost hear him reasoning with those suffering from the agony of worry. Who has not experienced that agony?

Years ago a precious Jewish woman attended our congregation. She was a mother to many. Unfortunately, she worried like the proverbial Jewish mother as well. Anxiety was a way of life for her. Of particular concern to her were her own grown children. Whenever I discussed her anxiety with her, she would say jokingly, "My maiden name means 'worry' in Yiddish. I guess I'm just living up to my name." Her name did mean "worry" in Yiddish.

In time, she was diagnosed with a fatal disease. We prayed for her healing, but unfortunately she continued to deteriorate. Naturally, the illness also caused her great anxiety. When she was near death, I visited her in the hospital. She told me she was very worried about her children. I told her she had to trust God to take care of them, since she couldn't. Finally, she truly relaxed for the first time as she gave them to God. Hours later, she went to be with the Lord.

Don't wait until you're near death to deal with anxiety. Choose trust over worry.

Today I Will

. . . decide to not "worry about anything; on the contrary . . . by prayer and petition, with thanksgiving" (Phil. 4:6), I will present my requests to God. Then I will leave it in his hands!

MW

The roar of your [God's] foes filled your meeting-place. . . . With hatchet and hammer they banged away. . . . They set your [God's] sanctuary on fire (Ps. 74:4–7a).

Dietrich Bonhoeffer was one of a handful of German pastors who stood up on behalf of our people during World War II. A study of his life reveals the secret of being able to stand in the midst of anti-Semitism and persecution. Bonhoeffer's love for the Jewish people and his defiance against the German government arose out of his lifestyle of daily Scripture meditation.

Soon after *Kristallnacht* (Crystal Night), November 9–10 (Cheshvan 15–16), 1938, when Nazis smashed the windows of Jewish-owned shops and set fire to countless synagogues, Bonhoeffer sent the following letter to church leaders throughout Germany: "I have been thinking a great deal about Psalm 74, Zechariah 2:8, and Romans 9:4 and 11:11–15. That leads us into very earnest prayer." Bonhoeffer's meditation on these Scripture passages—which all speak of God's faithfulness to Israel—reveals the life of a man who was in tune with the heart of God during dark times. We can only imagine what a difference it would have made if all Christians throughout Germany had meditated on these Scriptures.

Bonhoeffer was imprisoned in April, 1943 for his involvement in the plot to kill Adolf Hitler. He was so hated by the Nazi regime that he was executed just days before the war ended in 1945.

Today I Will

. . . pray that the Lord raises up more Dietrich Bonhoeffers in these last days.

CHESHVAN

15

חשון

Nov. 4, 1998
Oct. 25, 1999
Nov. 13, 2000
Nov. 1, 2001
Oct. 21, 2002
Nov. 10, 2003

Biblical
Jeroboam instituted a counterfeit festival (1 Kings 12:32–33).

Prayer Focus

DR

CHESHVAN

16

חשון

Nov. 5, 1998
Oct. 26, 1999
Nov. 14, 2000
Nov. 2, 2001
Oct. 22, 2002
Nov. 11, 2003

Prayer Focus

Adonai ELOHIM has given the ability to speak as a man well taught, so that I, with my words, know how to sustain the weary (Isa. 50:4).

The prophet says that God has given him *lashon limudim* (a disciple's tongue), that knows how to sustain the weary. This is the gift of encouragement. It is the opposite of flattery, which uses words to entice and manipulate. The flatterer does not bother to discern the true character of the other person, but says whatever he must say to win the person over to his own designs. The gift of encouragement also differs from a mere pep talk that seeks to prop up the weary with positive generalizations. Instead, it sustains the person by observing his strengths, and affirming them in specific terms.

An old Yiddish saying tells us that "words should be weighed, not counted." We will not sustain the weary through an abundance of words, but through words that are carefully chosen to identify with the weary; words that recognize his struggle and affirm the gifts that God has given him to succeed.

Today I Will

. . . look for strengths in my brothers and sisters who may be weary, and I will affirm them in specific terms.

RR

ADONAI doesn't see the way humans see—humans look at the outward appearance, but ADONAI looks at the heart (1 Sam. 16:7).

Nov. 6, 1998
Oct. 27, 1999
Nov. 15, 2000
Nov. 3, 2001 (4)
Oct. 23, 2002
Nov. 12, 2003

When King Sha'ul (Saul) becomes troubled by "an evil spirit from ADONAI" (1 Sam. 16:14), his servants recommend that he find someone to play soothing music for him on the harp. One servant recommends David, the son of Yishai (Jesse) of Beit-Lechem (Bethlehem), whom he describes as "a brave soldier [who] can fight" (1 Sam. 16:18).

David enters Sha'ul's service as an armor-bearer and personal musician. Later, when he offers to fight the giant Philistine who challenges the army of Israel, Sha'ul tries to dissuade him: "You're just a boy, and he has been a warrior from his youth!" (1 Sam. 17:33)

Is David a mere boy, or a warrior? Events prove that the servant has seen something that his master cannot see. David has looked beyond mere appearances to discern the God-given ability that rests upon him.

How readily we are led astray by outward appearances in our appraisal of others (and of ourselves)! Like Sha'ul, we are quick to accept the evidence of our senses and ignore the more subtle inward qualities of a person. We are dazzled by the one who eventually proves to be empty while we ignore the one who is truly gifted. We can assess accurately only as we become sensitive to God's purposes.

Prayer Focus

Today I Will

. . . seek to evaluate others, as well as myself, with a sensitivity to God's perspective.

RR

Nov. 7, 1998 (4)
Oct. 28, 1999
Nov. 16, 2000
Nov. 4, 2001
Oct. 24, 2002
Nov. 13, 2003

Prayer Focus

That they may be completely one, and the world thus realize that you sent me (John 17:23).

Amazing! The Messiah made the unity of his people the key to his redemptive purpose on earth. Before going to Gat-Shemanim (Gethsemane), he prayed the above prayer. Many believers in Yeshua have taught that unity is to be feared. Unity is sometimes decried as the world system of the anti-Messiah. Let us recognize that *false* unity which comes from the evil one is the counterfeit of *true* unity which comes from the Messiah. Yeshua's prayer will definitely be answered.

Rabbi Sha'ul (Saul; i.e., Paul) also tells us that God's appointed leadership is a means for bringing us to unity, to "the standard of maturity set by the Messiah's perfection" (Eph. 4:13). Unity is born of shared commitments and values that are foundational and convictional. Such a unity is shared between Yeshua and the Father. This unity will encompass every biblical congregation, in every city and every nation. The result will be that the world will believe in Yeshua. We will see the unity of Israel and the nations under the rule of the Messiah in the *Olam HaBa* (Age to Come). Do you share God's heart for the unity expressed in Yeshua's prayer?

Today I Will

. . . help usher in *tikkun ha'olam* (world restoration) by praying for the unity of Yeshua's body on earth.

DJ

It is he who puts down one and lifts up another (Ps. 75:7[8]).

Nov. 8, 1998
Oct. 29, 1999
Nov. 17, 2000
Nov. 5, 2001
Oct. 25, 2002
Nov. 14, 2003

It was 1896, and Theodor Herzl, the assimilated Jewish journalist who was to become the "father of modern Zionism," had recently published a book on the establishment of a Jewish state. One day, a very excited man with the long gray beard of a prophet came charging into the room of an astonished Herzl, proclaiming that he was there to help him in his mission. Though Herzl was initially skeptical, this Gentile evangelical minister, William Henry Hechler, proved true to his declaration. He not only promoted Herzl's vision; he stood by him with prayer and encouragement until Herzl's death in 1904, and remained a great friend to the Zionist movement until his own death in 1931.

We often question the divine appointment of people because they don't fit our preconceptions. However, God's ways and thoughts are higher than ours. It may seem unlikely that God would choose a non-religious Jew to lay the groundwork for fulfilling his scriptural promises. Yet, it's just as odd to the natural mind that encouragement for such a project would come from a chaplain of the Vienna British Embassy rather than from the Orthodox Jewish world. Not only is God sovereign in his choices, he delights in confounding the wisdom of the world's wise.

Prayer Focus

Today I Will

. . . cease to question God's choices, or to doubt his wisdom concerning who he calls to do his work.

MM

Nov. 9, 1998
Oct. 30, 1999 (4)
Nov. 18, 2000 (4)
Nov. 6, 2001
Oct. 26, 2002 (4)
Nov. 15, 2003 (4)

Prayer Focus

It is those who live by trusting and being faithful who are really children of Avraham (Gal. 3:7).

It is not enough that in Adam we are created in the image of God. It is not enough that in Noach (Noah) we all have the same father. In Avraham (Abraham), the father of many nations, we receive an everlasting heritage of faith.

Avraham waited more than two decades for an heir to God's promises. The child (Isaac) came by faith to an old man with a barren wife. Through faith, one must wait in patience for great things to grow up!

The *Talmud* tells the story of Choni, a miracle worker in the Second Temple period. Choni watched an old man planting a carob tree and said, "Why bother to plant a carob tree that takes seventy years to bear fruit?" The old man responded, "My grandchildren will be here. Just as there were carob trees when I came into this world, so there will be carob trees for them."

Choni couldn't understand. Then he fell asleep and actually saw the old man's grandchildren taking great delight in sucking the sweet juices from the pulp of a great carob tree. "How wise was that old man," he thought. Choni awoke and realized that his seventy-year sleep was a gift from heaven. Now he had eyes to see with clarity the old man's faith.

Today I Will

. . . take steps of faith to plant a tree in another's life.

JEF

The prayer offered with trust will heal the one who is ill (James 5:15).

Do you want more faith? The solution is not as mysterious as you might think. Faith comes from the Word of God abiding within us. Whether it comes from the gospel, a promise of God, or a statement about the character of God, faith rises in our hearts when the Word of God takes root within us. As we meditate on God's Word and allow it to trickle down into our hearts, the *Ruach HaKodesh* (Holy Spirit) produces faith within. Andrew Murray saw the truth of this when he wrote, "I did not understand that the secret of faith is this: There can be only as much faith as there is of the living Word dwelling in the soul."

Our forefathers understood this principle, as they often reminded God in their prayers: "Do as you have said," and "For you have spoken it." The Word gave them a reason to believe that their prayers would be answered. Let us recognize that our willingness to embrace God's words will determine the power that our words have with him in prayer.

Today I Will

. . . store up God's Word in my heart that I might have greater faith to pray.

Nov. 10, 1998
Oct. 31, 1999
Nov. 19, 2000
Nov. 7, 2001
Oct. 27, 2002
Nov. 16, 2003

Prayer Focus

DR

CHESHVAN 22 חשון

Nov. 11, 1998
Nov. 1, 1999
Nov. 20, 2000
Nov. 8, 2001
Oct. 28, 2002
Nov. 17, 2003

Prayer Focus

But you, Isra'el, my servant; Ya'akov, whom I have chosen, descendants of Avraham my friend (Isa. 41:8).

Amazing! God calls Abraham his friend. The King of the universe, the Holy One, invites a human being to become an intimate friend. Wondrous again is Yeshua's statement in John 15:15: "I no longer call you slaves . . . but I have called you friends." Those who follow him are not just his students or followers, but his friends.

But what does this friendship look like? How do we experience friendship with the God of Israel and with his Messiah? We must partner with God to work alongside him. Jewish tradition teaches that redemption is accomplished only by God working with men and women. How is this so? Because we are his highest creation.

Each day as we love others—as we pursue justice and goodness—we live out our friendship with God. In practical terms, we relate to God as our friend when we comfort a sad child, when we write a letter to a government official protesting an incident of gross injustice, when we lend an attentive ear to someone who is lonely, and when we make out a check to help alleviate suffering elsewhere in the world.

Today, we must make it a point to walk as God's friends by partnering with him to accomplish his work in the world. When the day is over, we will enjoy fellowship with his *Ruach* (Spirit), as he whispers to our souls, "Well done, my friend. We walked and worked together today."

Today I Will

. . . walk as God's friend by doing his work alongside him.

RN

Don't worry about tomorrow—tomorrow will worry about itself (Matt. 6:34).

Nov. 12, 1998
Nov. 2, 1999
Nov. 21, 2000
Nov. 9, 2001
Oct. 29, 2002
Nov. 18, 2003

O *if morgen zol Got zorgen* ("Let God worry about tomorrow"). This Yiddish phrase rhymes beautifully. Oh that we could learn Yiddish!

We can "what-if" our day away. There is the story of a man who had an apple stand. Next to him was another apple stand. Day after day he was being outsold and his income kept decreasing. He went to the rabbi and told him the dilemma. The rabbi went to the stand, saw what was happening, and told the man to increase the price of his apples over that of his competitor. Soon people began to buy more and more apples from him. He went to his rabbi, told him the story and asked why people would pay more. The rabbi said, "It was not the quality of your apples but the nature of your attitude. Your face and disposition devalued the way you looked at people and your product. Your worry pushed your customers away."

Worry can permeate our entire being. Not only will it push people away, it can also immobilize us emotionally. Let us cast our cares on Yeshua, for he cares for us.

Prayer Focus

Today I Will

. . . listen to what the Lord is saying to me about my situation and allow him to speak into my worry.

JR

Nov. 13, 1998
Nov. 3, 1999
Nov. 22, 2000
Nov. 10, 2001 (5)*
Oct. 30, 2002
Nov. 19, 2003

Prayer Focus

I am the real vine and my Father is the gardener (John 15:1).

In the above Scripture, Yeshua draws on vine imagery familiar to his hearers, and incorporates agricultural principles common to their experience. He does this to teach us the necessity of being fruitful followers. The "fruit" he has in mind is the same as that which Rabbi Sha'ul (Saul; i.e., Paul) refers to as the "fruit of the Spirit" (Gal. 5:22–23), and that which Yeshua himself describes in Matt. 7:16–20. Yeshua wants each of us to bear spiritual fruit.

Because fertile soil and adequate water were scarce in Israel, the gardener had to ensure that every part of his land, and every plant, was as productive as possible. He made every effort to make sure that each vine would produce as much fruit as it could. Branches bearing fruit were pruned (cut back) to produce even more fruit. The branches not producing fruit were not cut off, for this would have ended their "fruit-bearing lives" and would have undercut the gardener's ultimate purpose to do everything possible to increase his yield. Rather, the gardener would lift up the unproductive branches ("lift up" is the other common meaning of the Greek term usually translated "cut off" in John 15:2). This would better expose them to the beneficial effects of light and rain, and would give them a better opportunity to grow. Lifting up the unproductive branches was yet another part of the gardener's unceasing and tireless efforts to improve productivity.

Similarly, God will do everything possible to help us grow and be fruitful. He tenderly brings some of us to the sun and rain, to give us opportunities to be productive. However, God prunes those of us who are growing and producing well, for even greater fruitfulness. While the pruning is not always pleasant, the results are beneficial. Let us welcome whatever God does to help us grow.

Today I Will

. . . be responsive to the heavenly Gardener's efforts to make me more fruitful for him.

JF

I will put my *Torah* within them and write it on their hearts (Jer. 31:33[32]).

Perhaps you've heard the criticism that states: "Since we're no longer under the Law but under grace, Messianic Judaism is legalism." While it is true that we are no longer under the Law (in the Romans 6 context), neither has the Law been done away with. In Matt. 5:17, Yeshua says that he did not come "to abolish [the Law] but to complete" it. Today, under the New Covenant, our relationship to the Law has changed. No longer is it written on tablets of stone but on our very own hearts, that we might both intimately know the Law and desire to obey it.

Before I trusted in Messiah, I had a habit of going into the grocery store, pocketing some delectable snack and walking out—without paying for it! One week after I accepted Yeshua, I went to the local market and, without really thinking about it, grabbed a can of nuts, shoved it in my pocket, and walked out of the store.

I wasn't out of the market five minutes before I heard a voice inside of me, saying, "You shall not steal." Though I didn't yet know the Scriptures, I felt the conviction of sin in my heart. Eventually I repented. The *Ruach HaKodesh* (Holy Spirit) had written God's Law upon my heart.

What is our relationship to the Law? It is written on our hearts. All we need to do is listen and obey.

Today I Will

. . . obey the Law of God, which he has written upon my heart by his Spirit.

Nov. 14, 1998 (5)*
Nov. 4, 1999
Nov. 23, 2000
Nov. 11, 2001
Oct. 31, 2002
Nov. 20, 2003

Prayer Focus

JB

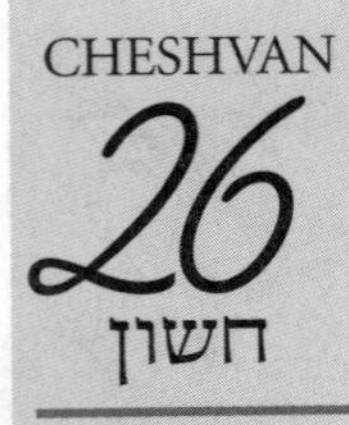
CHESHVAN 26 חשון

Nov. 15, 1998
Nov. 5, 1999
Nov. 24, 2000
Nov. 12, 2001
Nov. 1, 2002
Nov. 21, 2003

Prayer Focus

I wish everyone were like me; but each has his own gift from God, one this, another that (1 Cor. 7:7).

V*en ale mentshen zollen tsien oif eyn zait, volt zich di velt ibergekert* is Yiddish for "If all men pulled in one direction, the world would topple over." Students imitate their teachers. We sometimes imitate TV ads. We tend to imitate whatever has benefited others, thinking it will benefit us.

In the above Scripture, Rabbi Sha'ul (Saul; i.e., Paul) uses the word *thelo*, which may be translated in this context as "I wish" or "I desire." And what was Sha'ul's desire? That everyone be as he is; in this case, unmarried and thereby able to serve the Lord with all of his time and devotion.

What follows, however, is important. Each person has his or her own *charis* (gift) that befits who that person is, according to the design of the Creator. Everyone cannot do the same work. Thus, the distinctiveness of our labors, although knit together with others, is still important in Messiah's Kingdom.

Today I Will

. . . thank the Lord for giving me work and gifts in his Kingdom which are important and significant.

JR

I'll put up three shelters if you want—one for you, one for Moshe and one for Eliyahu (Matt. 17:4).

In what had to be the greatest spiritual experience of his life, Kefa (Peter), along with Ya'akov (James) and Yochanan (John), witnessed the transformation of Yeshua into all his glory. In a well-meaning but misguided gesture, Kefa volunteered to build dwellings for Yeshua, Moshe (Moses) and Eliyahu (Elijah).

It is, and has always been, human nature to memorialize divine events in the same way that Kefa offers to do here. Many churches, shrines, monasteries, mosques, statues, and monuments that now litter the Holy Land were erected with just such a purpose in mind.

The people who built those memorials meant for us to see them and remember what God had done. In itself, there is nothing wrong with this; it is important to remember the past. Unfortunately, history has also shown us that the greatest opponents of any new revival or move of God are those who were a part of the move of God which preceded it. Any time people choose to exalt a move of God above the Creator himself, they risk the danger of falling into mere religion and idolatry instead of a growing and changing relationship with God.

God didn't want Kefa to build memorials. Instead, God refocused his heart on the one deserving of worship, saying, "This is my beloved Son, whom I love, with whom I am well pleased. Listen to him!" (Matt. 17:5)

This is the key to maintaining a true relationship with the Lord: continually seek to "listen to him." Whenever we hang on to what God did *previously* or the way he did it *before*, we miss the fresh thing he is doing today.

Today I Will

. . . lay aside the past and set my heart to hear Messiah in a fresh way and respond to him in the "now" of my life.

Nov. 16, 1998
Nov. 6, 1999 (5)*
Nov. 25, 2000 (5)*
Nov. 13, 2001
Nov. 2, 2002 (5)*
Nov. 22, 2003 (5)*

Prayer Focus

JB

CHESHVAN 28 חשון

Nov. 17, 1998
Nov. 7, 1999
Nov. 26, 2000
Nov. 14, 2001
Nov. 3, 2002
Nov. 23, 2003

Prayer Focus

The existing authorities have been placed where they are by God (Rom. 13:1).

We may not always agree with those who govern us, but respect is another matter. David maintained respect even when King Sha'ul (Saul) hunted him. When we realize that leaders are "placed where they are by God," then respect for God's sovereignty should guide our attitudes and actions. Sometimes, however, the person in the position of authority should not be followed. Sometimes matters of conscience or observance of God's Law may require circumventing the law of the land.

Consider the story of Yehudah and Antoninus. Both were newborns in the days of the Emperor Hadrian. Rabbi Shim'on, head of the *Sanhedrin* (Jewish High Court) disobeyed Roman law by circumcising Yehudah, his son. (Circumcision was illegal in the days of Hadrian.) Mother and son were sent to Rome for trial. On the way, they stopped at an inn, where Yehudah's mother told her story. Deeply moved, the innkeeper's wife said, "Leave your baby here and take my son Antoninus to Rome. When the Emperor sees an uncircumcised child, you will be set free to return here."

The babies were exchanged. At Rome, the Emperor saw the uncircumcised baby and exclaimed, "What use is this law, if the God of Israel can make this baby whole?" The law was repealed. Mother and child were sent home. Back at the inn, the babies were exchanged once again. One grew up to become Rabbi Yehudah HaNasi, head of the *Sanhedrin*, and the other became Antoninus, Emperor of Rome and friend of the Jews.

Today I Will

. . . show respect for authority figures with whom I disagree, and recognize when obedience to God's law might require disobeying the law of the land.

JEF

How can you believe, when you receive glory [praise] from one another, and you do not seek the glory that is from the *one and* only God? (John 5:44 NASB)

Everyone looks for approval. From our earliest years, we thrive on our parents' approval, or starve for lack of it. Later, we receive approval from teachers, friends, and acquaintances. For most people, this approval helps shape our patterns of behavior, hopefully for the good. Due to the weakness of the flesh, however, the search for approval can easily become a hindrance to moral and spiritual development.

When we are born from above, a transformation begins. We have another Father whose approval is always separate from his love. God told David concerning his seed, "I will be a father to him, and he will be a son to Me; when he commits iniquity, I will correct him with the rod of men and the strokes of the sons of men, but My lovingkindness shall not depart from him" (2 Sam. 7:14–15 NASB). As this transformation continues, the approval of men begins to take a back seat to the approval of God. We can facilitate this transformation by viewing God as our unconditionally loving Father who works through our weaknesses and insecurities as we trust and obey him.

The word for "believe," in today's Scripture verse, can mean "to put confidence in." Even believers can struggle to put their confidence in God, because they find human approval so important. As God reveals his fatherly love, our confidence increases, and our hunger for men's approval decreases.

Today I Will

. . . choose to seek approval from my Father in heaven first. Pleasing him through obedience will be my greatest joy.

Nov. 18, 1998
Nov. 8, 1999
Nov. 27, 2000
Nov. 15, 2001
Nov. 4, 2002
Nov. 24, 2003

Prayer Focus

MW

CHESHVAN

30

חשון

Cheshvan usually has only 29 days.

Nov. 19, 1998
Nov. 9, 1999
Nov. 5, 2002
Nov. 25, 2003

Traditional *Rosh Chodesh* (the New Moon) Day 1

Prayer Focus

Nathan then said to David, "You are the man" (2 Sam. 12:7 NASB).

The *Talmud* (Sanhedrin 39a) tells the story of Rabbi Tanhum, who defeated the Roman Emperor in an argument. "'You have spoken well!' cried the Emperor." Unfortunately, the penalty for defeating the Emperor in an argument was be thrown to the lions!

Imagine an authority system so well-constructed that a man could safely go to the king and indict him of capital crimes! Israel's government—designed by God—was such a system! Its government reflected the fact that "we are but dust" (Psalm 103:14 NASB).

Within this system of government, the king could not function as a priest. The priest could not own land or possess wealth, so as to become a political power. The prophet could challenge both king and priest. The United States Constitution recognizes these same biblical truths by distributing power through a tripartite system of checks and balances.

What is the lesson we can learn from God's government? We believers walk in the great privilege of God's indwelling presence, but we must continually remember that "we have this treasure in earthen vessels" (2 Cor. 4:7 NASB). Just as King David was not perfect and was exposed as a sinner ("You are the man"), we, too, are not yet perfected in God. Let us be open to receive correction when we are faced with the accusation, "you are the man."

Today I Will

. . . consider whether I have people in my life like Nathan the prophet. If there are none, I will seek them out because I need them.

BC

As a bridegroom rejoices over the bride, your God will rejoice over you (Isa. 62:5).

When I perform a wedding, I speak of the bride "in all her beauty." But what if she is *not* so beautiful? She *is* beautiful because she is the bride. To the groom, the bride is always beautiful. In Hebrew, the word for "bride" is *calah*, which is derived from the word meaning "perfect." Literally, it means "the perfect one."

In the Scriptures, believers are called God's *calah*, his perfect ones. Does this make sense? Not really. But just as it is right for me to describe, "the bride in all her beauty," even if she is covered with blemishes, so it is right for God to call us his *calah*, his perfect one. Why? For two reasons. First of all, we are the bride of the Perfect One. Second, we are perfect in the eyes of the Bridegroom, the one who loves us with a perfect love. Even with all of our blemishes and imperfections, to God in his grace, we are his perfect ones.

Learn to see all things through his eyes, with his perfect love, and it will become so. We are his *calah*, his perfect ones.

Today I Will

. . . receive the love of the Bridegroom into my heart. He sees me as his beautiful one.

Nov. 20, 1998
Nov. 10, 1999
Nov. 28, 2000
Nov. 16, 2001
Nov. 6, 2002
Nov. 26, 2003

Biblical
Rosh Chodesh
(New Moon)

Traditional
Rosh Chodesh
Day 2
(except the years 2000–2001)

Prayer Focus

JC

KISLEV

2

כסלו

Nov. 21, 1998 (6)
Nov. 11, 1999
Nov. 29, 2000
Nov. 17, 2001 (6)
Nov. 7, 2002
Nov. 27, 2003

Prayer Focus

Do not murder (Exod. 20:13).

Four U. S. presidents were assassinated, contrary to the commandment, "Do not murder" (Exod. 20:13). Abraham Lincoln, the 16th president of the United States, was shot in a movie theater by an actor who was a confederate sympathizer. The murderer did not act alone. A number of co-conspirators simultaneously attempted to kill the vice-president and other cabinet members.

James Garfield, the 20th president of the United States, was in office only a few months before he was killed by a disgruntled office seeker. On the way to his 25th college reunion, he was struck down by a bullet that lodged in his spine. He died eighty days later.

William McKinley, the 25th president of the United States, was assassinated by an anarchist who fired two shots at close range. The president died eight days later.

John Kennedy, the 35th president of the United States, was killed by a communist sympathizer who shot him in the head with a bullet from a high caliber rifle.

The deaths of these presidents changed the course of history.

As momentous as these assassinations were, history was most radically altered when the Son of God was executed at the hands of his own creation. Surely, this act continues to change the course of human history by making it possible for us to receive forgiveness for our sins.

Today I Will

. . . seek to spread the word of life in a world so filled with death.

EK

Like someone who grabs a dog by the ears is a passer-by who mixes in a fight not his own (Prov. 26:17).

Zol ich azoi vissen fun tzores is Yiddish for "I should so know from trouble as I know about this." The expression is very much on target.

Often we find ourselves pulled into situations which are not our problem. Wanting to please the Lord, we feel we should help. Yet especially in situations where anger and unforgiveness are involved, we should remember to look before we leap.

Is it wise to jump into rough waters (especially when we are only marginal swimmers) in order to try to save someone from drowning? Could there be another more suited to the job? First tune into God's wisdom before making the situation worse! Occasionally a recipient of our kind intentions may turn on us and pull us down in the midst of the struggle. In jumping in to save the day, we often become distracted from the things God is calling us to do.

I am reminded of the student who was giving his defense for *semikhah* (ordination) before the board of his *yeshivah* (rabbinical school). He spent all week delving into the "difficult problems" of the Holy Books without studying the material foundational to his exam. When it came to the test, the first oral question was "recite the ten words of Moses [the Ten Commandments] handed down from Sinai." He could not remember the very foundation of his faith. He had been so busy arguing with the sages of the Holy Writ without attending to the business so important to his future that, of course, he failed.

When we become absorbed in the issues of others we often neglect our own affairs, In addition, we may unwittingly invite an unfriendly bite, or worse! Lack of propriety is not the wisdom of Messiah.

Today I Will

. . . prayerfully consider what the Lord wishes me to be involved in and I will prioritize my day accordingly.

JR

KISLEV

3

כסלו

Nov. 22, 1998
Nov. 12, 1999
Nov. 30, 2000
Nov. 18, 2001
Nov. 8, 2002
Nov. 28, 2003

Prayer Focus

KISLEV

4

כסלו

Nov. 23, 1998
Nov. 13, 1999 (6)
Dec. 1, 2000
Nov. 19, 2001
Nov. 9, 2002 (6)
Nov. 29, 2003 (6)

Biblical
On this day, Zechariah received a prophecy about hypocritical fasting and feasting (Zech. 7:1).

Prayer Focus

Everyone who hears these words of mine and acts on them will be like a sensible man who built his house on bedrock (Matt. 7:24).

Simon was an Orthodox Jew. He had a Gentile friend, James, who noticed that Simon owned four sets of false teeth.

One day James asked his friend why he had so many sets of false teeth. Surprised by the question, Simon explained, "My friend, as you know, I keep *kosher*. I have one set of teeth I wear when I eat milk products; I have another set for meat products; and the third set I use for Passover." After a moment of silence, James pressed further, "Well, then, what about the fourth set?" Simon snapped in response, "Is it any of *your* business if I want to eat a ham and cheese sandwich once in a while?"

Yeshua pointed out the hypocrisy of some *Perushim* (Pharisees) of his day. They prayed long public prayers and donned exaggerated forms of religious garb, in order to be heard and seen by men. They were more concerned about handwashing than about "mouth-washing." They were satisfied to dishonor their parents by manipulating the practice of dedicating their property to God, thus keeping it from their parents.

It is easy to become part of a spiritual institution and become too busy for God, settling, instead, for a ritualistic, self-serving show of righteousness. In the above Scripture, we are challenged to keep the fire alive in our hearts for the Word of God and service to Yeshua.

Today I Will

. . . ask God to help me put into practice what I believe.

EK

Do not follow the crowd when it does what is wrong (Exod. 23:2).

Nov. 24, 1998
Nov. 14, 1999
Dec. 2, 2000 (6)
Nov. 20, 2001
Nov. 10, 2002
Nov. 30, 2003

Being the runt of my neighborhood, I quickly had to learn how to survive and resist peer pressure. One day, the older kids concocted a test of courage for us younger boys. They challenged us to jump from the window of an old abandoned British military barrack in Camp Allenby. We all jumped successfully from the first floor onto a bed of sand. No one was hurt. When it came to jumping from the second floor, however, we became reluctant. The older kids started to tease us, "You're afraid to jump! You're chicken!" To prove that I was not a chicken, I jumped . . . and broke my leg.

All my "friends" later denied that they had told me to jump. Fear of reprisal overtook them. The biggest bullies were the first to shift the blame, "I didn't tell Joe to jump! You told him to jump! It's your fault!" Each of my so-called friends who had wanted to test my courage and had urged me to jump were now afraid to take responsibility for their actions.

I learned from this experience that strong people are not afraid to swim against the stream. This attitude, in fact, is what gave me the strength to follow Yeshua, even at the cost of being cast out of my home at the age of sixteen. Today, it is clear to me that I should owe no man anything other than the love of God. This is the only way I can be free from the pressures that come, even from "friends."

Prayer Focus

Today I Will

. . . not follow the crowd but obey the Lord my God.

JS

KISLEV

6

כסלו

Nov. 25, 1998
Nov. 15, 1999
Dec. 3, 2000
Nov. 21, 2001
Nov. 11, 2002
Dec. 1, 2003

Prayer Focus

Like someone from whom people turn their faces, he was despised; we did not value him (Isa. 53:3).

Did Messiah come as a striking prince among men? Have you ever meditated on his appearance? Yesha'yahu (Isaiah) tells us that he was "like someone from whom people turn their faces." Are you content with your appearance, or do you secretly believe that God could do more in your life were your appearance to improve?

The *Talmud* tells a story about a meeting between the ugly-looking Rabbi Joshua ben Hanania and the exquisitely gorgeous princess of the Roman Emperor. At the meeting, the princess addressed the rabbi in disgust, "I did not know that such great wisdom could exist in such an ugly vessel."

Unfazed, the rabbi asked the princess, "In what kind of vessels does your father, the Emperor, store the palace wine?"

"In vessels of clay," she responded.

The rabbi looked pensive. "Why not use vessels of the finest gold and silver worthy of such exceptional wine?"

Defiantly the princess ordered that all the palace wine be transferred to gold and silver containers. It was not long before the Emperor was drinking sour wine!

In the common, ordinary things of life God is glorified. The Creator has made all things according to his wisdom. Who can improve upon the wisdom of the Almighty?

Today I Will

. . . stop trying to make myself look better to others so that I can rest in the wisdom of God.

JEF

For we are not bold to class or compare ourselves with some of those who . . . measure themselves by themselves, and compare themselves with themselves (2 Cor. 10:12 NASB).

When Rabbi Joshua went to Athens to argue with the renowned philosophers there, they asked him, "Where is the centre of the world?" The rabbi pointed to a spot near his feet and said, "Here!" The Greeks responded, "How can you prove it?" Joshua answered, "Bring ropes and measure" (Bechorot 8b). Rabbi Joshua rightly discerned that his audience would never admit that their measuring devices were inadequate for the task.

Rabbi Sha'ul (Saul; i.e., Paul) expresses his confidence that the exact opposite is true for believers. God has given us *precisely* the tools we need—his perfect and absolute standard—by which to accurately measure ourselves. He invites us to know his views (1 Kings 2:3), his thoughts (Isaiah 55), even his personal presence (Ps. 16:11). This living connection with God sets us apart from the rest of the world (Exod. 33:15–16).

When we accept his standard, surrendering our right to self-definition (unlike the Corinthians described in the above Scripture) we gain a true understanding of ourselves. Let us yield our thoughts and our deeds to the one who can teach us the difference between that which is truly right, and that which merely *seems* right (Prov. 14:12).

Today I Will

. . . lay down my own measuring rod and invite the Lord to teach me how to measure according to his standard.

KISLEV

7

כסלו

Nov. 26, 1998
Nov. 16, 1999
Dec. 4, 2000
Nov. 22, 2001
Nov. 12, 2002
Dec. 2, 2003

Prayer Focus

BC

KISLEV

8

כסלו

Nov. 27, 1998
Nov. 17, 1999
Dec. 5, 2000
Nov. 23, 2001
Nov. 13, 2002
Dec. 3, 2003

Let no harmful language come from your mouth, only good words that are helpful (Eph. 4:29).

In the Hebrew language, *sipeyr* means "tell." From this Hebrew word we get the English word "sapphire." So what is God's ancient, holy language teaching us? When children of God speak to one another, sapphires should come from our mouths. Just as God's words are always precious jewels, utterances of great value, so too, our language should "appreciate," that is, *add value* to someone's life.

Messiah told us the same thing: "The good person produces good things from the store of good in his heart" (Luke 6:45). We may not have expensive possessions, much money, or vast resources to share with others, but we can always give them sapphires, priceless treasures that can change their lives and cost us nothing!

Treasure the Word of God in your heart and use your mouth to speak words of love, hope, encouragement, strength, and eternal life. These are worth more than millions. Learn to deal in sapphires. Give your wife a sapphire today. Give your husband, your children, your parents, boss, co-workers, and friends each a precious sapphire. Share these riches and watch the miracles they produce. Give away a sapphire today. For gold is expensive, diamonds are costly, but sapphires from the lips of God's children are free.

Prayer Focus

Today I Will

. . . give a sapphire—a word of life, a word of love, a word of encouragement, a word of salvation—to my wife, husband, children, parents, boss, friends, even to strangers. Then I will watch the miracle!

JC

Avraham built the altar there. . . bound Yitzchak his son and laid him on the altar (Gen. 22:9).

The *Akeydah* (binding of Isaac) was an unparalleled trial for Abraham, but it also included an act with which he was already familiar. On Mount Moriah, Abraham built an "altar," as he had so often done in the Land of Promise.

Genuine worship requires us to offer "our best"; God does not desire merely our gifts—he desires *us*. By demanding Isaac, who was more precious to Abraham than life, God showed that true worship requires the dedication of our "all." Yet God did not take Isaac from Abraham, but instead provided a substitute sacrifice. True worship demands our "all," but God accepts a sacrifice in its place. The ram that God provided on Mount Moriah was the first substitutionary offering. It was sacrificed so that Isaac might live to serve God. On that same mount, God planned to one day establish a whole system of substitutionary sacrifice in the form of Temple worship. Abraham prophetically named the place *Adonai Yir'eh* (The Lord will provide).

Two thousand years later the final substitutionary offering—Messiah himself—was sacrificed. In him, we offer ourselves fully to God, and yet, as with Isaac, we can live on to serve him.

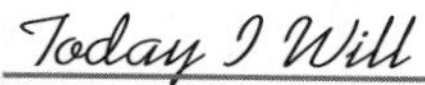

. . . present myself as a living sacrifice to God, dedicating myself wholly to him.

Nov. 28, 1998 (7)
Nov. 18, 1999
Dec. 6, 2000
Nov. 24, 2001 (7)
Nov. 14, 2002
Dec. 4, 2003

Prayer Focus

RR

KISLEV

10

כסלו

Nov. 29, 1998
Nov. 19, 1999
Dec. 7, 2000
Nov. 25, 2001
Nov. 15, 2002
Dec. 5, 2003

David comforted his wife Bat-Sheva (2 Sam. 12:24).

Here is perhaps King David's greatest moment. After his humiliating exposure before the nation, and the death of his newborn son, he could have turned and blamed Bat-Sheva (Bathsheba) for everything. "It was all your fault! You were bathing on that rooftop on purpose to cause me to sin! I wish I had never laid eyes on you!" We can well imagine such words being spoken. Yet, not from David. He shouldered the load of his sin like a true *mentsh* (Yiddish for a "person with integrity").

David went to the woman he had violated—through the abuse of his God-given power as king—and comforted her. He did not distance himself from her, but stood by her. He did not make her his scapegoat, but made her his companion. In so doing, he gave the world King Shlomo (Solomon); and Bat-Sheva became a symbol of the grace of God towards a king who chose not to hide his human frailties at the expense of another. David never shifted the blame to Bat-Sheva by claiming "she made me do it." David learned this truth and lived it well, to the benefit of the entire nation under his charge.

Prayer Focus

Today I Will

. . . seek grace to be a *mensch* in the sight of God and man. I will learn the art of saying, "I was wrong."

BC

You are to erect the tabernacle according to the design you have been shown on the mountain (Exod. 26:30).

Nov. 30, 1998
Nov. 20, 1999 (7)
Dec. 8, 2000
Nov. 26, 2001
Nov. 16, 2002 (7)
Dec. 6, 2003 (7)

The Lord makes this mysterious statement seven times in Scripture. Why was "the design" so important? The writer of the Book of Hebrews explains that the Tabernacle was "a copy and shadow of the heavenly original" (Heb. 8:5). The Tabernacle in heaven is not a simple structure, but complex in its design. It was necessary, therefore, for the earthly Tabernacle to reflect this careful detail.

David also tells us of God's involvement in building the Temple, another replica of the heavenly Tabernacle. David writes, "*Adonai*, with his hand on me, has given me good sense in working out these detailed plans" (1 Chron. 28:19). God was concerned that his house be built in a certain way, down to the smallest detail.

Many people think that God is concerned only with the big picture and not the details—spiritual areas, but not the nitty-gritty of daily life. Clearly, this is a Greek way of thinking and not typical of the Hebrew mindset.

Let us learn from the Tabernacle and the Temple the matter of detail. Let us remember that God desires that we pursue excellence, even in the smallest details of what he has called us to do in his kingdom.

Prayer Focus

Today I Will

. . . pay attention to detail as I serve the Lord.

DR

KISLEV

12

כסלו

Dec. 1, 1998
Nov. 21, 1999
Dec. 9, 2000 (7)
Nov. 27, 2001
Nov. 17, 2002
Dec. 7, 2003

Focus your minds on things above, not on things here on earth (Col. 3:2).

Do you ever sit down to pray and experience a loss of words? Over the years I have found that reciting passages of Scripture almost always gets the gears grinding in my mind and heart. It wakes up the inner man (who is sometimes snoozing) and prepares the way for times of intimate fellowship with the Lord.

Speaking and pondering God's Word prepares the mind for prayer. It takes our attention off of "things here on earth" and focuses our attention on "things above." God's abiding Word reminds us of God's overall perspective and invites us to see through his eyes. It aligns our hearts with the heart of God.

Would members of a symphony orchestra begin to play Beethoven's Fifth before tuning up their instruments? So we, too, should begin our day "tuning-up" in the presence of the Lord. Just as a tune-up quiets the motor of a car, Scripture meditation quiets our hearts before God. We can then be spiritually refreshed, at peace, and more prepared to enter into heartfelt conversation with our *Abba* (Father).

Prayer Focus

Today I Will

DR

. . . begin my times of prayer by reciting Scripture.

This is the greatest and most important *mitzvah.* And a second is similar to it (Matt. 22:38–39).

There are few things in our spiritual lives more important than understanding God's priorities. In the 1960s, the famous singing rabbi, Shlomo Carlebach, was sent by the Lubavitcher *rebbe* (head rabbi) to San Francisco to teach *halakhah* (the way of *Torah*) to young Jews. After a year, Carlebach told his *rebbe*, "I have a hundred who love *Shabbat* [Sabbath] and the *mitzvot* [God's commands]!" The *rebbe* replied, "I hear men and women are sitting together, and the men hear *kol ishah* (women's voices) during worship. This must stop." *Reb* [Rabbi] Shlomo replied, "*Rebbe*, please excuse me, but these one hundred have been far away in heart and spirit. If so soon I tell them they cannot sit together, seventy will leave; and if I tell them they cannot sing together, another twenty-nine will leave—and the one who will stay is a fool to whom I can teach nothing! What good is worrying about such a bandaid while the body is having a heart-attack?" The *rebbe* would not budge. So *Reb* Shlomo left the Lubavitcher community and became so fruitful in his work that there is virtually no synagogue in the Western world that does not sing Shlomo Carlebach's songs.

Right priorities are central to spiritual life. May we discern God's heart to better understand his priorities in our lives.

Today I Will

. . . pray, "Teach me, Oh Lord, your architecture for my life, and I will seek to build according to your design."

KISLEV

13

כסלו

Dec. 2, 1998
Nov. 22, 1999
Dec. 10, 2000
Nov. 28, 2001
Nov. 18, 2002
Dec. 8, 2003

Prayer Focus

BC

Dec. 3, 1998
Nov. 23, 1999
Dec. 11, 2000
Nov. 29, 2001
Nov. 19, 2002
Dec. 9, 2003

The things you heard from me . . . commit to faithful people, such as will be competent to teach others also (2 Tim. 2:2).

I once heard it said that every gift and every talent that the Lord bestows upon us is given with someone else in mind. In other words, he wants us to share all we receive. Our job is to receive, then turn around and give it way!

In the above Scripture, Rabbi Sha'ul (Saul; i.e., Paul) exhorts Timothy to pass on all he has been taught to faithful ones who will likewise teach others. Clearly this was already happening in Sha'ul's life. In this one verse, we find four generations of believers: Sha'ul; Timothy (Sha'ul's disciple); Timothy's disciples; and finally, those whom his disciples teach. How attentive we would be when receiving instruction if we only knew that we were not learning for ourselves alone, but for others we would later teach.

How closely would we pay attention to a teaching if we knew that, the following day, we would need to pass on the same information to someone else? A disciple is a learner who eventually is sent to repeat the process. Keep this idea in mind as you receive instruction and as you participate in any form of ministry training. Remember that you are called to pass on to others that which you receive.

Prayer Focus

Today I Will

. . . seek to pass on to someone else that which I have received from another so that the Kingdom of God may grow.

JB

True religion does bring great riches, but only to those who are content with what they have (1 Tim. 6:6).

Dec. 4, 1998
Nov. 24, 1999
Dec. 12, 2000
Nov. 30, 2001
Nov. 20, 2002
Dec. 10, 2003

A*z me ken nit vi me vil, tut men vi me ken* is Yiddish for "If you can't do as you wish, do as you can." The high-tech action movies of the nineties have left a certain impression on me. Although the hero may be a capable person or a *shlemiel* (a person prone to doing foolish things), he always manages to do one *great* thing. The movie ends and I go home also wanting to do a single *great* thing in my life.

Do you know much about the disciple Andrew? Very little is said of him in the *Brit Chadashah* (New Covenant Scriptures). Guess who found his brother Shim'on (Simon Peter) and brought him to Yeshua? Later, when there was no food for the multitude on the mountain, and everyone was trying to figure out how to feed the crowds, it was Andrew who found the lad with a few fish and some bread (John 6:8–9). What do you think the people said to him? "Are you *mishugah* (crazy)? It's not enough!" But look at what happened because of Andrew's behind-the-scenes work.

Being alert to what is needed to acomplish God's work can make us all *great* in the Kingdom. As humble servants, we can all be heroes.

Prayer Focus

Today I Will

. . . present my life to Yeshua for his use without being concerned about what he chooses to accomplish through me.

JR

KISLEV

16

כסלו

Dec. 5, 1998 (8)
Nov. 25, 1999
Dec. 13, 2000
Dec. 1, 2001 (8)
Nov. 21, 2002
Dec. 11, 2003

Prayer Focus

I will not take so much as a thread or a sandal thong of anything that is yours (Gen. 14:23).

Avram (Abram) had just achieved a major victory over the five kings from the east. His victory not only saved his nephew Lot, but also rendered a great service to the king of Sedom (Sodom), whom he addresses in today's Scripture passage. Yet Avram accepts none of the spoils of war, taking instead only food for his men. He lets his allies make their own decisions about the booty.

Avram always protected his allegiance to the Lord. Here, he exercised faith by rejecting the king of Sedom's offer of booty. Taking booty would have obligated Avram, making him a vassal of the king. Avram brushed aside the offer with the words *michut ve'ad serokh na'al* ("as a thread or a sandal thong"). In other words, "[I will accept] no booty from the thinnest thread for a shirt to the thickest thread for a shoe, nor anything in between! Only the Lord will receive credit for my wealth!" Avram boldly told the king.

Immediately, God rewards Avram's faith with the promise, "Don't be afraid . . . I am your protector; your reward will be very great" (Gen. 15:1). Faith requires a clean commitment on our part. Once the decision is made and acted upon, be assured God will respond. Avram exercised faith and exalted God in his life. God protected and rewarded him thereafter.

Today I Will

JEF

. . . exercise faith to magnify God in my life.

Do not eat the food of a stingy man . . . for he is the kind of man who is always thinking about the cost (Prov. 23:6–7 NIV).

Some of the greediest people I have met were, at one time, needy themselves. One would think that in their present circumstances they would be sensitive to the needs of others. Instead, they hoard their plenty as they once clung to their little. Once they would boast of how much they would give if wealth were theirs. Now that they're wealthy, they are as stingy as before.

The motivation behind this curious behavior is fear. The issue is not just whether money is their god, but whether money is more trustworthy to them than God himself. Like the stingy man in the verses above, they're always worrying about whether they will again be poor. They fail to realize two things: first, God sustained them when they were poor. As Rabbi Sha'ul (Saul; i.e., Paul) knew so well: "I have learned the secret of being content in any and every situation, whether well fed or hungry, whether living in plenty or in want" (Phil. 4:12 NIV). Second, they forget that, "he who is kind to the poor lends to the Lord, and he will reward him for what he has done" (Prov. 19:17 NIV). This truth teaches the opposite of what they fear and should lead us all into generous behavior.

Greed can rule us whether we are poor or wealthy. Whatever your financial condition, the time to conquer stinginess is now.

Today I Will

. . . replace the fear that leads to greed with the trust in God's faithfulness that leads to caring generosity.

KISLEV

17

כסלו

Dec. 6, 1998
Nov. 26, 1999
Dec. 14, 2000
Dec. 2, 2001
Nov. 22, 2002
Dec. 12, 2003

Prayer Focus

MW

KISLEV

18

כסלו

Dec. 7, 1998
Nov. 27, 1999 (8)
Dec. 15, 2000
Dec. 3, 2001
Nov. 23, 2002 (8)
Dec. 13, 2003 (8)

Prayer Focus

Sh'ol and Abaddon are never satisfied, and human eyes are never satisfied. (Prov. 27:20).

Yeshua told us that *HaSatan* (the Adversary) is the father of lies and that the whole world is under his influence. Therefore, it should come as no surprise that there is a fundamental deception that underlies the world system. It constantly promises something that it is unable to deliver—satisfaction. The illusion is that whatever we pursue—positions, possessions, or experiences—will somehow bring us inner peace. Yet it never happens. A more-desired object is always just over the next hill, and after climbing it, there suddenly appears one more obstacle to achieving our goal. Even if one is able to get hold of it, the result is still unfulfilling. It is not possible for the human soul to be satisfied with *things.*

This, however, is not bad, but part of the design of God. In Romans 8, we are told that the creation itself was subjected to futility so that the freedom for which every created being longs could only be found in the Creator. God uses this to bring people to himself and also to keep his children on the straight path. The journey can only be enjoyed when our eyes and hearts are not focused on the journey itself, but on him whose kingdom and manifest presence should be the goal of all we do.

Today I Will

. . . no longer allow the things of this world to blind me to their temporal nature and false promises. I will see beyond them to the place of contentment in the Lord, whose finished work has delivered me out of darkness and into his marvelous light.

MM

Where there is no counsel, the people fall; but in the multitude of counselors there is safety (Prov. 11:14 NKJV).

Dec. 8, 1998
Nov. 28, 1999
Dec. 16, 2000 (8)
Dec. 4, 2001
Nov. 24, 2002
Dec. 14, 2003

Yeder nar iz klug far zich is Yiddish for "Every fool thinks he is wise." In the above Scripture, we are told that a wise person will seek *tachbulah* (wise counsel giving good direction). The latter part of the Scripture should actually read "but in the multitude of counselors there is *teshua* (salvation or deliverance). *Teshua* comes from the same root as the name "Yeshua."

If we think that we can succeed in the ways of God without the help of others, we are like the *nar* (fool). A truly wise person will understand that good counsel is necessary for success.

The sages tell the story (Sanhedrin 91a) of a king who had an orchard. It was beautiful and full of fruit. The king, however, unwisely put a lame man and a blind man in charge of it. As a result, his orchard did not produce all that he expected from it. If the king had appointed wise overseers, what would the state of the orchard have been?

We too need good counsel to be successful.

Prayer Focus

Today I Will

. . . think about those whom the Lord has placed in my life to be wise counselors for me.

JR

Dec. 9, 1998
Nov. 29, 1999
Dec. 17, 2000
Dec. 5, 2001
Nov. 25, 2002
Dec. 15, 2003

Biblical
On this day, Ezra commanded Israelite men to separate from their pagan wives (Ezra 10:9).

Prayer Focus

He calls his friends and neighbors together and says, "Come, celebrate with me" (Luke 15:6).

K*ol hane'arim* is Hebrew for "all of the young lads." The words refer to the collective *aliyah* (going up) of boys under *bar mitzvah* age to the front of the synagogue on *Simchat Torah.* It is a joyous event and gives the boys a sense of community membership.

In Western thought, we tend to see ourselves as islands, individuals who do not require community involvement. Personal rights existed in ancient Israel, but a sense of belonging to the community guided the overall outlook. Even salvation was pictured corporately (although personal salvation was taught, too). Community blessing and community direction were all part of being Jewish. Rabbi Hillel urged, "Separate not thyself from the community" (Pirkey Avot 2:4).

The joy of imparting meaningful symbols to strengthen our young people's faith and identity—reminding them that they are carrying the torch of a great history of redemption—has for thousands of years been a normal part of community life in Israel. Without imparting this, the posterity and mission of our people is jeopardized.

Let us focus on the importance, even necessity, of being part of the greater *mishpachah* (family) of Israel and the community of faith, and the blessings of belonging to this *mishpachah* will impact our children and our children's children.

Today I Will

. . . reflect on the value of community for my family, and how I can help strengthen the community of the remnant of Israel.

JR

When the Messiah was executed on the stake as a criminal, I was too (Gal. 2:20).

Dec. 10, 1998
Nov. 30, 1999
Dec. 18, 2000
Dec. 6, 2001
Nov. 26, 2002
Dec. 16, 2003

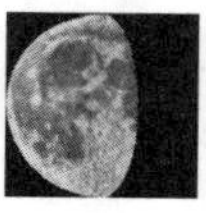

Biblical faith is centered on two great truths. The first is that God will fulfill his ultimate purpose for the creation and man's destiny in it. The second is that the *tzlav* (cross) is the key to that fulfillment.

The sinful nature of man will not thwart God's purpose. Human evil is characterized by selfishness. In selfishness we wound one another. Wounded people wound others. God's *Torah* is violated. We experience guilt, bitterness over our wounds, and develop a victim mentality. We feel guilty about the things we have done, and angry over the things others have done against us, including every kind of injustice, betrayal, and abandonment.

God's solution to our guilt is identification with our crucified and risen Messiah. God's solution to our pain from injustice is to identify with Yeshua. When we meditate on his crucifixion in the context of addressing our own pain, he replaces our bitterness and guilt with his compassion and forgiveness.

Identification with our crucified and risen Lord transforms us and restores the image of *HaShem* (God; literally, the Name). When we are filled with love and walk in his ways, we know that nothing can happen to us outside of his will. There is no victim mentality for the true believer.

Prayer Focus

Today I Will

. . . live the crucified and risen life through identification with Yeshua.

DJ

Dec. 11, 1998
Dec. 1, 1999
Dec. 19, 2000
Dec. 7, 2001
Nov. 27, 2002
Dec. 17, 2003

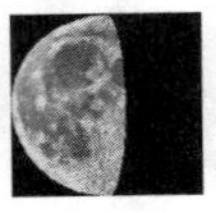

They put new wine into new wineskins and both are preserved (Matt. 9:17).

Having gathered as many apples as we could from the orchard, we were on our way to the local cider mill. The old Volkswagen van was so weighed down with sacks of apples that the tires looked like pears. When the trip was done, we had over ninety gallons of apple cider. That year we gave away a lot of cider.

I gave one gallon (in a glass jug with a screw-on top) to a friend who worked in a florist shop. He set it under the counter, planning to take it home at the end of the day, but he forgot. He continued to forget about the jar of cider, until one morning when he entered his shop and found it splattered with fermented cider and broken glass, smelling like a distillery.

This is precisely what Yeshua was speaking about in Matthew 9. The process of change that was taking place in the cider required a flexible container that could expand. Because glass does not have those properties, the result was an explosion!

In today's Scripture reference, Yeshua does not tell us to exchange one set of religious forms for another. He encourages us to embrace his unfolding plan for our lives. We have been filled with the new wine of the *Ruach HaKodesh* (Holy Spirit). In order for us to handle the changes that will inevitably result, we must be flexible in his hands.

Prayer Focus

Today I Will

. . . joyfully accept all that the Lord wants to do in my life. I will reject rigidity and brittleness, and embrace flexibility and growth.

MM

They began yelling at the top of their voices, so that they wouldn't have to hear him (Acts 7:57).

When I was in elementary school, Bible reading, prayer, even Christmas carols were still allowed in the public school system in the United States. As a Jewish child who had no personal experience with Christmas at home, I nevertheless found the songs to be very beautiful and enjoyable to listen to. However, I can still vividly remember my response to the song, "Come All Ye Faithful." I could listen to it up to the chorus, but then at the lyrics "Come let us adore Him, Christ the Lord," I would put my fingers in my ears and hum loudly to avoid hearing those words. I do not recall ever being taught to do such a thing, but that declaration seemed to be a threat to my very being.

It is an enormous tragedy that over the last 1900 years our people have stopped their ears to the message about Yeshua. It is not a message about some pagan god of the winter solstice, but about our very own Messiah bringing redemption to his own people. However, there is hope; for even as that little boy grew to manhood, the *Ruach HaKodesh* (Holy Spirit) in grace, lovingkindness, and mercy, removed the fear and uncovered my ears. Even so, he can do the same for the whole house of Israel.

Today I Will

. . . be encouraged to persevere in prayer for my non-believing family, knowing that perfect love casts out fear, and that the mercy of God is able to penetrate even the most resistant heart.

Dec. 12, 1998 (9)*
Dec. 2, 1999
Dec. 20, 2000
Dec. 8, 2001 (9)*
Nov. 28, 2002
Dec. 18, 2003

Prayer Focus

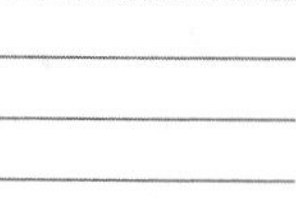

MM

Dec. 13, 1998
Dec. 3, 1999
Dec. 21, 2000
Dec. 9, 2001
Nov. 29, 2002
Dec. 19, 2003

Biblical
On this day, Haggai prophesied blessing for the Israelites (Hag. 2:10–19); Haggai received a prophecy for Zerubbabel (Hag. 2:20–23).

Traditional
Erev Chanukkah (the Eve of the Feast of Dedication)

The first candle is lit tonight.

Prayer Focus

Serve him truly and sincerely (Josh. 24:14).

No doubt about it! *Chanukkah* (the Feast of Dedication) is a fun holiday. The sights and sounds of this festival remind us of the great miracles that happened so long ago. The *chanukkiyah* (*Chanukkah menorah*, or lampstand) brings to mind the miracle of the Temple worship which was restored after the Syrian-Greeks defiled the House of God. Although there was only one day's worth of *kosher* (ceremonially acceptable) oil, we are told in the *Talmud* that the oil burned for eight full days until a new supply could be produced by the priests. Perhaps the greater miracle was found in that the army of the Maccabees was able to drive out the powerful Syrian-Greek forces of Antiochus Epiphanes. Mattathias and his sons realized that unless they stood against the pagan culture, the Jewish people would perish by sword or assimilation.

As we reflect on the history of *Chanukkah*, we realize that it was actually a test by the *Ruach* (Spirit) of God. The path was easy leading to compromise with the Hellenistic world. Many chose that route. But the road was narrower and more difficult that lead to God's kingdom. Putting it another way, *Chanukkah* was a battle of the gods! Who would prevail? Would it be the god of the world or the one true God of Abraham?

Every generation faces the same crossroads. Joshua called Israel to make the choice and responded to his own challenge, saying "as for me and my household, we will serve *Adonai*" (Joshua 24:15).

As we light the *chanukkiyah* this year, what will our choice be?

Today I Will

. . . choose the path of *HaShem* (God), even though it will probably be more difficult than the world's path.

BK

God raised him to the highest place and gave him the name above every name (Phil. 2:9).

Although *Chanukkah* (the Feast of Dedication) is not a festival specifically commanded in the Scriptures, we are told that Yeshua observed it in first-century Jerusalem (John 10:22). He certainly affirmed the importance of the Maccabean victory of 164 B.C.E. and celebrated the preservation of his people, Israel. A central part of the observance is the lighting of the nine-branched *chanukkiyah* (*Chanukkah menorah*, or lampstand) to commemorate the miracle of the oil.

We are told in the *Talmud* that as the Maccabees kindled the *Menorah* in the restored Temple, one day's worth of oil lasted for eight days until a new supply could be produced. Hence, we light one candle for each of the eight days. Why the ninth candle? We call this candle the *shammash* (servant). It is the first candle lit, kindled by the match; in turn, it gives light to the other eight candles. Although *shammash* means "servant," it is clearly exalted above the rest of the candles of the *chanukkiyah*. It stands taller than the others.

The *shammash* candle is a perfect picture of Yeshua the Messiah. He left his glory in heaven and humbled himself to become a *shammash* to mankind. Yet after his death, he was raised by the Father and exalted. We can only experience the light of God as we receive it from his Son, Yeshua, the Servant.

Thank you, *Abba*, for the light of your exalted servant, Yeshua *HaMashiach* (the Messiah)!

. . . seek to be a light in the world as I have received the light of Messiah.

Dec. 14, 1998 (מ)
Dec. 4, 1999 (מ/9/E)*
Dec. 22, 2000 (מ)
Dec. 10, 2001 (מ)
Nov. 30, 2002 (מ/9/E)*
Dec. 20, 2003 (מ/9/E)*

Traditional
Chanukkah (the Feast of Dedication) Day 1

The second candle is lit tonight.

Prayer Focus

BK

Dec. 15, 1998 (מ)
Dec. 5, 1999 (מ)
Dec. 23, 2000 (מ/9/D)*
Dec. 11, 2001 (מ)
Dec. 1, 2002 (מ)
Dec. 21, 2003 (מ)

Traditional *Chanukkah* (the Feast of Dedication) Day 2

The third candle is lit tonight.

Prayer Focus

Then came *Chanukkah* in Yerushalayim. It was winter, and Yeshua was walking around inside the Temple area (John 10:22–23).

There are two individuals in the Scriptures named Enoch. The first was the son of Cain. Cain had murdered his brother and was condemned to be a vagrant and a wanderer on the earth, away from the presence of the Lord. Cain fathered a son and built a city, calling them both Enoch. In order to find the peace for which he so fruitlessly yearned, Cain invested himself in these two symbols of his earthly, human achievement.

The other Enoch was a 7th-generation descendant of Adam, through his son Seth. Of this Enoch it was said that he walked with God, giving him pleasure, and that God took him without his seeing death.

The Hebrew for the name Enoch is Chanoch. It means "dedication," and is from the same root as the word used to refer to the Feast of Dedication—*Chanukkah.* In the days of the Maccabees, there existed a well-armed enemy seeking to subjugate Israel. However, that was not the heart of the conflict. Then, as now, the fiercer battle raged within the souls of the people—the battle over which direction they would take. Would they follow the path of the first Enoch, dedicating themselves to glorifying human ability and achievement, which was the focus of Hellenism? Or would they, like the second Enoch, dedicate themselves to walking with God in his ways, which transcend the power of death? This same choice is also ours today.

Today I Will

MM

. . . dedicate myself to walking with God.

She never left the Temple grounds but worshipped there night and day, fasting and praying (Luke 2:37).

Chanah (Anna) was born in 88 B.C.E., when the memory of Maccabean victories had degenerated into political intrigue and internal conflict. When she turned 11, conditions improved as Queen Alexandra began a 9-year peaceful reign over Israel. Some years later, Chanah married and the future looked bright. Unfortunately, in 69 B.C.E., the queen died, plunging the nation into another period of conflict, as her two sons vied for power. The issue was finally settled six years later when the Romans conquered Jerusalem. Chanah's husband died, possibly among the 12,000 killed by the Romans.

It would have been perfectly natural for Chanah, still young, to give herself to a new husband and begin afresh. Yet something motivated her beyond natural aspirations. Again, Israel was under foreign domination and Jerusalem was polluted by a pagan presence. Chanah desired that her people be free forever from the endless cycle of subjugation and bondage. Oh, that the redeemer would finally come to Zion! To this end, she committed herself through fasting and prayer.

Fifty-nine faithful years later, Chanah was present as Yosef (Joseph) and Miryam (Mary) carried the infant Yeshua into the Temple. "She came by at that moment and began thanking God and speaking about the child to everyone who was waiting for Yerushalayim to be liberated" (Luke 2:38).

Today I Will

. . . consider my own natural desires as nothing compared to the privilege of devoting my whole life to the fulfillment of God's plan of redemption for his people.

KISLEV

27

כסלו

Dec. 16, 1998 (מ)
Dec. 6, 1999 (מ)
Dec. 24, 2000 (מ)
Dec. 12, 2001 (מ)
Dec. 2, 2002 (מ)
Dec. 22, 2003 (מ)

Traditional
Chanukkah
(the Feast of Dedication)
Day 3

The fourth candle is lit tonight.

Prayer Focus

MM

KISLEV
28
כסלו

Dec. 17, 1998 (מ)
Dec. 7, 1999 (מ)
Dec. 25, 2000 (מ)
Dec. 13, 2001 (מ)
Dec. 3, 2002 (מ)
Dec. 23, 2003 (מ)

Traditional
Chanukkah
(the Feast of
Dedication)
Day 4

The fifth candle
is lit tonight.

Prayer Focus

The honor and spendor of the nations will be brought into it (Rev. 21:26).

Every people-group has its own cultural personality. Some aspects are good and reflect the attributes of God. Other aspects are evil—from the enemy.

Theologian and writer Reinhold Niebuhr addresses the subject of respecting culture. We are not to endorse everything in all cultures; nor are we to to demean peoples and cultures across the board. Rather, we are to view all cultures as transformed by the *ahavah* (love) of Messiah. That which is good is preserved; what is not is filtered out. In this way, a variety of cultures will all glorify the name of Yeshua.

Admittedly, certain aspects of the culture of our own people need to be transformed through Messiah and brought into line with his life and teaching. The foundation of Jewish culture, however, is a calling that did not anthropologically evolve, but came by unique revelation. Israel is to be *mamlechet cohanim* (a kingdom of priests) charged to bless all nations, bringing people to God and the ways of God to all peoples.

And whereas all followers of Yeshua have a priestly calling, the calling of the Jewish people is unique. This call is not merely to a ministry of *spoken* intercession, but one of prescribed ritual behavior—intercessory *practices* mandated by the Creator. *Chanukkah* (the Feast of Dedication) recalls the time when the Syrian-Greeks sought to completely destroy the Jewish culture and religion, denying this special calling of God.

God desires to preserve the Jewish culture. He is also interested in maintaining varieties of cultures that enrich the splendor of his Kingdom as his children seek to serve him together.

Today I Will

. . . respect the vast variety of peoples with an open heart of love.

DJ

Come, let's wipe them out as a nation; let the name of Isra'el be remembered no more! (Ps. 83:4[5])

One of the realities of living in Israel is the ever-present threat of war. Many of the peoples that surround us are controlled by the same spirits that motivated their ancestors who occupied those same geographical locations. When Asaph wrote this psalm three thousand years ago, he listed the names of those who sought Israel's destruction. The descendants of some of those named have that same agenda today. Looking at this situation can at times be overwhelming and not a little unnerving. Nevertheless, he points out that the opposition is ultimately aimed at the Lord and not just at Israel. Even during the time of the Maccabees, this little band of faithful Jews realized that they were fighting on behalf of God and not merely for themselves. God is the one who has made the investment in this place, and he is commited to protect both his interests and his Name.

God has an investment in all his people, those from Israel and those from among the nations. *HaSatan* (the Adversary) will, however, do all he can to stop the work of God and come against the people of God. His behind-the-scenes involvement was apparent when the Syrian-Greeks desecrated the Temple under the rule of their leader, Antiochus Epiphanes.

Our comfort is in knowing that since God himself and his purposes are the ultimate target, *he* is the one who will answer the challenge. We have no need to fear, since he is the "Most High over all the earth" (Ps. 83:18[19]), capable of handling every attack, no matter from which direction it comes.

Today I Will

. . . not fear whatever may come against me; for the Lord is a shield around me, and the one who lifts my head.

Dec. 18, 1998 (מ)
Dec. 8, 1999 (מ)
Dec. 26, 2000 (מ)
Dec. 14, 2001 (מ)
Dec. 4, 2002 (מ)
Dec. 24, 2003 (מ)

Traditional *Chanukkah* (the Feast of Dedication) Day 5

The sixth candle is lit tonight.

Prayer Focus

MM

In the year 2000, Kislev has only 29 days.

Dec. 19, 1998 (מ/10/C, D, E)
Dec. 9, 1999 (מ)
Dec. 15, 2001 (מ/10/C, D, E)
Dec. 5, 2002 (מ)
Dec. 25, 2003 (מ)

Traditional
Chanukkah (the Feast of Dedication) Day 6

The seventh candle is lit tonight.

Rosh Chodesh (the New Moon) Day 1

Prayer Focus

____
____
____
____
____
____
____
____

MM

Not by force, and not by power, but by my Spirit, says *Adonai-Tzva'ot* (Zech. 4:6).

The *Haftarah* (portion from the Prophets) that is read in the synagogue on the Sabbath of *Chanukkah* (the Feast of Dedication) spotlights the above verse as the theme of the holiday. In the fourth chapter of Zechariah, the prophet was shown a vision of a golden *menorah* (lampstand) like the one used in the Temple. On each side of the *menorah* stood an olive tree. From each of the trees, oil was fed into the seven lamp bowls at the top of the seven branched *menorah*. Zechariah was informed by an angelic guide that the two olive trees are the "two who have been anointed with oil; they are standing with the Lord of all the land" (Zech. 4:14). They are also referred to as the "two witnesses" in Revelation 11.

The *menorah* is a symbol of God's light and revelation in the world, specifically through Israel, but inclusive of all believers through the New Covenant. It is fed by the faithfulness of God's people who stand between a holy God and a lost world as prophets and priests. This message transcends the *Chanukkah* story and is relevant every day of the year. This assignment can never be accomplished by human effort, no matter how strong or noble. It is only by the grace of God that his *Ruach* (Spirit) flows in us and through us, to keep the *menorah* of his light ablaze.

Today I Will

. . . recognize that my heavenly Father desires to manifest his illuminating glory through me. I will offer myself fully to him, putting no confidence in my flesh, but allowing his *Ruach* free rein.

On the first day of the tenth month the tops of the mountains were seen (Gen. 8:5).

Suddenly, in the midst of a sky cloaked in darkness, a sliver of light appeared. At the same time, emerging from its watery shroud, a sliver of land appeared. These are two witnesses of the power of God to bring life to that which was devoid of it. Numerous other places in Scripture affirm this same message of resurrection and new life in connection with the appearance of the new moon. This is also what Yeshua taught regarding the new covenant, which he inaugurated by his death and resurrection. Those who enter into relationship with him reap the benefits of resurrection life.

It is no coincidence that Jeremiah 31 specifically speaks of that new covenant, ties it together with the promise of Israel's preservation and restoration, and speaks of the fixed order of the heavenly bodies as a sign of God's guarantee on the whole package. So whether we are partaking of the bread and the cup, or gazing up into the heavens at the beginning of each Hebrew month, let us be reminded that renewal and resurrection are available for us and for all Israel through the finished work of Yeshua.

Today I Will

. . . remember that the same gracious covenant that has made it possible to enter into a relationship with the God of Israel, has also guaranteed that he will always remain Israel's God.

Dec. 20, 1998 (מ)
Dec. 10, 1999 (מ)
Dec. 27, 2000 (מ)
Dec. 16, 2001 (מ)
Dec. 6, 2002 (מ)
Dec. 26, 2003 (מ)

Biblical
Rosh Chodesh
(the New Moon)

On this day, the mountain tops became visible after the flood (Gen. 8:5); Ezra began investigating the cases of Israelite men who had married pagan women (Ezra 10:16).

Traditional
Chanukkah
(the Feast of Dedication)
Day 7 (Day 6 for the year 2000)

The eighth candle is lit tonight (the seventh in the year 2000).

Rosh Chodesh
Day 2
(except the year 2000)

MM

TEVET

2

טבת

Dec. 21, 1998 (מ)
Dec. 11, 1999 (מ/10/F)
Dec. 28, 2000 (מ)
Dec. 17, 2001 (מ)
Dec. 7, 2002 (מ/10/F)
Dec. 27, 2003 (מ/10/F)

Traditional *Chanukkah* (the Feast of Dedication) Day 8 (Day 7 for the year 2000)

The eighth candle is lit tonight in the year 2000.

Prayer Focus

While it was still dark, Yeshua got up, left, went away to a lonely spot and stayed there praying (Mark 1:35).

Yeshua's life of prayer is a marvelous example to us! Being raised in a family of Messianic leaders, I remember that prayer was strongly emphasized by my parents. My father was a man of the night seasons. I would come down in the middle of the night to get a *nosh* (snack) from the refrigerator and would find him in the living room praying. My mother would rise at 5:00 every morning in order to have two good hours with the Lord before the kids woke up. These examples made a deep impression on me.

In a similar manner, Yeshua's prayer life profoundly impacted his disciples. On this occasion, he had been out ministering all day. He was physically and spiritually tired. He rose hours before dawn, left the city, and found a place where he could be alone with the Father. Hours later, his disciples found him. He was refreshed, restored, renewed, and ready to go.

If Yeshua needed to pray, then how much more do we need to pray? We need to learn from Yeshua's life and develop a life of prayer. If we give God our best time and are dedicated to prayer, then we will be empowered and led by the *Ruach HaKodesh* (Holy Spirit) every day.

During this Feast of Dedication, let us dedicate ourselves to prayer.

Today I Will

. . . make a commitment to pray every day. Help me, O Lord, to become like Yeshua and develop a pattern of prayer in my life.

DC

No one's heart has imagined all the things God has prepared for those who love him (1 Cor. 2:9).

My *bubbe* (grandmother) left me a set of dishes, service for sixteen, from the old country. You wouldn't call these beautiful dishes—in fact, they were downright ugly. They were green with gold trim, with a dull yellow tinge—definitely not my colors. I kept my *bubbe's* dishes safely wrapped in newspaper and out of the way . . . until the day my husband invited sixteen guests over for dinner.

I am not such a *balebusteh* (woman in command of her household) and I *kvetched* (complained) profusely as I dusted off the dishes, embarrassed, but having no alternative. As my guests arrived and sat at the table, I noticed one man eyeing his plate closely. "Oh, no," I thought. "I forgot to wipe it!" Mortified, I rushed to take the plate from him, but he stopped me. "Do you have any idea how much these dishes are worth?" he asked. This man, a porcelain expert, had recognized my *bubbe*'s old dishes as the work of a European master; they were worth a fortune! And what a beautiful yellow-green hue they had. The next day I went right out and purchased a new china cabinet and proudly exhibited my beautiful, priceless dishes.

How often we don't value the treasures that have been given to us. Similarly, the Scriptures tell us that no eye has seen and no ear has heard what God has prepared for his children who love him and who are dedicated to him.

May this last day of the Feast of Dedication be a time to dedicate ourselves to recognizing the wonderful blessings our Father has given us.

Today I Will

. . . dust off and appreciate the incredible riches that have been given to me in Yeshua, the Messiah of Israel.

TEVET

3

טבת

Dec. 22, 1998
Dec. 12, 1999
Dec. 29, 2000 (מ)
Dec. 18, 2001
Dec. 8, 2002
Dec. 28, 2003

Traditional *Chanukkah* (the Feast of Dedication) Day 8 for the year 2000

Prayer Focus

TEVET

4

טבת

Dec. 23, 1998
Dec. 13, 1999
Dec. 30, 2000 (10)
Dec. 19, 2001
Dec. 9, 2002
Dec. 29, 2003

From one man he has made every nation living on the entire surface of the earth (Acts 17:26).

For several years the Ku Klux Klan placed a cross in our city's main square during December. This act caused great controversy. Invariably, someone would knock the cross over during the night, which always got news coverage. Others would write notes expressing their opinion of the Klan, sticking them on a fence surrounding the cross. Most of what was written is not worth repeating. However, there was one exception. It simply contained the verse quoted above. I had never thought about the words "from one man he has made every nation" until I read them on that fence. That one verse, hand printed on an old piece of cardboard, exposed the mockery of the Klan's white supremacy.

The rabbis of old asked, "Why did the Creator form life from a single ancestor?" They answered, "So the families of mankind cannot boast that they sprang from superior stock, but instead might recognize their kinship with all men." Although every people-group, without exception, has sometimes forgotten this truth, we as Messianic believers must never forget it. When Kefa (Peter) declared that "God does not play favorites" (Acts 10:34), he was saying that Yeshua shed his blood for every individual in whose veins Adam's blood flows. When that biblical truth takes hold of our hearts, there is no room for prejudice, racism or anti-Semitism.

Prayer Focus

Today I Will

. . . ask the Lord to cleanse me of all prejudice, and to help me see all mankind as he does: made "from one man."

MW

The Y'vusi, the inhabitants of that region [Jerusalem]. . . . were thinking, "David will never get in here" (2 Sam. 5:6).

When the independence of the modern Jewish State was within weeks of being declared, Arab armies outnumbering the Israelis five-to-one stood poised to attack. "We shall push the Jews into the sea!" boasted *Haj* Amin el Husseini, the *Mufti* (Palestinian religious leader) of Jerusalem.

Golda Meir, a Russian-born Jewish woman raised in Milwaukee and living in Israel, was dispatched to the United States in early 1948. She was sent to raise the money needed to buy weapons that would save the infant state from death, even as it was being born.

Mrs. Meir told her antagonistic and uninterested audience of potential donors, "Our State will be born, and we will shed our best blood. You cannot affect whether or not this war will occur; that decision has already been taken. With what you do, you will only decide whether we will win or lose."

Golda was sent to try to raise twenty-five million dollars; she raised fifty-million—twenty-five million of it in one evening! At the eleventh hour, Israel had mustered the resources it needed to defend its rebirth into the modern era. Despite the boasting of the *Mufti*, the State of Israel was born.

The Scripture says, "No weapon made will prevail against you" (Isa. 54:17).

Today I Will

. . . stand in the name of Yeshua against the attacks of the enemy (Ps. 18:29).

TEVET

5

טבת

Dec. 24, 1998
Dec. 14, 1999
Dec. 31, 2000
Dec. 20, 2001
Dec. 10, 2002
Dec. 30, 2003

Biblical
On this day, Ezekiel learned that Jerusalem had fallen (Ezek. 33:21).

Prayer Focus

TEVET

6

טבת

Dec. 25, 1998
Dec. 15, 1999
Jan. 1, 2001
Dec. 21, 2001
Dec. 11, 2002
Dec. 31, 2003

Prayer Focus

Each of us should please his neighbor (Rom. 15:2).

It is good to be pleasing. We are supposed to please people and do things to comfort others and build relationships. But there is a big difference between pleasing people and being "people-pleasers." People-pleasers do not seek to merely express love and appreciation. Rather, they do their "pleasing" with ulterior motives. People-pleasers are not commited to the truth. They are willing to alter their ideas, views, personal feelings, even commitments, in order to receive personal benefit or praise.

Yeshua addressed this issue when he spoke about people who give alms in order to receive honor by men, "So, when you do *tzedakah* (charitable giving), don't announce it with trumpets to win people's praise, like the hypocrites in the synagoguges and on the streets" (Matt. 6:2).

We all succumb to the temptation to "people-please" at the expense of the truth, or at the expense of the gospel. Yochanan (John) tells us, "Many of the leaders did trust in him; but because of the *P'rushim* [Pharisees] they did not say so openly, out of fear of being banned from the synagogue; for they loved praise from other people more than praise from God" (John 12:42–43). Let us be pleasing people while avoiding the trap of becoming people-pleasers.

Today I Will

. . . seek the praise of God in all that I do.

JS

The word of *ADONAI* came to Yonah a second time: "Set out for the great city of Ninveh, and proclaim to it the message I will give you" (Jon. 3:2).

If there was ever anyone in need of a second chance from God, it was Yonah (Jonah). Having ignored the express command of God to go and preach to Ninveh (Nineveh), he ran in the opposite direction and ended up in the belly of a big fish. Disobedience to God may seem attractive at times, but the consequences are always deadly. Jonah learned that truth the hard way and turned from his sin in repentance. God is always quick to forgive in response to genuine repentance. He gave Yonah a second chance. But notice, God gave him a second chance to make right what he had done wrong. His first responsibility after getting out of the fish was to go to Ninveh.

When we repent, it's not enough to say, "I'm sorry." The question is, "What are we going to do to make it right?" God gave Yonah a chance to make it right and Jonah proved his repentance genuine by obeying God and going to Ninveh. When we go to God in repentance, it's not enough to say, "I'm sorry." God wants to know, "What will you do now to make it right?" I saw a bumper sticker one day that read, "If you love Jesus don't honk, obey." Well put!

God is a God who gives second, third, fourth, yes, even fifth chances. But the chance he always offers us is to obey him and make things right. Here is a little piece of Jewish wisdom: if God has given you a second chance to do something right, go and do it.

Today I Will

. . . take advantage of the opportunity God has given me to make right what has been wrong and to obey him.

Dec. 26, 1998 (11)
Dec. 16, 1999
Jan. 2, 2001
Dec. 22, 2001 (11)
Dec. 12, 2002
Jan. 1, 2004

Prayer Focus

DB

TEVET

8

טבת

Dec. 27, 1998
Dec. 17, 1999
Jan. 3, 2001
Dec. 23, 2001
Dec. 13, 2002
Jan. 2, 2004

We know that God causes everything to work together for the good of those who love God (Rom. 8:28).

Sometimes we make poor choices in life. Later, we pout over the grim consequences: a child born out of wedlock; a jail term for dealing drugs; uninspiring career options as a result of poor grades; a chronic disease but no health insurance. Is this the time to say, cheerfully, "God causes all things to work together for good . . . "?

The *Talmud* relates the experience of Rabbi Akiva while visiting an inhospitable town. He arrived in the evening and the innkeeper and home owners refused to grant him shelter. Rabbi Akiva was forced, with his candle, donkey and rooster, to spend the night in a field by the road. He lit his candle to study *Torah*, but the wind quickly blew it out. Then, a mountain lion attacked his donkey in the dark and carried it away. Still later, a weasel crept into the camp and stole the rooster. What a night! But Rabbi Akiva told himself, "This too is for the best."

At dawn, he awoke to discover the whole town had been ransacked and its inhabitants carried away by a band of marauding thieves. Had the townspeople given him shelter, had his candle remained lit, had his donkey brayed or his rooster crowed, he too would have been carried away with the rest. Rabbi Akiva gave thanks and continued on his way.

Prayer Focus

Today I Will

. . . commit myself to suspend judgment when I pass through the trials of life.

JEF

Of the descendants of Yissakhar, men who understood the times and knew what Isra'el ought to do, there were 200 leaders, and all their kinsmen were under their command (1 Chron. 12:32[33]).

Vladimir Jabotinsky was a volcano of Zionist vision, rhetoric and action, who trained and inspired modern Israeli leaders like Menachem Begin. When much of European Jewry was enjoying a false security at the end of the 19th century, inspired by the Age of Enlightenment which had been co-opted into Jewish religious circles as *Haskalah* (Enlightenment), Jabotinsky was screaming at the top of his lungs, "The ground of Europe is burning under your feet, and you do not smell the smoke! Get out while you can! Let us rebuild our Homeland!" Jabotinsky saw what very few around him could see, even though they were all looking at the same thing.

The *Tanakh* (1 Chron. 12:32) accords the tribe of Issachar the same compliment during the rise of King David. The Scriptures give us a thrilling and tantalizing summons, "ADONAI, God, does nothing without revealing his plan to his servants the prophets" (Amos 3:7). Happily, God's desire is for us to know what is going on. God is not playing hide-and-seek with us. Even when God tells us, "I am doing something new" (Isa. 43:19), he continues with an almost playful invitation for us to join with him, to know his mind, " . . . it's springing up—can't you see it?" (Isa. 43:19). We can, for we have the mind of Messiah.

Today I Will

. . . ask God to deepen my understanding of his plans for my generation, and seek to strengthen my connection to his purposes.

TEVET

9

טבת

Dec. 28, 1998
Dec. 18, 1999 (11)
Jan. 4, 2001
Dec. 24, 2001
Dec. 14, 2002 (11)
Jan. 3, 2004 (11)

Prayer Focus

BC

TEVET

10

טבת

Dec. 29, 1998 (מ)
Dec. 19, 1999 (מ)
Jan. 5, 2001 (מ)
Dec. 25, 2001 (מ)
Dec. 15, 2002 (מ)
Jan. 4, 2004 (מ)

Biblical
On this day, Ezekiel delivered his prophecy of the cooking pot (Ezek. 24:1); Nebuchadnezzar, King of Babylon, besieged Jerusalem (2 Kings 25:1).

Traditional
Asarah BeTevet (10th of Tevet) See Zech. 8:19

Prayer Focus

For *ADONAI* your God has chosen him . . . to stand and serve in the name of *ADONAI* (Deut. 18:5).

The first use of the phrase "in the name of *ADONAI*" is found in Deuteronomy 18. The context is the distribution of duties of the tribe of Levi within the camp of Israel. This specific phrase refers to the authority of the Lord. In the Scriptures, a person's name is his identity, and identity in the case of deity is always related to authority. In verses 19–20, we see this very clearly in describing a prophet who speaks "in the name of *ADONAI*" and correctly uses or misuses authority. It is clear, then, that speaking or praying "in the name of *ADONAI*" is always an issue of authority.

Yeshua commanded his disciples to approach the Father with the authority that God had given him. He said, "Whatever you ask for in my name, I will do" (John 14:13). We have no authority of our own. Rather, we are messengers empowered by the Messiah with delegated authority to do his will. It is with this authority that we can approach our Father in heaven. At the end of the verse it says, "If you ask for something in my name, I will do it." Elsewhere, Yeshua says that if we ask something of the Father in Yeshua's name, he will do it (see John 15:6). The Father will send Yeshua to perform whatever we have asked in the authority of his name.

Let us remember that we, like Aaron and his household, have also been chosen to minister "in the name of *ADONAI*."

Today I Will

. . . lift up prayers to the Lord in the authority of the Messiah's name.

JS

We are God's making, created in union with the Messiah Yeshua for a life of good actions (Eph. 2:10).

Do you like poetry? No? You may want to reconsider because poetry is very relevant to your life according to the Word of God. In the above Scripture, it is written, "We are God's making." In the Greek, it reads, "For we are his *poiayma*," from which we get the English word "poem." God is a poet, and you, if you've been born again, are his poem.

Sometimes we get very caught up in our works. Works are vital to a healthy walk, but if that's all we focus on, we miss the point. We *are* actually God's good work! In fact, we are his poem. God creates only works of beauty and works of grace. When we go our own way, or when we try God's way in our own strength and effort, life becomes a struggle, without rhyme or reason. But when we yield to the flowing and filling of his *Ruach* (Spirit), life becomes what it's *supposed* to be—a poem, written by the finger of God, perfect in rhyme and reason, styled with sweetness and grace, with appropriately placed rests and carrying a beautiful message.

If we follow the *Ruach* (Spirit) of the poet, our lives will actually become poems of God.

Today I Will

. . . think of one way I can yield my life to God as his poem.

TEVET

11

טבת

Dec. 30, 1998
Dec. 20, 1999
Jan. 6, 2001 (11)
Dec. 26, 2001
Dec. 16, 2002
Jan. 5, 2004

Prayer Focus

JC

TEVET

12

טבת

Dec. 31, 1998
Dec. 21, 1999
Jan. 7, 2001
Dec. 27, 2001
Dec. 17, 2002
Jan. 6, 2004

Biblical
On this day, Ezekiel delivered a prophecy against Egypt (Ezek. 29:1).

Prayer Focus

Write down the vision clearly on tablets, so that even a runner can read it (Hab. 2:2).

Over the past few years, I have met many people who were never able to accomplish the objectives God had set before them. The reason, in many cases, was their failure to develop a workable plan for realizing their vision and communicating that plan effectively to others who could help bring it about.

When the Lord called me to minister in Russia, he simply said, "Go and reach my people." I knew a plan was needed to fulfill God's word to my heart, but the only other clear direction I had was to return to St. Petersburg. So I went, trusting God would tell me more when I got there. He did and, eventually, the Messianic music outreach festivals were born.

However, these festivals didn't just "happen." An organizational structure had to be developed that would be simple, yet would allow as many people as possible to be involved. Then the vision had to be communicated and the laborers had to be gathered. It took enormous work to bring the vision to pass; but, eventually, I saw God's goals realized.

Has God given you a vision? Write it down, articulate it to others, and ask the Lord to give you a clear plan in order to accomplish it. Then step out in faith and be ready to work hard!

Today I Will

. . . take the first step to fulfilling the vision God has spoken to my heart. "Lord, revive that which you spoke to me long ago; your servant is listening."

JB

Because you are lukewarm, neither cold nor hot, I will vomit you out of my mouth (Rev. 3:16).

Jan. 1, 1999
Dec. 22, 1999
Jan. 8, 2001
Dec. 28, 2001
Dec. 18, 2002
Jan. 7, 2004

An aqueduct brought water to Laodicea. The water was cool and refreshing in the north, but by the time it reached Laodicea it was lukewarm. And you know what lukewarm water tastes like!

Yochanan (John) used this well-known situation to characterize the believers in Laodicea who were not super-active in the life of the Messiah, but who were also not altogether disinterested. The lukewarm taste in God's mouth regarding the state of these Jewish and Gentile believers was serious. God would spit them out of his mouth. The people were wealthy and claimed to have no needs, but from God's perspective they were poor. The Lord called them to repent.

In today's society, we are faced with the same temptations as were those Laodicean believers. We must therefore guard against the temptation of being unwilling to leave our "comfort zones," or becoming too busy to further the Kingdom of God on earth. We can learn a lesson from the Messiah, who said, "For where your wealth is, there your heart will be also" (Matt. 6:21). Let us reject lukewarmness and commit our whole lives to the Lord.

Prayer Focus

Today I Will

. . . seek to be poor in spirit—to be one who is fully dependent on God.

JR

Jan. 2, 1999 (12)
Dec. 23, 1999
Jan. 9, 2001
Dec. 29, 2001 (12)
Dec. 19, 2002
Jan. 8, 2004

In the *Tanakh* it is written, "*ADONAI* says, 'Vengeance is my responsibility; I will repay'" (Rom. 12:19).

Many of us have overly developed sensibilities when it comes to perceived insults, false accusations and the like. The Scriptures urge us to not be defensive but to leave room for wrath—God's wrath, that is. God is our defense and he will take up our cause, even if it is not as soon as we would hope. I've seen this principle born out in personal outreach on the streets.

Once, while handing out gospel tracts in Haifa, I and a few others with me were attacked by a group of *yeshivah bochers* (rabbinical students) and their rabbi. The rabbi saw one of our people with a bag full of tracts. He grabbed the bag with the tracts in it, swung it around over his head and let the bag sail into the middle of the street where it came crashing down on top of a passing car. The motorist braked his car to a screeching halt and went chasing after the rabbi. At this point, all the *yeshivah bochers* left and went to protect their rabbi. We were able to leave the site in relative peace and security.

God had taken care of that rabbi and he had taken care of us. He continues to do that in less dramatic ways in our daily lives. Sometimes, we rob ourselves of the joy of seeing him come to our defense because we seek to exact our own revenge. Let's experience the blessing of stepping back and watching God take up our cause.

Prayer Focus

Today I Will

. . . commit myself to being less defensive and allowing God to defend me in every situation.

DB

Sarah lived to be 127 years old; these were the years of Sarah's life (Gen. 23:1).

The *Torah* tells in great detail the story of Abraham commissioning his chief steward to find a suitable wife for his son Isaac. The emphasis of the Genesis account switches from father to son after Isaac brought Rebekah "into his mother Sarah's tent . . . and she became his wife" (Gen. 24:67). Indeed, although Abraham lived for another 35 years, it's no coincidence that his presence in Scripture is clearly diminished after the death of Sarah.

We are given more detail about the patriarchs than their wives; yet, without their godly wives, these men would not have been able to fulfill their callings (which was more than just having children!) Although ninety-nine percent of the recorded covenant promises were between God and Abraham, Sarah was always there, persevering alongside her husband. She walked in the kind of faith of which Yeshua spoke: "How blessed are those who do not see, but trust anyway!" (John 20:29)

Husbands and wives may have different gifts, but they are united in their calling. We who are married servants of the Lord, can therefore attain only that which God has called us to through being in love and harmony with our spouses, recognizing that our differences are complimentary rather than contradictory.

Jan. 3, 1999
Dec. 24, 1999
Jan. 10, 2001
Dec. 30, 2001
Dec. 20, 2002
Jan. 9, 2004

Prayer Focus

Today I Will

. . . give thanks with greater appreciation for the spouse the Lord has given me, and will endeavor to see the health of that relationship as central to the success of our service to God.

MM

TEVET

16

טבת

Jan. 4, 1999
Dec. 25, 1999 (12)
Jan. 11, 2001
Dec. 31, 2001
Dec. 21, 2002 (12)
Jan. 10, 2004 (12)

Prayer Focus

Love your enemies! Pray for those who persecute you! (Matt. 5:44).

The power to bless is stronger than the power to curse. God has provided us with the opportunity to choose one or the other. Just as our people stood before Mount Gerizim and Mount Ebal, and were faced with the choice of blessings or curses, so we today are presented with that same choice in serving the Lord.

One day I was handing out gospel tracts on Dizengoff Street in Tel Aviv. A Jewish man approached me and angrily said, "You're leading Israel astray and bringing a curse down on your head." Then he said, "I'm going to stand here and pray that God curse you. You pray to your Jesus that he curse me and we'll see whose God is stronger." I had never faced such a situation before, but I found myself saying to him, "You can pray a curse on me, but I'm going to pray that God bless you by giving you the knowledge that Yeshua really is the Messiah." He began to pray in Hebrew and I in English.

Several days later, a whole group was going to hand out tracts at the beach. We pulled into the parking lot, and who should be standing there, but this man who had pronounced the curse. Now he was surrounded by a whole group of Jewish believers in Yeshua. At that moment, I realized God was answering my prayer and revealing himself in a special way to this man. The power to bless is stronger than the power to curse.

Today I Will

. . . look for opportunities to bless rather than curse those who may mistreat me.

DB

It was God who sent me ahead of you to preserve life (Gen. 45:5).

Yosef (Joseph) had paid an enormous price to be sent ahead to preserve life. His brothers had nearly killed him at Shechem. He suffered heavily in his efforts to "preserve life"—thrown into a pit and sold by his brothers into slavery!

Yosef's troubles multiplied when he was cast into prison in Egypt for a bum rap and left to languish there for nearly a decade, with another two years besides. Yet despite foreign exile, injustice, and a lengthy prison term, Yosef here summarizes his life favorably.

Looking back with eyes of faith, Yosef sees that he has now become *av* (father, advisor) to Pharaoh. Early dreams of his brothers bowing before him have come true. His interpretation of Pharaoh's dreams of feast and famine have come to pass in time for him to rescue Egypt and his whole family, too! What's more, his father and brothers have come to live in his own mansion! What more could he ask for? God has turned every tear to joy. With a happy heart, Yosef can comfort his brothers with kindness and truth.

The psalmist says, "*Adonai* will fulfill his purpose for me" (Ps. 138:8). This promise can be realized not only for Yosef, but for anyone who walks in faith with the confidence that God will finish what he has begun. Can you believe that God is transforming your circumstances, too?

Today I Will

. . . view my whole life with eyes of faith.

TEVET

17

טבת

Jan. 5, 1999
Dec. 26, 1999
Jan. 12, 2001
Jan. 1, 2002
Dec. 22, 2002
Jan. 11, 2004

Prayer Focus

JEF

TEVET
18
טבת

Jan. 6, 1999
Dec. 27, 1999
Jan. 13, 2001 (12)
Jan. 2, 2002
Dec. 23, 2002
Jan. 12, 2004

Prayer Focus

Make your requests known to God by prayer and petition, with thanksgiving (Phil. 4:6).

Since childhood, I wanted to be a millionaire. I worked diligently toward that goal for most of my life and, as planned, went to college to earn a degree in business administration. During my second year, I had an encounter with the Lord and immediately felt a strong call to full-time ministry. I fought this call for many months, knowing that it meant giving up my dreams of immense wealth. Finally, however, I gave in, switching my major to Judaism and Early Christianity.

After graduation, I was ready for ministry but no doors opened to me. Instead, I began driving a bread truck, delivering Cohen's Kosher Rye Bread. Every day, I would drive my route, complaining to the Lord about what I had given up for him! One day, in my haste, I forgot to close the door latches on the bread trays and, when I slammed on the brakes to avoid going through a red light, all the bread came sliding forward on top of me. That's when God said, "You need to learn how to deliver physical bread with joy before you will be ready to deliver spiritual bread to anyone!" My attitude immediately changed. I began to praise him and soon I was in full-time ministry.

Are you complaining about your circumstances? Begin praising him right now!

Today I Will

. . . begin to praise God in the midst of difficulties and make my needs known to him with thanksgiving. I will focus upon him and not on the problem.

JB

Everyone will know that you are my *talmidim* [disciples] by the fact that you have love for each other (John 13:35).

Jan. 7, 1999
Dec. 28, 1999
Jan. 14, 2001
Jan. 3, 2002
Dec. 24, 2002
Jan. 13, 2004

When I was a boy, I had a poster on my bedroom wall with the familiar character, Charlie Brown, leaning on his elbows looking rather dour. The caption read, "I love humanity—it's people I can't stand." This theme of loving one another is significant, not only because of the many passages of Scripture that emphasize it, but because it is so lacking among believers today.

Rabbi Levi Isaac of Berdichev said, "Whether a man really loves God can be determined by his love for his fellow man." Unfortunately, we only pay lip service to this responsibility. We feel that in some cosmic way we fulfill this demand of Scripture just by being followers of Yeshua. We have a "say-so" love and not a "do-so" love, but God calls us to so much more. Our love of God is integrally connected to our love for others. It is only God's love in us that can empower us to love others. We love because he first loved us.

God's love is sacrificial; it holds nothing back. God's love is undeserved; the recipient can make no claim to that love. When we love one another, our love must be sacrificial and it must be extended, even to those whom we feel don't deserve it. We love because he first loved us, and when we love, the world will see the power of Yeshua in action.

Prayer Focus

. . . look to demonstrate the love of God to those I meet, especially those I find unlovely.

DB

TEVET

20

טבת

Jan. 8, 1999
Dec. 29, 1999
Jan. 15, 2001
Jan. 4, 2002
Dec. 25, 2002
Jan. 14, 2004

God said to Moshe [Moses], "*Ehyeh Asher Ehyeh* [I am/will be what I am/will be]" (Exod. 3:14).

In biblical Jewish understanding, a "name" was more than simply a series of sounds that, when pronounced together, formed a word. To the mind of an ancient Israelite, a name communicated the nature of the person.

In the case of deities, the name described a god's nature or function. When Moses asked for God's name in Exodus 3, he received a response that immediately set God apart from anything that could be fully communicated to or grasped by the human mind. God declared himself to be independent of all things and above all things, including all other gods. No name (in the biblical sense) could contain him, for everything was made by him. That is why he says, "I Am Who I Am." He is the eternal constant, "upholding all that exists by his powerful word" (Heb. 1:3).

The investors in Lloyds of London (the company that insures the treasures of the rich and famous) are simply referred to in the British press as "the names." This acknowledges the fact that they are some of the most wealthy and powerful people on earth. It might be nice to have some of those "names" as friends. But I would much rather have him who calls himself *Ehyeh* (I Will Be, or, I Am), the eternal constant of the universe, as my friend.

Has it hit you today that the ruler of the universe is your friend?

Prayer Focus

Today I Will

. . . smile in the knowledge that God is my friend.

DR

How blessed are those who reject the advice of the wicked, don't stand on the way of sinners or sit where scoffers sit! (Ps. 1:1)

Jan. 9, 1999 (13)
Dec. 30, 1999
Jan. 16, 2001
Jan. 5, 2002 (13)
Dec. 26, 2002
Jan. 15, 2004

Sometimes we look at life as a choice between following Messiah or being happy, but it's really not that way at all. In fact, we cannot be truly happy without following the Lord. When Yeshua gave the *derash* (sermon) on the Mount, he said, "How blessed are the poor in spirit. . . . How blessed are the meek. . . . How blessed are those who hunger and thirst for righteousness. . . . How blessed are those who make peace" (Matt. 5:3–9). That's a lot of blessedness. The word in Hebrew for "blessed" is *ashrey*. It doesn't just mean "blessed"; it also means "happy," or literally, "How happy!"

Ashrey is derived from the Hebrew word for "straight" or "right." For in the end, the way of happiness and the way of righteousness always turn out to be the same path.

Do you want to be happy? Stop seeking happiness. Seek righteousness instead. Seek what is right, believe what is right, receive what is right, do what is right, walk in what is right, live by what is right. All the rest will be added unto you. God's way is the way of true joy. Follow it and you'll be blessed, and not only blessed, but happy . . . and not only happy, but you'll arrive at that state in which you'll say, "*Ashrey*!" (How happy!)—with an exclamation point!

Prayer Focus

Today I Will

. . . remember that the way of righteousness and joy are the same path.

JC

Jan. 10, 1999
Dec. 31, 1999
Jan. 17, 2001
Jan. 6, 2002
Dec. 27, 2002
Jan. 16, 2004

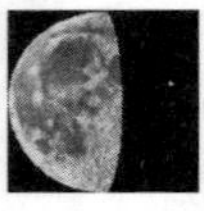

Prayer Focus

I am coming soon, and my rewards are with me to give to each person according to what he has done (Rev. 22:12).

Many believers seem uncomfortable with the idea of seeking reward from God, dismissing it as unspiritual and unnecessary. Yet the Bible does not deem it unworthy or unspiritual to work for a reward. Quite the contrary. From Genesis to Revelation, God uses the promise of reward and the threat of punishment to elicit from individuals proper behavior toward him and toward one another.

Perhaps our struggle over rewards reflects the ambivalence many of us experience over the place of desire and gratification in our lives. In his book, *The Weight of Glory*, C.S. Lewis writes, "If there lurks in most modern minds the notion that to desire our own good and earnestly hope for the enjoyment of it is a bad thing, I submit this notion has crept in from Kant and the stoics and is no part of the Christian faith. Indeed, if we consider the unblushing promises of reward and the staggering nature of the rewards God promised in the gospels, it would seem that our Lord finds our desires, not too strong, but too weak."

God promises to reward his children with good things, both here in this life and in the life to come. We need to cultivate in our own hearts a longing for the good things God wants to give us. He will surely reward us because he loves to give good things to his children.

Today I Will

. . . cultivate in my own heart a desire for the rewards that God promises to those who seek him.

DB

Let us keep paying attention to one another, in order to spur each other on to love and good deeds (Heb. 10:24).

Jan. 11, 1999
Jan. 1, 2000 (13)*
Jan. 18, 2001
Jan. 7, 2002
Dec. 28, 2002 (13)*
Jan. 17, 2004 (13)*

One of the most neglected responsibilities among believers today is the responsibility to encourage one another. The author of the Book of Hebrews says, "spur each other on to love and good deeds." All too often, we are sparing with our praise and so fail to spur one another on with the kind of encouragement that others may need to hear from us.

Yeshua was a wonderful model of encouragement for his followers. He considered his disciples his most important responsibility on earth. He said, "I am praying for them. . . . and in them I have been glorified" (John 17:9–10). Yeshua did not see his greatest work on the earth as raising the dead, turning the water into wine, multiplying the loaves and fishes, or healing the sick. He gloried in his disciples, the same disciples who slept while he prayed. They were, in a sense, his reward.

Often, we admire and heap praise on people who aren't even known to us; for example, media stars or accomplished athletes. Yet we are sparing with praise and encouragement for the ones closest to us, those we love the most. Have you ever noticed that when you're using a sprinkler to water grass, that the grass closest to the sprinkler is sometimes more brown and dried out than the grass further away from the sprinkler? So much energy and drive from the sprinkler goes to reach the farthest parts of the yard, that the grass closest to the source of water is left dry. This is true in our own lives when it comes to encouraging those close to us as well.

Be aware of the sprinkler syndrome! Let's be sure to encourage one another, especially those closest to us, and all the more as we see the day of Messiah's return approaching.

Prayer Focus

Today I Will

. . . actively look for ways to encourage others in my life.

DB

Jan. 12, 1999
Jan. 2, 2000
Jan. 19, 2001
Jan. 8, 2002
Dec. 29, 2002
Jan. 18, 2004

Pray for *shalom* in Yerushalayim; may those who love you prosper (Ps. 122:6).

The Scriptures exhort us to pray for the peace of Yerushalayim (Jerusalem). What does this really mean? Should we pray, for example, that the conflict between Jews and Arabs would cease? Such prayers are good, but I believe God is calling us to ask for more.

The Hebrew word translated *shalom* (peace) in the above passage involves sharing a deep unity and commitment to the well-being of another individual or group.

Throughout history, we have seen that putting an end to war does not necessarily guarantee lasting peace. Though the conflict may cease, hatred can still exist in the hearts of people. Hostility and violence in the Middle East cannot be stopped by giving back land, nor by any other human effort. There will never be true peace in Israel until the Prince of Peace, Yeshua, returns and transforms hearts. Only when he is ruling and reigning in people's lives will true peace come to Yerushalayim.

God is calling Messianic believers to pray for lasting peace and to work toward it as individuals. It means laying aside prejudice of every kind, loving the Arab people as well as our Jewish brethren, and praying for their salvation. Only then, through the transforming love of Yeshua, will true peace come to Yerushalayim.

Prayer Focus

Today I Will

. . . begin to pray for the true peace of Yerushalayim; for the salvation of both Jews and Arabs and the return of Yeshua to Zion!

JB

Jan. 13, 1999
Jan. 3, 2000
Jan. 20, 2001 (13)*
Jan. 9, 2002
Dec. 30, 2002
Jan. 19, 2004

Get yourself out of your country, away from your kinsmen and away from your father's house, and go to the land that I will show you (Gen. 12:1).

Did you ever notice that when the Lord spoke to Abram and promised him the Land, he did not tell him where to go? Imagine the Lord telling you something like that: "Just pack and I will show you." So, you hire a moving van, they load up your belongings and the driver asks, "Where to, buddy?"

"I'm not sure yet," you say. "Just start driving and the Lord will tell us." They will probably think you're crazy, and, if they agree *not* to dump your stuff out of the van, they will probably require you to pay a hefty sum in advance!

Abram obeyed God in that kind of situation! I think God did it that way so Abram would have to depend on God completely, every single day. That's what faith is all about—utter and complete dependence on God.

When we read that "God resists the proud but gives grace to the humble," it means that God resists those who rely solely on their own abilities and he gives grace to those who are dependent on him. Abram had such a dependence and it was "credited to his account as righteousness" (Rom. 4:3).

Are we dependent on the Lord today for direction, or are we independent, trying to do it our own way? Go God's way today!

Prayer Focus

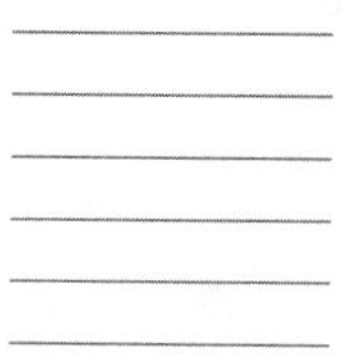

Today I Will

. . . repent of all independence in my life and, like father Abram, trust in God to lead me into his promised land for my life.

JB

TEVET

26

טבת

Jan. 14, 1999
Jan. 4, 2000
Jan. 21, 2001
Jan. 10, 2002
Dec. 31, 2002
Jan. 20, 2004

Yitzchak prayed to *ADONAI* on behalf of his wife, because she was childless (Gen. 25:21).

Yitzchak (Isaac) had done everything right! He had allowed his father Abraham to personally arrange the selection of his wife. Yitzchak had patiently stayed away from the nearby Canaanite women. Rivkah's (Rebekah's) identity as God's own choice was confirmed by supernatural signs. She was the one.

Amazingly, the girl was willing to make the journey into a distant land filled with danger, to be the wife of a man she had never seen. We can imagine the feelings that Yitzchak and Rivkah wrestled with as the years went by. The one thing necessary for the family of Abraham to fulfill its calling was the bearing of children . . . and now Miss Right could not do so!

Yitzchak married at forty years of age; his wife finally conceived when he was sixty. Those were a hard twenty years! Would Yitzchak have chosen Rivkah had he seen the immediate future, or the way Rivkah's brother Laban would treat their son Ya'akov (Jacob) in the more distant times to come? God does not tell us the future in detail because we would not respond to it correctly. Rivkah was God's exact choice, and God's choice is not defined by perfection as we define it. In Yitzchak and Rivkah's family, we behold God's perfect will being worked out through imperfect people. Such is godly life in the real world.

Prayer Focus

Today I Will

. . . yield myself to the simple fact that faith in God is not a ticket to smooth sailing through this life. "I pray, O God, let me choose your way in every circumstance."

BC

Don't forget to be friendly to outsiders; for in so doing, some people, without knowing it, have entertained angels (Heb. 13:2).

What was the sin of Sodom? Although the city is most commonly associated with sins of sexual perversion, it was judged for its lack of hospitality toward strangers. The two angels tested Lot's hospitality when they arrived in Sodom. Would Lot insist that they stay with him, or would he let them spend the night in the open square? The angels had just enjoyed Abraham's lavish hospitality on their way to Sodom. Now Abraham's nephew Lot showed that he too understood the importance of hospitality. Lot also indirectly indicted Sodom by not allowing the angels to remain in the city square, as he knew what fate awaited them. Indeed, when the angels accepted Lot's hospitality, the men of Sodom came to his very door to demand that he turn his guests over to them to be sexually assaulted.

The sages teach that it was a crime in Sodom to help anyone in need (Sanhedrin 109a, b). Because their city was so well-situated, "like the garden of *ADONAI*" (Gen. 13:10), the men of Sodom feared that poor strangers would take advantage of them and deplete their wealth. Let us learn a lesson from Sodom. The Scriptures warn us that prosperity is a snare, because it may make us closed-hearted to our brothers in need.

...look for opportunities to help a stranger or needy person around me.

TEVET

27

טבת

Jan. 15, 1999
Jan. 5, 2000
Jan. 22, 2001
Jan. 11, 2002
Jan. 1, 2003
Jan. 21, 2004

Prayer Focus

RR

TEVET

28

טבת

Jan. 16, 1999 (14)*
Jan. 6, 2000
Jan. 23, 2001
Jan. 12, 2002 (14)*
Jan. 2, 2003
Jan. 22, 2004

God loves a cheerful giver (2 Cor. 9:7).

Most people miss out on the joy of giving. Instead, we hang on to possessions as though *they* are what makes us happy. An old Yiddish proverb says, *Der veg iz der veister tsu de keshene* (The longest way is the one to the pocket). But reluctant charity is no charity at all. Have you ever asked someone for a favor and had them respond with a sour look and say, "Well, I suppose so. If you really need it." You're inclined to tell them, "Well, if it's all that painful, just forget it."

I think God must feel like saying that to us a lot. He loves a cheerful giver and that's why he made giving a part of worship. In ancient Israel, people were to bring their most prized possessions—the animals of their flock—and sacrifice them on the altar. This was worship that God found acceptable.

Today we don't sacrifice animals, yet the Lord still wants us to sacrifice. God doesn't need our money, he wants us. If he really does have us, that will be demonstrated in the way we give. Are we giving worshipfully and cheerfully in response to all he has given to us?

Prayer Focus

Today I Will

. . . commit myself to giving to God with a cheerful heart and in response to all that he has given me.

DB

You will receive everything you ask for in prayer, no matter what it is, provided you have trust (Matt. 21:22).

Jan. 17, 1999
Jan. 7, 2000
Jan. 24, 2001
Jan. 13, 2002
Jan. 3, 2003
Jan. 23, 2004

I was part of a singing group once that was scheduled to do a series of "peace" concerts in war-torn Northern Ireland. As Jews, we went with the message that Catholics and Protestants should stop fighting and behave as one in the Lord.

We were scheduled one afternoon to do a concert outside of Wellworth's department store in downtown Londonderry. The weather looked menacing, but we knew the Lord wanted us there. We prayed that there would be no rain and expected a miracle. As we arrived at Wellworth's, the menacing sky menaced no more; it broke out in a thunderous downpour. We felt quite let down by God, to tell you the truth. Hadn't we prayed in faith? Hadn't we gone there at the risk of our lives to serve him? At the last moment, our guide found another venue, a store around the corner, where we could set up and sing, even with the pounding rain.

Then, in the middle of our concert, BOOM! A bomb had gone off, right next door to Wellworth's, the place where we would have been had the Lord "answered" our prayers.

Be encouraged. God always hears your prayers, but sometimes his answer is "No!" You wouldn't want it any other way.

Prayer Focus

Today I Will

. . . look expectantly for God's creative and wise answers to my petitions.

SHEVAT

1

שבט

Jan. 18, 1999
Jan. 8, 2000 (14/A)
Jan. 25, 2001
Jan. 14, 2002
Jan. 4, 2003 (14/A)
Jan. 24, 2004 (14/A)

Biblical
Rosh Chodesh
(the New Moon)

On this day, Moses proclaimed to the Israelites God's commandments (Deut. 1:3).

Traditional
Echad BeShevat
(1st of Shevat)

The period between Shevat 1 and Adar 7 is a time to renew one's love for the study of *Torah* and keeping God's commandments.

Prayer Focus

The *Torah* was given through Moshe; grace and truth came through Yeshua the Messiah (John 1:17).

Grace and truth (*chesed ve'emet*) are two of the "Thirteen Attributes of Mercy" that Jewish authorities deduce from Exod. 34:6–7. In this passage of *Torah*, Moshe (Moses) implores the Lord, "I beg you to show me your glory!" (Exod. 33:18) The Lord explains to Moshe that it would be impossible to see his face, "because a human being cannot look at me and remain alive" (Exod. 33:20). Nevertheless, he allows Moshe to see his back, his glory, as it passes by. Then he proclaims his name (his thirteen attributes), including *chesed ve'emet.*

Similarly, Yochanan (John) writes that when Yeshua appeared, "We saw his *Sh'khinah* [Glory]. . . . No one has ever seen God; but the only and unique Son, who is identical with God and is at the Father's side—he has made him known" (John 1:14, 18). Yeshua, who is full of *chesed ve'emet,* embodies and makes known the attributes of mercy described in the *Torah.* In the above Scripture, we are told that Moshe gave the *Torah*; Yeshua, however, is the embodiment of *Torah.* Yochanan is not drawing a contrast between *Torah* and *chesed ve'emet*; rather, he is showing how Yeshua became the living *Torah,* so that we might know God more fully in all his attributes, including his *chesed ve'emet.*

When we say to God "Please, show me your glory," he points us to Yeshua.

Today I Will

. . . seek to know God's glory more fully by drawing closer to Yeshua.

RR

Weren't ten cleansed? Where are the other nine? Was no one found coming back to give glory to God except this foreigner? (Luke 17:17)

Jan. 19, 1999
Jan. 9, 2000
Jan. 26, 2001
Jan. 15, 2002
Jan. 5, 2003
Jan. 25, 2004

Yeshua passed through a village on his final journey to Jerusalem and encountered ten men with *tzara'at* (various forms of skin disease). According to the *Torah*, once a priest determined that someone had *tzara'at*, the person must remain outside the settlements of Israel, crying out, "Unclean! unclean!" (Lev. 13:45–46) Similarly, these ten men stood far off and cried out to Yeshua for mercy.

Yeshua heard their cry and then sent them in faith to the priests for examination. *En route*, all ten were cleansed, but only one—a foreigner from Samaria—returned to thank Yeshua. To him, Yeshua said, "Your trust has saved you" (Luke 17:19). They all trusted Yeshua enough to start on their way to the priests. Only one, however, had a faith that was acceptable to Yeshua.

Isaiah calls us all unclean. Like the ten, we stand far off from God and his redeemed people. Yeshua cleanses and restores us, but do we respond with thanks? All ten men received great blessing, but only the Samaritan had the faith that Messiah seeks.

As we see all he has done for us, let us open our mouths to give him thanks!

Prayer Focus

Today I Will

. . . recognize and thank God for all he has done for me, especially for the gift of salvation in Messiah Yeshua.

RR

SHEVAT

3

שבט

Jan. 20, 1999
Jan. 10, 2000
Jan. 27, 2001 (14)
Jan. 16, 2002
Jan. 6, 2003
Jan. 26, 2004

A *talmid* is not greater than his rabbi. . . . it is enough for a *talmid* that he become like his rabbi (Matt. 10:24–25).

Yeshua was a rabbi, and like the great rabbis throughout Jewish history, he had a group of men around him who listened to his every word. They were his *talmidim* (from the Hebrew root *lamad*, meaning "learn" or "study").

If you call Yeshua Lord, then you are one of his *talmidim*. He's your rabbi and teacher, and you are his *talmid*, his student.

As his *talmid*, your life ought to be dedicated to learning all you can from your rabbi, Yeshua. Greet each day as his *talmid*, seeking to receive a new gem of life from your master and teacher. Hang on to everything he wants to teach you; make his words more precious than food or drink. For you are his *talmid* and he is your rabbi!

Prayer Focus

Today I Will

. . . seek from the Lord a new lesson. I'm one of his *talmidim*!

JC

Avraham got up early in the morning, saddled his donkey (Gen. 22:3).

The *Talmud* notes that Abraham does something most unusual in this passage of Scripture. Why does he, a man of dignity and wealth, rise up early to saddle his own donkey? Surely it would have been more proper to leave this task to the two young men who accompanied him on his way to Mount Moriah. The sages explain that Abraham rose early in his zeal to obey God. He was so eager to carry out God's directive to offer up Isaac that he personally attended to every detail of the journey.

The *Torah* tells of another prominent man who also rose early to saddle his own donkey—Balaam the prophet. Like Abraham, he was motivated by great zeal, but not zeal to obey God. He was zealous to earn the commission offered him in exchange for cursing Israel. He saddled his own donkey like Abraham, but rode off in the opposite direction, in defiance of God's will.

Zeal is good; without it, we will accomplish little. However, we need to foster zeal for God above all else. A multitude of things demand our enthusiasm but count for little in the end. Let us avoid "the way of Bil'am Ben-B'or who loved the wages of doing harm" (2 Pet. 2:15), and instead follow "in the footsteps of . . . Avraham *avinu* [our father Abraham]," who loved righteousness (Rom. 4:12).

Today I Will

. . . reserve my greatest enthusiasm for the things that matter to God.

SHEVAT

4

שבט

Jan. 21, 1999
Jan. 11, 2000
Jan. 28, 2001
Jan. 17, 2002
Jan. 7, 2003
Jan. 27, 2004

Prayer Focus

RR

SHEVAT

5

שבט

Jan. 22, 1999
Jan. 12, 2000
Jan. 29, 2001
Jan. 18, 2002
Jan. 8, 2003
Jan. 28, 2004

Prayer Focus

Everyone is to obey the governing authorities (Rom. 13:1).

Fear of authority, in the sense of reverence, is crucial for spiritual health. Yet there is also a phobia that seeks to avoid authority if at all possible. God places authority in our lives for our benefit. Our first authority in life is our parents. There are also teachers, elders, civic authorities and employers. Many have seen in the commandment to honor our fathers and mothers the implication that we are to honor all authorities.

Our lives should be open to the proper role of authority, recognizing that all authority represents God's authority. Even if the authority does not always act with integrity, we are to respect and submit. There is a limit, or course: if we are told to violate the command of Scripture, God's commandment must override authority for God is ultimately in charge.

If we cannot change the authorities in our lives (for example, by changing jobs) then we are to trust the providence of God. A harsh authority can build character in us. This requires *emunah* (faith) in God. Remember, he often works through authority to conform us to the image of Yeshua.

Today I Will

. . . be rightly related to authority.

DJ

Whatever touches the altar will become holy (Exod. 29:37).

As Yeshua and his disciples made their way through the crowd, a woman who had been hemorrhaging for twelve years pushed through and grabbed the *tzitzit* (tassel) of Yeshua's garment (Luke 8:43; Num. 15:37–41). According to the *Torah*, this woman's condition made her unclean, and as such, everything and everyone she touched was rendered unclean (Lev. 15:25). However, her contact with Yeshua had the opposite effect. She was healed.

Like the altar of God, the holiness of Yeshua had the power to convey holiness to others. When Yeshua touched the leper in Matt. 8:3, the leprosy was cleansed. When the woman touched Yeshua's *tzitzit*, her hemorrhaging stopped. And when Yeshua took the hand of the dead daughter of the synagogue official (Luke 8:54), the little girl was brought back to life. All those conditions would have rendered anyone else unclean. But Yeshua is not just anyone. He is the Altar of God. In him sinful humanity and a holy God can meet. Because of his sacrifice, we can be sanctified when we encounter him.

Today I Will

. . . press in to touch the Holy Altar, Yeshua, for he is the only way that I can be cleansed of my sins.

SHEVAT

6

שבט

Jan. 23, 1999 (15)
Jan. 13, 2000
Jan. 30, 2001
Jan. 19, 2002 (15)
Jan. 9, 2003
Jan. 29, 2004

Prayer Focus

MM

SHEVAT

7

שבט

Jan. 24, 1999
Jan. 14, 2000
Jan. 31, 2001
Jan. 20, 2002
Jan. 10, 2003
Jan. 30, 2004

This is the genealogy of Yeshua the Messiah, son of David, son of Avraham (Matt. 1:1).

Other than Jerusalem, Hebron is probably the most important city mentioned in Scripture. Though numerous passages could be cited regarding this ancient place, the most significant ones are found in Genesis 15 and 2 Samuel 5. In the former, it is mentioned as the place where Abraham believed God and his faith was reckoned to him as righteousness. It was also the location of the actual cutting of the covenant between God and Abraham. The latter passage indicates that Hebron is the place where David was made king over the entire nation of Israel.

It is clear that the establishment of the Abrahamic covenant, which created the Jewish people, and the establishment of the Davidic dynasty are foundational, not only for Israel, but for all believers. The opening words of the *Brit Chadashah* (New Covenant Scriptures) inextricably connect Yeshua with both Avraham (Abraham) and David, and therefore, with these two events which occurred in Hebron. Yeshua is the representative of the Jewish people and also the king of Israel. He is the quintessential Israelite and the greater Son of David. All that he has accomplished and all that he will bring about rests on the foundations laid through these two men in Hebron.

Thus, even the very first verse of the *Brit Chadashah* recognizes that it is impossible to accurately understand the work of Yeshua without seeing the historical, national and spiritual womb from which he was born.

Let us not ignore the history which brought forth the characters and events whose far-reaching significance affect believers even to this day.

Prayer Focus

Today I Will

. . . remember that God does not work in a vacuum. What he does today and tomorrow has roots in what he has done in the past.

MM

My sheep listen to my voice (John 10:27).

Many believers wish they could hear God's voice better, but most fail to realize that the *Ruach HaKodesh* (Holy Spirit) often speaks to us through the words he has *already* inspired.

King Shlomo (Solomon) articulated this principle of spiritual life when he wrote, "My son, obey your father's command, and don't abandon your mother's teaching. Bind them always on your heart, tie them around your neck. When you walk, they will lead you; when you lie down, they will watch over you; and when you wake up, they will talk with you" (Prov. 6:20–22). If we desire to hear God's voice more clearly, we must internalize more of God's Word through Scripture meditation and memorization. The believer who does this will find the *Ruach HaKodesh* illuminating verses throughout the course of the day.

A lifestyle of Scripture meditation also helps us to better recognize the voice of God. Have you ever entered a room full of people talking and suddenly heard a voice you recognized? Similarly, the more we meditate on God's Word, the more we learn to differentiate between God's voice and our own thoughts.

As part of the Good Shepherd's flock, let us train our ears to better hear what Yeshua is saying to us.

Today I Will

. . . listen for God's voice as he speaks to me through his Word.

SHEVAT

8

שבט

Jan. 25, 1999
Jan. 15, 2000 (15)
Feb. 1, 2001
Jan. 21, 2002
Jan. 11, 2003 (15)
Jan. 31, 2004 (15)

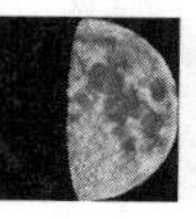

Prayer Focus

DR

SHEVAT

9

שבט

Jan. 26, 1999
Jan. 16, 2000
Feb. 2, 2001
Jan. 22, 2002
Jan. 12, 2003
Feb. 1, 2004

A young red female cow without fault or defect and which has never borne a yoke (Num. 19:2).

In the *Torah*, death is considered the ultimate source of defilement. Only the mixture of water and the ashes of the burned red heifer are able to wash away that defilement.

The strangest aspect of this ritual is that everyone who took part in preparing this cleansing formula was also rendered unclean by virtue of his participation in the process. The man who slaughtered the heifer, the priest who sprinkled its blood, the man who burned the carcass, and the one who gathered up the ashes all became unclean through their efforts. Nevertheless, the product of their labor made possible the cleansing of others (and themselves), satisfying the requirements of God.

This is a great mystery, but one that points to the even greater mystery of the cleansing death of Yeshua *HaMashiach* (the Messiah). All who were involved in that process became defiled through their actions: those who falsely accused him, those who judged him wrongly, those who turned him over to the Romans, those who beat and mocked him, those who did the crucifying, and all of us whose sin made his sacrifice necessary. Each part resulted in guilt and uncleanness for all involved.

The miracle is that the end result is the very means by which all are cleansed. Through his death and resurrection, the defilement of death is vanquished.

Prayer Focus

Today I Will

. . . walk in freedom, not carrying about my sins and past failures, for I know that my guilt and uncleanness have been washed away in the atonement of Messiah.

MM

"Until the land has been paid her *Shabbats*" . . . until seventy years had passed (2 Chron. 36:21).

Jan. 27, 1999
Jan. 17, 2000
Feb. 3, 2001 (15)
Jan. 23, 2002
Jan. 13, 2003
Feb. 2, 2004

Have you ever noticed that the number seven is the very foundation of the biblical calendar? There are seven days in a week. The seventh day is a Sabbath. The seventh month of the biblical year contains all the autumn sabbaths. Counting seven months from that seventh month brings us to the first month, which contains most of the spring sabbaths. Every seven years is a Sabbatical year and every seven Sabbatical years is a Jubilee year.

What an extraordinary gift the biblical calendar is! Nevertheless, the biblical calendar was largely ignored by Israel through the ages. God's people did not observe the Sabbatical or Jubilee years for four hundred ninety years! They presumed that the Lord no longer cared about the hard-to-keep commandments written down so long ago. But all that time, God was watching and waiting. He counted each of the seventy Sabbatical years that Israel had neglected over the course of five centuries, and, at the time of reckoning, he decreed that Israel would be exiled to Babylon—for seventy years! One year for each of the Sabbatical years that Israel had violated.

Are you ever tempted to neglect God's commandments because they were written down so long ago? Let us learn a lesson from our seventy years in Babylon and avoid presumption as well as God's judgment.

Prayer Focus

Today I Will

. . . ask the Lord to search my heart to reveal any presumption within me.

DR

SHEVAT

11

שבט

Jan. 28, 1999
Jan. 18, 2000
Feb. 4, 2001
Jan. 24, 2002
Jan. 14, 2003
Feb. 3, 2004

Prayer Focus

Miryam has chosen the right thing, and it won't be taken away from her (Luke 10:42).

When Yeshua arrived in Beyt Anyah (Bethany) with many disciples (Luke 10:38), Marta (Martha) knew that she was going to have a lot of work to do. In her culture, women often measured their worth by how well they performed "women's chores" like cooking and cleaning.

But Miryam (Mary) chose to sit at Yeshua's feet and listen to his teaching (Luke 10:39). In her culture, people sat on chairs for normal occasions or reclined on couches for banquets. One only sat "in the dust" at someone's feet (as the rabbis put it) if one were that person's disciple. Miryam was, therefore, making a radical statement, for women were not supposed to become disciples according to the culture of the day. Women were rarely trained as disciples. In one recorded exception, Beruryah (the wife of Rabbi Meir), had became so well educated that she was like a rabbi herself. Nevertheless, most men would not listen to her because she was a woman. Yeshua, however, welcomes Miryam as his disciple, to learn at his feet.

Marta wants help with the chores, but Yeshua commends Miryam for seeking to be a disciple (Luke 10:40–42). Too often we are like Marta, consumed by the things our culture demands that we accomplish. Yeshua wants us, most of all, to take the time to learn at his feet—to be his disciples.

Today I Will

. . . remember that whatever else I may be required to do, my first calling is to be Yeshua's disciple.

CK

ADONAI your God will keep with you the covenant and mercy that he swore to your ancestors (Deut. 7:12).

God will *keep* his covenant with you. The Hebrew root *shamar* (keep, guard, or watch) is the same word that was used to describe the watchmen on the ancient walls of Jerusalem. They were responsible for staying alert and keeping the city's inhabitants safe. That is how God will watch over the covenant he has made with us—lovingly and alertly. Our responsibility must be similar; the same Hebrew term is used for our relationship to the covenant in Deut. 7:12a. We must lovingly and alertly treasure and keep God's guidelines.

The covenant spoken of here is the one that God made with our ancestors at Mount Sinai. It is described as a covenant of *chesed* (grace)—not law! *Chesed* is a very strong word used to describe God's compassion, commitment and mercy toward us. Perhaps if we regarded this covenant from Sinai as a covenant of *chesed*, we would be more careful to treasure and follow the Lord's guidelines that were given through it.

In the *Sefer Torah* (Book of the *Torah*), this passage is found directly adjacent to the *Shema* (Deut. 6:4). The implication is clear. If I'm serious about the Lord being my God, if I'm serious about loving him with all my heart, my strength and my life, then I will more carefully and gratefully follow his instructions in the *Torah*.

Today I Will

. . . be more careful to treasure and follow the Lord's guidelines in the *Torah* because of my love for him.

SHEVAT

12

שבט

Jan. 29, 1999
Jan. 19, 2000
Feb. 5, 2001
Jan. 25, 2002
Jan. 15, 2003
Feb. 4, 2004

Prayer Focus

SHEVAT

13

שבט

Jan. 30, 1999 (16)
Jan. 20, 2000
Feb. 6, 2001
Jan. 26, 2002 (16)
Jan. 16, 2003
Feb. 5, 2004

Prayer Focus

So much learning is driving you crazy! (Acts 26:24)

Rachmiel Frydland was a learned and humble Messianic Jew. He had received his training in the *yeshivot* (rabbinical schools) of pre-war Poland. He began his studies under his father at the age of four; soon after, his ability to learn quickly brought him to Warsaw where he studied under the best teachers in the top *yeshivah* (rabbinical school). Then Rachmiel found the Lord.

Shortly thereafter, the Nazis invaded Poland and Rachmiel was on the run. After the war, he lived in England and then the United States where he continued his intensive studies in Semitic languages. He acquired two master's degrees and had completed his course work for a doctorate at New York University.

On one occasion when Rachmiel was sharing the good news about Messiah, he was challenged by ultra-Orthodox Jewish anti-missionaries. Their stock approach was to point to a lack of Jewish education as the reason why a Jewish person would accept Yeshua. They began examining Rachmiel. In response, Rachmiel recited in detail the particulars of his religious training and education. They listened intently, looking for a weakness. Unable to uncover any flaw, one turned to the other and said, "What a pity! All this education, and it is wasted on this belief in Jesus!"

Regardless of our educational background, impressive or unimpressive, an antagonist will always find a way to belittle our faith. Let us seek to please God and not men. Then we need not apologize for our limitations.

Today I Will

. . . use my background, whatever it may be, to share the Messiah Yeshua with others.

EK

I tell you that until heaven and earth pass away, not so much as a *yod* or a stroke will pass from the *Torah* (Matt. 5:18).

Jan. 31, 1999
Jan. 21, 2000
Feb. 7, 2001
Jan. 27, 2002
Jan. 17, 2003
Feb. 6, 2004

Yeshua may be alluding to an ancient Jewish story here to help reinforce his point about the authority of Scripture. Some early sages noticed that when Sarai's name was changed to Sarah (Gen. 17:15), the smallest Hebrew letter, *yod* (י), was taken from her name. The rabbis recognized how sorrowful an occasion this deletion must have been for the *yod*. They record that the *yod* cried out to God from generation to generation, complaining, "God, you have taken me out of the Bible! I am disgraced and humiliated! When will you stick me back in?" Finally, when Hoshea (Hosea) received the name Joshua (Num. 13:16), a *yod* was added in the Bible. "So you see," the sages pointed out, "not even a single *yod* can pass from the Bible."

Some of the teachers told another story. King Shlomo (Solomon) wanted to remove a *yod* from the Bible, but the *yod* cried out to God for help. "Don't worry," God assured the tiny letter, "A thousand Shlomos will be uprooted, but not a single *yod* will be removed."

Yeshua is probably alluding to these stories, reminding us that God's Word is eternal. We cannot pick and choose what we like to hear. We must pay attention to all that God has to say to us in the Scriptures.

Prayer Focus

Today I Will

. . . consider what areas in Scripture I need to be more obedient to.

CK

SHEVAT

15

שבט

Feb. 1, 1999
Jan. 22, 2000 (16)
Feb. 8, 2001
Jan. 28, 2002
Jan. 18, 2003 (16)
Feb. 7, 2004 (16)

Traditional
Tu BeShevat
(15th of Shevat)

Prayer Focus

As you come, the mountains and hills will burst out into song, and all the trees in the countryside will clap their hands (Isa. 55:12).

Tu BeShevat, the 15th day of the month Shevat, is also referred to as *Rosh HaShanah Le'Ilanot* (the New Year for Trees). It marks the end of the winter rainy season in Israel, and the renewal of the cycle of growth. Significantly, *Tu BeShevat* falls between mid-January and mid-February, not long after the Gregorian New Year. And in the Hebrew calendar it is one of four New Years, along with *Rosh HaShanah* in the fall, the first day of Nisan in the spring, and the first of Elul—the day of counting the tithe of cattle—in the late summer.

New beginnings are healthy, and we require more than one fresh start each year. Why a New Year for trees, though?

Perhaps trees can represent the whole order of nature, which is renewed yearly, and will be renewed in unimagined ways when Messiah returns. When we mark a new year for trees, we look ahead to the ultimate new beginning, when the creation itself "would be set free from its bondage to decay and would enjoy the freedom accompanying the glory that God's children will have" (Rom. 8:21).

Today I Will

. . . look at this world through the eyes of faith and imagine how even nature will be changed when Yeshua returns. I will also set aside some money to help plant trees in Israel.

RR

The person who is righteous will attain life by trusting and being faithful (Gal. 3:11; see also Hab. 2:4).

SHEVAT

16

שבט

Feb. 2, 1999
Jan. 23, 2000
Feb. 9, 2001
Jan. 29, 2002
Jan. 19, 2003
Feb. 8, 2004

During the last few centuries, some Jewish scholars have described Christianity as a religion based on faith, while Judaism is based on action. Perhaps a Church history of "faith without works" is to blame for this conclusion. However, during the first century Messianic Jewish revival, faith's place was acknowledged.

Talmudists living soon after the destruction of the Temple had much to say about faith toward God. Quite possibly they were influenced by New Covenant teaching on the subject. For example, in Makkot 24a, the rabbis taught that all the commandments are reduced to one, "The righteous shall live by his faith" (see Rom. 1:17). Rabbi Eliezer said (Sotah 48b), "Whoever has a piece of bread in his basket and says, 'What shall I eat tomorrow?' belongs only to them of little faith" (see Matt. 6:25–34). Were the rabbis quoting Yeshua and his disciples? In addition, Gen. 15:6—where Abraham believed God and was counted righteous—and Numbers 21—about healing through observing the serpent—are used by the rabbis as faith examples (see John 3:14–15)!

When Yeshua is asked how one might do God's works, he answers, "Here is what the work of God is: to trust in the one he sent!" (John 6:29) His message that faith and action are inextricably tied could not have been more Jewish!

Prayer Focus

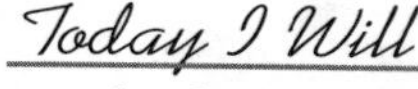

Today I Will

. . . do the most Jewish thing in the world. I will live by faith *and* action.

MW

SHEVAT

17

שבט

Feb. 3, 1999
Jan. 24, 2000
Feb. 10, 2001 (16)
Jan. 30, 2002
Jan. 20, 2003
Feb. 9, 2004

Prayer Focus

Don't owe anyone anything—except to love one another (Rom. 13:8).

God laid within the foundation of his *Torah* the principle of respect for others' property. The eighth commandment declares simply, "Do not steal" (Exod. 20:15[13]). Yet how many of us today violate this commandment when we fail to return what was borrowed, whether property (even something as small as a book) or money? Elisha's disciple understood the seriousness of this when he cried out, upon losing an axe head in the water, "Oh, no! . . . it was a borrowed one!" (2 Kings 6:5)

A story is told about a respected teacher of *Torah* who lived in Eastern Europe before the Second World War. For a certain time he owned a fish shop where he served mostly Gentiles. One day a man came in and bought some fish, but then became preoccupied and forgot to take his fish with him when he left the store. Noticing the fish on the counter, the teacher ran after the man, but it was too late. He tried to remember what the man looked like, but to no avail. The next day, the teacher gave away free fish to everyone who entered the store. Perhaps, he thought, the man who had left without his purchase would also enter and therefore receive the fish he had paid for.

Some might say the teacher went too far. But do we go far enough? Let those of us who have the *Torah* written on our hearts be examples of honesty and generosity.

Today I Will

. . . prayerfully begin paying all I owe to those I have borrowed from until I owe no man anything but love.

MW

Feb. 4, 1999
Jan. 25, 2000
Feb. 11, 2001
Jan. 31, 2002
Jan. 21, 2003
Feb. 10, 2004

By your tradition you make null and void the word of God! (Matt. 15:6)

The Breslovs do not have a head rabbi. When Rabbi Nachman, their founder, died, there was no one found worthy to replace him. It is the motto of the Breslovs that "it is better to have a dead rabbi and a live Judaism, than a dead Judaism and a live rabbi."

Yeshua also spoke of dead Judaism that embraced certain dead traditions. Our Jewish culture is rich with customs and practices that were first developed to bring us closer to God. It is good to practice traditions that are alive and meaningful. But to adhere to tradition when your heart is far from God, results in an empty formality with which God is not pleased. This is the hypocrisy of which Yeshua spoke.

Yeshua was not opposed to tradition. It was as much a part of the Judaism of his day as it is a part of our own today. However, he could not sanction the hypocrisy he saw among some of the *Perushim* (Pharisees) who used traditions as technicalities to circumvent the true meaning of God's commandments. Tradition should strengthen our relationship with *Torah*, not misdirect it.

The above Scripture passage challenges us to incorporate traditions for the purpose of expressing and enhancing our relationship with Yeshua so that God is glorified.

Prayer Focus

Today I Will

. . . seek to add meaning to my traditions by placing Yeshua, and all that he stands for, in the center of them.

EK

SHEVAT

19

שבט

Feb. 5, 1999
Jan. 26, 2000
Feb. 12, 2001
Feb. 1, 2002
Jan. 22, 2003
Feb. 11, 2004

You shall not add to the word which I am commanding you, nor take away from it (Deut. 4:2 NASB).

Rabbi Levi made the importance of every letter in the Scriptures clear. He noted that "even little things which are only ends of letters are actually mountains that can destroy the whole creation." For example, in the *Shema* (Deut. 6:4), it is written, "Hear O, Israel, the LORD is our God, the LORD is one" (NASB). The word for "one" is *echad*, which ends in the Hebrew letter *dalet* (ד). If you change the *dalet* to a *resh* (ר), by removing a small fraction of a stroke, the translation would be, "The LORD our God, the LORD is another."

Another example is the Scripture "You shall not worship any other god" (Exod. 34:14 NASB). The word for "other" ends in the Hebrew letter *resh* (ר). If you substitute the Hebrew letter *dalet* (ד), you get, "You shall not worship the One God."

Lev. 22:2 states, "Be careful . . . so as not to profane My holy name" (NASB). By changing the Hebrew letter *chet* (ח) to *hey* (ה) in the word "profane," the meaning will change to, "Do not praise my holy name."

Finally, in Isa. 8:17, it is written, "I will wait for the LORD" (NASB). If you change the *chet* (ח) in "wait" to the letter *hey* (ה), it will read, "I will smite the Lord." Thus, God is destroyed.

A change in letters changes the Scriptures. For this reason we must be careful that we do not add or detract from them. Our job is to heed and to obey.

Prayer Focus

Today I Will

. . . not add to Scripture, nor detract from it, but I will seek to understand and apply it correctly.

EK

A person does not live on food alone but on everything that comes from the mouth of *ADONAI* (Deut. 8:3).

Moshe's analogy between God's inspired words and food is a marvelous picture for understanding the need to internalize God's Word. Food is necessary because it contains the raw energy and nutrients the body needs to stay healthy and strong. If we don't eat every day, our bodies lose a hunger for food and eventually wither away and die. It is not enough for us to buy food or look at food. We must eat food if it is to give us the sustenance we need.

In the same way, the human spirit requires God's Word to maintain a healthy and strong spiritual life. God's Word accomplishes this because it is the overflow of God's spirit and life (John 6:53, 63). If we don't partake of God's Word every day, there is a good chance of losing our hunger for his Word; our spiritual life can potentially wither away and become as good as dead. We should be able to say with Job, "I treasure his words more than my daily food" (Job 23:12).

But do we eat God's Word as often as we eat our meals? Do we hunger for it every day? Or do we go for weeks without this spiritual sustenance? It is not enough to own the Scriptures or merely look at them. The Scriptures must be read and devoured. When we partake of God's Word in this way, we become spiritually strong and zealous for the Lord.

. . . feast on the Word of God.

Feb. 6, 1999 (17)
Jan. 27, 2000
Feb. 13, 2001
Feb. 2, 2002 (17)
Jan. 23, 2003
Feb. 12, 2004

Prayer Focus

DR

SHEVAT

21

שבט

Feb. 7, 1999
Jan. 28, 2000
Feb. 14, 2001
Feb. 3, 2002
Jan. 24, 2003
Feb. 13, 2004

The *Torah* is of the Spirit; but as for me, I am bound to the old nature, sold to sin as a slave (Rom. 7:14).

The ancient rabbis said that people were born with the *yetzer hara* (evil impulse), but that study of *Torah* could develop the *yetzer hatov* (good impulse).

Rabbi Sha'ul (Saul; i.e., Paul) describes such a struggle in Romans 7. But here the Law provides him no strength to fight the evil impulse! Romans 7, a chapter of spiritual defeat, uses the words "I," "me," or "my" many times. It pictures the best one can do to fulfill the Law through the flesh, by mere human strength (Rom. 7:18), as opposed to what one can do by the *Ruach*, the Spirit (Rom. 8:5–9).

Sha'ul declares that the Law can teach us right from wrong, but cannot transform our hearts unless it is written within us by grace (Rom. 8:2). Righteousness is a gift from God, paid for by Yeshua; we cannot achieve righteousness by mere human merit; we must embrace it as God's gift and live accordingly.

The rabbis teach that when the Messiah comes, he will slay the evil impulse in front of all the nations. For Sha'ul and those of us who know that God's Messiah *has* come, the *Torah* of God has been inscribed upon our hearts and we can live a new life in the *Ruach*, dead to sin and alive to God (Rom. 6:11).

Prayer Focus

Today I Will

. . . overcome temptation—not trusting in my ability to do so, but by trusting in God's gift of righteousness in Yeshua, and in his *Ruach*, which lives in me.

CK

All a person's ways are right in his own view, but *ADONAI* weighs the heart (Prov. 21:2).

A *mentsh tracht un Got lacht* is Yiddish for "Man thinks and God laughs." The *Talmud* teaches that a male at the age of thirteen becomes responsible for his own observance of the *Torah* (Pirkey Avot 5:24). It was once common for a girl to be confirmed at age twelve, but even this has changed and the *bat mitzvah* these days sometimes occurs at age thirteen.

Feb. 8, 1999
Jan. 29, 2000 (17)
Feb. 15, 2001
Feb. 4, 2002
Jan. 25, 2003 (17)
Feb. 14, 2004 (17)

When we are young, we believe that we are immortal, nothing can touch us and *oy*! are we smart. We know just what to do. Every parent's wish is that by the time of his *Bar Mitzvah* their son becomes a man. The truth is that we must train our young people in the knowledge that they do *not* know it all, and that neither do we.

The rite of passage of *bar/bat mitzvah* can be a blessed experience for our young people. But the tragic reality is that in modern times this rite of passage has too often become just a party. There is an old joke that the *bar/bat mitzvah* receives so many pens as gifts that instead of saying, "Today I am a man/woman," the saying should be, "Today I am a fountain pen."

We must become more focused on the meaning behind this event and the Word of God that defines it, and less focused on parties and gifts. Messianic Jewish families need to provide the proper *bar/bat mitzvah* training for their children, remembering always to make our redemption through Yeshua the centerpiece.

Prayer Focus

Today I Will

. . . become a man/woman in the truest sense by allowing the Lord to train me in his ways.

JR

SHEVAT

23

שבט

Feb. 9, 1999
Jan. 30, 2000
Feb. 16, 2001
Feb. 5, 2002
Jan. 26, 2003
Feb. 15, 2004

To act justly, love grace and walk in purity with your God (Mic. 6:8).

Here the prophet Micah exhorts us to God's highest standard. "To act justly" is to pursue God's order of righteousness in every sphere of our lives; thus we pray that *Malchut HaShem* (the Kingdom of God) will be established on earth as it is in heaven (Matt. 6:10). Justice is to be our goal and the motive for doing justice is love.

Love and justice are never contrary in the Scriptures. Indeed, in the above passage, Micah follows the words "to act justly" immediately with the words "love grace." They are tied together in one thought.

Finally, we are to walk with God in purity. As we walk with God, justice and grace become knit in our hearts.

The gospel empowers our lives when we identify with Yeshua's crucifixion, which can put to death the self-centered motives that steer us away from pursuing justice, love, and a pure walk with God. Yeshua's resurrection power through the *Ruach HaKodesh* (Holy Spirit) enables us to be people of love, justice and purity.

Yeshua's death and resurrection offer us the power to fulfill God's command given through Micah, the prophet.

Prayer Focus

Today I Will

. . . pursue God's righteousness with passion and love.

DJ

Eating without doing *n'tilat-yadayim* does not make a person unclean (Matt. 15:20).

Yeshua and his disciples were condemned because they did not practice *netilat-yadayim* (the traditional hand-washing ceremony before eating). However, nowhere in the Scriptures do we read of such a commandment.

Although "legalism" is not a term used in the Bible, it is clearly an issue in several passages of Scripture. But what exactly is legalism? Legalism is not a lifestyle empowered by grace to fulfill the *Torah* of God. Rather, it is self-righteousness and pride. It multiplies commandments and requires practices that are not rooted in the Word of God. The legalistic spirit has difficulty discerning between the lesser and the greater commandments.

Yeshua intentionally acted to break the chains of legalism in first century Israel. On *Shabbat* (the Sabbath), in defiance of the legalists, Yeshua healed the sick and walked through the fields with his disciples picking and eating grain. He said to the *Perushim* (Pharisees), "You pay your tithes of mint, dill and cumin; but you have neglected the weightier matters of the *Torah*" (Matt. 23:23).

Legalism destroys spiritual life, makes us narrow, and causes us to miss what is most important to God. We condemn those who differ from us in style of worship, language, and culture because of legalism. While legalism stresses external behavior, Yeshua emphasizes the motives of the heart (Matt. 5–7).

Let us ask the Lord to search our hearts to see if there is any trace of legalism within us; if any is revealed, let us repent and follow the way of Yeshua.

Today I Will

. . . be true to God's *Torah* and free from legalism.

Feb. 10, 1999
Jan. 31, 2000
Feb. 17, 2001 (17)*
Feb. 6, 2002
Jan. 27, 2003
Feb. 16, 2004

Biblical
On this day, Zechariah saw a vision of a man among the myrtle trees (Zech. 1:7).

Prayer Focus

DJ

SHEVAT

25

שבט

Feb. 11, 1999
Feb. 1, 2000
Feb. 18, 2001
Feb. 7, 2002
Jan. 28, 2003
Feb. 17, 2004

Dominion will rest on his shoulders (Isa. 9:6[5]).

Religion today appeals to self-centered interests and primarily addresses the state of one's inner peace. Many cults cater to these issues. Biblical faith, while not ignoring such concerns, teaches that the solution for inner unrest is dying to the self-centered life. Peace of mind and personal well-being are the result of being involved with and loving others.

But Biblical faith concerns itself not only with the individual but with the world as a whole; redemption is seen both as personal and national. Many prophets express hope for the day God's government will be established upon the earth. This is why we pray, "May your Kingdom come, your will be done" (Matt. 6:10).

Rabbi Joseph Soloveitchik, who has perhaps ordained more rabbis than any other man in history, has captured this orientation in his book *Halakhic Man.* He recognized the need to bring the truth of God's revealed Word into every aspect of life—personal and governmental.

Let us make God's goal our own—to apply the truth of *Torah* to every aspect of life.

Prayer Focus

Today I Will

. . . be an instrument of Messiah's government in every realm in which I have responsibility.

DJ

If you stop heeding discipline, you will stray from the principles of knowledge (Prov. 19:27).

Learning without doing can be dangerous. Do you say, "First I will learn what the right thing is, then I will do it"? Or do you say, "Learning includes doing; I cannot really learn without putting what I have learned into practice"? Here, the Scripture tells us that one will go astray morally if *musar* (discipline) is overlooked. This is sobering!

Rabbi Itzel Peterberger (1837–1907) told the following story at *Beyt HaMusar* (the House of Discipline) in Kovno one year during the *Yamim Nora'im* (Days of Awe). A little boy was wandering off the beaten path in a forest when he suddenly realized he was lost. Each turn took him deeper into the forest. After two days of wandering, he saw a figure in the distance. Running with joy, he embraced the man that he had found. "Surely," he thought, "This man will lead me out of the forest!"

But the man replied, "I wish I could be as happy as you are, my son. You've been lost for two days, but I've been lost here for over two weeks." The boy's heart sank. However, the old man continued, "Perhaps we can help one another. I at least know where not to go. By working together, we might find a way out."

Straying from God's path can have devastating results. Let us remain faithful in practicing what he has taught us so that we do not lose our way.

Today I Will

. . . accept God's boundaries and walk in his paths.

Feb. 12, 1999
Feb. 2, 2000
Feb. 19, 2001
Feb. 8, 2002
Jan. 29, 2003
Feb. 18, 2004

Prayer Focus

JEF

Feb. 13, 1999 (18/L)*
Feb. 3, 2000
Feb. 20, 2001
Feb. 9, 2002 (18/L)*
Jan. 30, 2003
Feb. 19, 2004

Prayer Focus

Whatever you want others to do for you, do so for them (Matt. 7:12 NASB).

According to rabbinic reckoning, there are 613 commandments in the *Torah*. Two hundred and forty-eight are positive commands that tell us what *to* do. Three hundred and sixty-five are negative commands that tell us what *not* to do. The 248 positive commands correspond to the number of separate parts in our body; the 365 negative commands correspond to the days of the year. Hence, all the days of the year we are to do all of the commandments with all the parts and joints of our body.

Yet, the respected Rabbi Hillel reduced all of the commands to one. As the story goes, a Gentile came to him seeking conversion to Judaism on the condition that Hillel teach him all of the commands while the man stood on one foot. Hillel agreed, saying, "What is hateful to you, do not do to your neighbour: that is the whole *Torah*, while the rest is the commentary thereof; go and learn it" (Shabbat 31a).

Yeshua did not say anything new, but restated the golden rule in the positive saying, "Whatever you want others to do for you, do so for them." It was an old rabbinic adage that captured the essence of the *Torah* in a single thought.

Today I Will

. . . seek to practice the golden rule by doing something good for another.

EK

In the beginning was the Word, and the Word was with God, and the Word was God (John 1:1).

The above Scripture quotes Gen. 1:1 and intentionally takes us back to the very beginning of the world, as Yochanan's (John's) readers clearly understood. When we return to the beginning, we find the Word himself there "face to face with God" (as the Greek indicates). This is a phrase that indicates the intimacy between the Word and God.

Yochanan uses the term "Word," the Greek translation of an Aramaic concept (*Memra*), found in the *Targums* (Aramaic paraphrases of Scripture) and familiar to his readers. The *Targums* consistently use *Memra* (Word) when speaking of God. So, in Genesis, it is the *Memra* who creates all things! In fact, when Yochanan says, "All things came to be through him" (John 1:3), he not only reinforces Yeshua's role as Creator, he also reaffirms that he is God.

The amazing truth here is that the Creator chose to become part of his creation, invading planet earth and entering human history as a baby. So Yochanan reminds us, using other *Targumic* terms to describe God, "The Word became a human being and lived with us, and we saw his *Sh'khinah* [Glory]" (John 1:14). Earlier, Yochanan described Yeshua as "the true light" who "gives light to everyone entering the world" (John 1:9), a process that began at his birth (Luke 1:79; 2:32).

As Yeshua sheds light on us, let us reflect his light to others (Matt. 5:14–16).

Feb. 14, 1999
Feb. 4, 2000
Feb. 21, 2001
Feb. 10, 2002
Jan. 31, 2003
Feb. 20, 2004

Prayer Focus

Today I Will

. . . enjoy Yeshua's light and gratefully share his light with others

JF

Feb. 15, 1999
Feb. 5, 2000 (18/B)*
Feb. 22, 2001
Feb. 11, 2002
Feb. 1, 2003 (18/B)*
Feb. 21, 2004 (18/D, L)*

Prayer Focus

Don't judge, so that you won't be judged (Matt. 7:1).

A mind submitted to the Word of God, transformed by meditating on the *Torah* and the life of Yeshua, can make solid moral distinctions. Yet our culture encourages moral equivocation. A murderer is excused because his condition is society's fault. An adulterer is no worse than the spouse who did not offer enough attention. Scripture is also used among believers in the spirit of moral equivocation. It is argued, "Don't judge, and you won't be judged" (Luke 6:37). With such broad application of God's Word, the adulterer is free to leave his wife and family, marry another, and continue in spiritual leadership. "We must not judge," we are told, but this self-protective outlook shields us from bearing the cost of taking a righteous stand.

Right and wrong are defined in God's *Torah*. The *Torah* provides a standard by which to evaluate people, congregations, businesses, governments, and especially ourselves.

Yeshua, the living *Torah*, is also our moral compass by which we can discern—and judge rightly—what is just, right and morally acceptable to God.

Let us not neglect our responsibility to make moral judgments in accordance with God's Word.

Today I Will

. . . use God's Word to distinguish between right and wrong, and to be a person of strong moral conviction.

DJ

Present yourself to God as someone worthy of his approval (2 Tim. 2:15).

No believer is called to ignorance. Every believer is called to study. If we are ignorant, for example, about answers to rabbinic objections regarding Messianic prophecy, then we are responsible to take the time to dig for those answers. The answers are there, but it's up to us to study and find them. Then we need never be ashamed.

Centuries ago, there was a rabbi who traveled from town to town with his *nahag* (horse boy). The *nahag* observed as the rabbi answered questions in each village. He thought to himself, "That's an easy job. I can do that." When he mentioned this to the rabbi, his wise master said, "Tomorrow we are traveling to a new town. You'll be the rabbi and I'll be the *nahag*." This pleased the *nahag*.

The next day, the rabbi watered the horses, and the *nahag* sat in the cart. As soon as they arrived in the town, a man ran up to the cart and asked the rabbi (really the *nahag*) the most difficult question he had ever heard. The *nahag* thought for a long time. Finally, he began to laugh. "That question is so easy, it's not worthy to be answered by a rabbi; I'm going to let my *nahag* answer it!"

Unfortunately, we don't have a rabbi standing by the horse. We'd better study!

SHEVAT

30

טבת

Feb. 16, 1999
Feb. 6, 2000
Feb. 23, 2001
Feb. 12, 2002
Feb. 2, 2003
Feb. 22, 2004

Traditional
Rosh Chodesh
(the New Moon)
Day 1

Prayer Focus

Today I Will

. . . choose a portion of the Scriptures about which I am ignorant, and I will study it until I am no longer ignorant.

MW

ADAR

1

אדר

Feb. 17, 1999
Feb. 7, 2000
Feb. 24, 2001
(18/C, L)
Feb. 13, 2002
Feb. 3, 2003
Feb. 23, 2004

Approximately every third year, a thirteenth month called Adar Sheyni (Adar II) is added to the calendar (See Appendix A, endnote 2). When this happens, all biblical and traditional commemorations are observed in Adar Sheyni.

Adar Sheyni
March 8, 2000
March 5, 2003

Biblical
Rosh Chodesh
(the New Moon)

On this day, Ezekiel prophesied against Pharaoh (Ezek. 32:1).

Traditional
Rosh Chodesh
Day 2

A New Covenant, the essence of which is not a written text but the Spirit. For the written text brings death, but the Spirit gives life (2 Cor. 3:6).

It is a common fault to separate what God unites. This distorts his revelation. Scripture tells us much about the Word and the Spirit. "For out of Tziyon [Zion] will go forth *Torah*, the word of *Adonai* from Yerushalayim [Jerusalem]" (Isa. 2:3). The Word was breathed out by God through the *Ruach HaKodesh* (Holy Spirit) in order that we might receive training in righteousness (2 Tim. 3:16–17). Holy men of old spoke the Word as they were "moved by the *Ruach HaKodesh*" (2 Pet. 1:21).

Today's Scripture passage indicates that when we separate the Word from the *Ruach* (Spirit), and seek to follow him by our own efforts, we become engaged in the practice of legalism; for "the written text brings death." On the other hand, when we take our focus from the Word, we end up floundering in subjective error and imbalance. Human beings cannot be transformed or live a life that is pleasing to God without his Word.

God wants us to depend on the *Ruach* and to know his presence, so that the Word might be fully effective in us. By meditating on the Word and by submitting our lives to it, we find ourselves transformed by the power of the *Ruach*. The balance must be struck for us to grow strong in the Messiah. We "know what God wants and will agree that what he wants is good, satisfying and able to succeed" (Rom. 12:2).

Today I Will

. . . be fully committed to living by God's Word and knowing the power of his *Ruach*.

DJ

All you who are thirsty, come to the water! You without money, come, buy, and eat! (Isa. 55:1)

ADAR

2

אדר

Feb. 18, 1999
Feb. 8, 2000
Feb. 25, 2001
Feb. 14, 2002
Feb. 4, 2003
Feb. 24, 2004

Adar Sheyni
(Adar II)
March 9, 2000
March 6, 2003

The prophet presents us with a choice: to partake freely of the true water that will satisfy us, or to "spend money for what isn't food, your wages for what doesn't satisfy?" (Isa. 55:2)

The *Midrash* (traditional commentary) tells us that the water is *Torah*; "the words of *Torah* are free; as it is said, 'Ho, every one that thirsteth, come ye for water'"(Numbers Rabbah 1:7). God's Word is free, but we must actively receive it. Why do we often spurn this gift for things that ultimately prove to be empty? Isaiah gives us a hint: "Let the wicked person abandon his way and the evil person his thoughts" (Isa. 55:7). "His way" in Hebrew means his own path, the ingrained habits that distract him, keeping him from spending time studying Scripture. We do not come and drink because we are engaged in too many other activities. We have established pathways in our lives that do not pass by the well of *Torah.* "His thoughts" refers to inner attitudes and values, many of which do not line up with God's teaching.

We do not come to God's Word because we do not consider it genuinely important. We need to forsake the habits and thoughts that sidetrack us so that we may drink deeply and steadily from Scripture.

Prayer Focus

Today I Will

. . . see what activities I can reduce so that I may have more time and energy for studying God's Word.

RR

ADAR

3

אדר

Feb. 19, 1999
Feb. 9, 2000
Feb. 26, 2001
Feb. 15, 2002
Feb. 5, 2003
Feb. 25, 2004

Adar Sheyni
(Adar II)
March 10, 2000
March 7, 2003

Biblical
On this day, the second Temple was completed (Ezra 6:15).

Prayer Focus

All the *mitzvot* [commandments] I am giving you today you are to take care to obey (Deut. 8:1).

This Scripture actually describes God's commandments in the singular (*kol hamitzvah*). The emphasis is not on following each one of God's instructions as separate or distinct parts. Instead, they need to be viewed as a whole, as the *Artscroll Tanach* reads, "the entire commandment." In other words, each part of the *Torah* is interconnected. Ya'akov (James) makes the same point as he reflects on this passage in James 2:8–12. This means we cannot treat Scripture as a dinner menu, selecting just those items which are most appetizing.

We are to *fully* follow God for our *entire* well-being. We should see ourselves as members of the "613 Club"—there are 613 commandments in the *Torah*, according to tradition—not the "600 Club" or even the "612 Club." As Yeshua himself makes clear, even the less significant *mitzvot* are important as well (Matt. 5:18–19).

Does this mean that if we can't keep the whole of *Torah* we might as well give up and not keep any of it? That's like the story of the bear who goes into the cornfield and fills his arms with ears of corn. As he leaves, he drops one ear. Dissatisfied with losing part of his haul, he throws down the rest and goes back to gather more. Again he drops an ear as he leaves the field. Again, dissatisfied, he throws away the remainder and returns to get more. He does this repeatedly. Eventually, he goes away hungry. But aren't we hypocrites if we keep only part of the *Torah*, and not all of it? A hypocrite is one who claims something for himself or herself that is not true. Our inability just makes us inconsistent. As many have pointed out, the only totally consistent people are those who are dead. We should follow God as completely as we can at our present stage of development and seek to grow into following his guidelines more fully.

Today I Will

. . . trust God to enable me to follow him more fully than yesterday.

You are to love *ADONAI* your God with all your heart, with all your soul, with all your strength and with all your understanding (Luke 10:27).

The core of our confession of faith is love for God. At times our rabbis have emphasized obedience to the *mitzvot* (commandments) and have neglected the importance of a passionate love for the Holy One of Israel. But obedience should always be a response to love. Yeshua said, "This is the greatest and most important *mitzvah* [commandment]" (Matt. 22:38). But few of our people have experienced the purifying power of loving God with reckless abandon.

I was in my office in Skokie, Illinois one day when three Lubavitcher *Chasidim* (Ultra-orthodox Jews) walked through the front door. They had noticed the yellow sign in our front window that declared, "We have *Mashiach* (the Messiah) now!" One of them spoke for the others and said, "We have just been with the Messiah." (They meant their *rebbe,* head rabbi, Menachem Schneerson, who was still alive at the time.) "We've been with the Messiah," he continued, "and he told us what God wants. God wants more *mezuzahs* [boxes containing several Scriptures, attached to the doorframes of the house] and more *tefillin* [phylacteries; boxes containing several Scriptures, worn on the head and arm]." With that, they turned and walked out and I was left with my mouth hanging open. If only they knew what God really wants. It's not more *mezuzahs.* It's not more *tefillin.* It's more love. God wants us to love him with a reckless abandon. Only through Yeshua can we love the Lord in this way.

Today I Will

. . . commit myself to falling in love with God all over again and rekindle my passion and adoration for him with all my heart, soul, and strength.

Feb. 20, 1999 (19)
Feb. 10, 2000
Feb. 27, 2001
Feb. 16, 2002 (19)
Feb. 6, 2003
Feb. 26, 2004

Adar Sheyni
(Adar II)
March 11, 2000 (23)
March 8, 2003
(23/F)

Prayer Focus

DB

ADAR

5

אדר

Feb. 21, 1999
Feb. 11, 2000
Feb. 28, 2001
Feb. 17, 2002
Feb. 7, 2003
Feb. 27, 2004

Adar Sheyni
(Adar II)
March 12, 2000
March 9, 2003

Prayer Focus

He is like someone building a house who dug deep and laid the foundation on bedrock (Luke 6:48).

It is undeniably true that the integrity of any structure is determined by the foundation upon which it rests. The Scriptures teach that this is just as applicable in spiritual matters as in physical ones. Rabbi Sha'ul (Saul; i.e., Paul) said that Yeshua *HaMashiach* (the Messiah) was the only foundation that could be laid (1 Cor. 3:11). Beyond that, the durability of what was built would be directly related to the value of the material used. The end result would be evident when tested by fire. Nevertheless, there are people and groups that claim to have Yeshua as their foundation, and have built sincerely, but have constructed something that is not square.

What is often overlooked is that the foundation itself must be secure. This is why Yeshua speaks of digging deep and reaching bedrock before laying the foundation. The bedrock upon which Yeshua rests is the *Torah* of God. The entire body of truth contained in the *Torah* is important, not just the prophecies that point to his coming. If we don't regard *Torah* as the foundation of revelation, we set the groundwork for aberrant views about Yeshua and, hence, faulty structures. With a sturdy scriptural foundation we will always be able to discern what is true.

Today I Will

. . . like David, cry out, "Open my eyes, so that I will see wonders from your *Torah*" (Ps. 119:18).

MM

You are to love *ADONAI* your God with all your heart, all your being and all your resources (Deut. 6:5).

Mazel Tov! *Mazel Tov*! (Congratulations!) The young man is greeted with enthusiastic expressions of praise and blessing. He is complimented on how marvelously he chanted from the *Torah* and sang his *Haftarah* (portion from the Prophets). His speech—a masterpiece of enlightened commentary, *midrashic* (homiletic) stories and *Yiddishkeit* (Jewishness)—was spiced with humor and wrapped in pronouncements of gratitude toward the rabbi who trained him, and the parents who made it all possible. Today he is a man, able to be counted as part of a *minyan* (a quorum of ten Jewish men needed for prayer), and fully able to participate as an adult in the religious life of the Jewish community.

The young man is now responsible for keeping all of the commandments of the *Torah.* Yet he is not called a *bar mitzvot* (son of the commandments) but a *bar mitzvah* (son of the commandment). The obvious question is, "Which one commandment would be the most appropriate to illustrate the full range of his new spiritual responsibility?"

The answer, given in the above Scripture passage, was Yeshua's response (Mark 12:29–30) to a similar question. That commandment, along with love for our neighbor, carries the full intent of every requirement of the *Torah.* If the *bar mitzvah* boy, as well as the rest of us, will make that first commandment the absolute priority of life, then we will all be children of the commandment and of the one who gave it.

Today I Will

. . . become a son or daughter of the Commandment by making my relationship with the God of Israel the highest priority of my life.

ADAR

6

אדר

Feb. 22, 1999
Feb. 12, 2000 (19)
March 1, 2001
Feb. 18, 2002
Feb. 8, 2003 (19)
Feb. 28, 2004 (19)

Adar Sheyni
(Adar II)
March 13, 2000
March 10, 2003

Prayer Focus

MM

ADAR

7

אדר

Feb. 23, 1999
Feb. 13, 2000
March 2, 2001
Feb. 19, 2002
Feb. 9, 2003
Feb. 29, 2004

Adar Sheyni
(Adar II)
March 14, 2000
March 11, 2003

Prayer Focus

Kefa said to Yeshua, "It's good that we're here, Lord. I'll put up three shelters if you want—one for you, one for Moshe and one for Eliyahu" (Matt. 17:4).

It's encouraging to see that even Kefa (Peter) could come up with a bad idea. After all, who could blame him for wanting to help? There he was, standing before Moshe (Moses), Eliyahu (Elijah) and the glorified Messiah. I certainly would have been at a loss for something interesting to say, wouldn't you? What could any earthly person say in conversation with these three men? Perhaps I would have asked Moshe where his body was secretly buried. Or Eliyahu, "Why did you panic after the Mount Carmel victory?" I would have sounded more foolish than Kefa.

Kefa's suggestion was a terrible idea because these men were in the heavenly realm; they needed shelters about as much as a fish needs a raincoat.

God's advice to Kefa, after the dust of his mistake cleared, coincides with advice he gave earlier to mankind in general, "Even a fool, if he stays silent, is thought wise" (Prov. 17:28). To Kefa, he said, "This is my Son, whom I love. . . . Listen to him!" (Matt. 17:4) Sometimes, the last thing needed is for us to say something.

Thank God for Kefa. He walked on water; yes, but he also had moments of glorious fallibility. There is hope for us all!

Today I Will

. . . let go of perfectionism and allow the human errors of the godly ones in Scripture encourage me.

BC

Don't you realize that Yeshua the Messiah is in you? (2 Cor. 13:5)

ADAR

8

אדר

Feb. 24, 1999
Feb. 14, 2000
March 3, 2001
Feb. 20, 2002
Feb.10, 2003
Mar. 1, 2004

Adar Sheyni
(Adar II)
March 15, 2000
March 12, 2003

I was visiting a beautiful old *shul* (synagogue) that I had not been in for over twenty years. The Jewish community had mostly moved away, so the attendance on that *Shabbat* (Sabbath) morning was not much more than a *minyan* (quorum of ten Jewish men). Since I was a visitor, I was offered an *aliyah* (the privilege of being called up to chant the blessings over the *Torah*). When I told the elderly rabbi my name, he told me that he had known my grandfather.

After the service and the customary *kiddush* (prayer of sanctification over a cup of wine), an old man followed me into the hallway and stood looking at me intently. He started to say: "You look more like . . . " In my mind, I immediately finished his sentence for him, "You look more like a rabbi than the Rabbi" (with my full beard and dark suit, I had heard it numerous times). I was shocked, however, by what he did say. "You look more like Jesus Christ than any man I've ever seen." Hardly knowing how to respond, I stuttered through a brief conversation with him. I never found out who he was or what he knew about Yeshua, but this old Orthodox Jewish man had seen a reality that we believers often forget. He had seen Yeshua in me.

Prayer Focus

Today I Will

. . . walk conscious of who it is that dwells in me.

MM

ADAR

9

אדר

Feb. 25, 1999
Feb. 15, 2000
March 4, 2001
Feb. 21, 2002
Feb. 11, 2003
March 2, 2004

Adar Sheyni
(Adar II)
March 16, 2000
March 13, 2003

Prayer Focus

As high as the sky is above the earth are my ways higher than your ways (Isa. 55:9).

Joseph Vactor was born in Hungary before World War I. He lived his entire life as a devout, God-fearing Orthodox Jew. In 1944, the Germans led the last of the Hungarian Jewish community on a long winter march, on foot, to the death camps. Joseph and his brother, David, were among them. During this death march, Joseph noticed a corpse on the side of the road. It was apparent from the clothing that the dead man had been an Orthodox Jew. In the hand of this Jewish man was something made of black leather that looked like a billfold. Joseph bent down and quickly took it from the dead man's hand. Only when they were already in the death camp of Bergen-Belzen did Joseph open the little leather pouch. It was not a billfold. It was a copy of the *Brit Chadashah* (New Covenant Scriptures) in Hungarian. This was the only book that Joseph and David had to read during the days of their captivity.

Many years later, in 1974, when I was attending the *yeshivah* (rabbinical school) in Jerusalem, I drove a group of Orthodox Jewish men to look for a place to build a new settlement in Judea. However, I forgot that the back seat contained some correspondence courses that I had written for sharing the gospel. As I was driving down to Tekoa in the Judean Mountains, I looked in the mirror and saw these Orthodox Jews reading the materials. At the end of the trip, Joseph and David Vactor pointed to the pamphlets and asked: "Who wrote this?" I answered that I had. They asked, "And do you believe what is written here?" "Yes!" I said to them. "We do too!" they joyfully replied. Since that day, until Joseph's recent death, our paths have not separated.

Today I Will

. . . pray for my Orthodox Jewish brothers, that they, like Joseph Vactor and his brother, would learn about Yeshua and come to believe in him.

JS

How blessed are those who do not see, but trust anyway! (John 20:29)

Feb. 26, 1999
Feb. 16, 2000
March 5, 2001
Feb. 22, 2002
Feb. 12, 2003
March 3, 2004

Adar Sheyni
(Adar II)
March 17, 2000
March 14, 2003

Many look for miracles as the proof they need to trust in God. This is particularly true of our people. Rabbi Sha'ul (Saul; i.e., Paul) said, "Jews ask for signs" (1 Cor. 1:22). Toma (Thomas) wanted evidence, and so do we. Yet Yeshua promised a special blessing for those who trusted.

Jewish tradition does, in fact, encourage us to recognize God's handiwork in the everyday experiences of life, not simply in supernatural signs and wonders. In the *Amidah* (Standing Prayer) we are called to praise the Lord, "For your miracles that are with us every day." All of life can be considered one giant miracle that God is continually performing before us. God reveals himself through the supernatural as well as through the manifold acts of his providence. Somewhere between providence and miracle we can, through faith, find the reality of God's daily presence in our lives. That is where we must anchor our souls. Whether we see him working providentially, in phenomenal answers to prayer, or through miracles, let's be content for him to decide. The sign we should seek is the sign of his coming; the wonder we can experience daily is his transforming power that makes us more like Yeshua.

Prayer Focus

Today I Will

. . . believe in Yeshua's transforming power. I will look for that special blessing he promises to those who believe without seeing.

DB

ADAR

11

אדר

Feb. 27, 1999 (20/M)
Feb. 17, 2000
March 6, 2001
Feb. 23, 2002 (20/M)
Feb. 13, 2003
March 4, 2004 (מ)

Adar Sheyni
(Adar II)
March 18, 2000
(24/M)
March 15, 2003
(24/M)

Traditional
Ta'anit Ester
(the Fast of Esther)
in the year 2004.
See Apendix C,
Chart 3, note 5.

Prayer Focus

Anyone who slanders is a fool (Prov. 10:18).

A wise religious teacher headed a small community where one man caused problems by his gossip. The gossip turned into backbiting and slander, and his venomous remarks hurt his victims. Many complained to the teacher, who summoned the slanderer.

The accused appeared to be very remorseful. He apologized to the teacher and seemed ready for penance. The teacher said, "I want you to take your pillow case, fill it with feathers, and bring it to me." Thinking that this was his penalty, he obeyed. The teacher then said, "Now I want you take this pillow case filled with feathers to the top of the nearby mountain and empty it." He readily obeyed and watched as the many feathers were carried by the wind and tossed about the mountainside. Some fell upon the rocks on the side of the mountain; some floated to the ground at the bottom of the mountain; still others were carried off into the distance. He returned to the teacher and reported that he had completed the discipline. Then the wise teacher said, "Now I want you to find every feather and return it to the pillow case."

It's easy to slander a person, and to say "I'm sorry" when you get caught. But it's impossible to undo the damage that has been done.

Today I Will

. . . use my tongue to say nice things about others.

EK

Here is the final conclusion, now that you have heard everything: fear God, and keep his *mitzvot* [commandments]; this is what being human is all about (Eccles. 12:13).

Feb. 28, 1999
Feb. 18, 2000
March 7, 2001
Feb. 24, 2002
Feb.14, 2003
Mar. 5, 2004

Adar Sheyni
(Adar II)
March 19, 2000
March 16, 2003

The renowned medieval rabbi Moses Maimonides (the Rambam), wrote in his *Guide to the Perplexed* that King Shlomo (Solomon) not only knew every one of God's commandments by heart, he also knew the divine reason behind each one. Yet, King Solomon's wisdom deserted him at a critical point in his life. He had built everything, tasted everything, drunk everything, and had married over 700 women! Yet, what he concluded was *most* important is summarized in the verse above.

Given the chance to go back and do it over again, Shlomo would not have violated the commandments of God, even knowing that God's grace would meet him later in his repentance. In Ecclesiastes, we sense that we are listening to a man with one driving compulsion: to convey this message to succeeding generations, "It is not worth it."

Shlomo emphatically warns us to embrace eternal values, even when we are young, when eternity seems far away. This warning is his most lasting legacy, enduring beyond his spectacular Temple, which lay in ruins only four centuries after it was built—many centuries before Messiah came to walk among us.

The thought expressed at Shlomo's most lucid moment is the message we must share with our own generation. Yeshua himself commissioned us to share this truth, calling us to declare God's eternal Kingdom (Matt. 10:7) to a pleasure-seeking world unaware of the eternal bottom line.

Prayer Focus

Today I Will

. . . seek to grow as a model of eternity-minded living and to share with others King Solomon's final conclusion as explained in today's verse.

BC

ADAR

13

אדר

March 1, 1999 (מ)
Feb. 19, 2000 (20)
March 8, 2001 (מ)
Feb. 25, 2002 (מ)
Feb. 15, 2003 (20)
March 6, 2004
(20/M)

Adar Sheni
(Adar II)
March 20, 2000 (מ)
March 17, 2003 (מ)

Biblical
On this day, Haman's plan to annihilate the Jewish people was to be implemented (Esther 3:13); the Jews were given the right to defend themselves (Esther 8:12).

Traditional
Ta'anit Ester (the Fast of Esther)

Erev Purim (the Eve of the Feast of Lots)

Prayer Focus

MM

Their defense has been taken away from them . . . . Don't be afraid of them! (Num. 14:9)

In one of our congregational Purim plays, based on the Book of Esther, we performed the scene where Vashti received word from the king to come to his party and display her great beauty. Angered by this, Vashti (appropriately renamed Smashti for the sake of our parody) demolished a table and several chairs. With a few swift kicks and swipes of the hand, all that remained was a heap of wood. Was our actress a martial arts expert or endowed with incredible strength? Not at all. Prior to the play, the furniture had been sawed through in numerous places leaving only slivers of wood holding them together. Yet, to the unsuspecting audience, they appeared to be perfectly sound.

Returning from the Promised Land, the ten spies discouraged Israel because what they had witnessed there seemed too substantial to conquer. What could they do against fortified cities with massive walls and giants inside? Yet Joshua and Caleb sought to help Israel see with the eyes of faith. Regardless of how things appeared, there was no need to fear. God had already gone ahead of them and "sawed through" the enemy's defenses. All that Israel needed to do was strike and their enemies would fall.

Today I Will

. . . not fear obstacles and challenges that are beyond my natural abilities, for I know that if God has said to go forward, he has already made a way.

Who knows whether you didn't come into your royal position precisely for such a time as this (Esther 4:14).

It was a most difficult time for our people. Large numbers of Jews had fled after the destruction of the Temple in 586 B.C.E. to a more friendly place—Persia (modern-day Iran). Yet after a few generations, things became difficult there as well. An anti-Semitic government official named Haman convinced King Ahasuerus that these foreigners were a detriment to his country and that they must be annihilated. Lots were cast, setting the date of destruction for Adar 13. Terror gripped the Jewish community. However, God always has a way of escape, so that his covenant people may endure.

Previous to Haman's wicked plot, a beautiful Jewish girl named Esther had won a contest and had become Ahasuerus's new queen. Although she had previously hidden her Jewish background, Esther was challenged by her cousin, Mordecai, to stand up for her people in their time of trouble. This must have been an incredible test of faith for a young woman who was experiencing the privileges of being queen. Yet Esther realized that her true calling was to speak out for her people, no matter what the cost. The courage of her faith is reflected in her famous answer to Mordecai, "I will go in to the king, which is against the law; and if I perish, I perish" (Esther 4:16).

The holiday of *Purim* (the Feast of Lots) is a celebration of the deliverance of Israel, largely due to the faithfulness of Esther. To Messianic believers, there are no coincidences. God orchestrates the details of our lives. Perhaps we have been placed in our own sticky situations in order to share Yeshua's love "for such a time as this" (Esther 4:14).

Today I Will

. . . seek to see the hand of God on my life in the place where he has planted me.

March 2, 1999 (מ)
Feb. 20, 2000
March 9, 2001 (מ)
Feb. 26, 2002 (מ)
Feb. 16, 2003
March 7, 2004 (מ)

During Hebrew leap years, *Purim* (the Feast of Lots) is celebrated in Adar Sheyni (Adar II). The 14th and 15th days of Adar Rishon (Adar I) are referred to as *Purim Katan* (Little Purim).

Adar Sheyni (Adar II)
March 21, 2000 (מ)
March 18, 2003 (מ)

Biblical
On this day, the Jewish people celebrated their victory over Haman and all who followed his evil plan (Esther 9:17).

Traditional
Purim (the Feast of Lots) Day 1

BK

March 3, 1999
Feb. 21, 2000
March 10, 2001 (20)
Feb. 27, 2002
Feb. 17, 2003
March 8, 2004

Adar Sheyni
(Adar II)
March 22, 2000
March 19, 2003

Biblical
On this day, Ezekiel prophesied against the nations (Ezek. 32:17).

Traditional
Purim
(the Feast of Lots)
Day 2

Shushan Purim
(Susa Lots)
See Esther 9:18

Prayer Focus

The Jews resolved and took upon themselves . . . and all who might join them . . . [to] observe these two days in accordance with what was written (Esther 9:27).

Although *Purim* (the Feast of Lots) is usually labeled as a "minor" holiday, it has a major message for all believers. Due to the great deliverance of the Jewish community in Persia, *Purim* is celebrated with expressions of joy. It has become customary to read the entire *megillah* (scroll) of Esther in the synagogue while role-playing the intriguing story. It is not uncommon to spot several Esthers and Mordecais in the crowd, as many people come in costume to add to the festivities. As the words of the *megillah* are read, the mention of "Haman" brings a chorus of boos and hissing, while the mention of "Mordecai" elicits cheers of joy. *Groggers* (noisemakers) are heard throughout the synagogue as we celebrate the day of redemption for those who had been slated for destruction.

It is understandable that the Jewish community celebrates the day of *Purim*; yet, today's Scripture verse tells us that many non-Jews also joined in the festival. And why not? These people understood that the God of Israel was the one true God.

Another reason for the universal significance of *Purim* is that if Haman had accomplished his evil plan of annihilation, how would Messiah have been born? Indeed, *Purim* should be a celebration for all people who place their faith in the trustworthiness of God to keep his promises. In Yeshua, the promises of God are "Yes" and "Amen" (2 Cor. 1:20).

Get out your *grogger*! This is something for all of us to celebrate!

Today I Will

. . . walk steadfastly with the Lord, knowing that all his promises to me will come to pass.

BK

The leopard will lie down with the goat, the calf and the lion and the yearling together (Isa. 11:6 NIV).

In the Age to Come, the lion will lie down with the calf. Until then, if a lion and a calf lie down together, you can be sure the calf is not going to get a good night's sleep. Likewise, if a lion comes over to your house, the best thing for you to do is let him have his way. It's never a wise policy to be unnecessarily rude to a lion. You're not going to domesticate him. He's not going to fit into your lifestyle or daily routine. He's a lion! Let him have his way.

The Scriptures call God *Ari* (Hos. 11:10), the Hebrew word for "lion." One of the biggest mistakes we can make is to think that God should adjust to our lives—to fit our schedules, our doctrines, our ways. God is a lion and we must relate to him as such. We should never try to "domesticate" him. We must not expect God to conform to our ways. We must agree to be transformed by what God wants and to allow our lives to be changed by his surprising, mighty, and unbridled reality.

Do you want abundant life? Come to the living God, the Mighty and Awesome One. He is the lion. Let him have his way, and you'll be forever changed.

Today I Will

. . . let the Lord have his way in my life.

ADAR

16

אדר

March 4, 1999
Feb. 22, 2000
March 11, 2001
Feb. 28, 2002
Feb. 18, 2003
March 9, 2004

Adar Sheyni
(Adar II)
March 23, 2000
March 20, 2003

Prayer Focus

JC

ADAR

17

אדר

March 5, 1999
Feb. 23, 2000
March 12, 2001
March 1, 2002
Feb. 19, 2003
March 10, 2004

Adar Sheyni
(Adar II)
March 24, 2000
March 21, 2003

Prayer Focus

Let him smother me with kisses from his mouth (Song of Sol. 1:2).

You may think of worship as singing a song, saying a blessing, being quiet, shouting out, kneeling down, reciting praises, and so on. But the essence of worship is not that. You'll find it hidden in the Greek word for worship used throughout the *Brit Chadashah* (New Covenant Scriptures). The word *proskuneo* speaks of "reverence." It comes from two words: *pros* which means "towards" and *kuneo* which means "kiss."

What is worship? It is to kiss God. Some find worship in the the Song of Shlomo (Solomon). They see in it an allegory describing our relationship with God. Its very first words are, "Let him smother me with kisses from his mouth, for your love is better than wine."

God wants to kiss you in his love. Likewise, worship is to kiss God. Is it too simple for you? Maybe worship is more simple than you imagined. It's as simple as kissing someone you love. In the same way, your relationship with God is the most intimate relationship and deepest love you can ever experience. How can you be in such a relationship without kissing? What is true worship? A kiss from your heart. Learn true worship. It's more simple and natural, more intimate and wonderful, than you ever imagined. It's as simple as a kiss.

Today I Will

. . . close my eyes and just start thinking of God's mercy, kindness, grace, and love.

JC

I will bless *Adonai* at all times; his praise will always be in my mouth (Ps. 34:1[2]).

I knew as soon as I preached the message that Friday night at our *Erev Shabbat* (evening of the Sabbath) service that I was in trouble. Don't ask me how I knew, I just knew. Today's wonderful Scripture verse had been on my heart for weeks. I wanted to give a strong, encouraging message to the congregation about praising God in all things. However, there is an axiom in teaching the Word of God that you can't truly teach it until you have lived it.

A few days later I woke up sicker than I could remember, with nausea, fever, headaches and vomiting. I got up at five in the morning and went downstairs so as not to awaken my family. I seriously contemplated driving myself to the emergency room. Suddenly, the verse I had preached on *Shabbat* came back to me, "I will bless *Adonai* at all times . . . " I groaned in my spirit, "This is not the time, Lord!" Yet the verse would not leave me.

In the midst of my pain, I began to praise God. I focused my mind and my heart on him—as much as I could. Suddenly, the pain became more bearable. I kept praising God. Miraculously, my mind began to clear and I felt better. I called my doctor, who prescribed medicine for me, and the battle was soon over.

We need to praise God when things are going badly as well as when they are going well. When we enter the realm of blessing God, it gives him the chance to work in our lives. Victory is on the way, and when it comes, we will *really* be able to praise him!

Today I Will

. . . seek to praise the Lord through both good and bad. If I'm down, I will praise the Lord, knowing that deliverance is on the way.

March 6, 1999 (21/N)
Feb. 24, 2000
March 13, 2001
March 2, 2002 (21/N)
Feb. 20, 2003
March 11, 2004

Adar Sheyni (Adar II)
March 25, 2000 (25/N)
March 22, 2003 (25/N)

Prayer Focus

DC

March 7, 1999
Feb. 25, 2000
March 14, 2001
March 3, 2002
Feb. 21, 2003
March 12, 2004

Adar Sheyni
(Adar II)
March 26, 2000
March 23, 2003

Prayer Focus

He [Saul] stood head and shoulders taller than anyone else in Isra'el (1 Sam. 9:2).

King Sha'ul (Saul) collapsed with fear when he saw Goliath. He had never faced an enemy in combat who was taller than he. Sha'ul's confidence was shaken and he was unprepared for even the *idea* of battle with Galyat (Goliath). Galyat was a missile aimed directly at the heart of King Sha'ul.

On the other hand, nestled away from the spotlight was young David ben-Yishai (son of Jesse). In the wilderness of Judah, when his sheep were being attacked by one predator after another, the young king-to-be was training for battles against overwhelming odds. He had killed a bear and wrestled a lion to death, grabbing it forcefully by the mane. Upon seeing Galyat, David had the faith to instantly proclaim, "Your servant has defeated both lions and bears, and this uncircumcised P'lishti [Philistine] will be like one of them" (1 Sam. 17:36).

Our most precious time in life is when we are being trained by the living God for our calling; becoming molded by the Master Potter into a royal vessel. Often during this process we can see no more clearly into the future than king David did, as he cared for his sheep in the sleepy grazing fields of the Judean wilderness.

Today I Will

. . . ask God to keep my heart free of fear and my confidence firmly in him, knowing that God has made all things—even my attackers (Isa. 54:16).

BC

Now, *Adonai*, take my life. I'm no better than my ancestors (1 Kings 19:4).

The rabbis told stories about the ancient teacher Choni the Circle-Drawer, who was noted for his holy *chutzpah* (boldness). After a long period without rain, people begged Choni to secure rain for them, so Choni drew a circle and declared, "God, I am not stepping outside this circle until it rains." Immediately the rain began to pour, and the water rose until the people thought there would be a flood. "Choni, Choni, make the rain stop!" they cried. So Choni drew another circle and God stopped the rain.

The rabbis modeled Choni after Eliyahu (Elijah), another man of holy *chutzpah* who called down fire from heaven and announced rain even before a cloud had appeared in the sky. Eliyahu had acted at God's bidding (1 Kings 18:36).

But even Eliyahu struggled, doubting his mission. Like Moses (Exod. 17:4), Jeremiah (Jer. 20:14–18), and John the Immerser (Matt. 11:3–6), Eliyahu faced a crisis in his ministry; he had given his best and had seen great results, but wicked Queen Jezebel had only become more determined to destroy him. Eliyahu was a person just like us (James 5:17).

We may struggle at times with what God is calling us to do, but God will still use us. God used Eliyahu more powerfully after this incident than he did before it.

Today I Will

. . . remember that the prophets were people just like me, and God can use me the way God used them.

March 8, 1999
Feb. 26, 2000 (21)
March 15, 2001
March 4, 2002
Feb. 22, 2003 (21)
March 13, 2004
(21/N)

Adar Sheyni
(Adar II)
March 27, 2000
March 24, 2003

Prayer Focus

CK

ADAR 21 אדר

March 9, 1999
Feb. 27, 2000
March 16, 2001
March 5, 2002
Feb. 23, 2003
March 14, 2004

Adar Sheyni
(Adar II)
March 28, 2000
March 25, 2003

Prayer Focus

Give us the food we need today (Matt. 6:11).

A*z me vil nit alt verren, zol men zich yungerheyt oifhengen* is Yiddish for "If you want to avoid old age, hang yourself when you are young."

Do you remember how tough it was when you were twelve and wanted to be sixteen? Then it was wanting to be eighteen. Eventually, thirty arrived, or even worse forty, and you saw the future racing toward you too quickly.

Many of us live either in the past or in the hope that something will come about to change our future, like winning the lottery. This way of thinking stems from forgetting to live in the present. Let us remember that our lives are happening today.

The daily morning preliminary prayers in the *siddur* (prayer book) contain many petitions for God's blessing on our lives today. Living our lives instead of "thinking about living" is an important part of living the joyful life.

Today I Will

. . . not live in the past or future but in the present.

JR

I am giving you a new command. . . . In the same way that I have loved you, you are also to keep on loving each other (John 13:34).

The *Torah* instructs us to love our neighbors as ourselves (Lev. 19:18). Why, then, does Yeshua call the above commandment "new"?

The Old Covenant idea of loving one's neighbor emphasizes fair treatment, "Don't take vengeance on or bear a grudge . . . rather, love your neighbor" (Lev. 19:18). In a sense, it means that we are to treat other people in the same way that we want them to treat us.

In the above passage, however, Messiah is talking about a different kind of love—an *agape* (divinely empowered, sacrificial love). He taught about this kind of love in his *derash* (homily) known as the Sermon on the Mount (see Matt. 5:44); he demonstrated it on the mount called Gulgolta (Golgotha). In laying down his life for us, Yeshua set the precedent for our relationships with one another. We are to love one another sacrificially, preferring others to ourselves.

The greatest testimony of Yeshua living within us ought to be our love one for another. Many times, Jewish visitors to our congregation have told me that it was this kind of love—the kind that prefers one another and is modeled after 1 Corinthians 13—that impressed them the most.

Do you feel and demonstrate this kind of love toward others? This is Yeshua's new commandment to each of us.

Today I Will

. . . ask the Lord to fill me with *agape* love. "Lord, help me to be selfless rather than selfish, to be willing to lay down my life for others."

March 10, 1999
Feb. 28, 2000
March 17, 2001
(21/N)
March 6, 2002
Feb. 24, 2003
March 15, 2004

Adar Sheyni
(Adar II)
March 29, 2000
March 26, 2003

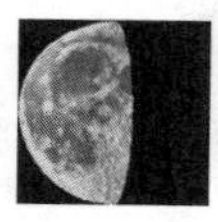

Prayer Focus

March 11, 1999
Feb. 29, 2000
March 18, 2001
March 7, 2002
Feb. 25, 2003
March 16, 2004

Adar Sheyni
(Adar II)
March 30, 2000
March 27, 2003

Prayer Focus

Let the children come to me and stop hindering them . . . the Kingdom of God belongs to such as these (Luke 18:16).

Yeshua welcomed children and recommended child-like faith to his adult followers. Adults tend to mess things up through pride and pretentiousness. Children learn those behaviors from adults. They tend to come without airs, without pretensions. That kind of openness and honesty is what is needed for all who come to God.

I remember having a Jewish couple in our home for dinner. They were not yet believers, and as we sat around the table, there was an uncomfortable pause at the point when we would normally pray. The awkward silence was broken by my two-year-old, Isaac, who extended his hands and said, "Pray to Yeshua, Daddy?" Everyone smiled. I explained our custom of praying which we then did. The ice was broken and we had a meaningful opportunity to witness over the meal. We can learn a lot about the Lord from children.

We would do well to cultivate an appreciation and love for children, like that of Yeshua, and seek opportunities to minister to them. Most of all, we should look to cultivate a child-like faith in our own hearts, for such is the way of the Kingdom of God.

Today I Will

. . . seek to minister the good news of Messiah to children that he has brought into my life.

DB

A large crowd of *cohanim* [priests] were becoming obedient to the faith (Acts 6:7).

March 12, 1999
March 1, 2000
March 19, 2001
March 8, 2002
Feb. 26, 2003
March 17, 2004

Adar Sheyni
(Adar II)
March 31, 2000
March 28, 2003

Leviticus 13 contains very detailed instructions for the priests of Israel in diagnosing leprosy. After a thorough investigation, if someone was found to have this terrible skin disease, he was forced to live outside of mainstream society all the days of his life.

Leviticus 14 tells the priests how to determine if someone has been healed of this ailment, and if so, what the proper procedure for reinstating him into the community was. However, there is a missing piece. There is no indication of "how" to get healed. In the fifteen hundred years from the giving of the *Torah* to the coming of Yeshua, there is no biblical evidence that there was anyone other than Moses's sister Miryam (Num. 12:13–15) and Na'aman the Syrian (2 Kings 5) who was ever healed of leprosy.

When Yeshua came, this changed dramatically. Not only did he and his disciples cleanse lepers (Matt. 10:8; 11:5), but the healed lepers were instructed to show themselves to the priests in observance of Leviticus 14 (Matt. 8:2–4; Luke 17:12–14). Imagine the impact. From never being called on to deal with healed lepers, the priests were suddenly swamped with requests. God's Word came to life and took on new meaning. Is it any wonder that, as today's Scripture passage says, "a large crowd of *cohanim* were becoming obedient to the faith"?

Yeshua is the one who fills in the missing pieces and by doing so, causes faith to rise up in our hearts.

Prayer Focus

Today I Will

. . . recognize that God makes no mistakes. Even if I don't have all the answers, Yeshua holds the missing pieces.

MM

March 13, 1999
(22, 23/O)*
March 2, 2000
March 20, 2001
March 9, 2002
(22, 23/O)*
Feb. 27, 2003
March 18, 2004

Adar Sheyni
(Adar II)
April 1, 2000
(26/O)*
March 29, 2003
(26/O)*

Biblical
On this day, King Jehoiachin was freed from prison (Jer. 52:31).

Prayer Focus

Just as you used to offer the parts of your body in slavery to impurity . . . so now offer them in slavery to righteousness (Rom. 6:19).

The Book of Yonah (Jonah) records that when God called his prophet, "Yonah . . . prepared to escape to Tarshish" (1:3). He tried to escape! As you know, Yonah wound up getting into a lot of trouble, not to mention getting into a fish. But then *ADONAI* [the LORD] called him again. This time the Scripture says, "Yonah set out and went to Ninveh [Nineveh], as *ADONAI* had said. . . . " (3:3) First he prepared to escape. Then he set out and went. In other words, with the same eagerness that Yonah rebelled against God, he now obeyed.

If we want real fruitfulness and holiness in God, then we need to simply serve the Lord with the same commitment as we once served sin. When we served sin, we didn't just *serve* sin, we *indulged* in sin. We didn't do it half-heartedly, we went all the way.

We need to serve God in the same way. We must not just *serve* God; we need to serve him with zeal and excitement! When we obey God, we must not just *obey*, but do so with all our hearts. We didn't sin with half our hearts. So in the same way, we must not walk with God half-heartedly.

We once sinned with excellence; let us serve the Lord with excellence. We must never just *serve* the Lord, but serve the Lord with joy, delight, and all the gusto and strength we have! We were once great at serving sin. Let us be even greater at serving the living God.

Today I Will

. . . serve the Lord with zeal and excitement!

JC

People with good sense are slow to anger, and it is their glory to overlook an offense (Prov. 19:11).

If we want to be in fellowship with the Father, the Messiah, and his *Ruach* (Spirit), we must break the habit of being easily offended. Yes, we need to confront significant sin, but small slights and minor irritations can simply be overlooked. A person who has not yet been healed of rejection can be easily hurt by many little things. This hurt may turn to bitterness.

In the life of a congregation, people who are easily hurt also become offended on behalf of others. Sometimes they start factions based on their mutual hurts. Through such a bitter pool, many can become polluted. Scripture outlines two ways to avoid this sin.

First, we must deal with those who have offended us in a biblical manner, according to the standards described in Matthew 18. We must begin by going alone, then with one or two; finally we are to approach the entire congregation.

Second, we must remember to walk in love so that a multitude of smaller slights are overlooked. This is possible when we know Yeshua and identify with the pain of his crucifixion and the victory of his *techiyah* (resurrection).

Today I Will

. . . not be easily offended by my brothers.

March 14, 1999
March 3, 2000
March 21, 2001
March 10, 2002
Feb. 28, 2003
March 19, 2004

Adar Sheyni
(Adar II)
April 2, 2000
March 30, 2003

Prayer Focus

DJ

March 15, 1999
March 4, 2000
(22/L)*
March 22, 2001
March 11, 2002
March 1, 2003
(22/L)*
March 20, 2004
(22,23/O)*

Adar Sheyni
(Adar II)
April 3, 2000
March 31, 2003

Biblical
On this day, King Jehoiachin was released (2 Kings 25:27).

Prayer Focus

You have shown your strength to both God and men and have prevailed (Gen. 32:29).

Do you desire to win? Do you secretly divide the world into winners and losers? Are you extra friendly with the winners in life and perhaps a little cautious with life's losers?

Ya'akov (Jacob) competed fiercely his whole life in order to win. He was even given a name which means "heel-grabber" or "supplanter." Ya'akov was accused by his twin brother of usurping both the blessing and the rights of the firstborn (Gen. 27:36). He also competed successfully with his uncle Lavan (Laban) for wealth and the right to transplant his family to the Promised Land (Gen. 31:43).

In Genesis 32, Ya'akov stands alone at the banks of the Yabbok (Jabbok) River, just outside the Promised Land. Stripped of his possessions, including his family, he could not return to Lavan's land nor move forward through Eysav's (Esau's) country. An assailant attacked him, and the struggle lasted all night. Shortly before dawn, the assailant crippled him for life. But Ya'akov would not let the attacker depart. Clutching, grabbing, holding on, he cried out, "I won't let you go unless you bless me" (Gen. 32:26). So the Lord renamed him Yisra'el (Israel), for he had prevailed against God and man.

Would you rather be a fast, vigorous Ya'akov or a halting, crippled Yisra'el? What does your answer tell you about your spiritual condition?

Today I Will

. . . stop being competitive toward those around me and allow the Lord to lift me up.

JEF

He also saw a poor widow put in two small coins (Luke 21:2).

One of our first lessons in Hebrew school concerned *tzedakah* (the act of charitable giving). We would put money in the "*tzedakah* box," and fill "Israeli tree" cards by placing dimes in the slots. In both cases, my mother supplied the coins.

Our synagogue also had bigger givers. Though I was young, I remember being disturbed that halls and auditoriums were named after them. I wondered how their children—some of whom I knew—felt about it. Something just didn't seem right. It's interesting how our consciences can sometimes receive *Torah* truth directly from God's heart. This was years before I heard Yeshua's teaching about givers who "announced [their giving] with trumpets to win people's praise" (Matt. 6:2).

My early lessons in giving had little impact on my teen years. Though I was generous to friends, I never gave much thought to charitable giving. It wasn't until a few weeks after meeting Yeshua that this sleeping area of my life awoke. I was in a congregation when the time for offerings arrived. I didn't have much money; in this case, I had just a five dollar bill. The money, however, was mine (not my mother's). I knew that giving it would change my life.

That day I experienced the joy of worshipping ADONAI *Tzidkeynu* (the LORD our Righteousness) through the privilege of giving sacrificially. I have never regretted it.

Today I Will

. . . consider the joy of giving, especially when the amount is sacrificial.

March 16, 1999
March 5, 2000
March 23, 2001
March 12, 2002
March 2, 2003
March 21, 2004

Adar Sheyni
(Adar II)
April 4, 2000
April 1, 2003

Prayer Focus

MW

March 17, 1999
March 6, 2000
March 24, 2001
(22,23/D,O)*
March 13, 2002
March 3, 2003
March 22, 2004

Adar Sheyni
(Adar II)
April 5, 2000
April 2, 2003

Prayer Focus

The heavens declare the glory of God (Ps. 19:1[2]).

How large our problems loom in our eyes, but let's stop and gain a little perspective. Today's airplanes zoom us across the country at about 600 miles per hour. Seems pretty fast, until we think of the speed of light: 186,000 miles . . . per second! At this mind-boggling speed, it would take us only a little over eight full minutes to travel the 93 million miles to the sun. From there to the next nearest star would take us over four years.

Let's expand this a bit: we would have to travel 103,000 years at the speed of light to get across the 300 billion stars that make up our Milky Way galaxy; to get to our nearest neighboring galaxy, the Magellanic Clouds, would require more than another million years. Remember, too, our galaxy is just one of over 200 billion galaxies in the heavens. The farthest celestial object that we can discern today is about 15 billion light years away, and that's if you travel 186,000 miles each second.

Stop for a moment, ponder these distances, and then remember the words of the Scripture: "[God] has counted the handfuls of water in the sea, measured off the sky with a ruler, gauged how much dust there is on the earth, weighed the mountains on scales, . . . the hills in a balance" (Isa. 40:12); this unbelievably vast universe is in the palm of his hand.

This same God loves and cares for us!

Today I Will

. . . lift my eyes to the heavens and reflect on the wonder of God's creation, remembering that he cares for me. Awesome!

Please say that you are my sister, so that it will go well with me for your sake (Gen. 12:13).

As parents, we must ask the question, "What type of example are we setting for our children?" Look at our father Avram (Abram). Shortly after the Lord commissioned Avram to go up to the land of Canaan, he went down to the land of Egypt (Gen. 12:10). In Egypt, Avram agreed with Sarai his wife to tell the Egyptians that Sarai was his sister. A second time (in the above passage), Avram repeated the same story; this time to the people of Gerar in the Negev.

When Yitzchak (Isaac) was faced with the same problem, what did he do? He did exactly what his father did! The Scripture tells us, "The men of the place asked him about his wife, and out of fear he said, 'She is my sister.' He thought, 'If I tell them she's my wife, they might kill me in order to take Rivkah [Rebekah]. After all, she is a beautiful woman' "(Gen. 26:7). The child learned from the parent.

Let us remember that our children look upon our actions and learn from them much more than they do from our speeches.

Today I Will

. . . consider what type of example I am setting for my children, and whether it is one that will lead them in the ways of the Lord.

Adar usually has 29 days. During leap years, however, Adar Rishon (Adar I) has 30 days and Adar Sheyni (Adar II) has 29.

March 7, 2000
March 4, 2003

Traditional *Rosh Chodesh* (the New Moon) Day 1

Prayer Focus

JS

March 18, 1999
April 6, 2000
March 25, 2001
March 14, 2002
April 3, 2003
March 23, 2004

Biblical
Rosh Chodesh
(the New Moon)

The New Year

On this day, the Flood waters dried up (Gen. 8:13); the Tabernacle was set up (Exod. 40:2, 17); Ezra began his journey from Babylon to Jerusalem (Ezra 7:9); Ezra's investigation ceased (Ezra 10:17); Hezekiah began consecrating the second Temple (2 Chron. 29:17); Ezekiel received a prophecy against Egypt (Ezek. 29:17); the Ezekiel Temple will be purified (Ezek. 45:18).

You are to begin your calendar with this month; it will be the first month of the year for you (Exod. 12:2).

L*eshanah tovah!* (To a good year!). It may seem unusual to offer a new-year blessing on Nisan 1, but from God's perspective it is perfectly appropriate. You see, the Lord has his own calendar in heaven (Lev. 23:2). It does not begin on Tishri 1 or January 1, but on Nisan 1 (see Exod. 12:2). In fact, the months in the Hebrew calendar are referred to in Scripture as "the first month," "the second month," etc. When Scripture refers to dates (e.g., "the second month"), it is always reckoning time relative to the date of the exodus—the first month of the year.

Our people celebrated the new year exclusively on Nisan 1 (then called Aviv 1) until the time of the Babylonian exile. It was then that we adopted the Babylonian calendar as our own, including the names of the months and the new year celebration. Did you know that the name of the first month in the Babylonian calendar is Tishri, and that Tishri 1 is . . . you got it! . . . the Babylonian new year?

Tradition is good, but sometimes it is important to prioritize our traditions in light of *Torah* (see Appendix B). God had a good reason for making Nisan the first month of the year. It was because Nisan was the month in which he brought our people out of the land of Egypt (Deut. 16:1). By remembering each day that biblical dates are reckoned in relation to the month of Nisan—the month of the exodus—we can be thankful for that great redemption all year!

Today I Will

. . . commemorate the New Year by remembering that the Lord is my Redeemer and Deliverer.

DR

May your Kingdom come, your will be done on earth as in heaven (Matt. 6:10).

A well-known talmudic story concerns a disagreement over a minor ceremonial issue about a certain stove. In order to prove his view right, Rabbi Eliezer asks God to do several extraordinary miracles. Each one comes to pass. Still, the other rabbis decide to choose the majority opinion over his view.

This incident reveals the method used by the rabbis to "discover God's mind" on important issues. It also raises the question of how Messianic Jews ought to approach the subject of discerning God's will in a matter.

First, it must be remembered that God wants us to know his will even more than we want to know it ourselves. He will go out of his way to reveal his will if we're open to hearing it. Second, God never leads us to do anything that is contrary to his Word. For example, he would never ask us to commit adultery. Finally, God reveals his will in many ways. He will sometimes speak specifically through his Word, giving us an inner prompting to guide us. He might even speak in a still small voice (1 Kings 19:12–13). He also uses the counsel and wisdom of others to confirm his will for us.

Most important for the believer is to know that discerning God's will depends on first having a personal relationship with him.

Today I Will

. . . seek God's will for me in the confidence that as I ask him for wisdom, he will generously grant it to me (see James 1:5).

March 19, 1999
April 7, 2000
March 26, 2001
March 15, 2002
April 4, 2003
March 24, 2004

Prayer Focus

MW

NISAN

3

ניסן

March 20, 1999 (24)
April 8, 2000 (27)
March 27, 2001
March 16, 2002 (24)
April 5, 2003 (27)
March 25, 2004

Prayer Focus

Delight yourself in *ADONAI*, and he will give you your heart's desire (Ps. 37:4).

I have experienced the fulfillment of this promise many times in my life. I have also discovered that it never seems to work when I delight myself in the Lord in order to receive the desires of my heart. Delighting in the Lord must be its own separate desire, a glorious end in itself.

As we continue to delight in the Lord, our desires become purified. Those based totally on self-indulgent motives are in time revealed for what they are, while those which will not divert our focus from the Lord are in time realized. Other desires may become modified as we begin to perceive circumstances in a new light. We may want to move to a certain area of town, but as we delight in the Lord, he may shift our desire to another area, revealing that as his will.

Answers to some desires seem small, but they can powerfully communicate God's love. Once I prayed for a small mica disk to fit into a copy of a primitive phonograph I was making. Such a part had not been manufactured for this purpose in sixty years. A few months later I looked down while worshipping under a tree near my house, and there was the part—which ended up fitting perfectly! The love I felt from my Father was even more important than the fulfillment of my original desire.

Today I Will

. . . enjoy delighting in the Lord with the knowledge that he enjoys granting me the desires of my heart.

MW

Run your lives by the Spirit. Then you will not do what your old nature wants (Gal. 5:16).

Ruach is the Hebrew word for "wind" (it even sounds like the wind). It's also the Hebrew word for "Spirit." *Ruach HaKodesh* literally means "the Holy Wind" or "the Holy Spirit." This means that when we live our lives in opposition to the Spirit—when we walk in sin—it's like walking against the Wind, so we become tired. Aerodynamically, walking against the wind creates drag. So when we live our lives in opposition to the *Ruach*, life becomes a drag. God doesn't want that. That's why he calls us to walk with the Spirit, in the way of love, faith and purity. It's a life of dying to self.

It's not too hard to live God's way; it's very hard not to. Walking with the Lord is actually the easiest path. The Spirit is the *Ruach*, so when we walk in him, the Wind is with us! If we walk with the *Ruach*, with the Wind at our backs, we won't get tired, and life won't drag. Yeshua said, "Come to me, all of you who are struggling and burdened, and I will give you rest. . . . For my yoke is easy, and my burden is light" (Matt. 11:28–30).

Is life a drag? Do you want real life? The answer, my friend, is blowing in the *Ruach*. It's as simple as turning around. Walk in the Spirit, and life won't be a drag, but a breeze!

Today I Will

. . . lay down one burden, sin, or anything creating "drag" in my life, and I will take one step to walk in the way of love, faith, and purity.

NISAN

4

ניסן

March 21, 1999
April 9, 2000
March 28, 2001
March 17, 2002
April 6, 2003
March 26, 2004

Prayer Focus

JC

NISAN

5

ניסן

March 22, 1999
April 10, 2000
March 29, 2001
March 18, 2002
April 7, 2003
March 27, 2004 (24)

He has removed our sins from us as far as the east is from the west (Ps. 103:12).

Here is an amazing truth. In the above Scripture, we are told that God has removed our sins as far as the east is from the west. This was written long before it was an established fact that the earth is round. It says, "as far as the east is from the west," not "as far as the north is from the south." The earth is a sphere and it spins on an axis; thus, we have two poles, a north pole and a south pole. If you head north or south, you come to an end at either pole. So if the Word of God said, "He has removed our sins from us as far as the north is from the south," you could measure the distance in thousands of miles.

But unlike north and south, east and west never meet. The directions east and west are infinite; east and west are thus infinitely separate. Likewise, in salvation, he has removed our sins an infinity away!

The Bible is awesome! Even more awesome is his love toward us. Rejoice and be very glad, for we are totally free. He has removed our sins, our past, our hindrances, our failures . . . as far as the east is from the west!

Prayer Focus

Today I Will

. . . write down any sin or failure that I'm troubled about, give it to God and ask for forgiveness. Then, as a sign of believing in his promise, I will tear up the paper, accept God's total forgiveness, and walk in freedom!

JC

He took the five loaves and the two fish and, looking up toward heaven, made a *b'rakhah* (Matt. 14:19).

March 23, 1999
April 11, 2000
March 30, 2001
March 19, 2002
April 8, 2003
March 28, 2004

Do you want to perform a beautiful miracle? Learn from the master rabbi, Messiah, who was given two fish and a few loaves of bread to feed thousands of hungry people. It was clearly too little for the need, but he didn't complain. Instead, he lifted what he had up to the Father and gave thanks for it. Undoubtedly, he said the *motzi* (the Hebrew blessing over bread):

> *Barukh atah* ADONAI, *Eloheynu melekh ha'olam, hamotzi lechem min ha'aretz. Ameyn.*
>
> Blessed are you, O LORD our God, king of the universe, who brings forth bread from the earth. Amen.

Take note: he didn't focus on all the bread he *didn't* have. Rather, he gave thanks for the little bread he *did* have. And then the miracle happened! The bread multiplied!

How do we perform the miracle of multiplying bread? The answer is simple. When we don't have enough in life, we should stop complaining. We should stop focusing on what we lack, and just give thanks. We need to take all the things we wish we had more of, lift them up to God and say the *motzi.* For when we give thanks to God, we receive the power to perform the miracle of multiplication. The blessings of our lives will begin to multiply, our hunger will turn to fullness, and "not enough" will become "more than enough."

Let's perform our first miracle today—by saying the *motzi* and multiplying that bread!

Prayer Focus

Today I Will

. . . write down ten blessings of God in my life that I haven't thanked him for in a long time, or ever. Then I will spend time lifting them up and giving thanks to him.

NISAN

7

ניסן

March 24, 1999
April 12, 2000
March 31, 2001 (24)
March 20, 2002
April 9, 2003
March 29, 2004

Biblical
On this day, Ezekiel received a prophecy against Egypt (Ezek. 30:20); the Ezekiel Temple will be atoned for (Ezek. 45:20).

Prayer Focus

He gave gifts to mankind (Ps. 68:18).

Moshe (Moses) grew up in the household of Pharaoh, accustomed to making laws obeyed by a consenting multitude. He was a general, experienced in leading large armies across vast deserts. He was uniquely gifted for his calling. Fifteen hundred years later, God gave the job of establishing congregations among the Gentiles to Rabbi Sha'ul (Saul; i.e., Paul) of Tarsus, an experienced Jewish religious leader, a Pharisee of Pharisees who studied at the feet of Rabbi Gamli'el (Gamaliel).

Denying gifts that God has given us will not make us humble. It will not make us spiritual. God rejoices in how he has made us, and summons us to yield ourselves to his leading, so that we may use all that we are to serve his purposes (Rom. 6:13, 19).

Of course, it is important to recognize that human gifts only go so far. While Moshe's leadership skills were crucial during the trek from Egypt to Israel, they were useless when the need was the parting of the Red Sea.

Is it not uplifting to consider that while we seek to be worthy stewards of the natural gifts we have been given (Matt. 25:14–28), God is well able to bring us challenges that force us to humbly tap into God's ability (Matt. 14:28–29)?

Today I Will

. . . ask God for the grace to see myself accurately. I will use the gifts the Lord has given me, and I will not grieve my Creator by walking in pride because of them (1 Cor. 4:7).

BC

Rejoice with those who rejoice, and weep with those who weep (Rom. 12:15).

The Ba'al Shem Tov (Master of the Good Name), who founded *Chasidism* (an ultra-Orthodox Jewish sect), believed that being a good Jew was based not so much on what you knew, but on what you felt. While such a view may be open to question, one thing is certain: feelings play an important role in the life of a believer. How understanding God is in this regard!

He does not tell us *not* to have feelings; he gives us guidelines for handling them. Spirituality does not mean having no feelings. Yeshua wept (John 11:35) and he rejoiced (Luke 10:21). Rabbi Sha'ul (Saul; i.e., Paul) wrote openly of his feelings of despair (2 Cor. 1:8), as well as his confidence (1 Cor. 2:4). In the *Tanakh* we see that King David danced for joy (2 Sam. 6:14) and admitted grief when the occasion warranted (1 Sam. 30:4).

If Abraham had not loved Isaac, there would have been no majesty in his willingness to sacrifice him on Mount Moriah. If David had not loved Jonathan, there would have been no majesty to the triumph of friendship over jealousy.

Love, joy, sadness, courage and fear are all part of the existence God has given us. In short, godliness is not measured by how flat the graph of your emotions may be; it is measured by how you allow the choices arising from those feelings to be governed by the Word and the *Ruach* (Spirit) of the living God.

Today I Will

. . . allow the Lord to govern my emotions.

March 25, 1999
April 13, 2000
April 1, 2001
March 21, 2002
April 10, 2003
March 30, 2004

Biblical
Yeshua arrived in Beyt Anyah (Bethany) on Nisan 8/9 (John 12:1).

Prayer Focus

BC

NISAN

9

ניסן

March 26, 1999
April 14, 2000
April 2, 2001
March 22, 2002
April 11, 2003
March 31, 2004

Prayer Focus

You meant to do me harm, but God meant it for good—so that it would come about as it is today, with many people's lives being saved (Gen. 50:20).

The *Talmud* (Ta'anit 21a) tells the story of Nachum who "was blind in both of his eyes, his two hands and legs were amputated, and his whole body was covered with boils and he was lying in a dilapidated house on a bed, the feet of which were standing in bowls of water in order to prevent the ants from crawling on him." In the midst of all this suffering, Nachum would say, "This also is for the best" (*Gam zu letovah*). Therefore, he was given the nickname "the Gamzu Man" (*Ish Gamzu*).

Yosef (Joseph) was very much like Nachum. In the midst of his suffering, he trusted in God. Yosef knew that God was in charge of all things, and was able to see the bigger plan. He would not let himself get bogged down in retribution, bitterness, harshness or the dark side of God's plan. Thrown into a pit, sold into slavery, imprisoned unjustly, Yosef could have become very bitter. But God showed him the larger picture. Nachum came to the same conclusion. How about you?

Today I Will

. . . look at the bigger picture and remember that the Lord is ultimately in charge of my life.

JR

On the tenth day of this month, each man is to take a lamb or kid for his family (Exod. 12:3).

One of the essential elements of the first *Pesach* (Passover) was a hand-chosen lamb that was sacrificed. As the blood of the sacrifice was applied to the doorposts of their homes, the people who obeyed God's command (both Jews and Gentiles) were spared the judgment inflicted by God.

We should not overlook the preparation that went into selecting this important sacrificial animal. The *Torah* tells us that the people were to bring the lamb into their home four days before the actual sacrifice. They were to carefully scrutinize the lamb in order to verify that it met the qualifications for a sacrifice. It had to be an unblemished lamb (Exod. 12:5). Clearly, God was showing our forefathers that since they were imperfect, a sinless sacrifice was required to pay the price for their sins. Nothing short of perfection would suffice since God is perfectly holy. If the lamb had any defect or broken bone, it was disqualified. These problems could be confirmed during the four-day period in which the lamb was brought into the home.

What a picture of the Messiah to come! Yeshua entered the city of Jerusalem on the tenth of Nisan as though he were presenting himself for inspection (John 12:1, 12). There was great debate about his identity; some rejected him, yet many welcomed him (John 12:13) with cheers of "*Barukh haba BeSheym Adonai*" (Blessed is he who comes in the Name of the Lord)!

Messianic believers today concur with the assessment of Yochanan (John) who cried out, "Look! God's lamb! The one who is taking away the sin of the world!" (John 1:29)

Today I Will

. . . be thankful that the blood of God's lamb, Yeshua, is applied to the doorpost of my heart.

March 27, 1999 (25/P)
April 15, 2000 (28/P)
April 3, 2001
March 23, 2002 (25/P)
April 12, 2003 (28/P)
April 1, 2004

Biblical
On this day, the Passover lambs were chosen (Exod. 12:3); the Israelites camped at Gilgal (Josh. 4:19); Ezekiel saw the future glorious Temple (Ezek. 40:1); Yeshua rode into Jerusalem on a young donkey as crowds proclaimed him the Messiah (John 12:12–16); Yeshua and his disciples entered the Temple area and then returned to Beyt Anyah (Bethany) (Mark 11:11).

BK

March 28, 1999
April 16, 2000
April 4, 2001
March 24, 2002
April 13, 2003
April 2, 2004

Biblical
On this day, Yeshua and his disciples left Beyt Anyah (Bethany) for Jerusalem (Mark 11:12); Yeshua cursed a fig tree (Mark 11:12–14); Yeshua cleansed the Temple, ridding it of merchants (Mark 11:15–17).

Prayer Focus

In his forebearance, he had passed over . . . the sins people had committed in the past (Rom. 3:25).

In the *Midrash* (traditional commentary) on Ruth 2:14, we read this about the Messiah: "The phrase 'dip your morsel in the vinegar' refers to his sufferings, as it is said, 'But he was wounded for our transgressions'" (Isa. 53:5). After this statement we find the following interesting comparison: "Rabbi Berekiah said in the name of Rabbi Levi: 'The future Redeemer [Messiah] will be like the former Redeemer [Moses]. Just as the former Redeemer revealed himself and later was hidden from them . . . so the future Redeemer will be revealed to them and then be hidden from them. . . . He who believes in him will live, and he who does not believe will depart to the Gentile nations and they will put him to death'" (Midrash Ruth 5:6).

In our efforts to reach others with the truth about Messiah, we often expend our energies trying to show how Yeshua was like Moses. This is like pointing out how many ways the original Rembrandt is like the copy! Although Moses instituted the first covenant, the Book of Hebrews states that there was still a need for a second one (8:7). The blood of Yeshua the Messiah instituted this new covenant.

We have the original, the perfect, the complete, and we never need to be ashamed of the one whom we declare and represent.

Today I Will

. . . give God thanks for the great redemption which he has given me through the atoning death of his Son.

RP

ADONAI your God will bring you back into the land your ancestors possessed, and you will possess it (Deut. 30:5).

I was brought to Eretz Yisra'el (the Land of Israel) when I was just a baby. I was raised in Yerushalayim (Jerusalem). As a youth, I learned to know and to love this Land through my feet. I walked with the Zionist youth movement all over the Land. We walked from Sea to Sea; that is, from the Mediterranean to the Sea of Galilee. We walked over the hills of Yerushalayim and the Negev desert. We walked and learned the biblical stories on the sites where they had taken place.

Eretz Yisra'el is God's real estate. He has chosen it and calls it "My Land." It is the only land in which the *Shekhinah* (Glory of God) dwelled for over five hundred years. Eretz Yisra'el is the stage where our history has been played out.

Today, Eretz Yisra'el is the gathering place for our people from all corners of the world. For thousands of years, Jews have been looking forward to the events that we are currently witnessing. Our people are coming home to Israel. They are returning because of their deep love for this Land. The love for the Land is rooted in a love for what God has promised to do here, and what he is doing here now. Have you been to Eretz Yisra'el?

Today I Will

. . . be open to the possibility that the "you" in the above Scripture refers to me.

March 29, 1999
April 17, 2000
April 5, 2001
March 25, 2002
April 14, 2003
April 3, 2004 (25/P)

Biblical

On this day, Yeshua and his disciples left Jerusalem at evening (Mark 11:19); in the morning, they noticed the cursed fig tree had withered (Mark 11:20); Yeshua returned to Jerusalem; his authority was questioned (Mark 11:27–33); Yeshua taught at the Temple and Mount of Olives (Mark 12–13); Yeshua taught in parables and rebuked the religious leaders (Matt. 21:28–24:5); Yeshua predicted that in two days he would be handed over to be crucified (Matt. 26:1–2); Yehudah of Keriot (Judas Iscariot) conspired with religious leaders to betray him (Matt. 26:14–16).

Traditional

Ta'anit Bekhorim (the Fast of the Firstborn) in the year 2001. See Appendix C, Chart 3, note 5.

JS

March 30, 1999
April 18, 2000
April 6, 2001
March 26, 2002
April 15, 2003
April 4, 2004

Biblical
On this day, Haman's edict was written (Esther 3:12).

Traditional
The removal of *chameytz* (leaven) from the house takes place tonight.

Prayer Focus

The Egyptians tried to flee, but *ADONAI* swept them into the sea (Exod. 14.27).

How easy and natural it is to rejoice when our enemies suffer misfortune, especially if it comes to them when they are in the midst of acting against us. Rabbinic literature records an *aggadah* (popular legend) that when the ministering angels in heaven saw the Egyptians drowning, they began to rejoice. God, however, rebuked them and said, "The works of my hands are perishing, so why are you rejoicing?"

We must always remember that even those we do not get along with are made in God's image. The Messiah died for them no less than he died for us. We are told to pray for them, not rejoice at their suffering. In this way we will be like our Father in heaven. "For if we were reconciled with God through his Son's death when we were enemies, how much more will we be delivered by his life, now that we are reconciled!" (Rom. 5:10)

Today I Will

. . . ask the Lord to help me see others through his eyes, to love my enemies just as God loves me.

RP

In his forebearance, he had passed over . . . the sins people had committed in the past (Rom. 3:25).

There is no Jewish festival that has more meaning and symbolism than *Pesach* (Passover). The *seder* (service) reminds us of the events leading up to the exodus from Egypt and God's intervention on behalf of our ancestors. The meal includes bitter herbs which graphically depict our slavery. The *charoset* (apple-nut mixture) speaks of the sweetness of our redemption. The shankbone of the lamb, the central element of the *seder* meal, explains the reason for the holy day. As God was about to send the angel of death throughout Egypt, he proclaimed that there would be deliverance for every household which had the blood of the perfect lamb applied to its doorpost. Upon seeing the blood of the sacrifice, God would *pesach* (pass over) that house and not allow the death of the firstborn son (Exod. 12:13).

Pesach is not just about the history of our people. It is also about God's plan of redemption for all nations. What a perfect picture of the death of Messiah on our behalf! Yeshua—the perfect lamb of God—died to take away the sin of the world (John 1:29). By faith, we have applied the blood of his sacrifice to the door of our lives, and God must pass over us! It is not by works of righteousness but only by the free gift of the Father.

Let us rejoice in our two-fold deliverance: from physical death in Egypt and from spiritual death in eternity. For Messianic Jews, Passover becomes a double blessing!

Today I Will

. . . meditate on all that God did to deliver me at *Pesach*.

March 31, 1999
April 19, 2000
April 7, 2001 (25/P)
March 27, 2002
April 16, 2003
April 5, 2004

Biblical
Pesach
(Passover)
begins at twilight

On this day, Josiah restored the celebration of Passover to Israel (2 Chron. 35:1); Yeshua celebrated the Passover with his disciples (Luke 22:13–14).

Traditional
Ta'anit Bekhorim
(the Fast of the Firstborn)

Prayer Focus

BK

NISAN 15 ניסן

April 1, 1999 (מ)
April 20, 2000 (מ)
April 8, 2001 (מ)
March 28, 2002 (מ)
April 17, 2003 (מ)
April 6, 2004 (מ)

Biblical
Matzot
(the Feast of Unleavened Bread)
Day 1
Annual Sabbath

On this day, the Israelites entered Egypt (Exod. 12:40–41), left Egypt (Exod. 12:6–13, 29–31), and began eating the produce of the Promised Land (Josh. 5:11); Yeshua prayed on the Mount of Olives (Luke 22:15–46), and was arrested, tried and crucified (Luke 22:47–23:49).

Traditional
The first day of Passover

Prayer Focus

____

____

____

BK

This cup is the New Covenant effected by my blood (1 Cor. 11:25).

It seems that the symbols associated with our holy week of *Pesach* (Passover) are almost unlimited! Every food, every prayer, every Scripture reading beckons us to understand the depths of our redemption. Perhaps the custom that brings it all into focus is the central cup of the *Pesach seder* (Passover service): the Cup of Redemption. During the course of the meal, we drink from the various cups of wine or grape juice to remind us of the great truths of the season. The rabbis stipulated that four cups should be at the table to highlight the four promises to Moshe (Moses) spoken in Exod. 6:6–7.

The Cup of Sanctification starts the holy occasion. The Cup of Plagues is sipped as we tell how our Redeemer brought us out of Egypt. The fourth cup is called the Cup of Praise. We recite the *Hallel* (Praise Psalms 113–118). However, right after the main meal is the third cup—the Cup of Redemption—which points to the fact that we were "bought back; redeemed" from Egyptian slavery.

Some 1500 years after that first Passover, Yeshua of Nazareth celebrated the *seder* with his Jewish disciples. What an amazing fulfillment they could see as Yeshua took the Cup of Redemption and said, "This is my blood . . . shed on behalf of many, so that they may have their sins forgiven" (Matt. 26:28). From that point on, true disciples of Yeshua could not only celebrate the redemption from Egypt, but also the spiritual redemption found through faith in God's Messiah. What a blessing it is for Messianic Jews and Gentile believers to lift up the Cup of Redemption and call on the Name of the Lord (Ps. 116:13)!

Today I Will

. . . remember the price that was paid for my sins on that first-century Passover day in Jerusalem.

Now if I, the Lord and Rabbi, have washed your feet, you also should wash each other's feet (John 13:14).

Of the many ceremonies of the *Pesach seder* (Passover service), an essential one is the *netilat yadayim* (washing of hands). An Orthodox Jew will cleanse his hands through this ceremonial washing in the traditional basin. This custom is a reminder that we must be cleansed to partake of the food which God has graciously provided. In fact, there are two separate washings at the *seder* meal—emphasizing, even more, our need for cleansing.

As we look back at the last *Pesach* of Yeshua, we realize that the Messiah taught many lessons from the traditions of our fathers. When this *seder* came to the moment of the *netilat yadayim*, a rather shocking thing happened. Usually a servant would come out with the water basin (the *seder* participants would not normally be bothered with such a menial task—after all, it is a night to recline at the table in celebration of freedom from slavery). At this point, however, Messiah got up from the table, took the water basin, and began to wash the disciples' hands and feet. Taken aback, some of the disciples insisted that Yeshua stop.

The water basin at the *seder* conveyed an important lesson to them . . . and to us! If the Messiah humbled himself to serve others in this way, how much more should we, his disciples, do the same? This is the lesson of *netilat yadayim*.

Today I Will

. . . seek out ways in which I can serve others, that they may see Messiah in me.

NISAN

16

ניסן

April 2, 1999 (מ)
April 21, 2000 (מ)
April 9, 2001 (מ)
March 29, 2002 (מ)
April 18, 2003 (מ)
April 7, 2004 (מ)

Biblical

Matzot (the Feast of Unleavened Bread) Day 2

On this day, the manna stopped (Josh. 5:11–12); Hezekiah finished consecrating the Temple (2 Chron. 29:17).

Traditional

The second day of Passover

Bikkurim (the Feast of First Fruits)

Sefirat Ha'Omer (Counting of the Omer)
In rabbinic tradition, the fifty-day count to *Shavu'ot*/Pentecost (the Feast of Weeks) begins on Nisan 16. In contrast, the Scriptures state that the counting should begin on the Sunday in the middle of *Matzot* week (Lev. 23:11–16). See Appendix B, endnote 6.

BK

April 3, 1999 (מ)
April 22, 2000 (מ)
April 10, 2001 (מ)
March 30, 2002 (מ)
April 19, 2003 (מ)
April 8, 2004 (מ)

Biblical
Matzot
(the Feast of Unleavened Bread)
Day 3

Traditional
The third day of Passover

Nisan 17–20 is called *Chol Hamo'ed* (Intermediate Days). In Israel, this period begins on Nisan 16.

Prayer Focus

BK

Let us celebrate the *Seder* not with leftover *chametz* . . . but with the *matzah* of purity and truth (1 Cor. 5:8).

Spring cleaning! It is a busy time of the year. Yet it seems that this much-needed chore is actually the idea of God himself! Every year at this time, we are told in the *Torah* to clean out the *chameytz* (leaven) from our dwelling places as we commemorate Passover (Exod. 12:15).

Why bother? The word *chameytz* can actually be translated as "decay," "corruption," or just plain "sour." Because of this description, we can see many spiritual lessons in the removal of *chameytz* at Passover. It is actually symbolic of a bigger problem—sin. Indeed, our transgressions decay our existence, taking us away from God's perfect plan for our lives. *Chameytz* also reminds us that a corruption may set in if we choose our own ways instead of the abundant life which Yeshua offers. Because it is sour, *chameytz* represents what sin does to us: it can turn us into sour, bitter people!

By contrast, *Matzah* (unleavened bread) can also be translated "sweet." Our people were told to replace the *chameytz* with pure, unleavened *matzah*. How true it is that when sin is removed from our lives, the sweetness of God's blessings can take over! As we eat the *matzah* during the eight days of Passover, may we know afresh the sweetness of our walk with Yeshua.

Today I Will

. . . clean out any spiritual *chameytz* and let the sweetness of the *Ruach HaKodesh* (Holy Spirit) show forth to those around me.

When I am lifted up from the earth, I will draw everyone to myself (John 12:32).

One of the foundational doctrines of our Messianic faith is the resurrection of Yeshua. Many people appreciate the wonderful teachings of Yeshua. Some even acknowledge him as a great rabbi. Yet, it is his resurrection from the dead that sets him apart from any other person in history! We would expect such an important event to be foreshadowed in the Jewish Scriptures.

The Roman Church tried to create a picture of the resurrection by messianizing the pagan celebration of *Ishtar* (Easter), which is still observed. However, there is a biblical holy day which clearly foreshadows this triumph of Messiah's life. In the *Torah*, we are told that on the day after the Sabbath during *Pesach* (Passover) week there is to be a special observance called *Bikkurim* (the Feast of First Fruits).

This holy day was to be a time of thanksgiving for the ingathering of the barley harvest, the first grain to ripen in Israel every spring. As part of the Temple ceremony, the priest was to take some of the barley, lift it up, and wave it to the Lord in the sight of all the people (Lev. 23:9–16). While this ceremony would turn people's attention to the harvest aspect of the festival, *Bikkurim* was to also have a deeper, spiritual meaning.

This spiritual picture comes into focus when Yeshua tells his disciples that his body will be like the grain of barley that must die in order to produce more fruit. Yet he would also be lifted up in the resurrection and "waved" before the people for all to see. No wonder many in Israel were drawn to Yeshua, the living Redeemer! Yeshua not only died on Passover, but he rose on *Bikkurim* in perfect fulfillment of the *Torah*. Have you celebrated the Risen One in your heart today?

Today I Will

. . . walk in the newness of life which Yeshua obtained for me by his death and resurrection.

April 4, 1999 (מ)
April 23, 2000 (מ)
April 11, 2001 (מ)
March 31, 2002 (מ)
April 20, 2003 (מ)
April 9, 2004 (מ)

Biblical
Matzot
(the Feast of Unleavened Bread)
Day 4

Bikkurim
(the Feast of First Fruits) and *Sefirat Ha'Omer* (Counting of the Omer) in the year 1999, 2000, 2002, and 2003. These dates are based on the Scriptural teaching to celebrate the festival on the Sunday in the middle of *Matzot* week (Lev 23:11–16). See Appendix B, endnote 6.

Traditional
The fourth day of Passover

BK

NISAN

19

ניסן

April 5, 1999 (מ)
April 24, 2000 (מ)
April 12, 2001 (מ)
April 1, 2002 (מ)
April 21, 2003 (מ)
April 10, 2004 (מ)

Biblical
Matzot
(the Feast of Unleavened Bread)
Day 5

Traditional
The fifth day of Passover

Prayer Focus

He was wounded because of our crimes, crushed because of our sins (Isa. 53:5).

One of the most striking symbols of the traditional *Pesach seder* (Passover service) is the special holder for the three *matzot* (sheets of unleavened bread). Known for generations as the *matzah tash* (unleavened bread holder), this ritual bag contains three separate compartments, each of which holds a piece of *matzah*. The rabbis have debated the original meaning of this rather unusual custom, which dates back perhaps two thousand years. The consensus has been that the *matzah tash* represents some kind of unity. Some consider it the unity of our forefathers: Abraham, Isaac and Jacob. Another view speculates that the *matzah tash* represents the unity of our people Israel: the *cohen* (priest), the Levite and the Israelite.

Adding to the mystery is the fact that during the *seder* we take out the middle *matzah*, break it in two, wrap it in a napkin, and hide it, to be found later. One half of the broken *matzah* is given a special name: the *Afikomen* (Coming One). While earlier explanations fall short of explaining the mystery of the three-in-one unity of the *matzah tash*, the Messianic view is intriguing.

Many believe it was the middle *matzah* that Yeshua took out at his last *seder*. After breaking it, as was customary, he shared it with his disciples, adding "This is my body, which is being given for you" (Luke 22:19). The *Afikomen* depicts what the *Mashiach* (Messiah) came to do on our behalf.

Like the *matzah*, he was "pierced" and "broken" as he died for the sins of Israel and for all nations. He was "wrapped" and hidden in a burial tomb, only to "reappear" at his resurrection! As the name implies, the "Coming One" will return to establish his Kingdom. Perhaps the *Afikomen* is not so mysterious after all!

Today I Will

. . . give thanks for the rich customs which remind me of what God has done for me through his Son, Yeshua.

BK

I will put my Spirit in you; and you will be alive. Then I will place you in your own land (Ezek.37:14).

On the *Shabbat* (Sabbath) that occurs during the week of Passover, the *Haftarah* (portion from the Prophets) that is read in the synagogue is Ezek. 37:1–14. In spite of the fact that there were numerous suitable Scriptures to choose from, the ancient sages of Israel picked one that especially expresses the heart of Passover. Though many things come to mind when we think of Passover, how often do we connect it with revival? Yet looking at the history of Israel, it is plain to see that the two go hand-in-hand.

After forty years of wandering in the wilderness, Israel crossed the Yarden (Jordan), circumcised their men (renewing the covenant), and celebrated the first Passover in the Land. Years later, after decades of sin and neglect, Judah's King Hezekiah held a glorious two-week-long Passover celebration for the whole nation, which led to spiritual revival. This same pattern is seen under the rulership of King Josiah, and again with Ezra and the exiles who returned to Yerushalayim (Jerusalem) from Babylon.

In a vision, Ezekiel saw the revival of the people of God, coming out of the graveyard of the world, returning to the Land of their fathers, and receiving the *Ruach* (Spirit) of God. This would become the ultimate victory that Yeshua the Messiah accomplished on Passover.

Today I Will

. . . see the celebration of Passover not just as a commemoration of the past, but as an ongoing experience of revival in which I can participate, flowing like a river from the first Passover in Egypt to its fulfillment at the end of days.

April 6, 1999 (מ)
April 25, 2000 (מ)
April 13, 2001 (מ)
April 2, 2002 (מ)
April 22, 2003 (מ)
April 11, 2004 (מ)

Biblical
Matzot
(the Feast of Unleavened Bread)
Day 6

Bikkurim
(the Feast of First Fruits) and *Sefirat Ha'Omer* (Counting of the Omer) in the year 2004. This date is based on the Scriptural teaching to celebrate the festival on the Sunday in the middle of *Matzot* week (Lev. 23:11–16). See Appendix B, endnote 6.

Traditional
The sixth day of Passover

Prayer Focus

MM

April 7, 1999 (מ)
April 26, 2000 (מ)
April 14, 2001 (מ)
April 3, 2002 (מ)
April 23, 2003 (מ)
April 12, 2004 (מ)

Biblical
Matzot
(the Feast of Unleavened Bread)
Day 7
Annual Sabbath

Traditional
The seventh day of Passover

Prayer Focus

The nations will know . . . when, before their eyes, I am set apart through you to be regarded as holy (Ezek. 36:23).

Israel is God's picture book, teaching the world that he exists and is supreme over all he has created. Israel is also God's picture book, graphically displaying his purpose for all mankind. God invites anyone to open this book and understand his ways.

We learn from the portrait of Israel that God is a just and righteous God who wants us to order society according to his *Torah.* If we do, there will be blessing; if not, there will be a curse. The picture book of Israel also teaches us about sowing and reaping, righteous courts, and accountable leaders. In the days of King David and during the early reign of King Shlomo (Solomon), we see a glorious foreshadowing of God's ultimate Kingdom on earth.

The nation of Israel also provides a picture of God's long-suffering love. Centuries pass and Israel is faithfully restored to her Land in fulfillment of prophecy. Israel's feasts are pictures too. Passover is a picture of God's deliverance.

Israel is not God's only picture book. We are also a picture book. The Scriptures call this being a "witness." What kind of a picture book are we?

Today I Will

. . . be a true witness, a picture of God's grace and righteousness.

DJ

Look, I will send to you Eliyahu the prophet (Mal. 3:23).

Perhaps the most renowned and beloved of the Jewish prophets is Eliyahu *HaTishbi* (Elijah the Tishbite). This could be because of the awesome miracles which were performed through the hand of this humble servant of God. We also admire his incredible boldness as he confronted the pagan prophets of *Ba'al* on Mount Carmel (1 Kings 18). Likewise, Eliyahu has always captured the attention of our people because of his mysterious ascension into heaven on a fiery chariot (2 Kings 2).

It doesn't surprise us, therefore, that this man of faith is given special mention in the last verses (Mal. 4:5–6[3:23–24]) of the *Nevi'im* (Prophets) as the one who will prepare the way of restoration before the days of *Mashiach* (Messiah). On account of this distinction, the rabbis of old placed great emphasis on Eliyahu as the one who would announce the coming of *Mashiach*. Hence the fifth cup at our *Pesach seder* (Passover service)—*kos* Eliyahu (cup of Elijah).

This cup is set on the table, filled to the brim, but left untouched during the *seder*. The hope is that Eliyahu himself will show up at our *seder*, drink from the cup and announce that *Mashiach* is finally here! What a beautiful tradition it is; and yet how tragic.

There was a man who came to our people in the first century and claimed to be sent by God to prepare the way for the *Mashiach*. Yochanan (John) came in the spirit and even with much of the physical appearance of Eliyahu. Yeshua the Messiah said of him "if you are willing to accept it, he is Eliyahu, whose coming was predicted" (Matt. 11:14). Although both Yochanan and Yeshua were rejected by many, God will still fulfill his promise to send Eliyahu. Are we ready for him to join us at our *seder*?

Today I Will

. . . contemplate the message of the Cup of Eliyahu and prepare for the return of Messiah.

April 8, 1999 (מ)
April 27, 2000 (מ)
April 15, 2001 (מ)
April 4, 2002 (מ)
April 24, 2003 (מ
April 13, 2004 (מ)

Biblical
Bikkurim (the Feast of First Fruits) and *Sefirat Ha'Omer* (Counting of the Omer) in the year 2001. This date is based on the Scriptural teaching to celebrate the festival on the Sunday in the middle of *Matzot* week (Lev. 23:11–16). See Appendix B, endnote 6.

Traditional
The eighth day of Passover (in diaspora only)

In addition to having *seders* on Nisan 15–16, the Ba'al Shem Tov instituted the custom of having a third seder on Nisan 22 called the "Meal of Messiah." It is a time for the *Chasidim* (ultra-Orthodox Jews) to remember that the Messiah is coming soon.

BK

April 9, 1999
April 28, 2000
April 16, 2001
April 5, 2002
April 25, 2003
April 14, 2004

Prayer Focus

Kefa followed him at a distance (Matt. 26:58).

Following at a distance is a good way to become lost, as anyone who has tried to follow a friend's car through city traffic can tell you.

The prophet Elisha was not one to follow at a distance. When his master Eliyahu (Elijah) was about to depart from this world, he stayed close beside him. Three times the older prophet urged Elisha to stay back, but he refused, and followed his master beyond the Yarden (Jordan) River. There he saw Eliyahu taken up by a whirlwind into heaven. Because of his persistence, Elisha received a double portion of Eliyahu's spirit and crossed back over the Yarden with great power (2 Kings 2).

Kefa's (Peter's) master also departed from this world, but in a far less glorious way. Kefa wanted to remain a disciple, but after Yeshua was arrested and led away to the *Cohen HaGadol* (High Priest), it seemed wise to keep some distance from Yeshua. Following at a distance is a good way to become lost; Kefa soon found himself denying that he even knew Yeshua.

Like Kefa, we follow at a distance when we avoid identifying too openly with Yeshua, when we consider it too costly or risky to be his disciple. To reach our spiritual destination without becoming lost, we must stay close beside him.

Today I Will

. . . follow Yeshua closely by openly declaring my loyalty to him, even at the risk of mockery or rejection.

RR

Dani'el resolved that he would not defile himself with the king's food or the wine he drank (Dan. 1:8).

April 10, 1999 (26)*
April 29, 2000 (29/G)*
April 17, 2001
April 6, 2002 (26)*
April 26, 2003 (29/G)*
April 15, 2004

Biblical
On this day, Daniel received a prophecy about the end times (Dan. 10:4).

Talk about a potentially tragic life! As a young Jewish boy, Daniel was taken captive from Yerushalayim (Jerusalem) by the hated Babylonians. He became separated from his parents and was forced to serve in the king's court. Daniel could have become bitter against God and given up his faith. Instead, at this critical juncture in his life, he made a decision to faithfully serve the God of Israel. This decision affected his entire life, the course of Israel's history, and even the fate of the great Babylonian empire.

In Hebrew, Daniel and his three friends are described as *yeladim* (usually translated "children," but "young teenagers" would be more accurate). Rabbi Ibn Ezra believed that Daniel was fifteen years old.

Daniel and his friends were instructed to eat the king's meat and drink his wine. Why was this bad? The meat was unclean according to the biblical laws of *kashrut* (ritual cleanness), probably including the meat of animals the *Torah* called unclean or of animals that had been strangled. The wine had likely been offered to idols and could have drawn God's people into idolatrous ceremonies. Daniel resolved (literally, "set his heart") to separate from the world and follow God. He chose to take his stand on this issue and God blessed him for it.

Decisions to live for the Lord begin in the heart. We must choose not to compromise with the world, but to be like a city set on a hill for all to see. As the world gets darker, let us become brighter. Let us follow the example of this young, godly Jewish boy who chose God and changed the world.

Prayer Focus

Today I Will

. . . purpose in my heart to serve the Lord. I will not compromise with the world, but I will let the light of Yeshua shine brightly within me.

DC

April 11, 1999
April 30, 2000
April 18, 2001
April 7, 2002
April 27, 2003
April 16, 2004

***Elohi! Elohi! L'mah sh'vaktani?* (which means, "My God! My God! Why have you deserted me?") (Mark 15:34)**

At the height of the pain and torture of crucifixion, Yeshua cried out a meditation from the Word of God: "My God! My God! Why have you deserted me?" Contrary to the understanding of many, Yeshua was not admitting a loss of faith in uttering these words. Rather, he was, in a very Jewish way, indicating his meditation on the whole text of Psalm 22—a Messianic passage—by quoting the first verse. Yeshua knew that the Psalm spoke of God's faithfulness as it stated, "In you our ancestors put their trust; they trusted, and you rescued them. . . . For he has not despised or abhorred the poverty of the poor; he did not hide his face from him but listened to his cry" (Ps. 22:4[5], 24[25]).

The Lord will never desert us. How can we be sure of this in our hour of trial? By meditating on the promises of *HaShem* (God; literally, "the Name"), even as Yeshua did. Then we will be as prepared as he was to carry the *tzlav* (cross).

Prayer Focus

Today I Will

. . . meditate on God's promises so that my faith will be prepared to withstand life's trials and the temptations of the Adversary.

DR

Fools say in their hearts, "There is no God" (Ps. 14:1).

April 12, 1999
May 1, 2000
April 19, 2001
April 8, 2002
April 28, 2003
April 17, 2004 (26)*

What the Bible calls "fools" are not people with a limited brain capacity, but people who simply do not acknowledge God. The greatest fools, however, are those who do know God, but choose not to follow him. In lieu of following God, they choose to play "god" in their own lives. These fools can be found among Jews as well as Christians.

One of the most famous fools recorded in Scripture is a rich man who comforted himself with the words, "You're a lucky man! You have a big supply of goods laid up that will last many years. Start taking it easy! Eat! Drink! Enjoy yourself!" (Luke 12:19) The passage continues as God said to him, "You fool! This very night you will die! And the things you prepared—whose will they be?" (Luke 12:20) In spite of all his possessions, this rich man was not rich in God. Thus, he was a fool.

But there is another type of fool spoken of in the Scriptures—those who choose to be fools for Messiah's sake (1 Cor. 4:10). To the world, Messianic Jews may appear to be fools because we have embraced the message of a crucified Messiah. In reality, however, we are partakers of the wisdom of God. Rabbi Sha'ul (Saul; i.e., Paul) reminds us, "For the message about the execution-stake is nonsense to those in the process of being destroyed, but to us in the process of being saved it is the power of God. . . . For God's wisdom ordained that the world, using its own wisdom, would not come to know him. Therefore God decided to use the 'nonsense' of what we proclaim as his means of saving those who come to trust in it" (1 Cor. 1:18, 21).

Prayer Focus

Today I Will

. . . share the good news of Yeshua with others, even though I may be perceived as a fool.

NISAN

27

ניסן

April 13, 1999
May 2, 2000
April 20, 2001
April 9, 2002
April 29, 2003
April 18, 2004

Traditional
Yom HaSho'ah
(Holocaust
and Ghetto
Uprising Day)

Prayer Focus

In all their troubles he was troubled (Isa. 63:9).

Undoubtedly, it is the most horrific part of a long history of pain and suffering. It is known as the Holocaust, a term uniquely used to describe the planned destruction of the Jewish people by the Nazis during World War II. How can one comprehend the murder of six million Jews—which included one and a half million children? The fact that an additional five million non-Jews perished in the concentration camps should also make *Yom HaSho'ah* (Holocaust Day) a day for *all* people to contemplate.

While the satanic plot to destroy the Jewish people will never be fully comprehended, it has left many living casualties who struggle with the impossible question: Where was God in all this? There are no simple answers, but we must have the courage to look at the different aspects of this tragic time. In the above Scripture, Isaiah the prophet tells us about God's heart. God was not absent from his universe when Israel was afflicted; indeed, he grieved over the suffering of his people. Why didn't he act? Actually, he acted more than we might think. Although one-third of our people perished in Europe, we should stop to consider the two-thirds who survived, many of whom helped to establish the modern State of Israel.

We may never entirely understand the events of that day, but let us listen carefully to our Father to know exactly what he was feeling. Justice will prevail, if not now, then most definitely in the *Olam HaBa* (the Age to Come). Many people are tempted to blame God for such evil; rather, we should ask the question, "Where was man?" The Holocaust underlines the fact that mankind can shrink to incredible lows if we turn away from God's ways. What does *Yom HaSho'ah* mean to you?

Today I Will

. . . repent of any attitude or action which is inconsistent with the character of God.

BK

The angel of *ADONAI*, who encamps around those who fear him, delivers them (Ps. 34:8).

God promises special protection to his loved ones who fear him and serve him. That protection doesn't come by removing us from trials and difficult circumstances. His special care is most clearly seen when we are in the midst of trouble.

One day I was singing with a group on Ben-Yehudah Street in Jerusalem. A crowd of Israelis had gathered around us to enjoy our music and listen to the message of Yeshua. Suddenly, we were attacked by four *yeshivah bochers* (rabbinical students) seeking to disrupt our evangelistic efforts. Just when I thought we might be martyred right there in Jerusalem, a very big Israeli man jumped in between us and the students. He was at least six feet tall, completely bald, and terrifying! He stuck his finger in the faces of these students and said to them in Hebrew, "You touch them and I'll touch you." The seminary students backed off and we were able to continue our ministry. The Bible says, "the angel of *ADONAI*, who encamps around those who fear him, delivers them." I just never knew that the angel of *ADONAI* looked like that!

God, in his mercy, provides covering and protection for his servants in many different forms. We can trust him, no matter what the circumstances. He will be with us to preserve and protect us.

April 14, 1999
May 3, 2000
April 21, 2001 (26)*
April 10, 2002
April 30, 2003
April 19, 2004

Prayer Focus

Today I Will

. . . walk in the fear of the Lord, confident of God's protection no matter what the circumstance.

DB

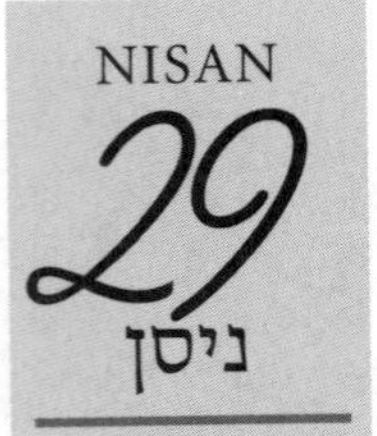

April 15, 1999
May 4, 2000
April 22, 2001
April 11, 2002
May 1, 2003
April 20, 2004

This is why I suffer as I do. But I am not ashamed, because I know in whom I have put my trust (2 Tim. 1:12).

Rabbi Sha'ul (Saul; i.e., Paul) was writing to his *talmidim* (disciples) from prison. He had suffered and was continuing to suffer much hardship for proclaiming his faith in Yeshua. Nevertheless, nearing the end of his life, he was still able to write with great confidence concerning his own salvation and eternal life with the Lord. This is because he had placed his trust fully in Yeshua.

Compare Rabbi Sha'ul's thinking to that of the first-century rabbi who was the architect of modern-day Judaism, but who did not know Yeshua. The *Talmud* (Berakhot 28b) states, "When Rabbi Yochanan ben Zakai fell ill, his disciples went in to visit him. When he saw them, he began to weep. His disciples said to him, 'Lamp of Israel, pillar of the right hand, mighty hammer! Wherefore weepest thou?' He replied, ' . . . Now that I am being taken before the Supreme King of Kings . . . there are two ways before me, one leading to Paradise and the other to *Gehinnom* [Hell], and I do not know by which I shall be taken, shall I not weep?'"

As believers in Yeshua, we are set apart by our hope and assurance of salvation. That hope springs from true faith in God's provision, his Messiah, through whom we can and do know our destiny. Let's rejoice in the assurance God has given us through faith in Messiah Yeshua.

Prayer Focus

Today I Will

. . . walk in the confidence of my salvation in Yeshua, and will look for ways to share that same hope with others.

DB

It is a narrow gate and a hard road that leads to life, and only a few find it (Matt. 7:14).

April 16, 1999
May 5, 2000
April 23, 2001
April 12, 2002
May 2, 2003
April 21, 2004

Traditional
Rosh Chodesh
(the New Moon)
Day 1

Prayer Focus

EK

Robert Frost wrote beautiful poetry. In one of his best-known and best-loved poems "The Road Not Taken," he wrote,

> Two roads diverged in a yellow wood,
> And sorry I could not travel both
> And be one traveler, long I stood
> And looked down one as far as I could
> To where it bent in the undergrowth;
>
> I shall be telling this with a sigh
> Somewhere ages and ages hence:
> Two roads diverged in a wood, and I—
> I took the one less traveled by,
> And that has made all the difference.

There are two paths. We could take the beaten path. We could broaden out our doctrine and attract more people. We could embrace replacement theology or downplay the deity of Yeshua. We could compromise in order to multiply our congregational attendance and finances. We could justify it, saying that it will help us expand our outreach and improve our programs. We could, but we won't.

Our path is an unpopular one. Yeshua was not popular. Neither will we be if we follow him. We have chosen the path that leads to ostracism, persecution and tribulation. Yet, we are called to be unspotted in the world. By taking the narrow path—the road less traveled — we will not feel comfortable. But it will make all the eternal difference.

Today I Will

. . . travel the road less traveled, the one Yeshua would take.

April 17, 1999 (27, 28/A)
May 6, 2000 (30/A)
April 24, 2001
April 13, 2002 (27, 28/A)
May 3, 2003 (30/A)
April 22, 2004

Biblical
Rosh Chodesh (the New Moon)

On this day, the Lord spoke to Moses in the Tent of Meeting (Num. 1:1); a census of Israel was taken (Num. 1:18).

Traditional
Rosh Chodesh Day 2

Prayer Focus

For who has despised the day of small things? (Zech. 4:10 NKJV).

I have a precious photograph, taken around the turn of the century, of a rag-tag group on a barren stretch of sand in the west-central region of what was then called Palestine. Just one hundred people with shovels. They were proclaiming the existence of a Jewish city they called Tel Aviv. Today, less than one hundred years later, that sand is a Jewish metropolis. That picture is pasted in my Bible to remind me that I am not sowing into God's plans for only my generation's sake.

If an obscure Jewish novelist named Herzl could write a small book, entitled *The Jewish State*, that would change human history; if a handful of Jewish individuals whose names are long forgotten could teach Zionism to Eastern European Jewish children who later grew up to become Ben-Gurion, Meir, Jabotinsky and Begin, then perhaps what I do each day may not be as inconsequential as it sometimes seems.

On dark hilltops millennia ago, a young Israeli sang into the darkness to comfort his soul, as he stood watch over sheep appearing to hold no more promise than the wool on their backs. Three thousand years later, we are still singing that young man's songs. The *Brit Chadashah* (New Covenant Scriptures) sums up the life of that youth with these precious words: "King David, after he had served his own generation by the will of God, fell asleep [died]" (Acts 13:36 NKJV).

Today I Will

. . . remember that I live not only for myself. The destiny of countless futures is bound up in the choices I make. This is why the Jewish sages taught that saving one life saves an entire world (Baba Batra 11a). I will settle for no less than serving my generation by the will of God.

BC

You are to come to the place where *ADONAI* your God will put his name. . . . which is where he will live (Deut. 12:5).

Even before Israel crossed the Yarden (Jordan), God declared that he would choose a place somewhere in this Promised Land in which to manifest his Name. That place, Yerushalayim (Jerusalem), was captured and established under King David. Under David's son, Shlomo (Solomon), the Temple was built on that spot. At the dedication of this Temple (1 Kings 8), Shlomo prayed that God would meet the needs of Israel when they came before the Lord in the Temple, or if they would pray toward Yerushalayim, in faith, from a distance. To this day, in synagogues around the world, *Torah* scrolls are located so that when the worshippers face them they are also looking towards Yerushalayim.

Why was prayer efficacious when directed toward the Temple and toward the holy city? That was the place where God provided the means for sinful humanity to reconnect with him by sacrifices, providing forgiveness and purification.

Similarly, turning to Yeshua in faith is how we touch the manifestation of God's presence, where forgiveness and cleansing can be realized. We can still face Yerushalayim when we pray. However, the answer to our prayers comes not from the place, but from the person—Yeshua—who gave his life for us in Yerushalayim and will, one day, return there to reign.

Today I Will

. . . remember that all my needs are met by turning towards the one who is the living Temple of God.

IYYAR

2

אייר

April 18, 1999
May 7, 2000
April 25, 2001
April 14, 2002
May 4, 2003
April 23, 2004

Biblical
On this day, Solomon began building the Temple (2 Chron. 3:1–2).

Prayer Focus

MM

IYYAR

3

אייר

April 19, 1999
May 8, 2000
April 26, 2001
April 15, 2002
May 5, 2003
April 24, 2004
(27,28)

Prayer Focus

Ya'akov was left alone. Then some man wrestled with him until daybreak (Gen. 32:24).

Weighing most heavily on Ya'akov's (Jacob's) mind when he fled his home was that his brother Eysav (Esau) was planning to kill him. Twenty years later, Eysav approached with an army of four hundred men, apparently unappeased by the passage of time. Ya'akov sent away his wives, children, servants and livestock to protect them from the impending attack. However, before the encounter with Eysav took place, an event of greater significance occurred. Ya'akov, left alone, spent an entire night wrestling with the *Mal'akh* (Angel) of the Lord.

The outcome was that Ya'akov's nature was changed. He went from being one who was totally self-sufficient to one who understood dependence; from one who got what he wanted by his own cleverness, to one who could not stand without God's help. Ya'akov became Yisra'el (Israel). The consequence of this transformation was that when the two brothers met, instead of shedding blood, they embraced each other and shed tears of joy.

Ya'akov could have done nothing on his own to resolve the conflict. The supernatural breaking of his heart and will had a supernatural effect on Eysav as well, and his heart softened toward his younger brother. The solution to hostile situations that face us, often as a result of our own sin, can be found in allowing the Lord to change *us* first. Such faith will release God's power to work in the areas we fear most.

Today I Will

. . . get alone with the Lord and let him do his work in me, instead of relying on my own cleverness.

MM

Those who carried loads held their loads with one hand and carried a weapon in the other (Neh. 4:17[11]).

It was *Erev Yom Kippur* (the evening of the Day of Atonement) in Israel. On this most solemn evening, I was in the synagogue with my two youngest sons and future son-in-law. Looking down the narrow aisle, I could see several rows ahead of me to where one man stood, his entire body wrapped in his *tallit* (prayer shawl). Swaying in prayer, oblivious to all else, he presented the classic picture of the devout Jew that has been with me since childhood. However, there was one element that had not been part of my memories of *shul* (synagogue). It was the M-16 rifle leaning against the wall alongside of the worshipper.

In Israel, military readiness is a reality that permeates every aspect of life. Surrounded by hostile forces, we cannot take our security for granted—even, or perhaps most especially, on the eve of *Yom Kippur*. On *Yom Kippur*, 1973, Israel was attacked by her enemies.

This is how it is spiritually for all true believers, whether living in Israel or not. We are called to be vigilant because we have an enemy who roams around like a roaring lion, seeking whom he may devour. At moments when we desire to draw closer to God, this enemy often comes against us the hardest. Therefore, our weapons must be readily at hand at all times.

Today I Will

. . . remember that the weapons of our warfare are not carnal but are powerful through God, and I will maintain my vigilance in order that the evil one will find no place of entrance in my life.

April 20, 1999
May 9, 2000
April 27, 2001
April 16, 2002
May 6, 2003
April 25, 2004

Traditional
Yom HaZikkaron
(Remembrance Day)

Prayer Focus

MM

IYYAR

5

אייר

April 21, 1999
May 10, 2000
April 28, 2001
(27, 28)
April 17, 2002
May 7, 2003
April 26, 2004

Traditional
Yom Ha'Atzma'ut
(Israel Independence Day)

Prayer Focus

RR

If one of yours [an Israelite] was scattered to the far end of the sky, *ADONAI* your God will gather you even from there (Deut. 30:4).

The *shalosh regalim* (the three pilgrimage festivals given in the *Torah*) inextricably link the cycle of the Jewish year to the Land of Israel. Each festival has an agricultural component that can be fulfilled only in the Land of Promise. Hence, Jewish longing to return to the Land is reinforced in the biblical practice of Jewish religion.

Well over a century ago, the British Prime Minister Benjamin Disraeli, himself of Jewish background, noted this connection: "The vineyards of Israel have ceased to exist, but the eternal Law enjoins the children of Israel still to celebrate the vintage. A race that persists in celebrating their vintage, although they have no fruits to gather, will regain their vineyards."

As Disraeli foresaw, the eternal Jewish bond to the Land of Israel demanded a fulfillment in history. No event celebrates that fulfillment better than *Yom Ha'Atzma'ut,* the fifth of Iyyar, May 14, 1948, when an independent Jewish state was again declared in the Land. This same event also marks the imprint of God upon modern history. The Jewish return to the Land is the product not only of Jewish aspiration, but of a biblical promise and God's intervention to fulfill it. He is still at work, bringing his Word to pass.

Today I Will

. . . pray for spiritual awakening in the Land of Israel, confident that this is part of God's promise of restoration for the Jewish people.

Not neglecting our own congregational meetings, as some have made a practice of doing (Heb. 10:25).

IYYAR

6

אייר

April 22, 1999
May 11, 2000
April 29, 2001
April 18, 2002
May 8, 2003
April 27, 2004

It would seem that one of the most difficult disciplines for believers in Yeshua is commitment to regular worship and fellowship with others who know Messiah. This is especially crucial for brand-new believers. It can often be the difference between someone following the Lord or walking away from Yeshua altogether. Of the many Jewish people that I have seen make professions of faith in Messiah, only those who have made the commitment to regularly being with God's people—worshipping and fellowshipping in a congregation—have grown in Messiah and are walking effectively with him today.

A man was in a store purchasing some clothing when the clerk behind the checkout counter noticed from his identification that his customer was a rabbi. The clerk asked the rabbi what synagogue he served. When the rabbi told him, the man replied, "Oh, that's my synagogue." At this, the rabbi perked up, "That's strange," he said. "I've been the rabbi there for five years and I've never seen you before." The clerk responded, "Come on, rabbi, I didn't say I was a fanatic."

We who desire to serve Yeshua must commit ourselves to regular fellowship and worship with God's people. Someone might say, "I don't get anything out of my congregation." Well, maybe that's because that person is not looking to put anything in to begin with. When we regularly attend services in obedience to God's Word, with the desire to serve him there among his people, we will certainly find both joy and purpose in our worship experience.

Prayer Focus

Today I Will

. . . recommit myself to regular fellowship and worship, and to give as much as I am able to the ministry of my local congregation.

DB

IYYAR

7

אייר

April 23, 1999
May 12, 2000
April 30, 2001
April 19, 2002
May 9, 2003
April 28, 2004

Prayer Focus

The very rock that the builders rejected has become the cornerstone! (Ps. 118:22)

When asked how he produced such marvelous sculptures, the brilliant Italian artist Michelangelo responded that he just chipped away all the stone that didn't belong and released the piece within. He had the ability to look at a block of marble and see the beauty that it contained. Tragically, many among the first-century Jewish leadership in Israel—the God-ordained builders of the Kingdom of God—did not have the gift of being able to see the inner beauty of a person. They rejected the precious stone that God had chosen to be the foundation of his spiritual house—Yeshua—and stumbled over him like debris.

However, before we are quick to judge their error, it would be wise to examine our own hearts. For even those who have recognized the living stone, Yeshua, often miss the precious value of the living stones that God has selected to be built together with him into that spiritual Temple. Rabbi Sha'ul (Saul; i.e., Paul) exhorted us to see one another, not according to external characteristics, but as new creations in Messiah. For it is the Lord who has chipped away, and is still chipping away all the pieces that don't belong in our lives. He is releasing the masterpieces he has created within us that we can all see in one another by looking through Messiah's eyes.

Today I Will

. . . reject all carnal judgments about my brothers and sisters, and see them as God sees them.

MM

I haven't sinned against you—even though you are seeking every chance you get to take my life (1 Sam. 24:11[12]).

At this point in King David's life, he must have felt like someone had pronounced that old Yiddish curse on him, "May all your teeth fall out except one, and may that one have a toothache!" He had been anointed by God at the hand of the prophet Shmu'el (Samuel), began to ascend succesfully in King Sha'ul's (Saul's) ranks by valiant military service, succeeded as a leader, and married the king's daughter. Just when everything seemed to be going right, the king went insane.

Sha'ul heard David being praised among the people more highly than himself, and he simply went mad. David was reduced from a leader of the army to a refugee hiding in caves. When his enemy came within reach of his spear, David had to heed God's restraint, and not touch the Lord's anointed (1 Chron. 16:22)! He did, however, wisely make sure to hold up the proof of his innocence publicly before his former comrades, who had swallowed Sha'ul's lies about him, and were hunting him like a game-fowl. What was all this trial and denial for?

God was deliberately forming the David who would unite Yisra'el (Israel) and build Yerushalayim (Jerusalem) on the anvil of betrayal with the hammer of injustice. Having watched what Sha'ul had become, David learned what sort of king he did not desire to be.

. . . thank God for the chance to be trained by him, through success and even trial.

IYYAR

8

אייר

April 24, 1999 (29, 30/H)
May 13, 2000 (31)
May 1, 2001
April 20, 2002 (29, 30/H)
May 10, 2003 (31)
April 29, 2004

Prayer Focus

BC

IYYAR

9

אייר

April 25, 1999
May 14, 2000
May 2, 2001
April 21, 2002
May 11, 2003
April 30, 2004

The Kingdom of Heaven . . . will be like ten bridesmaids who took their lamps and went out to meet the groom (Matt. 25:1).

After the Lord created woman from Adam's side, the *Torah* says, "He brought her to the man-person" (Gen. 2:22). The rabbis deduced from this verse that the Lord attended the marriage ceremony of Adam and Eve, and they concluded that it is a *mitzvah* (good deed) to serve as an attendant at a wedding. Thus the Jewish wedding came to incorporate a procession of family and friends eager to fulfill this *mitzvah* for the beloved bridegroom and bride, often by torch light.

The ten virgins of Yeshua's story were to be part of such a procession. Five had brought extra oil and were prepared to fulfill the *mitzvah.* Five others seemed equally eager, but failed in the end. They had not made preparations to complete what they had begun. Perhaps their anticipation of the bridegroom's appearance was half-hearted, for it did not translate into perseverance.

Messiah warns at the end of his story: "So stay alert, because you know neither the day nor the hour" (Matt. 25:13) in which the Son of Man will return. He is noting our all-too-human tendency to start well and fade away, especially in matters of obedience. Salvation is a gift, but we will be ill-prepared for Messiah's return if we follow him without a concrete commitment to persevere.

Prayer Focus

Today I Will

. . . correct any habits or attitudes in my life that reveal a waning eagerness to follow Messiah.

RR

Think about the fields of wild irises, and how they grow . . . won't he much more clothe you? (Matt. 6:28–30)

IYYAR
10
אייר

April 26, 1999
May 15, 2000
May 3, 2001
April 22, 2002
May 12, 2003
May 1, 2004
(29, 30/H)

In this passage of the *Brit Chadashah* (New Covenant Scriptures), Yeshua informs us that we should have faith to believe that God will provide for all of our needs. Even the need for clothing, he tells us, is not outside the realm of God's concern for us.

A number of years ago I was in need of new clothes. My wife was continually sewing up holes in my shirts and slacks, but to no avail; new ones kept appearing. It was downright embarrassing. Then one day, a friend of ours told us that she had a closet full of men's clothes that I might be interested in. A millionaire friend of hers had given them to her to distribute to the needy, and from her perspective, I fit that category. As it turned out, all of the clothes were of the finest quality, custom tailored, and fit me perfectly. Not only that, but the millionaire had his initials sewn onto every shirt pocket. They read "G.O.D."

God wants us to remember that he will provide for all of our needs. Do you have a need? Don't worry about it. Instead, put it in the hands of our heavenly Father who clothes even the wild irises of the fields.

Prayer Focus

Today I Will

. . . put aside all worries and trust in the Lord to provide for all of my needs.

DR

IYYAR

11

אייר

April 27, 1999
May 16, 2000
May 4, 2001
April 23, 2002
May 13, 2003
May 2, 2004

How blessed is the man who perseveres through temptation. . . . he will receive as his crown the Life which God has promised to those who love him (James 1:12).

During the year since Rita's husband had left her, she had developed a serious medical condition that required extensive treatment. Then Rita suddenly lost her job when her manager was ordered to cut his work force in half. "Why is all this happening to me?" she asked. "Why is God allowing all this trouble in my life?"

When we experience trials, we often ask, like Rita, "Why is this happening to me?" David writes, however, "*ADONAI* tests the righteous" (Ps. 11:5). Rabbi Eleazer comments on this verse, "When a man possesses two cows, one strong and the other feeble, upon which does he put the yoke? Surely upon the strong one! Similarly, God tests none but the righteous, as it says, 'The Lord trieth the righteous'" (Genesis Rabbah 55:2).

To ask God, "Why is this happening to me?" is the wrong question. It is better to ask God *how* he will bring us through the trial and what he is teaching us; how God will use it to perfect our faith and prepare us to receive as our crown the Life promised by God. Like Rita, we cannot always avoid trials, but we can choose to respond with the right question: not "Why?" but "How?"; *how* is God going to use this trial to bring blessing into my life?

Prayer Focus

Today I Will

. . . thank God for the trials in my life and look for the blessing that he wants to bring about through them.

RR

Avram gave him a tenth of everything (Gen. 14:20).

April 28, 1999
May 17, 2000
May 5, 2001
(29, 30/H)
April 24, 2002
May 14, 2003
May 3, 2004

Why does Abram give a tithe to Melchizedek? The laws of tithing would not be written for another four hundred years, but Abram is already familiar with the practice of dedicating the best to God as a way of honoring him. Centuries before, Abel brought the "firstborn of his sheep, including their fat" (Gen. 4:4), and God accepted this offering. Years later, Abram's grandson Jacob promised to honor the Lord with the tithe to signify that the LORD is God (Gen. 28:20–22).

The tithe, then, honors God; but why give it to Melchizedek? This mysterious figure is a priest of *El Elyon* (God Most High). Abram recognizes *El Elyon* as the one true God and gives the tithe to Melchizedek, God's representative. As a worshiper of God, Abram is eager to express honor to him. He does not view the tithe as a tax or an obligation, but as a way to dedicate *all* that he has to the Lord. Thus he fulfills the command that will be given four hundred years later—to love the Lord your God with all your heart, with all your soul, and with all your substance (*me'odekha*). *Me'odekha* can also refer to one's possessions or wealth. By giving the tenth to God, we dedicate all we have to him.

Prayer Focus

Today I Will

. . . give the Lord the first and best of my increase, thereby dedicating all I have to him.

RR

IYYAR 13 אייר

April 29, 1999
May 18, 2000
May 6, 2001
April 25, 2002
May 15, 2003
May 4, 2004

Regard it all as joy, my brothers, when you face various kinds of temptations (James 1:2–3).

Sometimes when people ask how we're doing, we give them a "going through" answer. "Well, I'm *going through* a lot." or "I'm *going through* tough times." It doesn't sound encouraging, but with the Lord it is.

In the Hebrew Scriptures, *derekh* is an important word. *Derekh* means "the way, the road, the path, the journey." God's people are always on a *derekh*, a journey in life. Messiah said, "I am the *Derekh* (Way)." That is why the first Messianic Jews and Gentiles were called the people of the *Derekh*—people of the Way (Acts 24:14).

What's so encouraging about *going through* things? The blessing is that you're going "through" them! At Isa. 62:10, God commands, "Go on through! Go on through!" If you're going "through" things, you're obeying God! It's a holy thing! People on the *derekh* of God don't dwell on their problems, they go "through" them.

So when you say, "I'm going through a lot," be encouraged! Messiah gives you the power to "go through" and "get through" anything. You might say, "You don't know what *I'm* going through." You're right. I just need to know you're "going through," and with eyes of faith you will see that the end of the trial is near! You're on the *derekh*. So go on through! And he'll see that you get through just fine.

Prayer Focus

Today I Will

. . . keep going, persevere, press on, and *make it through.* He will give me the victory.

JC

If any of you . . . is on a trip abroad, nevertheless he is to observe Pesach. But he will observe it in the second month on the fourteenth day (Num. 9:10–11).

My grandmother marks down all of her special days on a new calendar each year. It includes all the birthdays, wedding anniversaries and *yahrtzeits* (death anniversaries) in our family. Why does she go to this trouble? Because she loves to send cards; in a way, it's her part-time job. The older I get, the more meaningful it is to receive a card from my grandma. When I open her cards, knowing how much she loves me, I can't help but think, "She remembered . . . amazing! My special days are her special days, too."

The Lord has his special days and one of them is the fourteenth day of the first month. He just loves that date. Like a birthday, wedding anniversary or *yahrtzeit*, it's engraved on his heart. Is he sentimental? Maybe more than we realize. Many don't think the Lord is concerned with little details like dates, but I would beg to differ based on the above Scripture.

Here, the *Torah* tells us that if an Israelite did not celebrate *Pesach* (Passover) because he was far away on a journey, he could not merely celebrate *Pesach* on a day of his own choosing or not celebrate it at all. God had an alternative date for him to celebrate a belated *Pesach*—day 14 of the second month, which is today—exactly one month after Passover.

God just loves that date—the 14th of the month. On Nisan 14, and Iyyar 14, the Lord remembers every detail of the redemption he brought us. And when his special day is our special day, he is happy.

Today I Will

. . . reflect on the events of the Exodus and make it a special day. If I know of someone who was unable to observe *Pesach* on Nisan 14, I will help them prepare for this evening's Passover meal (*seder*).

April 30, 1999
May 19, 2000
May 7, 2001
April 26, 2002
May 16, 2003
May 5, 2004

Biblical
Pesach Sheyni
(Belated Passover)
begins at twilight
(see Num. 9:6–14)

On this day, Hezekiah and the Israelites celebrated a belated Passover in accordance with God's Law (2 Chron. 30:15).

Prayer Focus

DR

May 1, 1999 (31)
May 20, 2000 (32)
May 8, 2001
April 27, 2002 (31)
May 17, 2003 (32)
May 6, 2004

Biblical
On this day, the Israelites came to the Desert of Sin (Exod. 16:1); Hezekiah and the Israelites began celebrating a belated *Matzot* (Feast of Unleavened Bread) (2 Chron. 30:13).

Prayer Focus

Without a prophetic vision, the people throw off all restraint (Prov. 29:18).

Have you ever considered the relationship between *chazon* (prophetic vision) and the keeping of the *Torah*? How are they related? In addition to "prophetic vision," *chazon* can also mean "prophetic revelation" or "current revelation." Thus, we might translate the passage, "Where there is no current prophetic revelation, there is *lawlessness*."

God's *Torah* needs to be proclaimed—to groups, to congregations, to society. If not, lawlessness, paganism, secular control and sin will pervade. Moshe (Moses), for example, was the voice of God to the children of Israel after they left Eygpt. Through him, God revealed his will, his direction and his laws. Moshe was God's prophetic voice. As long as the word of the Lord was proclaimed, the people followed the laws of God. When Moshe departed to the mountain to receive the commandments from the Lord, the people fell into idolatry, gross sin and lawlessness. The prophetic voice had ceased.

Today, we are called to be prophetic voices to our people and our nation. Like Moshe, we must proclaim God's Word and call our people back to him. We are the salt of the earth, called to preserve godliness and prevent decay. Let's begin our work today!

Today I Will

. . . pray, "Lord, make me a prophetic voice to my people and my nation. Give me boldness to speak the truth in love and not hide my light."

JB

For he himself is our *shalom* [peace]—he has made us both one and has broken down the *m'chitzah* [dividing wall in the Temple] which divided us (Eph. 2:14).

May 2, 1999
May 21, 2000
May 9, 2001
April 28, 2002
May 18, 2003
May 7, 2004

In Messiah Yeshua, God has established a unity of Jews and Gentiles that goes beyond human efforts or expectations. It is a supernatural unity brought about through the blood of Yeshua. Those of us who know Messiah are *mishpachah* (family). Despite the social and cultural differences, we have a bond that is stronger than flesh and blood.

In the movie *The Frisco Kid*, Gene Wilder plays a hapless rabbi who, upon coming to America, faces disaster upon disaster. He is robbed and beaten and ends up alone. Wandering through fields in the middle of Pennsylvania, he spies what he thinks are fellow Jews out plowing in the field. He discovers they are not Jews but Amish folk. Later, the rabbi strikes up a lasting bond of friendship with a rough-hewn cowboy played by Harrison Ford. Ford is about as Jewish as a ham sandwich, but he takes Wilder under his wing and helps him make his way across the country. It's a delightful story that illustrates this point: what looks like *mishpachah* isn't always *mishpachah*. What may not look much like *mishpachah* may, in fact, be the best *mishpachah* we could ever want.

As followers of Messiah, we are united with people from every tribe, tongue and nation. God has joined us together in a deep and profound unity that will never obliterate our distinctiveness, yet can make us truly one in him.

Prayer Focus

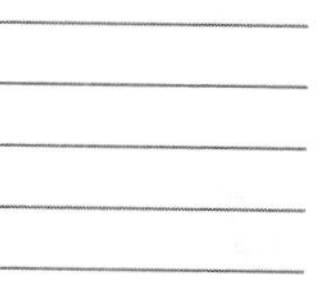

Today I Will

. . . commit myself to set aside any prejudice I may have towards my Jewish or Gentile brothers or sisters in Messiah.

DB

May 3, 1999
May 22, 2000
May 10, 2001
April 29, 2002
May 19, 2003
May 8, 2004 (31)

Biblical
On this day, Noah and his family entered the ark; the flood began (Gen. 7:11).

Prayer Focus

Do not let yourselves be conformed to the standards of the '*olam hazeh* [this world] (Rom. 12:2).

The *Torah* says that Noah was "perfect" and "righteous" in his generation (Gen. 6:9; 7:1). The sages debate whether this is a statement of praise or of criticism. The first view commends Noah for preserving his faith and obedience even in the midst of great wickedness. The second view holds that Noah can only be considered faithful and obedient in contrast to such great wickedness. Born into a later, better generation, he would not seem righteous at all. What is clear in Noah's story is that faith in God can never be a product of the day in which we live. Our generation is one of particularly ungodly values. We may appear spiritual if we view ourselves only by its light, but we will never then reach the full purpose of God in our lives.

Noah was perfect in his generation because he "walked with God" (Gen. 6:9). Whether this perfection was truly great faithfulness, or only great relative to the surrounding imperfection, it stemmed from his nearness to God. Our walk with God makes us stand out in the day in which we live.

Today I Will

. . . re-examine my ways and attitudes in the light of Scripture, instead of merely comparing myself to those who are in the world.

RR

Since I am going and preparing a place for you, I will return to take you with me (John 14:3).

Hidden in the Jewish marriage tradition is a divine mystery. The journey toward marriage begins with the Jewish groom visiting the house of the bride, paying a bridal price, and sealing the marriage covenant. The bridegroom would then leave the bride and return to his father's house. The two would then spend a year in separation during which time they would be considered husband and wife. These were the Days of Preparation. For the groom, it was the time to prepare a house for the bride. For the bride, it was the time to prepare *herself* for marriage and for her new life with the bridegroom.

Two thousand years ago, the Bridegroom of our souls, Messiah, visited our house, paid the great bridal price to set us free, and then returned to prepare a place for us in his father's house. So what are the days in which we live? These are the Days of Preparation.

If you are Messiah's bride, you are not here on earth to get caught up in money, success, circumstances or self-centeredness. These are your Days of Preparation for eternity. Use them wisely, saying good-bye to the old, pressing on to the new, and becoming more and more beautiful in his eyes.

Today I Will

. . . write down one area I need to let go in order to give myself wholeheartedly to the Bridegroom.

IYYAR

18

אייר

May 4, 1999
May 23, 2000
May 11, 2001
April 30, 2002
May 20, 2003
May 9, 2004

Traditional
Lag Be'Omer
(33rd of the Omer)

Prayer Focus

JC

May 5, 1999
May 24, 2000
May 12, 2001 (31)
May 1, 2002
May 21, 2003
May 10, 2004

Church Tradition

The Council of Nicea was convened on Iyyar 19, 4085 (May 20, 325 C.E.). This council officially changed the date of the observance of Passover in the Church from Nisan 14 (the biblical date) to the first Sunday after the first full moon after the first day of Spring. This was done so that the Church would have "nothing in common" with the Jewish people.

Prayer Focus

MW

Was someone already circumcised when he was called? Then he should not try to remove the marks of his circumcision (1 Cor. 7:18).

Rabbi Sha'ul (Saul; i.e., Paul) was not referring in the above verse to a physical operation when he used the word "circumcised," even though history does record rare instances where assimilated Jews of the time were given primitive "uncircumcision" operations. Most scholars agree that Sha'ul was using the word "circumcised" here to refer to Jewish identity, just as in Acts 10:45, where Luke used the word "circumcised" to refer to Jewish believers. The great "apostle to the Gentiles" was laying down a biblical principle to first-century Jewish believers—a principle that would not again be applied by a significant number of Messianic Jews until modern times.

Historically, a message in direct oppostion to this verse has been communicated by Church leaders, from the Council of Nicea (325 C.E.) which forbade believing Jews from continuing Jewish observance—to the forced conversions of *Marranos* [Jewish converts] in fifteenth-century Spain.

How might history have been different if Messianic Jews had been encouraged to keep their identity? We will never know. But with the proliferation of modern Messianic synagogues, an identifiable Messianic community has arisen. Now families worship the Messiah through their rich Jewish heritage. Today, the Jewish "remnant" is visible worldwide, and the body of believers is becoming increasingly aware of their "Jewish roots" through the teaching and example of Messianic Jews. The message is being proclaimed to the Jewish community worldwide that Messianic Jews are, as the Scriptures encourage, still Jewish!

Today I Will

. . . praise God for my Messianic Jewish calling and recommit myself to that call through keeping my Jewish identity, as Rabbi Sha'ul encouraged so many years ago.

Even gold is tested for genuineness by fire (1 Pet. 1:7).

May 6, 1999
May 25, 2000
May 13, 2001
May 2, 2002
May 22, 2003
May 11, 2004

Biblical
On this day, the cloud of glory lifted for the first time from above the Tabernacle (Num. 10:11–13).

Prayer Focus

Recently, our synagogue in Israel was fire-bombed. Through this experience we felt our faith tested and purified, drawing us much nearer to Yeshua.

During the first century, when Peter wrote this exhortation, persecution was common. The early Messianic Jews gave living testimony to Yeshua as the promised Redeemer. As a result, thousands entered the Kingdom of God, entire cities heard the news of Messiah, and Messianic congregations were established. In the process, Messianic Jews took a lot of heat.

The testing of our faith comes every day, usually in smaller, more figurative fires. Nonetheless, our response to these purifying trials can bring honor to our beloved King. If I measure success or well-being by asking, "Is everything going smoothly?" then I am setting up a false goal, foreign to the life of believers who have gone before me. In the eternal scheme of things, it does not matter whether or not I arrive at the store before closing time. What matters is that my faith in the living God is real and growing, and responding to challenges, both small and great.

Today I Will

. . . view the difficulties and pressures in my life as opportunities to draw near to God and to glorify Yeshua in the way I deal with them.

ES

IYYAR

21

אייר

May 7, 1999
May 26, 2000
May 14, 2001
May 3, 2002
May 23, 2003
May 12, 2004

The righteous person suffers many evils, but ADONAI rescues him out of them all (Ps. 34:20).

Believers who love to claim promises are not apt to claim "trouble" as one of God's commitments to them. Some are apt to claim *no trouble.* They'll have to wait until heaven for that. For those still here on earth, the question may be asked, "What good is a promise like Psalm 34, even if it's accompanied by a promise of deliverance from trouble? After being delivered, aren't we back in the same place we were before the trouble came?" The Scripture shouts a resounding "no" to that question. And the "no" is not the general kind—it's the kind of "no" that the rabbis proclaimed when they meant, "On the contrary, it's all for the best." Scripture provides very specific promises that accompany trouble. Two come to mind.

The first is in Heb. 12:11, which declares that God uses hardship or trouble to train us. Those who trust him through it will "produce a harvest of righteousness and peace." What a promise!

The second promise is found in 2 Cor. 1:4, where Rabbi Sha'ul (Saul; i.e., Paul) says that God comforts us in our trouble so we can comfort others in their affliction. Doesn't that make the trouble "worth the trouble"?

God hasn't promised us a rose garden. But he has promised us a vegetable garden, bearing wonderful bounty for his kingdom.

Prayer Focus

Today I Will

. . . thank God for the troubles he allows to come my way, because I know that he will turn them to good in specific ways, and ultimately he will deliver me from them all.

MW

Having exposed himself to death and being counted among the sinners (Isa. 53:12).

May 8, 1999 (32, 33)
May 27, 2000 (33)
May 15, 2001
May 4, 2002 (32, 33)
May 24, 2003 (33)
May 13, 2004

True sacrifice is a rare thing. Sometimes it's confused with courage, which involves a choice to face life's challenges. Sacrifice, on the other hand, involves a choice to give that which is most precious. David said "I refuse to offer to ADONAI my God burnt offerings that cost me nothing" (2 Sam. 24:24). The media often emphasize the "heroic courage" of celebrities who endure tragedy bravely. But true heroes are not just courageous. They are also sacrificial when the need arises.

There have been many sacrificial acts in Jewish history. Often these have occurred in times of great persecution. During World War II, Jewish leaders marched ahead of their people to death, comforting them as they went. Likewise, some righteous Gentiles, during that period, sacrificed their lives for Jewish people.

The paramount sacrifice in history was performed by a person that Isaiah calls the "arm of *ADONAI*" (53:1). Though some Jewish commentators say that chapter 53 refers to Israel, Isa. 53:12 and 59:16 confirm that such a sacrificial intercession for others could only be accomplished when the eternal "arm of *ADONAI*" came as a man. Hence, the most noble choice a man can make is also an attribute of the God in whose image we were created!

Let's consider that loving sacrifice is part of who God is, and who we, too, are called to be.

Prayer Focus

Today I Will

. . . choose to lay my life down for others, the choice of Yeshua, who said "This is why the Father loves me: because I lay down my life. . . . I lay it down of my own free will" (John 10:17–18).

MW

IYYAR

23

אייר

May 9, 1999
May 28, 2000
May 16, 2001
May 5, 2002
May 25, 2003
May 14, 2004

Get yourself out of your country, away from your kinsmen and away from your father's house, and go to the land that I will show you (Gen. 12:1).

It had been a while since I walked through the old Jewish neighborhood in Baltimore. Everything looked just as I had remembered it, only a bit more worn. It was easy to reflect on what might have been if we had not left. But we had. We had followed the leading of the *Ruach HaKodesh* (Holy Spirit) to move to Israel. The choice we made was not based on earthly reasoning or personal gain, but on what would best serve the purposes of the God of Abraham, who—as he did with Abraham—had also revealed himself to us.

In our lives, choices face us at every turn of the road. While we do not cast off our minds, the decision-making process must embrace the fact that our heavenly Father always knows what is best. Often pain must be endured when we answer the Lord's call. There is the pain of the loss of family, homes, and the comfort zone of the familiar. There is also the pain of criticism from those who do not understand. Yet, could we "seek first his [God's] Kingdom and his righteousness" (Matt. 6:33) and make any other choice?

Any temptation to consider what might be gained by choosing a different road will not stand when we are secure in the goodness and wisdom of our God.

Prayer Focus

Today I Will

. . . put my hand to the plow and not look back.

MM

If the world hates you, understand that it hated me first (John 15:18).

May 10, 1999
May 29, 2000
May 17, 2001
May 6, 2002
May 26, 2003
May 15, 2004
(32, 33)*

It was about 2:00 A.M. and very dark. Several individuals climbed on top of our Messianic synagogue in Israel and broke through the roofing material to lower explosives and flammable material into the building. After igniting it, they fled. The ensuing explosion ripped off that section of the roof. The heat of the fire warped the steel beams, totally destroying our office and everything in it. The entire building was blackened by smoke and the electrical system was damaged, but the sound equipment, the Ark, and the *Torah* were not harmed.

There is a striking parallel between the actions of these individuals and those in Luke 5:19, who also went up on a roof and broke through in order to lower their paralyzed friend down to Yeshua. In both cases the goal was to get to Yeshua. In the latter case, the goal was to receive healing from him for their friend. In our case, the goal was to stop Yeshua's healing work in our community. Yeshua is, by the decree of the Almighty, the one who has pre-eminence in all things. People are going to be judged according to how they respond to him. The thoughts and intentions of every man's heart will be revealed in that response. The more we identify with him, the more those same attitudes and actions will be directed towards us.

Prayer Focus

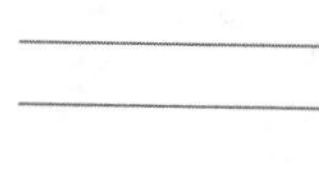

Today I Will

. . . count my own popularity or unpopularity as nothing compared to the surpassing value of knowing Yeshua and making him known to others.

MM

May 11, 1999
May 30, 2000
May 18, 2001
May 7, 2002
May 27, 2003
May 16, 2004

Prayer Focus

Sin is crouching at the door—it wants you, but you can rule over it (Gen. 4:7).

Rabbi Isaac comments on the phrase, "Sin is crouching at the door," saying, "At first it is like a [passing] visitor, then like a guest [who stays longer], and finally like the master of the house" (Genesis Rabbah 22:6). God warns Cain that he must resist sin and master it, or else it will master him. Like his parents, Adam and Eve, Cain encounters a clear choice: obedience and blessing, or disobedience and death. And like his parents, he makes the wrong choice.

We may also see the choice clearly enough, yet find ourselves without the strength to make the right decision. God's intention is to provide the means to obey his Word. Once we choose God's way, the power will be there, as it would have been even for Cain.

With the coming of the Messiah, it became clear that we could have the power to master sin. As Sha'ul (Saul; i.e., Paul) says, "For sin will not have authority over you; because you are not under legalism but under grace" (Rom. 6:14). God's grace does not give us the freedom to sin, but the power in Messiah to rule over the sin that crouches at our door.

Today I Will

. . . examine my heart for any excuses I still use to justify sinful behavior in my life. I will not allow sin to rule me, but I will master it through Messiah.

RR

Let us keep paying attention to one another, in order to spur each other on to love and good deeds (Heb. 10:24).

May 12, 1999
May 31, 2000
May 19, 2001
(32, 33)*
May 8, 2002
May 28, 2003
May 17, 2004

Two of Jacob's offspring became involved in rather sordid episodes, recorded in the Book of Genesis. Dinah, "went out to visit the local girls" (Gen. 34:1) and was raped by Shechem, prince of the country. Shechem was eventually killed, along with all his men, by Dinah's vengeful brothers—Simeon and Levi. The *Midrash* (traditional commentary) faults Dinah for contributing to this tragedy by going out from the shelter of her family (Genesis Rabbah 80:1–5).

Similarly, Judah "went off from his brothers" (Gen. 38:1) and married a Canaanite woman. Before the story ended, Judah had lost his two oldest sons as well as his wife, and he had fathered an heir by his own daughter-in-law, Tamar, who had disguised herself as a harlot. Like his sister Dinah, Judah inherited trouble when he left the circle of his family.

In our day of extreme individualism, it is easy to forget that God calls us into community. We may enter his Kingdom one-by-one, but once there, we need to understand how dependent we are upon one another. By God's design we can receive strength through the brothers and sisters who stand with us. Let us not lightly leave the shelter of our spiritual family.

Prayer Focus

Today I Will

. . . stay in close touch with my brothers and sisters, to give and receive encouragement in our walks with the Lord.

RR

May 13, 1999
June 1, 2000
May 20, 2001
May 9, 2002
May 29, 2003
May 18, 2004

Biblical
On this day, the earth was completely dry after the Flood (Gen. 8:14).

Prayer Focus

When Ach'av saw Eliyahu, Ach'av said to him, "Is it really you, you troubler of Isra'el?" He answered, "I haven't troubled Isra'el, you have" (1 Kings 18:17–18).

The *Talmud* (Baba Batra 23b) describes a discussion in a *yeshivah* (rabbinical school) that concerned property law. If a bird falls within fifty cubits (about seventy meters) of a person's property, it belongs to the property owner; if outside that range, it belongs to whoever finds it. At this point, Rabbi Jeremiah chimes in, "If one foot is within fifty cubits and the other beyond, how do we decide?" The next line says (no kidding), "It was for [asking] this [question] that they turned Rabbi Jeremiah out of the *Beth Hamidrash* [*yeshivah*]."

I empathize with Rabbi Jeremiah. Messianic Judaism is questioning one of the cornerstones of Western civilization: the dichotomy between Judaism and Christianity. There is not one God for the Jews and another for the nations. Messianic Judaism strikes at the heart of the false notion that God has replaced the Jewish people (see Romans 11:11–24), which has been the foundational thinking in much anti-Semitic theology. We Messianic Jews ask our people, "Why can't Yeshua of Nazareth be the Messiah for the Jews?" To the Church world, we ask, "How can adherence to the New Testament, which clearly directs Jewish believers *not* to abandon their Jewishness (Acts 21:18–25), necessitate a departure from Judaism?"

For asking such questions, one may be tossed outside, but when one brushes the dust off and looks up, one finds oneself in wondrous company.

Today I Will

. . . seek the Lord for courage to ask good questions, and I will pray for courage to respond to the answers as one hungry to be ruled by truth.

BC

If I forget you, Yerushalayim [Jerusalem], may my right hand wither away. . . . if I fail to count Yerushalayim the greatest of all my joys (Ps. 137:5–6).

The age-old Jewish vision for the restoration of Jerusalem testifies to the endurance of hope and the power of persevering prayer. For nearly two millennia, pious Jews have beseeched God daily: "Return to Jerusalem, your city of mercy, and dwell within it as you have proclaimed, and build it soon, even in our day, a building forever." Then, through a few days of battle in June of 1967, the Lord responded. Israeli troops recaptured the Old City of Jerusalem from the hands of the Jordanians who had held it since 1948. It had been under continuous Gentile rule since the days of the Roman Empire. When the Western Wall was liberated, the Israeli soldiers wept like small children.

There is a connection between the centuries of prayerful longing and those few days of battle. God heard the cries of his people and responded, even though his response seemed like a long time in coming. A united Jerusalem testifies to Jewish hope and perseverance; but even more powerfully, it displays the faithfulness of the God of Israel, who continues to oversee human history. When the proper time arrives, he intervenes in that history to accomplish his Word.

Today I Will

. . . actively place my hope in the faithfulness of God, even in areas where he seems to be absent or disinterested.

May 14, 1999
June 2, 2000
May 21, 2001
May 10, 2002
May 30, 2003
May 19, 2004

Traditional
Yom Yerushalayim
(Jerusalem Day)

Prayer Focus

RR

May 15, 1999
(34/B)*
June 3, 2000
(34/B)*
May 22, 2001
May 11, 2002
(34/B)*
May 31, 2003
(34/B)*
May 20, 2004

Prayer Focus

You will be a kingdom of *cohanim* [priests] for me, a nation set apart (Exod. 19:6).

The entire nation of Israel, not just the tribe of Levi, was set apart, consecrated to God for his purposes. We were called to be a light to the nations. Unfortunately, our people have not entirely lived up to this holy calling. Today, the majority of our people remain in unbelief.

But God has still called us to be that light, a remnant according to the election of grace. In Yeshua, we are consecrated by God to be a light both to our people and to all of the nations. We have an obligation to live lives that are set apart unto God, so that people will see and be drawn to Messiah Yeshua. Henry Varley, a 19th century British evangelist, once said, "It remains for the world to see what the Lord can do with a man wholly consecrated to [Messiah]." As we commit ourselves to living consecrated lives, the world will wake up and take notice. Unfortunately, the world too often sees us in a state of compromise, not consecration.

God has called us to be set apart for his purposes, that he might receive the glory, and that others may be drawn to him. We have a priestly ministry to exercise. As we consecrate ourselves to God, our own people and the entire world will see and be drawn to Yeshua.

Today I Will

. . . consecrate myself unto the Lord God of Israel. I will set myself apart from all those things that deter me from being holy unto him.

DB

You will know the truth, and the truth will set you free (John 8:32).

Throughout the centuries, rabbis have been aware that the *Tanakh* (Hebrew Scriptures) prophesied that Messiah would be humiliated and also exalted. Three different explanations for this are found in the Babylonian *Talmud.*

One view is that if the Jewish people are unworthy, Messiah will come "humble . . . riding on a donkey" (see Zech. 9:9). If we are worthy, he will come "with the clouds of heaven" (see Dan. 7:13).

In a second view, the two roles of Messiah are fulfilled by two different Messiahs: *Mashiach* Ben-David (Messiah Son of David), the King Messiah, and *Mashiach* Ben-Yosef (Messiah Son of Joseph), the suffering Messiah.

In a third view, the Messiah supposedly came to earth when the Second Temple was destroyed, and is presently suffering affliction with his people. He will bring about Israel's salvation when they hear his voice and repent.

These three views provide sincere explanations for the dual roles of Messiah. However, they are sincerely wrong. The truth is that one Messiah was to come in two different eras, for two distinct purposes. He came first to atone for the sins of his people and to bring peace to those who would repent and receive him. He will return again to establish his Kingdom of peace on earth. This truth, revealed in the *Brit Chadashah* (New Covenant Scriptures), is the key that unlocks the truth about the two roles of Messiah.

. . . investigate the truth of Messiah from a study of the Scriptures.

May 16, 1999
June 4, 2000
May 23, 2001
May 12, 2002
June 1, 2003
May 21, 2004

Biblical
Rosh Chodesh
(the New Moon)

On this day, Ezekiel received a prophecy against Egypt (Ezek. 31:1).

Prayer Focus

EK

May 17, 1999
June 5, 2000
May 24, 2001
May 13, 2002
June 2, 2003
May 22, 2004 (34)

Prayer Focus

How blessed you are when people insult you and persecute you . . . because you follow me! (Matt. 5:11).

The Messiah revealed from the beginning of his ministry that his followers would encounter persecution. This persecution would not be the ordinary difficulties of life, or even the difficulty of living a moral life in the midst of an immoral world. Rather, Yeshua called his disciples to "suffer on account of my name" (Acts 9:16). When we identify with the Messiah, we draw the fire of persecution upon ourselves.

Believers around the world are encountering such persecution today. In China and Vietnam, they are harassed, beaten, and imprisoned by governments. In Sudan they are kidnapped and sold into slavery by Islamic militias. In Saudi Arabia they face execution for sharing their faith. Rabbi Sha'ul (Saul; i.e., Paul) seemed to have our day in mind when he told Timothy, "All who want to live a godly life united with the Messiah Yeshua will be persecuted" (2 Tim. 3:12).

But what of believers in lands like ours, lands where there is little or no real persecution? Do we identify with the rest of the body of Messiah, so that their suffering becomes our own? The writer of the Book of Hebrews instructs us, "Remember those in prison and being mistreated, as if you were in prison with them and undergoing their torture yourselves" (Heb. 13:3). We must remember our imprisoned spiritual brothers and sisters, and pray for them consistently with perseverance.

Today I Will

. . . begin the practice of praying for my persecuted brothers and sisters in Messiah throughout the world.

RR

We are the aroma of the Messiah (2 Cor. 2:15).

SIVAN

3

סיון

May 18, 1999
June 6, 2000
May 25, 2001
May 14, 2002
June 3, 2003
May 23, 2004

The Chafetz Chayyim (Rabbi Yisrael Meir HaCohen) once met a fellow Jew who had the habit of working on *Shabbat* (Sabbath). *Reb* (Rabbi) Yisrael simply took the man's hand between his own hands and wept over it, saying, "*Shabbat, Shabbat.*" After several moments, the other man broke into weeping also. Thereafter, the worker was found in *shul* (synagogue) every *Shabbat.*

Reb Yisrael was so committed to and enamored of Judaism, as he understood it, that he radiated its concerns from the innermost core of his being—without words. Scripture tells us that through Yeshua's atonement, God has written his *Torah* on our hearts (Jer. 31:31). We can feel what God feels. We can radiate the heart of God to those who do not know him. The scent of God is on us, like the perfume of a beloved spouse in whose embrace we have lingered long.

When Moshe (Moses) was coming down from the mountain of God's presence, he had a radiance of which he seemed unaware (Exod. 34:30). Are you aware that God is in you? You are a walking letter from God to humankind (2 Cor. 3:2). You are also the balm and ointment for the scars upon the world's soul (2 Cor. 1:4). You are more than you realize.

Prayer Focus

Today I Will

. . . be mindful of the privilege God has accorded me—to stand before humankind with the imprint of Messiah upon my heart.

BC

May 19, 1999
June 7, 2000
May 26, 2001 (34)
May 15, 2002
June 4, 2003
May 24, 2004

Prayer Focus

Yeshua deserves more honor than Moshe [Moses](Heb. 3:3).

The rabbis teach that Moshe *Rabbeynu* (Moses our Rabbi) is the greatest of all the prophets of Israel. They go on to say that the Rambam (Moses Maimonides) is the next greatest. There's a rabbinic saying, "From Moses to Moses, there is none like Moses." In other words, between Moses the giver of *Torah* and Moses Maimonides, there has been none greater. The author of the book of Hebrews tells us otherwise. We are told that Yeshua "deserves more honor than Moshe" (Heb. 3:3).

Moshe's glory began to fade after he came down from Mount Sinai. But of Yeshua we read, "We saw his *Sh'khinah* [Glory], the *Sh'khinah* as of the Father's only Son" (John 1:14). Moshe was a faithful member of the house of Israel, but Yeshua is the builder of the house of Israel. Moshe was the servant; Yeshua is the Son. Moshe spoke of the future, Yeshua fulfilled all the promises from the past. "The *Torah* was given through Moshe; grace and truth came through Yeshua the Messiah" (John 1:17).

There have been times when I've handed out gospel tracts, wearing a Jews for Jesus T-shirt, and Orthodox Jews have come up to me and said, "We are Jews for Moses." Now I respond by saying, "If you really were Jews for Moses, you'd be for Yeshua, too." Yeshua said, "If you really believed Moshe, you would believe me; because it was about me that he wrote" (John 5:46). If we properly honor Moshe *Rabbeynu*, all the glory will go to Messiah Yeshua.

Today I Will

. . . make a commitment to glorify Yeshua—Israel's greatest prophet, my Rabbi and Savior, and the Messiah.

DB

God raised up this Yeshua! And we are all witnesses of it! (Acts 2:32)

According to Jewish tradition, King David died on *Shavu'ot* (the Feast of Weeks). David is still in his tomb, but Yeshua is not. The fact that God has raised Yeshua from the dead—delivering him from his tomb—means that he is Lord and Messiah.

In Brooklyn, New York, there are many *Chabad Chasidim* (ultra-Orthodox Jews) who still hope that their *rebbe* (chief rabbi), Menachem Schneerson, will rise from the dead and thereby prove that he is the Messiah. Unlike them, we have a living Messiah!

The prophet Isaiah foretold of the Messiah's suffering and resurrection: "After forcible arrest and sentencing, he was taken away; and none of his generation protested his being cut off from the land of the living for the crimes of my people. . . . After this ordeal [suffering], he will see satisfaction" (Isa. 53:8, 11). As the long-awaited Suffering Servant, Yeshua died for our sins and was resurrected before hundreds of witnesses! Today he lives to intercede on our behalf in the heavenly tabernacle.

Today I Will

. . . put my trust fully in Yeshua, knowing that he is alive and able to help me.

SIVAN

5

סיון

May 20, 1999
June 8, 2000
May 27, 2001
May 16, 2002
June 5, 2003
May 25, 2004

Traditional
Erev Shavu'ot
(Eve of the Feast of Weeks)

Prayer Focus

KK

SIVAN

6

סיון

May 21, 1999 (מ)
June 9, 2000 (מ)
May 28, 2001 (מ)
May 17, 2002 (מ)
June 6, 2003 (מ)
May 26, 2004 (מ)

Traditional
Shavu'ot
(the Feast of Weeks)
Day 1

This date for *Shavu'ot* is based on the rabbinical custom of counting fifty days from Nisan 16 (See Appendix B, endnote 6).

Prayer Focus

Mount Sinai was enveloped in smoke, because ADONAI descended onto it in fire (Exod. 19:18).

Of all the *shalosh regalim* (three pilgrimage festivals) which Israel was commanded to celebrate in Yerushalayim (Jerusalem), *Shavu'ot* (the Feast of Weeks) stands out as the most dramatic. According to tradition, it was at this time—fifty days after the first Passover in Egypt—that our people came to Mount Sinai to receive the *Torah*. As God spoke to Moshe (Moses), there were incredible signs and wonders which testified that Israel was in the presence of *HaShem* (God; literally, "the Name"). Fire, smoke, and lightning were all seen that day at the mountain. Hence, *Shavu'ot* has been celebrated as the time when Israel received the *Torah* and entered into a new covenant relationship with ADONAI (the LORD).

Interestingly, part of the *Haftarah* (portion from the Prophets) read on this holy day is Ezekiel 1. This passage of Scripture was undoubtedly chosen because the prophet Ezekiel had a vision of the *Shekhinah* (Glory of God), as represented by the strong wind, the cloud, and the fire. Tragically, it was during Ezekiel's day that the *Shekhinah* departed from Israel at the destruction of the first Temple (Ezek. 10:18–19).

While our people pray for the return of the *Shekhinah*, we often overlook an important event—a *Shavu'ot* in first-century Jerusalem: "The festival of *Shavuot* arrived, and the believers all gathered together in one place. Suddenly there came a sound from the sky like the roar of a violent wind, and it filled the whole house. . . ." (Acts 2:1–2) What a sign to our people! As they worshipped on *Shavu'ot,* reading from the prophet Ezekiel, the manifestations of the *Shekhinah* returned! Little wonder that 3,000 Jewish believers were spiritually born on that day. As we celebrate *Shavu'ot* today, do we see the life-changing power of the *Ruach HaKodesh* (Holy Spirit) in our lives?

Today I Will

. . . die to my own ways and let the *Ruach* (Spirit) of God be revealed in my life.

BK

The harvest is rich, but the workers are few (Matt. 9:37).

SIVAN

7

סיון

May 22, 1999 (מ)
June 10, 2000 (מ)
May 29, 2001 (מ)
May 18, 2002 (מ)
June 7, 2003 (מ)
May 27, 2004 (מ)

Traditional
Shavu'ot
(the Feast of Weeks)
Day 2
(in diaspora only)

This date for *Shavu'ot* is based on the rabbinical custom of counting fifty days from Nisan 16 (See Appendix B, endnote 6).

Shavu'ot (the Feast of Weeks) has many wonderful lessons. For the Jewish community, it is the annual celebration of receiving the *Torah* at Mount Sinai. To remind us of this event, we eat dairy foods because the Word of God is the milk of our spiritual lives. The *Torah* is the foundation of the whole Scripture, leading us into abundant and eternal life in the presence of our heavenly Father. Historically, we also know that *Shavu'ot* was the time of the wheat harvest in the Land of Israel. As this early grain was brought in, our people rejoiced in God's provision and were confident that there would be a good fall harvest (Lev. 23:15–21).

As is the case with each of God's appointed times, there are historical lessons as well as spiritual applications to be found in this festival. It was during this time of year that Yeshua walked with some of his disciples through fields in the Galil (Galilee). The early grain was turning white, beckoning for harvest. What a picture of our people Israel! Despite the fact that some opposed Yeshua and his claims, there were many in Israel who were ripe for spiritual harvest. They were ready to welcome the Messiah into their lives upon hearing the good news. In fact, a great Jewish harvest is recorded in the Book of Acts during *Shavu'ot* (2:41).

If the early grain ripened to harvest, how much more will God's promise of a latter-day harvest come to pass! Yeshua called for workers in his day. What are we doing to help in the great harvest in our own day?

Prayer Focus

Today I Will

. . . say, "*Hineyni* (Here I am), Lord! Show me how I might be part of the harvest in the Jewish fields."

BK

SIVAN

8

סיון

May 23, 1999
June 11, 2000
May 30, 2001
May 19, 2002
June 8, 2003
May 28, 2004

Biblical *Shavu'ot* (the Feast of Weeks) in the years 1999, 2000, 2002, and 2003. Annual Sabbath

This date for *Shavu'ot* 1999, 2000, 2002, and 2003 is based on the Scriptural teaching to count fifty days from the Sunday in the middle of *Matzot* week (Lev. 23:11–16). See Appendix B, endnote 6.

Prayer Focus

The Good News about the Kingdom will be announced throughout the whole world as a witness to all the *Goyim* [nations]. It is then that the end will come (Matt. 24:14).

In May 1992, while flying home from a ministry trip to Russia, I was reading Matthew 24 and came upon the above passage. I'd read it many times before, but now it jumped out at me in a way it never had before.

As I pondered the word "nation," I recalled from my study of Greek that the word used in the original language is *ethnos*, from which we derive the word "ethnic." I understood more clearly than ever that Yeshua was talking not merely about countries, but the "people groups" within those countries.

Suddenly I realized that, although thousands of missionaries and evangelists were working in the former Soviet Union since the Iron Curtain was torn down, there were not even a handful who were focused on reaching the three million Jewish people scattered throughout this great land. I felt the Lord stirring my heart to make a deeper commitment to reaching our people in the former Soviet Union. Within the year, I was led to organize the Messianic music festivals that, since 1993, have reached hundreds of thousands with the gospel.

As Messianic Jews, we understand the priority of the gospel being "to the Jew especially, but equally to the Gentile" (Rom. 1:16). Let us, as a movement, now take the responsibility Messiah has given us to bring the good news to our brethren in every corner of the globe. Until all Jewish people scattered throughout the nations hear the good news, Messiah will not return.

Today I Will

. . . pray for laborers to go to every Jewish community in the world where our people have been scattered.

JB

There is a remnant, chosen by [God's] grace (Rom. 11:5).

It has been said that truth is never determined by a majority vote. Similarly, it has never been "the moral majority," but rather the holy minority, through whom God has accomplished his plan and purpose. As Jewish believers, we must recognize that we have a special role to play as the remnant among our people Israel. My grandfather, Fred Kendall, began a ministry of sharing the gospel with the Jewish people and called it Israel's Remnant. People used to come into the storefront looking for pieces of carpeting from the Holy Land!

One aspect of being part of a remnant is that you need to be visible. You need to be different. The remnant is distinguishable from the whole, but it can only exist by standing out. Some of our Messianic brothers and sisters would much rather blend in and be invisible. Some seek to blend into the rest of Israel by hiding their lights under a bushel. They never let anyone know of their faith in Yeshua and so fail in their responsibility as part of the remnant. Others seek to blend in to the rest of their church, foregoing their Jewish distinctive. These, too, fail to fulfill their responsibilities as part of the remnant.

As Messianic Jews, we must hold our Jewishness and our "Jesusness" in full view, for all the world to see. Only then can we truly fulfill our calling as "a remnant, chosen by [God's] grace."

Today I Will

. . . look for ways to affirm my faith in Yeshua and my Jewish identity in him.

SIVAN

9

סיון

May 24, 1999
June 12, 2000
May 31, 2001
May 20, 2002
June 9, 2003
May 29, 2004 (35)

Prayer Focus

DB

May 25, 1999
June 13, 2000
June 1, 2001
May 21, 2002
June 10, 2003
May 30, 2004

Biblical
Shavu'ot (the Feast of Weeks) in the year 2004. Annual Sabbath

This date for *Shavu'ot* 2004 is based on the Scriptural teaching to count fifty days from the Sunday in the middle of *Matzot* week (Lev. 23:11–16). See Appendix B, endnote 6.

Prayer Focus

Pray that the Lord of the harvest will send out workers to gather in his harvest (Matt. 9:38).

One of the most unique and meaningful words in the Bible is *hineyni*. If you learn how to say it right, it can change your life. *Hineyni* comes from the Hebrew word *hiney*, for which we have no comparable word in English. *Hiney* means, "Behold! There it is! Look! Whoa! Hey! Here!" So when *hiney* becomes *hineyni*, it means, "Behold me! Here I am!"

In the sixth chapter of Isaiah, the prophet is overcome with a sense of unworthiness. But when he hears a divine voice say, "Whom should I send?" (Isa. 6:8), he shouts out, "*Hineyni*!" ("I'm here!")

The Lord asks you the same question: "Whom should I send?" He has a calling on your life. It will require you to step out against your fears. He's waiting not just to hear you say, "Here I am," but "*Hineyni*!" with an exclamation point. You need to be unequivocal and unconditional. "*Hineyni*! Here I am Lord. Send me. Wherever you lead, I will go!" Say it with joy, excitement, and with your whole heart. "*Hineyni*! Here I am. Send me!" And he will.

Today I Will

. . . say, "*Hineyni*!" to the Lord with an exclamation point!

JC

The voice of *ADONAI* in power. . . . The voice of *ADONAI* cracks the cedars (Ps. 29:4–5).

No heart is so hard that the voice of the Lord cannot reach it. The cedars of Lebanon were the strongest construction material known in biblical times, but they were no barrier to the Lord.

My mother—my wonderful Jewish mother—often reminded me of the cedars of Lebanon. She was so hardened to the Messiah that it seemed nothing would soften her heart. "I'll believe in your Yeshua when my rabbi tells me to," she would say. For more than twelve years, my husband and I prayed for her, but she showed no sign of openness.

Then one day, she became ill with cancer. For the first time in her life, she felt helpless, and in her time of need, she asked Yeshua for help. As her health deteriorated, her heart began to soften. As she neared the end, she slipped into a coma. One of the nurses told me that patients in a coma can often still hear, so I didn't give up. Moments before her death she told us that she had accepted Yeshua. The voice of the Lord reached my mother that day, as she lay unconscious to the world but conscious to the voice that pierced through her darkness, that tore down the cedars of hardness she had erected in her heart. He can do the same for those you love.

Don't give up hope for your loved ones who don't yet believe in Yeshua. He is able to speak to the hardest heart, until the final moment. The voice of *ADONAI* cracks the cedars of Lebanon.

Today I Will

. . . be encouraged to pray for those I love, even if I see no sign that their hearts will ever be softened. I will trust that the voice of the Lord can reach even them.

May 26, 1999
June 14, 2000
June 2, 2001 (35)
May 22, 2002
June 11, 2003
May 31, 2004

Prayer Focus

SIVAN

12

סיון

May 27, 1999
June 15, 2000
June 3, 2001
May 23, 2002
June 12, 2003
June 1, 2004

Biblical *Shavu'ot* (the Feast of Weeks) in the year 2001. Annual Sabbath

This date for *Shavu'ot* 2001 is based on the Scriptural teaching to count fifty days from the Sunday in the middle of *Matzot* week (Lev. 23:11–16). See Appendix B, endnote 6.

Prayer Focus

I tell you that unless a person is born again from above, he cannot see the Kingdom of God (John 3:3).

According to the rabbis, there are different ways of being born again. In various places, the *Talmud* says that one can be born again when he comes of age, when he is married, when he undergoes *semikhah* (ordination), and when he becomes the head of a rabbinic academy.

As a ruler in Israel, Nakdimon (Nicodemus) had experienced all these "new births." But this is not the new birth that Yeshua spoke of. The new birth Yeshua spoke of was not the mark of some passage of time or change of life. Rather it was descriptive of an entirely *new* life.

Eventually, Nakdimon was born again through belief in Yeshua. At first he had been proud and skeptical, but God changed his heart. It was Nakdimon who called on the chief priests to hear Yeshua before they judged him (John 7:51). It was Nakdimon who brought myrrh and aloes to anoint the body of Yeshua for burial (John 19:39). Finally, we learn in the *Talmud* (Jerusalem Talmud, Sanhedrin 43:1) that Nakdimon was openly identified as a follower of Yeshua. As a result, he lost his considerable wealth and standing within the Jewish community. Nakdimon may have been the first rabbi to be truly born again.

What about you? Have you experienced the new birth that Rabbi Nakdimon experienced? Have you told others of the new birth that Rabbi Yeshua offers those who believe in him?

Today I Will

. . . stand with Rabbi Nakdimon and other Jews who have received new birth in Yeshua the Messiah. I will look for ways to live my life so that others can experience this new birth as well.

DB

For your love is better than wine (Song of Sol. 1:2).

The Bible has a love song—the Song of Shlomo (Solomon)—which some consider a beautiful allegory about a bridegroom and bride, representing God and us. At its beginning, the bride says of the bridegroom, "For your love is better than wine." Significantly, the Hebrew reads *ki-tovim dodeykha miyyayin*, not "your love" but "your loves [plural] are better than wine."

We, as the bride, must speak these words, for God not only has love for us, but has abundant "loves." When you lean on the Lord, as a child learning to walk, God loves you with one love. But when you fall and need comfort, he loves you with another love. When you're young in him, zealous and naïve, he loves you with one love. When you are old in the Lord, deeply rooted and wise, he loves you with another. The love with which he loves you today is a new love, not an old love. He loves you tonight, not with this morning's love, nor this morning with last night's love. His love is new every morning and every moment.

God has many loves for us, more than enough for a lifetime. Receive the new love he has for you right now as you say with your heart, "Your loves are more delightful than wine."

Today I Will

. . . praise God in a new way or sing to him a new song of praise, acknowledging his abundant loves.

May 28, 1999
June 16, 2000
June 4, 2001
May 24, 2002
June 13, 2003
June 2, 2004

Prayer Focus

JC

May 29, 1999 (35)
June 17, 2000 (35)
June 5, 2001
May 25, 2002 (35)
June 14, 2003 (35)
June 3, 2004

I have always made it my ambition to proclaim the Good News where the Messiah was not yet known (Rom. 15:20).

People can be ambitious in many areas. To some, career goals are most important, while others seek their children's success. One is not much better than the other. When all is said and done, the question is whether we have lifted the Messiah to the place of highest importance in our lives.

Joseph Rabinowitz, a Messianic Jewish leader in nineteenth-century Russia, expressed the ambition of his life with the following story:

"My position is to be compared with one who went out to the ocean in a ship and suffered a shipwreck with all on board. Now all of those who are shipwrecked try to get to some firm ground on which to save themselves. If one after struggling for life finds a rock, the moment he feels he is on firm ground, he will shout to those still struggling in the sea. And if some are beyond the reach of his voice, he will try to raise something—a stick or flag—to attract their attention and call them to head for the rock. Now that is my position. Russia is like the ocean, the Jews there are like shipwrecked people, and since, by God's mercy, my feet are on the Rock [Yeshua], I have tried to do what that person I spoke of tried to do. I am shouting to my shipwrecked people to come to the Rock."

Prayer Focus

Today I Will

. . . signal to the shipwrecked people God lets me meet that Yeshua is the Rock on which it is safe to build their lives.

KK

I will spare seven thousand in Isra'el, every knee that hasn't bent down before Ba'al (1 Kings 19:18).

SIVAN

15

סיון

May 30, 1999
June 18, 2000
June 6, 2001
May 26, 2002
June 15, 2003
June 4, 2004

Biblical
On this day, the Israelites arrived at the Desert of Sinai (Exod. 19:1; 12:6–13, 29–31).

Prayer Focus

Let's face it: this was not much comfort to Eliyahu (Elijah). He seemed to be the only Jew in his era still following the God of Israel. Out of a nation numbering millions, God said there were seven thousand faithful ones—less than one tenth of one percent.

We in the Messianic Jewish movement have nothing to complain about. By the estimate of the Federation of Jewish Agencies in 1990, somewhere between eight and fourteen percent of American Jews profess some kind of positive faith in Yeshua of Nazareth. Do we feel outnumbered? Open our eyes, Lord, so we may see those who are with us (2 Kings 6:17).

Are we tired of the fight? So was Eliyahu, who, in his exhaustion even threw a fit of self-pity: "'Enough!' he said. 'Now *Adonai*, take my life. I'm no better than my ancestors.' Then he lay down under a broom tree and went to sleep" (1 Kings 19:4–5). But God's manner of dealing with the prophet seemed comical to me. God completely ignored the prophet's complaints! After feeding him and letting him rest, God simply issued him his next marching order. Almost as an afterthought, God told him of the seven thousand who had remained faithful to the God of Israel.

Let us detour around the delusional luxury of self-pity and seek God for our marching orders. Who knows how many millions are among Israel right now who already know Yeshua as Messiah, and have not yet surfaced? We are walking by faith (2 Cor. 5:7) into the Messianic revival to come. So be it. Faith is the only way (Heb. 11:6).

Today I Will

. . . look at my people, not through the lens of human sight, but through the filter of faith.

BC

May 31, 1999
June 19, 2000
June 7, 2001
May 27, 2002
June 16, 2003
June 5, 2004 (36)

Give a reasoned answer to anyone who asks you to explain the hope you have in you (1 Pet. 3:15).

Many think this verse refers to intellectual arguments for our faith. There is a place for such a presentation. However, Kefa (Peter) is more likely asking us to be ready to testify to the power of the *Ruach HaKodesh* (Holy Spirit) in our own lives. We should share what God has actually done for us—his restoration of marriage and family, his healing of soul and body, his supernatural answers to prayer. Our *shalom* (peace) and our confidence provide evidence. A life of intimacy with God always conveys a testimony of security and renewal. These are also reasons for faith.

The person who experiences the presence and power of the *Ruach* (Spirit) has powerful reasons for his faith. Consider today how your walk with the Lord provides a powerful apologetic for Yeshua.

Prayer Focus

Today I Will

. . . be prepared to share with others what Messiah has done in my life.

DJ

A large crowd of *cohanim* were becoming obedient to the faith (Acts 6:7).

June 1, 1999
June 20, 2000
June 8, 2001
May 28, 2002
June 17, 2003
June 6, 2004

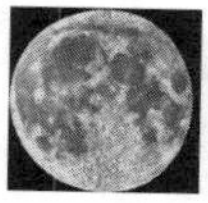

Have you ever heard the story of Rabbi Isaac Lichtenstein? For forty years he was the district rabbi of Tapio-Szele in Hungary. At the beginning of his rabbinical career, he confiscated a *Brit Chadashah* (New Covenant Scriptures) from a teacher who served under him, and buried it in the back of his library.

Forty years later, during a period of severe persecution of the Jews, Rabbi Lichtenstein became interested in Yeshua. The persecution had been promulgated by so-called Christians who killed Jews in the name of Jesus. Other Christians, however, condemned the persecution and defended the Jewish community. Rabbi Lichtenstein wondered which ones were Yeshua's true disciples. To try to find an answer, he searched in the hidden corner of his library for the *Brit Chadashah* he had buried there so many years ago.

Rabbi Lichtenstein later wrote of his experience while reading the *Brit Chadashah*, "A sudden glory, a light, flashed through my soul. I looked for thorns, and gathered roses; I discovered pearls instead of pebbles; instead of hatred, love; instead of vengeance, forgiveness; instead of bondage, freedom; instead of pride, humility; instead of enmity, conciliation; instead of death, life, salvation, resurrection, and heavenly treasure." Rabbi Lichtenstein became a Messianic Jew.

The life of Rabbi Lichtenstein is a reminder that we must not neglect sharing the *Brit Chadashah* with the leaders of our people. Some of the most educated rabbis have not rejected Yeshua, but simply have a misconception of who he really is.

Prayer Focus

Today I Will

. . . consider ways that I can bring a knowledge of Yeshua to the leaders of my own people.

DR

June 2, 1999
June 21, 2000
June 9, 2001 (36)
May 29, 2002
June 18, 2003
June 7, 2004

Prayer Focus

Rabbi, which of the *mitzvot* [commandments] in the *Torah* is the most important? (Matt. 22:36)

A man asked Messiah for the most important commandment, and for two thousand years we've missed the answer. We think he answered, "Love the Lord your God with all your heart, soul, mind and strength." Actually, he answered, "*Shema Yisra'el, Adonai Eloheynu, Adonai echad*" (Hear, O Israel; the Lord our God, the Lord is one). *Then* he said, "And you are to love *Adonai* your God with all your heart, with all your soul, with all your understanding and with all your strength" (Mark 12:29–30). This is the *Shema*, recited by virtually every Jewish worshiper in every synagogue, every week, throughout the world. The first answer Messiah gave when asked what was the most important command was one word—*shema* (hear, listen, pay close attention).

We rush around, but the Lord told us to stop and listen. We seem to ignore that. Before we can do great things for God, we have to learn to listen. Stop and listen. He's God. We're not. We need to let him speak to our hearts. When we listen, we truly learn to know him. Then we can really love him and love others.

Take time today to listen to him and know him. He has something to say to you.

Today I Will

. . . stop rushing around, even to do things for God. I will be still and *listen* to the Lord.

JC

Afterwards, the people of Isra'el will repent and seek *ADONAI* their God and David their king (Hos. 3:5).

June 3, 1999
June 22, 2000
June 10, 2001
May 30, 2002
June 19, 2003
June 8, 2004

Over the years I have heard godly leaders, Jewish and Gentile, say that Israel will not be spiritually awakened until the Messiah Yeshua returns. As *Yehudim Meshichim* (Messianic Jews), we need to know what the Word of God says, and then make this information the foundation of our lives.

The above passage is one of many prophecies that speak of a great turning to God within Israel in the Latter Days. The prediction states that Israel will be without king, Temple, and homeland for a period of time and then will return to the Land. However, the physical restoration of Israel is paralleled by the spiritual restoration. Jewish people will not only seek God, but specifically "David their king" (i.e., the Messiah).

In the early 1970s, tens of thousands of Jewish people, suddenly and miraculously, accepted Yeshua the Messiah. Today, there are hundreds of Messianic congregations throughout the world. There is a growing movement in Israel and we have seen a revival in Russia of which we could have only dreamed!

Now is the "day of salvation" for Israel. Pray and believe that your family will be saved. Expect to see Jewish communities turn to the Messiah. Let us pray for and expect to see the greatest spiritual awakening of our people since the days of the Book of Acts!

Prayer Focus

Today I Will

. . . pray for the nation of Israel and for our people everywhere to know the Messiah Yeshua. Lord, use me in this great spiritual revival to bring many to you.

DC

June 4, 1999
June 23, 2000
June 11, 2001
May 31, 2002
June 20, 2003
June 9, 2004

Seek first his Kingdom and his righteousness (Matt. 6:33).

I recently visited the ancient port city of Akko (Acre) in northern Israel. Beneath the current street level are the ruins from the Crusader occupation (the twelfth and thirteenth centuries). I saw massive buildings constructed by the sweat and blood of thousands of hands. Dining halls, dormitories, dungeons, and a cathedral—all once filled with real people who had dreams and hopes and aspirations—are now tourist sights.

Historians call their conquests "the Crusader Kingdom." But what did it accomplish? Death and destruction were promulgated in the name of religion. Unfortunately, death and destruction are often the end result of seeking a kingdom other than God's, even when the seekers believe that their mission is a holy one. God's Kingdom is not spread by the warrior's sword or the builder's trowel, but by the power of the *Ruach* (Spirit).

Prayer Focus

Today I Will

. . . build for eternity so I don't just leave behind tourist attractions.

MM

Didn't the Messiah have to die like this before entering his glory? (Luke 24:26)

June 5, 1999 (36)
June 24, 2000 (36)
June 12, 2001
June 1, 2002 (36)
June 21, 2003 (36)
June 10, 2004

Have you ever heard a relative of yours say, "Jews don't believe in a dead and resurrected *Mashiach* (Messiah)"? Our loved ones would like us to think that the Messianic Jewish view of Messiah falls outside the realm of traditional Judaism, but is this really the case?

Recently I picked up a book entitled *To Live and Live Again: An Overview of Techiyas HaMeisim Based on the Classical Sources and on the Teachings of Chabad Chassidism.* In it, Rabbi Nisan Dovid Dubov (an emissary of *Chabad-Lubavitch* in England) writes, "there are indications that *Mashiach* could possibly be a righteous individual who has already lived and died and will then be resurrected as *Mashiach* . . . according to this view, a righteous individual deemed to be the *Mashiach* will live, then die on account of the sins of his generation, but will eventually be resurrected."

Rabbi Dubov represents an increasing number of Orthodox Jews who have come to believe in the possibility of a Messiah who could die and then be resurrected. Such a view, they argue, is in full agreement with the great rabbis of old who believed in the Messiah son of Joseph, the Suffering Servant! After centuries of neglecting this doctrine, many of the most zealous and learned among our people are getting up to speed. Let us be encouraged by their insights and remind our less traditional brethren of them—while at the same time pointing them to Yeshua.

Prayer Focus

Today I Will

. . . tell my Jewish family and friends that even the Orthodox are starting to believe in a Messiah who dies for our sins and is resurrected from the dead.

DR

June 6, 1999
June 25, 2000
June 13, 2001
June 2, 2002
June 22, 2003
June 11, 2004

Give a reasoned answer to anyone who asks you to explain the hope you have in you (1 Pet. 3:15).

When I first came to know the Lord in 1970, I was a freshman at the University of Cincinnati. The Lord supernaturally moved me to begin to study the Scriptures a minimum of two hours a day—along with my other studies, no less! At the same time, the Lord opened a door for our small group of Messianic Jewish students on campus to have interaction with an Orthodox Jewish group. Thus began a two-year dialogue on the Messiah that changed my life.

It is one thing to hand someone a tract with a hundred Messianic prophecies on it and quite another to sit down with religious Jews (and, occasionally, rabbis) and go through these same passages, verse by verse, in Hebrew and English. I had never really studied these remarkable passages, much less in their original Hebrew, and now I found myself debating them with Orthodox Jews! I knew I had to study these passages, and soon! Because of the research I did and the subsequent discussions I had with these Jewish students, my faith became stronger. I now *knew* that Yeshua was the only person who could possibly have fulfilled all of these predictions about the Messiah.

By studying the Messianic prophecies, we come into a deeper faith that Yeshua is the Messiah of Israel. We also become more confident in sharing our Messianic faith with our own people.

Prayer Focus

Today I Will

. . . study the Messianic passages, know them thoroughly, and boldly share my faith with everyone who asks me.

DC

Woe to you when people speak well of you (Luke 6:26).

After David Ben-Gurion declared the Jewish State on May 14, 1948, he wrote in his diary, "The country went wild with joy, but I could not rejoice. I knew the war we faced." Ben-Gurion and the *Yishuv*—the Jewish population in the land of Israel—had not done what was easy; they had done what was right. American President Theodore Roosevelt spoke of how he handled moments like this when he said, "If I must choose between peace and righteousness, then I choose righteousness."

Integrity is the commitment to do the right thing under pressure. Scripture calls us to develop this quality as believers if we truly desire fellowship with *HaShem* (God; literally, "the Name"). We are not to be contentious people; we are to seek the peaceful path when it can be found (Heb. 12:14). However, if our integrity is on the auction block, we are not to sell at any price. If that means battle, then battle it must be, and may our God be with us. A coward dies a thousand deaths; the valiant man, but one. Courage is as much a part of walking with God as purity, for without courage, there can be no integrity. Without integrity, there can be no true intimacy with the living God. "When they saw how bold Kefa and Yochanan were . . . they recognized them as having been with Yeshua" (Acts 4:13).

Today I Will

. . . ask God to fill my heart with courage so that I can stand my ground in matters of righteousness (Psalm 15).

June 7, 1999
June 26, 2000
June 14, 2001
June 3, 2002
June 23, 2003
June 12, 2004 (37)*

Biblical
On this day, Mordecai's decree allowing the Jews to defend themselves was written (Esther 8:9).

Prayer Focus

BC

June 8, 1999
June 27, 2000
June 15, 2001
June 4, 2002
June 24, 2003
June 13, 2004

Prayer Focus

Yeshua suffered death outside the gate, in order to make the people holy through his own blood (Heb. 13:12).

Did you ever wonder why Messiah had to go outside the gate to be crucified? In ancient times, you would never bury someone inside a Jewish city nor carry out an execution inside its walls. Criminals had to be executed outside the city gates. This is one reason Messiah was crucified outside the walls of Jerusalem.

But there's another reason. God purposefully decided that this most important event would not take place in heaven, on a throne, in a Temple, or inside the holy city; it would take place "outside the gate." Why? Because Messiah came to earth to save those who are outside—outside the gates, outside his mercy, outside his holiness, outside his love. That's everyone.

Therefore, if you are his disciple, you too must go outside the gate. You too must go to the sinners and to the rejected. Real love always steps outside the gate. This is why Messiah died outside the gate. Therefore, that is where you too must go. Go "out" to the outcast, to the stranger, to the despised, and to the lepers of this world, for Messiah died outside the gate.

So, in the Kingdom of Heaven, going "out" is the "in" thing to do.

Today I Will

. . . go "outside the gate" with the love of Messiah.

JC

For God's free gifts and his calling are irrevocable (Rom. 11:29).

What is God's calling to Israel? The Abrahamic covenant states that Abraham's seed will bring blessing to all the nations. Thus, Israel plays a mediatory role in bringing God to the nations. But how is this accomplished? Intercession is the key. Intercession is prayer that brings God's blessings into the lives of others. Even Israel's life is a unique form of intercessory prayer. Her sacrifices called forth the coming of Yeshua. The *Torah* life calls forth the day when all the nations of the world will obey God's rule. Israel's very existence is a testimony to God's faithfulness!

In an overlapping but somewhat different way, all disciples of Yeshua participate in this mediatory calling and ministry of intercession. The Messiah's supper illustrates the meaning of Messiah's death and releases his power as a type of corporate intercession for the redemption of the world. In various ways, our lives prove God's existence and faithfulness to a doubting world, and our prayers call forth his blessing.

Let us see ourselves today as priestly members of God's kingdom, who have an irrevocable call to intercede for *tikkun ha'olam* (world restoration).

June 9, 1999
June 28, 2000
June 16, 2001 (37)*
June 5, 2002
June 25, 2003
June 14, 2004

Prayer Focus

Today I Will

. . . fulfill my calling to intercede as a priest in God's Kingdom.

DJ

June 10, 1999
June 29, 2000
June 17, 2001
June 6, 2002
June 26, 2003
June 15, 2004

He explained to them the things that can be found throughout the *Tanakh* concerning himself (Luke 24:27).

We need to assert our confidence in the prophecies concerning Messiah in the Jewish Scriptures. Many rabbis and anti-missionaries have tried to discount the evidence for the Messiahship of Yeshua. But they have to do some fancy footwork to come to that conclusion. Yeshua opened the eyes of the disciples on the road to Amma'us (Emmaus) by instructing them in the prophecies and Scriptures of the coming of Messiah. Wouldn't you love to have been able to sit in on that discipleship session?

I used to distribute a pamphlet entitled, "The Law and the Prophets at the Flatbush Yeshiva." The pamphlet posed a scenario where various Bible characters were applying for admission to the Flatbush *Yeshivah* (rabbinical school). Each character was given the final question, "What do you believe about Jesus?" Moshe (Moses) answered the question by quoting Deut. 18:18, "I will raise up for them a prophet like you from among their kinsmen." Moshe was expelled from the *yeshivah.* King David answered the question by quoting Ps. 110:1, "*Adonai* says to my Lord, 'Sit at my right hand, until I make your enemies your footstool.'" David was expelled. Micah answered by quoting Mic. 5:2(1), "But you, Beit-Lechem [Bethlehem] . . . out of you will come forth to me the future ruler of Isra'el . . . " Isaiah was asked and answered with Isa. 53:5, "But he was . . . crushed because of our sins . . . and by his bruises we are healed." These and other Bible characters interviewed were dismissed for citing evidence that Yeshua is Messiah.

Brothers and sisters, we stand in good company by believing in Yeshua. Let's renew our confidence in the Word of God—the predictions of the Hebrew prophets and the proclamations of the *Brit Chadashah* (New Covenant Scriptures). Messiah has come!

Prayer Focus

Today I Will

. . . renew my confidence in Yeshua as the one who fulfilled all the promises of the prophets of Israel.

DB

On you will fall the guilt for all the innocent blood that has ever been shed on earth (Matt. 23:35).

When we suffer for obeying God's will, we must never forget that sooner or later God will vindicate us. Yeshua pointed out that Abel's blood cried out to God on his behalf (Gen. 4:10–11), so that he spoke, even though he was dead (Heb. 11:4). Later rabbis reported that the blood of Zechariah spurted up like a fountain in the Temple until the Babylonians destroyed the Temple and avenged his murder. The way the Hebrew Bible is arranged, Abel was the Bible's first martyr, and Zechariah the last (2 Chron. 24:20–22).

The aristocrats who ruled Yerushalayim (Jerusalem) for the Romans were about to execute Yeshua, the greatest of the prophets, the Messiah. This was the climax of the previous generations' sins, and invited God's judgment on the current generation—the generation from approximately 30 C.E. to 70 C.E. (Matt. 23:36). This judgment was fulfilled when the Temple was destroyed in 70 C.E. (Matt. 23:38; 24:2). Yet Yeshua promised a different era, one in which his people would welcome him to Yerushalayim (Matt. 23:39).

Yeshua's blood testifies not only of vindication, but of forgiveness; his "sprinkled blood . . . speaks better things than that of Hevel [Abel] (Heb. 12:24).

Today I Will

. . . trust that whatever the cost of serving Yeshua, he will, someday, vindicate me.

June 11, 1999
June 30, 2000
June 18, 2001
June 7, 2002
June 27, 2003
June 16, 2004

Biblical
On this day, the rain that caused the Flood ended (Gen. 7:11–12).

Prayer Focus

CK

June 12, 1999 (37)*
July 1, 2000 (37)*
June 19, 2001
June 8, 2002 (37)*
June 28, 2003 (37)*
June 17, 2004

The foxes have holes, and the birds flying about have nests, but the Son of Man has no home of his own (Matt. 8:20).

When Yeshua was immersed in the Yarden (Jordan), a voice from heaven said, "This is my Son, whom I love; I am well pleased with him" (Matt. 3:17). The voice identified Yeshua as the Son of God. Later, the crowds identified Yeshua as Ben-David (Son of David). Yet Yeshua most often referred to himself as Ben-Adam (Son of Man).

In the above Scripture, Yeshua said that Ben-Adam had nowhere to lay his head. "Ben-Adam" was a glorious Messianic title (Dan. 7:13; Matt. 24:30), but it also described the Messiah as humble, as one who fully identified with the humanity he came to save, even the lowliest and most rejected among men. As Ben-Adam, Yeshua declared that when he returns in glory, he will judge the nations according to their treatment of the naked, sick, hungry, and imprisoned. When Yeshua returns, he will say to them, "Yes! I tell you that whenever you did these things for one of the least important of these brothers of mine, you did them to me!" (Matt. 25:40)

The Messiah is Ben-Adam, a glorious figure who takes on our humanity so fully that he records our service to others, especially when it is to the poor and needy, on his own account.

Prayer Focus

Today I Will

. . . recognize Yeshua in the hurting and needy people I encounter, and treat them accordingly.

RR

All the people gathered with one accord in the open space in front of the Water Gate (Neh. 8:1).

John Donne said, "No man is an island." Nowhere is this saying truer than in a *kehilah* (congregation). Just as the revival in Nehemiah's day would never have occurred if the repairers of the wall had not "gathered with one accord," so we will not experience God's reviving power in our lives without uniting in him. Though Messiah loved the whole world, he spent most of his time on earth in the company of twelve disciples and seventy-two others with whom he shared his life. After his death and resurrection, this small congregation, turned the world upside down. Assisting in this revival were fellowships which sprouted up in communities everywhere the good news was shared. Messianic Jews and Gentiles were called to build close loving relationships with others in synagogues (James 2:2) and were cared for by those called to oversee the flock (1 Pet. 5:2).

The *Talmud* has an interesting account about those who separate themselves from fellowship. The rabbis of old tell us that two angels will place their hands on them and say, "This person who separated himself from the community shall not witness its deliverance."

If you want to witness the good things God will do for those he has called you to love, stick around!

Today I Will

. . . be thankful to God for the congregation I attend. If I don't attend one now, I will ask for God's help in finding one, in order to obey Heb. 10:25 by "not neglecting our own congregational meetings, as some have made a practice of doing."

June 13, 1999
July 2, 2000
June 20, 2001
June 9, 2002
June 29, 2003
June 18, 2004

Prayer Focus

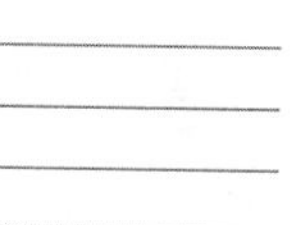

MW

June 14, 1999
July 3, 2000
June 21, 2001
June 10, 2002
June 30, 2003
June 19, 2004
(38/A,D)

Traditional
Rosh Chodesh
(the New Moon)
Day 1

Prayer Focus

The heart knows its own bitterness, and no stranger can share its joy (Prov. 14:10).

A certain Jewish play opens with a scene inside a synagogue. Two old Jewish men are sitting across from each other. After what seems like an eternity of silence, one groans, "My daughter-in-law! May she buy a hotel with a thousand rooms, and die in every one of them!" This sudden eruption always brings the house down with laughter as the audience imagines this curse in graphic detail.

Every human heart erupts periodically, pouring out those things hidden within. When it happens to us, we are often stunned that what causes us unspeakable pain might seem funny to others.

In Messiah we are better able to connect with one another than are those who are in the world—to "rejoice with those who rejoice, and weep with those who weep" (Rom. 12:15). Yeshua told his disciples that one of the ways the world would recognize that they were his followers was "that [they] keep on loving each other" (John 13:34).

Lonely humanity will notice that our love for and sensitivity toward one another is different from what surrounds them. They will see Messiah Yeshua in us.

Today I Will

. . . Seek opportunities to "do what is good to everyone, and especially to the family of those who are trustingly faithful" (Gal. 6:10). I will call on God to cause this love to lead many to the knowledge of him.

BC

The time has come, God's Kingdom is near (Mark 1:15).

With these words Yeshua began his public ministry. Yeshua also taught us to pray, "May your Kingdom come, your will be done on earth as in heaven" (Matt. 6:10). The *Malchut HaShem* (Kingdom of God) is the realm where God's rule is established. Our people have been preserved by a hope for the Kingdom of God—a day when the rule of God would be established over all the earth. Israel and the nations will experience unity under the rule of the Messiah in the *Olam HaBa* (the Age to Come). The whole human family will know the joy and fulfillment that come through living according to God's ways.

Yeshua ushered in this Kingdom in part, but the fullness of these hopes will await his return. His *Malchut* (Kingdom) encompasses all the dimensions of our lives, including our personal devotional lives, family lives, economic lives, and even recreational lives. Every aspect of life can reflect the glory of his rule. The Kingdom, like a mustard seed (Matt. 13:31–32), will continue to grow and fill the earth. When the Messiah returns, his Kingdom will be fully established over the earth.

We pray, "May your Kingdom come, your will be done" to confess the wisdom and glory of his ways, that we might live according to his rule in everything. The glory of our Father and his *Malchut* are to be our foundational motivating passions. Even if we are engaged in the lowliest work, we can do it to the glory of his Kingdom. This gives joy and meaning to the most mundane endeavors.

Today I Will

. . . reflect God's Kingdom rule in every aspect of my life.

June 15, 1999
July 4, 2000
June 22, 2001
June 11, 2002
July 1, 2003
June 20, 2004

Biblical
Rosh Chodesh
(the New Moon)

Traditional
Rosh Chodesh
Day 2

Prayer Focus

DJ

TAMMUZ

2

תמוז

June 16, 1999
July 5, 2000
June 23, 2001 (38)
June 12, 2002
July 2, 2003
June 21, 2004

They do not come to trust because the god of the *'olam hazeh* [this world] has blinded their minds (2 Cor. 4:4).

It is easy to become discouraged at the unbelief of our people, our friends, and especially our family members. We feel that if only we could say the right words or have the right book or tract at the right time, then surely they would believe. But no one was ever argued into God's Kingdom.

Once I met with a Jewish attorney who prided himself in his great intellect and ability to argue a point. He told me confidently that he could never believe in Yeshua because, while Yeshua was dying, he cried out in accusation against God, "My God! My God! Why have you deserted me?" I was eager to show him the passage from Psalm 22 which Yeshua quoted when he hung on the *tzlav* (cross). I explained how Psalm 22 was a Messianic prediction. His eyes grew wide as he realized the connection, but immediately his face clouded over and he said to me, "The disciples must have put these words in Yeshua's mouth to make it seem like he was fulfilling this passage." I was thunderstruck. First he said that the words of Yeshua proved he wasn't the Messiah. Then, he changed his tune to say that Yeshua never said those words to begin with!

The capacity for human unbelief knows no bounds. Instead of being surprised and discouraged by this unbelief, we should pray without ceasing, for only through the power of the *Ruach HaKodesh* (Holy Spirit) can unbelief be turned to faith in the Lord.

Prayer Focus

Today I Will

. . . make or renew a commitment to pray for my unbelieving family and friends, that by the power of God's *Ruach* (Spirit) they would come to know that Yeshua is Messiah.

DB

You are to name him Yeshua [which means, "*Adonai saves*"], because he will save his people from their sins (Matt. 1:21).

TAMMUZ

3

תמוז

June 17, 1999
July 6, 2000
June 24, 2001
June 13, 2002
July 3, 2003
June 22, 2004

Jesus is a fine name for the Messiah. It's an English transliteration of his Greek name—*Iesous*, which is actually a Greek translation of his original Hebrew name—Yeshua. Yeshua is a beautiful name. Its meaning—"the Lord saves"—is even more beautiful.

It's also beautiful because you are in it. Think about it. Why does Messiah have anything to do with salvation? Only because of you. "Yeshua" therefore actually means "*ADONAI* [the LORD] saves *you*!" Your salvation is in his name. His love for you is in his name.

God has, with all his heart, become your salvation, the answer to all your needs. If you were the only one in the world who needed salvation, he would still have sacrificed his life for you to become your Yeshua. He made this sacrifice to save you personally, and personally is the only way you can respond to his salvation. He's not salvation until you can say, "My Yeshua, my Salvation."

If you haven't said that yet, say it today. His holy name already has you inside of it, and that's something truly beautiful.

Prayer Focus

Today I Will

. . . spend intimate time with the Lord. I will return to the intimacy of my Savior and friend. I'm in his name!

JC

June 18, 1999
July 7, 2000
June 25, 2001
June 14, 2002
July 4, 2003
June 23, 2004

For I have made myself known to him, so that he will give orders to his children and to his household after him to keep the way of *ADONAI* (Gen. 18:19).

One of our greatest desires, as followers of Yeshua, is to see our families come into the *Malchut HaShem* (Kingdom of God). Whether it is our children, parents, brothers, sisters, grandparents, cousins, aunts or uncles, we want to know that their names are written in the *Sefer HaChayyim* (Book of Life), and that we will all be in eternity together.

I was raised in a godly Messianic Jewish home, by parents who were in the ministry and who believed strongly in family salvation. They prayed for families to know the Lord, and it happened.

One of the teachings I heard while growing up was from this wonderful Scripture passage about Avraham (Abraham). God said that he has made himself known to Avraham so that he would give orders to his children to keep the way of *ADONAI* [the LORD]. God actually went beyond family salvation and said that this extended to his "household" as well. Some have guessed that Avraham had a household of 2000–3000 people because of his great wealth. This meant that, including family and household, Avraham was spiritually training up a "congregation" of thousands, and they all believed in the one true God!

The fact that God wants to save families is taught all through the Scriptures. Examples of family salvation include Noah, Jacob, Joseph, Rahab, Joshua, Cornelius and Timothy, to name just a few. Family salvation is God's will! Have faith, pray for your families, and share with them as God opens the door. What a glorious day it will be when our families are united with us in the Messiah!

Prayer Focus

Today I Will

. . . exercise faith for my family to come to know the Messiah Yeshua. I will stand on the Lord's promises and the examples in Scripture for my family's total salvation.

DC

The disciplining that makes us whole fell on him, and by his bruises we are healed (Isa. 53:5).

The talmudic sages discuss the death of Messiah in Sukkah 52a. They call the Messiah who will be killed *Mashiach* Ben-Yosef (Messiah Son of Joseph) because our patriarch Yosef suffered injustice in order to save his family and others from famine. The *Talmud* also says that the second Psalm, in which God describes his Son, refers to that Messiah. The sages cite the prophet Zechariah (12:10), and agree that when *Mashiach* Ben-David (Messiah Son of David), the conquering Messianic king, comes to earth, Israel will recognize him by the pierce-marks on his body.

The idea of Messiah suffering on earth, and then returning in power, is not a non-Jewish contrivance superimposed onto Jewish texts. Some have alleged that one can only be "duped" into believing that Yeshua is the Messiah if one is talmudically unlearned. This talmudic text (Sukkah 52a) alone makes that assertion untrue. Thus, Messianic and talmudic Judaism part company on one point only: Messianics believe the prophets show that this Messiah had to come before the destruction of the Second Temple (Dan. 9:24–27), and therefore had to be Yeshua. Talmudic Judaism believes that the Messiah is yet to come, and therefore cannot be Yeshua.

As Messianic Jews, we have confidence in the one in whom we have believed (2 Tim. 1:12), and we look forward to the day when all our people will know him, too. Truly, in that day, "ADONAI will be the only one, and his name will be the only name" (Zech. 14:9).

Today I Will

. . . cultivate my inner life before God as if Messiah will return this very night (Matt. 25:1–13).

June 19, 1999 (38)
July 8, 2000 (38)
June 26, 2001
June 15, 2002 (38)
July 5, 2003 (38)
June 24, 2004

Biblical
On this day, Ezekiel received visions of God (Ezek. 1:1).

Prayer Focus

BC

TAMMUZ

6

תמוז

June 20, 1999
July 9, 2000
June 27, 2001
June 16, 2002
July 6, 2003
June 25, 2004

I would rather stand at the threshold of the house of my God than dwell in the tents of wickedness (Ps. 84:11 NASB).

Many Jewish *chatunot* (marriages) are celebrated at this time of year. The one person no one wants to be around is the *aveyl beyn chatanim* ("mourner among bridegrooms," the wet blanket). The opposite is a *lirkod beshtey chatunot* (one who likes "to dance simultaneously at two weddings," a joyful person). In family and congregational settings there are wet blanket believers and joyful believers. Messiah prefers that we be full of joy. How can we be?

In the above Scripture, *bacharti* ("I would rather") is best translated "I choose." Joyful believers choose the place of God's dwelling. David chose to dwell where God dwelt. Abraham did, too.

Let us also choose to live in the place where the Lord dwells rather than in "the tents of wickedness." There we will find joy enough to dance at two weddings!

Prayer Focus

Today I Will

. . . spend time in the courts of the Lord, who is the source of my joy.

JR

Obey your leaders (Heb. 13:17).

Liberty is a value embraced by many people—liberty from the restrictive social and moral codes of the past; liberty from grades in school; liberty from the consequences of extra-marital sexual relations, liberty from work and from want; liberty from authorities and accountability.

Liberty and freedom are attractive words. However, the meaning of liberty and freedom are used quite differently in the biblical context than they are used today. Both the secularist libertine and the committed follower of Yeshua seek a position where our desires are fulfilled and where we can experience spontaneous action. However, the content of that action is quite different.

The libertine secularist seeks freedom from all restrictions. The *talmid* (disciple) of Yeshua seeks to be so transformed by the *Ruach HaKodesh* (Holy Spirit) that conformity to *Torah* is the desire of his heart. What he automatically desires is what God desires. This is true liberty. "Bondage" is to be kept from serving God according to his *Torah.*

Let us be *free* to obey the Lord, and let us encourage others to do the same.

Today I Will

. . . run in the path of God's *mitzvot* (commands), for he has set my heart free.

TAMMUZ

7

תמוז

June 21, 1999
July 10, 2000
June 28, 2001
June 17, 2002
July 7, 2003
June 26, 2004 (39)

Prayer Focus

DJ

TAMMUZ

8

תמוז

June 22, 1999
July 11, 2000
June 29, 2001
June 18, 2002
July 8, 2003
June 27, 2004

Your word is a lamp for my foot and light on my path (Ps. 119:105).

Chazak, chazak, venitchazeyk! (Be strong, be strong, and we will be strengthened!) This is recited by the congregation after each book of the *Torah* is completed in *shul* (synagogue).

Being strong in the Messiah involves receiving his strength, his encouragement, his blessing. The word "blessing" comes from the root word *barakh*, which refers to a situation where the blesser imparts something to the one to be blessed. As Messianic Jews, we must always ask ourselves, "Are we blessing others out of the great supply of all we have received from Messiah?"

One way in which we are called to be a blessing is to be a source of light in the world—a beacon of encouragement and strength to those around us. The source for this light is revealed in the passage above. The source of our light is the Word of God.

In this psalm the word for lamp is *neyr*, meaning "a lesser light such as a candle glistening." The word for light, *or*, means "light of day." The word for path, *nativ*, conveys the idea of moving along a course.

This generation is desperate for spiritual direction, a source of light, of strength, of encouragement. Let us consider how we can bless them with the message of God's Word.

Prayer Focus

Today I Will

. . . be strong through the Messiah's light and gain his *berakhah* (blessing), so that I can be a blessing to others.

JR

You make me know the path of life (Ps. 16:11).

Lechayyim! Have you ever considered the meaning of this blessing? *Chayyim* means "life" and *le* means "to." So *lechayyim* means "to life!" It's amazing that this would be the blessing of our people, for no other people has been so persecuted and crushed. No other people has known so thoroughly the meaning of death, and yet the miracle is . . . we live, for God chose us to be his witness.

We must learn the blessing of being a people "to life." It's not enough for us to just be "of life." We must be *lechayyim*—"to life." We must always choose those things that are "to life," and reject those things that are not "to life." Things like bitterness, self-pity, lust, hopelessness, unforgiveness, and selfishness are not *lechayyim*; they're not "to life," but "to death." Also, coldness and fear, not loving your wife or husband, worldliness, possessiveness, greed, pride, gossip, and negative words are all "to death."

But we are called to be *lechayyim*! So we must choose to follow only what is "to life." Celebrate the life of God and everything related to it. God is the God of life and his people are a people of life. Live a life that says in word, deed and spirit, "To life! To life! *Lechayyim*!"

Today I Will

. . . choose the way of life over the way of death.

TAMMUZ

9

תמוז

June 23, 1999
July 12, 2000
June 30, 2001 (39)
June 19, 2002
July 9, 2003
June 28, 2004

Biblical
On this day, Nebuchadnezzar broke through the wall of Jerusalem at the height of famine (Jer. 39:2; 52:6).

Prayer Focus

JC

June 24, 1999
July 13, 2000
July 1, 2001
June 20, 2002
July 10, 2003
June 29, 2004

Prayer Focus

God saw everything that he had made, and indeed it was very good (Gen. 1:31).

We Jews are creation-oriented. We say a blessing over even seemingly little things: *Barukh atah* A*DONAI*, *Eloheynu, melekh ha'olam, borey peri hagafen.* (Blessed are you, O LORD, our God, king of the universe, who creates the fruit of the vine.) Some believers forget to celebrate the fact that our God is the great Creator. Scary end-times scenarios propel some to overemphasize God as the Redeemer of a sick society and neglect to exalt his role as Creator of the world.

Don't get stuck recounting only the world's ills and the devil's plans. Look around you! Look at the magnificent sky which our King set in place. Look at the trees whose branches reach to the heavens in the posture of prayer and praise. Gaze into the faces of children and read the stories of bunny-love in their eyes. Call to mind the magnificent people in your congregation—all different, all gifted, all amazing human beings.

See in your mind's eye the infant Yeshua. If ever our God showed his stamp of approval on the physical world, it can be known through reflection on the wonder of the Incarnation. So high did our King value this world that he sent his Son to share in its physical reality.

Today, as you check off the many activities listed on your to-do list, look around . . . just look around. See God's majesty in what he has made, and be glad.

Today I Will

. . . make it a point to be aware of God's *kavod*, revealed in his wonderful creation.

RN

The Son of Man is Lord even of *Shabbat* (Mark 2:28).

TAMMUZ

11

תמוז

June 25, 1999
July 14, 2000
July 2, 2001
June 21, 2002
July 11, 2003
June 30, 2004

Yeshua's conflict with the *Perushim* (Pharisees) came over the definition of what constitutes work on the *Shabbat* (Sabbath). His disciples were plucking ears of grain to eat on *Shabbat,* clearly legal according to the *Torah* (Deut. 23:25). According to the Scripture, "work" would have been putting the sickle into the harvest and gathering it. The *Perushim,* however, had added additional laws, including those that forbade the plucking and chafing of grain on *Shabbat.* These laws—which constituted a "fence" around the *Torah*—were added to prevent the Hebrew people from violating God's *mitzvot* (commandments). Perhaps because of this, the *Perushim* had fallen into the trap of following the letter of the *Torah* and missing its spirit. Yeshua challenged their interpretation of God's *mitzvot,* saying, "*Shabbat* was made for mankind, not mankind for *Shabbat*" (Mark 2:27). Just as God stands above his laws and they are subject to him, so the law of *Shabbat* was subject to Yeshua's judgment.

As the Messiah, Yeshua is the fulfillment of the *Torah* and the Prophets, including the *Shabbat.* How does Yeshua enrich the meaning of *Shabbat*? *Shabbat* means "rest," and truly Yeshua's atonement is the only way that God's rest can enter into our hearts and lives. The Messiah said, "Come to me, all of you who are struggling and are burdened, and I will give you rest. . . . you will find rest for your souls" (Matt. 11:28–29). How do we enter the Messiah's rest? It begins by coming to him, totally yielding ourselves to him in every area of our lives.

Let us seek to serve God in all we do and to find God's will in all matters. When we do this, Yeshua promises that we will find a true *Shabbat* for our souls.

Prayer Focus

Today I Will

. . . yield every area of my life to you, Lord, that I may come into the *Shabbat* rest of the Messiah (Heb. 4:1–11).

DC

June 26, 1999
(39, 40)
July 15, 2000
(39, 40)
July 3, 2001
June 22, 2002
(39, 40)
July 12, 2003
(39, 40)
July 1, 2004

Prayer Focus

God will fill every need of yours according to his glorious wealth (Phil. 4:19).

There they are, every *Shabbat* (Sabbath). After we bless the wine at our *Shabbat* dinner, we next turn to bless the two *challot* (braided loaves of egg bread). These beautifully twisted loaves are not only delicious, they remind us of an important truth. During our people's wanderings in the wilderness, God promised to provide daily *manna* during the six work days. However, in order for his people to truly rest on the *Shabbat*, God said he would provide a double-portion on Friday so that they would not have to worry about their own sustenance on *Shabbat* (Exod. 16:22–24).

What a wonderful reminder that double-portion was, encouraging our people to truly trust in God's provision. As we bless the two *challot*, God would have us expand the same truth. Sometimes we are tempted to meet our own needs by endlessly seeking our own "kingdom." God, through the Messiah Yeshua, still wants us to cease from our labors and trust in his provision for all our needs.

Our weekly *Shabbat* is a tremendous practical way to show our trust in the Lord. As we bless the two *challot* every week, may we be reminded that it is a good "*challah*-day" because of God's promises to those who walk with him.

Today I Will

. . . apply the meaning of the two *challot* in my life by trusting that God, through Yeshua, will provide all that I need.

BK

He went to Sh'khem, where a man found him wandering around in the countryside (Gen. 37:14–15).

I recently read a story wherein the author masterfully wove together many seemingly unconnected episodes in the lives of numerous people. By the end of the book, it was evident that all the pieces had been necessary and worked together. Many of the characters never met nor even knew of the others who had dramatically impacted their lives. If this human writer could put together such a cohesive conclusion from such far-flung facts, I thought, how much more is the Author of life able to cause all things to work together for the good of those who love him!

Some have speculated on the identity of the man who found Joseph wandering in the fields and who then told him where to find his brothers. The focus in today's Scripture passage, as in the rest of the story of Joseph, is on the providentially arranged encounters that brought him from shepherding in the valley of Hebron to exaltation in Egypt—where all the nations of the region came to him for food. God's nature has not changed over the last 3700 years. Whether or not all the connections are obvious to us, he is involved in orchestrating the course of the universe, including the destiny of nations and even the smallest details of our lives.

Today I Will

. . . see my life as an exquisitely written story, continually flowing from the pen of an unparalleled author. I will not fret or fear when there are unexpected twists and turns in the plot, but confidently continue on, knowing there is a glorious ending.

June 27, 1999
July 16, 2000
July 4, 2001
June 23, 2002
July 13, 2003
July 2, 2004

Prayer Focus

MM

June 28, 1999
July 17, 2000
July 5, 2001
June 24, 2002
July 14, 2003
July 3, 2004 (40)

Whoever acknowledges me in the presence of others I will also acknowledge in the presence of my Father in heaven (Matt. 10:32).

Yeshua has given us the responsibility of confessing him before others. However, some of us treat our faith in Yeshua as though it were a crime, and our confession is forced out of us rather than joyfully proclaimed.

I once led a group of Messianic Jewish college students on a trip to Israel. A number of the students were new believers, so I wanted to keep our faith in Yeshua quiet, lest they be treated harshly and become discouraged. I was the first one to be questioned by the security officers of El Al (the Israeli airline) . Slowly but surely his questions forced me to declare what I didn't want to say: "We are Jews who believe in Jesus." The man then looked out over the sea of people waiting to pass through security and yelled in a loud voice, "How many of you are from the Jews for Jesus group?" Sixteen college students sheepishly raised their hands. As a result, the team had numerous chances to share their faith, not only with the security guards, but with many of the passengers on the plane.

Jewish believers often struggle with openly confessing their faith to fellow Jews and even to their own family members. Although the discomfort and pain that come with confessing Yeshua can be deep, the reward of confessing him outweighs it all. Our confession can lead our family or friends to come to know the Messiah. It also leads to his advocacy for us. If we confess him, he will confess us.

Prayer Focus

Today I Will

. . . resolve to be open about my faith in Yeshua the Messiah. I will take steps to make my faith known to any of my family or friends who don't yet know about my belief in Yeshua.

DB

Messiah executed on a stake as a criminal! To Jews this is an obstacle, and to Greeks it is nonsense (1 Cor. 1:23).

For the Jewish mind, the *tzlav* (cross) has become a symbol of the Church's contempt for the Jewish people. But long before that happened, Rabbi Sha'ul (Saul; i.e., Paul) said that the *tzlav* is an obstacle for Jews and nonsense for Greeks (i.e., Gentiles). Sha'ul was right. It's an absurd idea to everyone—Jews as well as Gentiles—that the Son of God should die on a *tzlav*. To die a hero, admired by everybody, is one thing, but to die hanging on a tree in dishonor and agony is a different matter.

A piece of third-century graffiti on the Palatine Hill in Rome shows a young man who is looking at a *tzlav* upon which hangs a man whose head has been substituted with the head of a donkey. Underneath is scrawled the words, "Alexamenos worships his God." Someone who knew this Alexamenos was ridiculing his faith in the crucified and suffering Messiah. At the same place, another inscription in a different handwriting says, "Alexamenos is faithful."

Whether the response is ridicule or encouragement, we have been called to proclaim Messiah's crucifixion, the atoning sacrifice for sin. Let us do it with boldness and love.

Today I Will

. . . contemplate the *tzlav* of Yeshua and what he suffered for me, that I may be strong enough to suffer for his sake. KK

June 29, 1999
July 18, 2000
July 6, 2001
June 25, 2002
July 15, 2003
July 4, 2004

Prayer Focus

June 30, 1999
July 19, 2000
July 7, 2001 (40)
June 26, 2002
July 16, 2003
July 5, 2004

Avraham, when he was put to the test, offered up Yitzchak as a sacrifice (Heb. 11:17).

Are you ready for the test of God? Testing will come. God tests all his children. Testing forges character and makes plain one's spiritual strength. God will test you in order to prove your character.

Avraham (Abraham) faced a terrifying test of faith. He responded to God's test by obediently offering up his son Yitzchak (Isaac). Moved by the sole desire to please him, Avraham trusted God. We call this motivation the holy desire for *kiddush HaShem* (sanctifying God's Name). Avraham faced the heat with a holy desire to sanctify, or set apart, his life for the glory of God!

Now, consider the process of purifying steel. Temperatures of 3500 degrees Fahrenheit are applied to iron ore. Oxygen from the molten metal reacts with unwanted elements such as silicon, phosphorus, sulfur, and excess carbon to form slag, an impurity, which is removed.

At the *akeydah* (binding) of Isaac, Avraham surrendered his most prized possession. In doing so, his character was tested and made pure. Avraham learned in a new way that Yitzchak belonged solely to God.

To forge character, God will test us and remove our impurities. During times of testing, do not take your eyes off him. Remember that your purity will always remain. You will shine, purified by the refiner's fire.

Prayer Focus

Today I Will

. . . face the heat in my life with a desire to shine brightly for God.

JEF

A spring will be opened up for the house of David . . . to cleanse them from sin and impurity (Zech. 13:1).

Moshe (Moses) left his community for forty days and forty nights to go on a divinely supported journey. He had no food and no water. He finally ascended Mount Sinai, where he communed with God and received the Ten Commandments, the foundation of the Law.

Upon his return, he saw the Israelites frolicking and worshiping the golden calf. He rebuked them and smashed the Ten Commandments in his anger. Then he ascended the mountain a second time, when he once again received the commandments from God. Upon Moshe's return he found a different scene. The people readily received him and assented to do all that he said. By receiving Moshe, they received God.

God sent Yeshua, who, like Moshe, descended the "mountain" to deliver the "Word of the Lord" to his people. However, the first descent brought widespread rejection. Israel as a nation failed to embrace him. Our people are frolicking and worshiping idols, but have not accepted God's sent one, Yeshua. Like Moshe, Yeshua will once again descend for his people. It is this second time that they will look to him and "mourn for him" (Zech. 12:10). They will repent and in that day "a spring will be opened up" for our people "to cleanse them from sin and impurity" (Zech. 13:1). "It is in this way that all Isra'el will be saved" (Rom. 11:26).

Today I Will

. . . seek to obey Yeshua the first time he comes for me.

TAMMUZ

17

תמוז

July 1, 1999 (מ)
July 20, 2000 (מ)
July 8, 2001 (מ)
June 27, 2002 (מ)
July 17, 2003 (מ)
July 6, 2004 (מ)

Traditional
Shiv'ah Asar BeTammuz (the 17th of Tammuz)
See Zech. 8:19

Prayer Focus

EK

TAMMUZ

18

תמוז

July 2, 1999
July 21, 2000
July 9, 2001
June 28, 2002
July 18, 2003
July 7, 2004

Traditional
Beyn HaMetzarim
(Between the Straits)
From Tammuz 18–
Av 8

Prayer Focus

You are a letter from the Messiah . . . written not with ink but by the Spirit of the living God (2 Cor. 3:3).

Rabbi Daniel Zion was the chief rabbi of the Bulgarian Jewish community for over 23 years. During the years of World War II, he was one of my main role models and a man very dear to me.

One day Rabbi Zion was looking at the sunrise while praying, and Yeshua appeared to him in a vision. After that, Rabbi Daniel's faith in Yeshua became a well-known "secret" in the Jewish community of Bulgaria. His position was so honored and his services so highly esteemed, however, that no one would openly criticize the rabbi. The rabbi remained well within the boundaries of the Jewish community in Bulgaria and did not stop living as an Orthodox Jew.

In 1943, the government of Bulgaria made a decision, under German pressure, to send all Bulgarian Jews to the death camps in Poland and Germany. But due to Rabbi Zion's influence with King Boris II, 86 percent of Bulgaria's 50,000 Jews were saved. When Nazi Germany occupied Bulgaria, Rabbi Zion, as the spiritual leader of the Jewish community, became the object of persecution and ridicule. He was publicly flogged in front of the Great Synagogue of Sofia.

In 1949, the rabbi immigrated to Israel with his community and lived the rest of his life as the chief rabbi of Bulgarian Jews, though everyone knew that he believed in Yeshua. Rabbi Daniel wrote hundreds of songs that we still use to this day in our Messianic congregation in Jerusalem.

Rabbi Zion was truly a "letter from the Messiah."

Today I Will

. . . consider how I can be a letter to my people from within the Jewish community.

JS

Adonai forbid that I should do such a thing to my lord, Adonai's anointed (1 Sam. 24:7).

Zol Gott op-hiten! ("May God prevent it!") is a Yiddish phrase often heard among older Jewish people. It expresses the desire for good and not evil and implies an awareness that God must, at times, intervene to save us from ourselves.

In his book *Eichmann in My Hands*, Peter Z. Malign (who played a key role in the capture of Nazi war criminal Adolf Eichmann) writes, "Evil does not exist in isolation. It is a product of amorality by consensus. Could it happen again?" Our reply, of course, is *zol Gott op-hiten*! But we can't just say it; we have a responsibility to do something about it.

In the above Scripture, David knew something. He knew that God was going to hold him to the highest standard of personal holiness and to the truth. No amount of clever argument can cover up what is true.

Yeshua continually challenges the motives of people's hearts. His standard is uncompromising. With him, there is no such thing as a little white lie, no such thing as a little sin, just because everyone is doing it.

The rabbis of old noted that the Hebrew alphabet starts with the letter *alef* (א). In the middle of the alphabet is the letter *mem* (מ), and the last letter is *tav* (ת). Together, the three letters form the Hebrew word *emet* (truth). Truth is always the essence of the Jewish faith.

Today I Will

. . . refuse to compromise Yeshua's standard of truth and righteousness.

July 3, 1999 (41/I)
July 22, 2000 (41/I)
July 10, 2001
June 29, 2002 (41/I)
July 19, 2003 (41/I)
July 8, 2004

Prayer Focus

JR

TAMMUZ

20

תמוז

July 4, 1999
July 23, 2000
July 11, 2001
June 30, 2002
July 20, 2003
July 9, 2004

Prayer Focus

Just as a deer longs for running streams, God, I long for you (Ps. 42:1[2]).

When my husband was in seminary, he received a rather odd homework assignment: he was to spend twenty minutes a day with his wife, just talking. Every single day. No exceptions.

I can't tell you how good that was for our marriage. After the course was over, we continued to do that exercise daily because we enjoyed the closeness we had developed. However, as the demands of life and the pressures of work increased, little by little, we skipped a day here, a day there; pretty soon, we stopped having our talks.

As his job demanded that he travel more and more, our time together eroded even further. Our relationship became strained. Yes, we still loved each other. Yes, we were still committed to each other. But an entire dimension of our relationship—the emotional closeness—went by the wayside. It was our loss. It took some time, but we learned our lesson and are now protecting that special time together at all costs.

Our relationship with God is no different. We can be committed to him, we can love him, but if we don't take that twenty minutes a day talking with him, relating to him, and just being together, a whole beautiful facet of our relationship will atrophy. The loss will be ours.

Today I Will

. . . set side twenty minutes to spend with the Lord, just talking with him, listening, and enjoying our closeness.

Go and tell his *talmidim* [disciples], especially Kefa, that he [Yeshua] is going to the Galil ahead of you (Mark 16:7).

There is a story of two men standing outside *shul* (synagogue). One of the men is reviling a man named Rubenstein incessantly. The other man eventually asks, "*Nu*? [So?] How do you know so much about Rubenstein?" The reviler replies, "Oh, him? We've been best friends for years!"

It is an ironic truism that those closest to us are best acquainted with our weaknesses. This was never more true than in regard to Kefa's (Peter's) relationship with Yeshua. Kefa, who had promised he would never abandon Yeshua, denied three times that he ever knew him. After Yeshua's execution, Kefa was most likely off by himself, drowning in anguish and humiliation. Then came God's message to the three women who came to anoint Yeshua's dead body with spices: "Go and tell his *talmidim*, especially Kefa." There is such grace in the words "especially Kefa." News of the resurrection was probably not half so sweet to Kefa's ears as was God's open embrace.

Kefa was no Yehudah (Judas). Kefa had simply fallen prey to his own humanity, and that is not a crime for which God withdraws his grace. Elsewhere, Scripture tells us, "God does not take away life, but plans ways so that the banished one may not be cast out from him" (2 Sam. 14:14 NASB). So then, even as we stumble, God is furnishing the means for us to rise again (Prov. 24:16). Bless his merciful Name.

Today I Will

. . . not let my sins distract me from God's faithfulness to me, even in my weakest moments (2 Tim. 2:13).

TAMMUZ

21

תמוז

July 5, 1999
July 24, 2000
July 12, 2001
July 1, 2002
July 21, 2003
July 10, 2004 (41/I)

Prayer Focus

BC

TAMMUZ

22

תמוז

July 6, 1999
July 25, 2000
July 13, 2001
July 2, 2002
July 22, 2003
July 11, 2004

Prayer Focus

Mashiach will be cut off and have nothing. The people of a prince yet to come will destroy the city and the sanctuary (Dan. 9:26).

The *Talmud* records some peculiar changes that occurred in the Temple about 40 years before its destruction. The lot for the goat to be sacrificed on *Yom Kippur* ceased to come up on the right hand of the *Cohen HaGadol* (High Priest) as it had previously. The crimson cloth put out on *Yom Kippur* would not turn white as it had before. The western light ceased to burn. Finally, the doors of the Temple no longer opened of themselves.

The Temple was destroyed in 70 C.E. after about three years of being under siege by the Romans. Jerusalem was leveled. That splendid city which housed the *Shekhinah* (Glory of God) ceased to be the center of Jewish life.

What was the cause of such destruction? Some rabbinic sources explain the reason for the fall of Jerusalem as the sin of "hate without a cause." Although the rabbis do not explain this in more detail, those who embrace this theory are close to the truth.

The prophet Daniel spoke of a Messiah who would come and be killed as a sacrifice; then the city and the Temple would be destroyed. Yeshua was the *Mashiach* (Anointed One, Messiah). He came to give us eternal life with him. Nonetheless, he was hated without a cause and was killed about 40 years before the destruction of the Temple. He who was sinless became our atonement because of his love for those who hated him.

Today I Will

. . . seek to explain the love of Messiah to those who hate him.

EK

Let every person be quick to listen but slow to speak, slow to get angry (James 1:19).

R*eden iz gut, shvaigen noch besser* is Yiddish for "Speech is good, silence is even better." In the above Scripture, the Greek word for angry, *orgay*, means "anger with the connotation of vengeance."

How many times we wish to punish others with our words and thoughts! The Scripture warns us to be "quick to listen." In the context of chapter 1 and chapter 3, where arguments of a violent nature are spoken against, this warning extends to avoiding the judgments we make by not abiding in "God's Word" (James 1:18).

The Scripture tells us to be "slow to speak," especially regarding judgments when we are not fully aware of the truth of a matter.

Let us heed Ya'akov's (James's) warning and remember, "The tongue has power over life and death; those who indulge it must eat its fruit" (Prov. 18:21).

Today I Will

. . . guard my tongue from quick responses and judgments that do not conform to the Word of truth.

TAMMUZ

23

תמוז

July 7, 1999
July 26, 2000
July 14, 2001 (41/I)*
July 3, 2002
July 23, 2003
July 12, 2004

Prayer Focus

JR

July 8, 1999
July 27, 2000
July 15, 2001
July 4, 2002
July 24, 2003
July 13, 2004

He will return and gather you from all the peoples to which *Adonai* your God scattered you (Deut. 30:3).

There has been an ongoing tension in the Messianic movement for many years over the issue of *aliyah* (returning to Israel). Some have been tirelessly devoted to calling and shepherding our people back to the Land. They believe, according to numerous Scriptures such as Ezekiel 37, that as a result of the Jewish people's return to the Land, the Lord will pour out his *Ruach* (Spirit) upon them and they will be saved. Others, deeply committed to bringing the gospel to our people, have argued that it makes no difference where Jewish people die. If they die without Messiah, they are eternally separated from God.

While working in Russia, I have become convinced that both of these views contain elements of truth. The restoration of the Jewish people is *both* spiritual and physical. Just as salvation involves both soul and body, the restoration of the Jewish people includes both the spiritual restoration of our people to God through Messiah and their physical restoration to the Land.

Messianic Jews must understand and be committed to this idea of dual restoration. I think that very soon anti-Semitism will grow in Russia and the doors to Israel will slam shut. Perhaps millions of Jews will be left behind. The immense task of getting them back to Israel may fall heavily upon us. Are you prepared to help?

Prayer Focus

Today I Will

. . . pray, "Lord, I commit myself to your complete plan of restoration for the Jewish people. I give myself to the dual task of bringing your people back spiritually through Yeshua and back physically to the Land of Promise."

JB

Even though he was the Son, he learned obedience through his sufferings (Heb. 5:8).

The fear of pain has weakened Western civilization and made it soft on morality and on commitment to causes. Pain is something that needs to be mastered by the individual, just like eating a hot chile pepper.

July 9, 1999
July 28, 2000
July 16, 2001
July 5, 2002
July 25, 2003
July 14, 2004

I remember my daughter going to a shop on Ben-Yehudah Street in Jerusalem to have her ears pierced. She knew that she would experience some pain. But she was willing to submit to this pain because she considered it worthwhile. Women become pregnant, fully aware that there will be pain involved as the child is born. Men in Israel enter the army, and even volunteer for the best fighting units, with the full knowledge that training is painful. Athletes enter competition realizing that, without pain, there is no victory.

Common to all of these examples is the fact that pain is often a means to gain. The Messiah suffered pain on the *tzlav* (cross) so that we might have everlasting life. We need to know that even when the pain is not by our own choice, God can use it for good if we allow him. Overcoming pain is a means to learning more about ourselves and about the Lord.

Prayer Focus

Today I Will

. . . remember that without pain there is no gain, even in the things of God.

JS

TAMMUZ

26

תמוז

July 10, 1999
(42, 43/J)*
July 29, 2000
(42, 43/J)*
July 17, 2001
July 6, 2002
(42, 43/J)*
July 26, 2003
(42, 43/J)*
July 15, 2004

Prayer Focus

Rabbi, how often can my brother sin against me and I have to forgive him? (Matt. 18:21–22)

There are two types of forgiveness taught in the Scriptures. Transactional forgiveness is intended to restore the relationship between the one who has seriously sinned and the one who has been wronged. The repentant one says, "I was wrong, will you forgive me?" He desires to make restitution and the relationship can be restored. This is the right way to deal with a relationship where wrong has been committed. Without repentance in such a situation, it would be inappropriate to overlook evil and maintain ongoing fellowship as if nothing happened.

Non-transactional forgiveness is the type reflected in the prayer of Yeshua on the *tzlav* (cross): "Father, forgive them; for they don't understand what they are doing" (Luke 23:34). When there is no possibility for an ongoing relationship, this type of forgiveness can free us from bitterness and the desire for revenge. This is especially helpful when the one who has wronged us is unreachable, even dead. We can practice this type of healing forgiveness as we identify with our crucified and risen Lord, God's *Mashiach* (Messiah).

Today I Will

. . . walk in forgiveness according to the teaching of God's Word.

DJ

It is easier for a camel to pass through a needle's eye than for a rich man to enter the Kingdom of God" (Matt. 19.23–24).

The "needle's eye" was not a small gate in Jerusalem's walls, as many teach. No such gate by that name existed, and this interpretation first appeared during the Middle Ages. It is far more likely that Yeshua was using a well-known teaching technique to make his point. He chose for his image the largest animal known in the Land of Israel (the camel) and the smallest opening in any man-made object of that time (the needle). By combining them, he demonstrated that "humanly, this is impossible" (Matt. 19:26).

But he may have also been referring to a *Midrash* (traditional commentary). In the *Midrash* on Song of Solomon we find this interesting parallel: Rabbi Jassa said, "The Holy One, blessed be He, said to Israel: 'My sons, present to me an opening of repentance no bigger than the eye of a needle, and I will widen it into openings through which wagons and carriages can pass'" (*Midrash* on the Song 5:2).

According to the *Midrash*, "repentance" is the meaning of the needle's eye. Without it, we cannot see the Kingdom of God nor continue to enjoy its blessings. Our part is very small, and in fact we are not even able to repent as we should. But if we will turn to God in repentance, he is there to broaden the way for us, no matter what our situation may be.

TAMMUZ

27

תמוז

July 11, 1999
July 30, 2000
July 18, 2001
July 7, 2002
July 27, 2003
July 16, 2004

Prayer Focus

Today I Will

. . . ask the Lord to help me overcome those "impossible" sins, which I cannot defeat with my own strength.

RP

TAMMUZ

28

תמוז

July 12, 1999
July 31, 2000
July 19, 2001
July 8, 2002
July 28, 2003
July 17, 2004
(42, 43/J)*

Prayer Focus

We thank you, *ADONAI*, God of heaven's armies, the One who is and was, that you have . . . begun to rule (Rev. 11:17).

Almost two thousand years lie between us and the first Jews who confessed Yeshua as Messiah, but on God's timeline we stand at the same point as they did. The decisive acts of salvation through Yeshua belong to the past, and the return of Yeshua belongs to the future—for them as well as us.

Meanwhile, like first-century Messianic Jews, we have to listen to scoffing words, such as, "Where is this promised 'coming' of his?" (2 Pet. 3:4) The response of the first believers was not to give a detailed timetable for the return of Yeshua, but to repeat what they had heard from Messiah himself, "You too, be ready! For the Son of Man will come when you are not expecting him" (Luke 12:40).

The decisive battles of World War II were fought after the allied forces had invaded Normandy in June, 1944. The victory had been won, but peace proper did not come until the spring of 1945.

Yeshua has won the decisive battle over sin, death and the Adversary. Let us walk in spiritual victory and be ever watchful for his peace-bringing return.

Today I Will

. . . live my life as if Messiah were crucified yesterday, risen today and returning tomorrow.

KK

I could wish myself actually under God's curse and separated from the Messiah, if it would help my brothers (Rom. 9:3).

July 13, 1999
Aug. 1, 2000
July 20, 2001
July 9, 2002
July 29, 2003
July 18, 2004

Whenever I read Rom. 9:3, I am astounded by the level of dedication it indicates that Rabbi Sha'ul (Saul; i.e., Paul) had towards the salvation of his own people.

Sha'ul knew of the great riches inherent in the love of God, and that nothing, not even famine, persecution or sword, could separate him from it. He knew of the joys of heaven, as well as the realities of *Geyhinnom* (hell). Despite all this, he was willing to be cut off from eternity with the Lord, if it meant that other Jewish people would be saved.

What compassion he had, especially when we consider that it was some of his own brothers who were causing Sha'ul his greatest miseries and problems. They rejected, ostracized, persecuted and beat him. They incited riots against him, even stoning him and leaving him for dead. Still, he remained so committed to their salvation that he was willing to sacrifice his own heavenly reward.

Many Jewish believers have felt the pain of rejection and humiliation when we have told our family and friends that we had accepted Yeshua. Despite this, God is calling us to love them, forgive them, and share with them the good news. By the power of the *Ruach HaKodesh* (Holy Spirit), we can!

Prayer Focus

Today I Will

. . . ask the Lord to remove any bitterness or rejection from me so I can love my own people with his love, and see them as he does.

JB

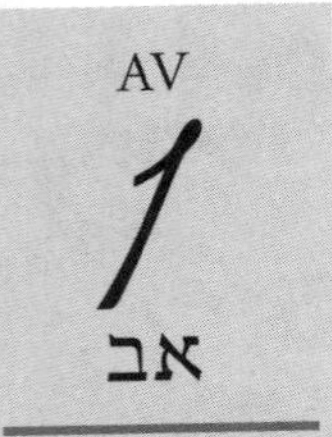

July 14, 1999
Aug. 2, 2000
July 21, 2001
(42, 43/J, C)
July 10, 2002
July 30, 2003
July 19, 2004

Biblical
Rosh Chodesh
(the New Moon)

On this day, Aaron died on Mount Hor (Num. 33:38); Ezra arrived in Jerusalem (Ezra 7:9).

Traditional
The first nine days of Av are set apart as a time of mourning for the destruction of Jerusalem and the Temple.

Prayer Focus

MM

Aharon's staff . . . had sprouted not only buds but flowers and ripe almonds as well (Num. 17:23).

During the years that I lived on a farm, I put up a number of fences. Sometimes the wooden posts which we set into the ground were not sufficiently cured. After a few days in the damp soil, they would sprout small branches with leaves. Though these little sprouts lasted only about a week, it was still a sight to see. How much more dramatic was the sprouting of Aharon's (Aaron's) rod! After only one night sitting on *dry* ground, it produced an entire season's cycle of growth. What a picture of resurrection!

Resurrection is God's mark of authenticity and confirmation. Of the twelve rods that were put before the ark of the covenant, only Aharon's brought forth new life, signifying God's choice of his family for the priesthood. In Ezekiel 37, the Lord declares that his choice of Israel would also be dramatically clear when Israel would be raised up from death and restored both physically and spiritually. Finally, *Mashiach* (Messiah) himself was "powerfully demonstrated to be Son of God spiritually, set apart by his having been resurrected from the dead" (Rom. 1:4). Glory be to the living God who has unimaginable power to bring forth life from the dead!

Today I Will

. . . count my old nature dead that I might walk in the power of Yeshua's resurrection life.

Openly acknowledge your sins to one another, and pray for each other, so that you may be healed (James 5:16).

The *Talmud* says, "Great is repentance, for it brings healing to the world." Ya'akov (James) appears to be dealing with something more modest—healing for individuals—but he agrees that repentance is essential. When we confess our sins, we accept God's verdict on them and renounce them. We assume responsibility for them. In God's plan, this action—repentance—prepares the way for healing. David said, "When I kept silent, my bones wasted away because of my groaning all day long. . . . When I acknowledged my sin to you, when I stopped concealing my guilt, and said, 'I will confess my offenses to ADONAI'; *then* you forgave the guilt of my sin" (Ps. 32:3, 5).

Many, of course, are ill without harboring unconfessed sin, but modern medicine has recognized the connection between emotional and physical wholeness. Likewise, the Scriptures speak of healing as physical, emotional, and spiritual. Confession restores us to inner wholeness, which is often reflected in outward wholeness.

What about "healing to the world"—of which the *Talmud* speaks? When we confess corporately, as Daniel did (Dan. 9:4–19), acknowledging not only our own sins, but also those of our people, we open the door for healing on a corporate scale. Such repentance is truly great!

Today I Will

. . . acknowledge not only my own sins, but also those of my people, and ask for God's forgiveness.

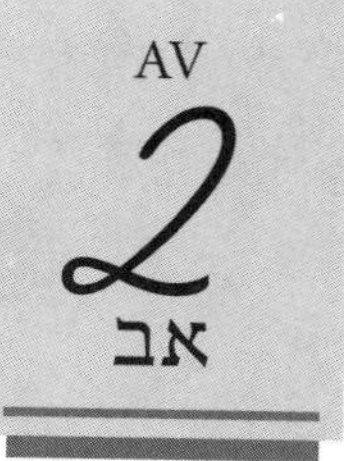

July 15, 1999
Aug. 3, 2000
July 22, 2001
July 11, 2002
July 31, 2003
July 20, 2004

Prayer Focus

RR

AV

3

אב

July 16, 1999
Aug. 4, 2000
July 23, 2001
July 12, 2002
Aug. 1, 2003
July 21, 2004

Prayer Focus

ES

Your sins have been forgiven (Luke 7:48).

How often do we take this simple statement of Yeshua's for granted? Have we placed ourselves comfortably out of reach, where we no longer respond personally when we hear these words from our Redeemer? Once while counseling someone who was heart-broken by his own sin and the mess he had made of his life, I reflected on my own condition. "How am I different?" I wondered.

The prophets of old proclaimed the central achievement of Messiah: "making an end of sin" (Dan. 9:24). God has promised, "I will forgive their wickednesses and remember their sins no more" (Jer. 31:34[33]). "By his knowing [pain and sacrifice], my righteous servant makes many righteous" (Isa. 53:11).

If we have forgotten the blessedness of being forgiven ("How blessed are those whose offense is forgiven, those whose sin is covered!" [Ps. 32:1]), we have drifted alarmingly off course. Our relationship with the Most High began with dramatic cleansing, atonement, and transformation from the darkness of our self-will to the light of his chosen path for us. We can only find peace in our own spirits and joy amidst the evil of the world by doing what the sin-forgiven woman did. She washed Yeshua's feet with tears of repentance and joy, anointing them with the fragrant oil of loving worship. Repenting of our sins will transform our lives every day.

Today I Will

. . . carry with me the above words of my master, who himself bore my sins. I will take deeply to heart that each of my many sins has been forgiven.

Tears may linger for the night, but with dawn come cries of joy (Ps. 30:5[6]).

July 17, 1999 (44)
Aug. 5, 2000 (44)
July 24, 2001
July 13, 2002 (44)
Aug. 2, 2003 (44)
July 22, 2004

One of the best-known traditions in the Jewish wedding ceremony is the breaking of a glass under the groom's heel at the end of the ceremony. The shattering sound is greeted with joyous shouts of "*Mazel Tov*!" (Congratulations!) There are several explanations for this ceremony, but the most common is that this act commemorates the destruction of the Temple.

The rabbis have taught that even at times of greatest joy, such as weddings, we should not forget to grieve over the destruction of the Temple. Such is the nature of life. Joy is often tempered with sadness, and the troubles we experience in this life often intrude upon the happy moments.

God wants us to share his eternal perspective. He wants the joy of his presence and his promises for the future to be real even during our moments of deepest sadness. The joys and the sorrows of this world are temporal. No matter what struggles and disappointments we may face, no matter what sadness we may endure, joy always comes with the dawn. In God we have eternal hope. A new day is dawning when he will wipe away all sorrow, sadness, and tears from our eyes.

Prayer Focus

Today I Will

. . . walk in the joy of the Lord and allow whatever sorrow I must face to be tempered by the promise of his future grace.

DB

AV

5

אב

July 18, 1999
Aug. 6, 2000
July 25, 2001
July 14, 2002
Aug. 3, 2003
July 23, 2004

Evening, morning and noon I complain and moan; but he hears my voice (Ps. 55:18).

It is significant that David cried out to the Lord three times a day. These times corresponded to the Temple services, when sacrifices were lifted up to God (Ps. 141:2; see also Pss. 5:3; 88:13; 92:2).

David is not the only righteous man mentioned in the Scriptures whose prayer times corresponded to the schedule of the Temple sacrifices. Daniel also followed this pattern: "On learning that the document had been signed, Dani'el went home. The windows of his upstairs room were open in the direction of Yerushalayim; and there he kneeled down three times a day and prayed, giving thanks before his God, just as he had been doing before" (Dan. 6:10[11]). Peter and John also followed this custom (Acts 3:1; see also Acts 10:9). Finally, the Gentile believer Cornelius set his prayer times to correspond to those of the Temple offerings (Acts 10:30).

How often do we stop what we are doing to devote ourselves to prayer? We can learn from our forefathers and make it our goal to pray in the evening, in the morning and at noon as they did. Thus, we will be obeying the command to "pray regularly" (1 Thess. 5:17).

Prayer Focus

Today I Will

. . . begin a lifestyle of praying three times a day.

DR

This brother of yours was dead but has come back to life—he was lost but has been found (Luke 15:32).

July 19, 1999
Aug. 7, 2000
July 26, 2001
July 15, 2002
Aug. 4, 2003
July 24, 2004 (44)

When the *Perushim* (Pharisees) and Scribes criticized Yeshua for spending time with "sinners and tax collectors," Yeshua told them a story about two types of *teshuvah* (repentance).

A father had two sons. The younger one wandered off but finally returned to his father, who joyfully prepared a great feast for the whole household. The older son, who had remained with his father all along, petulantly refused to participate. He was in his father's house but would not join the celebration.

The younger son experienced a "crisis of *teshuvah*"; he had to change direction completely in order to return to his father. The older son, on the other hand, required a "custom of *teshuvah*." Though he had remained with his father, he had turned away from him in heart. The older son resented his father's forgiveness of his brother and felt that his father owed him for all of his years of faithfulness.

When Yeshua told this story, he did not reveal the ending. The older son represented his critics, and the choice that lay before them was theirs alone. Would they repent, embrace their Father's grace, and enter his joy, or resent what they heard in Yeshua's message and remain without these blessings. The same choice confronts us and all who dwell in our Father's house. We may not require a "crisis of *teshuvah*." We must still follow the "custom of *teshuvah*" and return in heart to *Avinu* (our Father) daily.

Prayer Focus

Today I Will

. . . return to the Lord in my heart and receive his grace and forgiveness.

RR

AV

7

אב

July 20, 1999
Aug. 8, 2000
July 27, 2001
July 16, 2002
Aug. 5, 2003
July 25, 2004

Biblical
On this day, the Temple was set on fire (2 Kings 25:8–9).

Prayer Focus

The Messiah redeemed us from the curse pronounced in the *Torah* by becoming cursed on our behalf (Gal. 3:13).

This plain statement must not be watered down. The Messiah has become a curse for us. It is not enough that he died. There is the additional fact that he hung publicly as a dead man.

Messiah's death was painful and agonizing. With the blows inflicted, he suffered immeasurably. His death was not pretty. He underwent the penalty prescribed for covenant-breakers: "A curse on anyone who does not confirm the words of this *Torah* by putting them into practice" (Deut. 27:26). Though he never broke the *Torah* himself, still he became a curse, "because a person who has been hanged has been cursed by God" (Deut. 21:23).

The Jewish commentator Rashi compares this statement in Deuteronomy to the execution of a certain bandit who was convicted and hanged for his crimes. It was soon discovered that the convicted man was the twin brother of the king! It was impossible for the people who observed the hanging not to see the king's character as tarnished too! It was as though the king had become accursed for the crimes of his brother! It is dishonoring to God when one of his children, created in his image, is hanged from a tree.

God's sense of justice demanded that Messiah become a curse to redeem us. Yeshua carried out his mission unflinchingly. Are you awed by the price God paid to set you free? Are you inspired by Messiah's example of loving obedience? Are you willing to be considered accursed for identifying with Yeshua?

Today I Will

. . . reflect God's love, even to those who treat me harshly.

JEF

He who conceals his sins will not succeed (Prov. 28:13).

The wrongs we commit against one another do not simply go away. If they are left unaddressed, these wrongs can destroy a friendship. Confession and repentance (*teshuvah*) must be embraced or the alternative will be inevitable—a trail of dead friendships at the end of our lives.

Confession—the "I am sorry" part—must be faced. Honest regret must be expressed. But confession apart from *teshuvah*—the "I won't do it again" part—is just a dead work. It has been compared to a man who seeks ritual purification through immersion in water while holding a defiling dead reptile in his hand. Put another way, it is like a surgeon who sterilizes his equipment and then proceeds to perform surgery without washing his hands or putting on sterile gloves. *Teshuvah* requires a change in behavior, a return to God, a forsaking of the pattern of sin. Transgressions against our fellow man require restitution and reconciliation with the one who was wronged.

Yeshua taught, "So if you are offering your gift at the Temple altar and you remember there that your brother has something against you, leave your gift where it is by the altar, and go, make peace with your brother. Then come back and offer your gift" (Matt. 5:23–24).

Today I Will

. . . resurrect a languishing friendship by expressing my heartfelt sorrow and following it up with actions that will reconcile me with my friend.

AV

8

אב

July 21, 1999
Aug. 9, 2000
July 28, 2001 (44)
July 17, 2002
Aug. 6, 2003
July 26, 2004

Prayer Focus

JEG

AV

9

אב

July 22, 1999 (מ)
Aug. 10, 2000 (מ)
July 29, 2001 (מ)
July 18, 2002 (מ)
Aug. 7, 2003 (מ)
July 27, 2004 (מ)

Traditional
Tish'ah Be'Av
(the 9th of Av)
See Zech. 7:3–5; 8:19

There are exactly fifty days between *Tish'ah Be'Av* and *Rosh HaShanah.*

Prayer Focus

RR

The grace of *ADONAI* is not exhausted . . . his compassion has not ended. [On the contrary,] they are new every morning! (Lam. 3:22–23)

Tish'ah Be'Av (the 9th of Av) is a day burdened with grief. On this day, the first Temple was destroyed by Babylonians and the second Temple by Romans. Numerous other disasters have also fallen on this day, culminating in the expulsion of Jews from Spain in 1492. *Tish'ah Be'Av* is only one day, but its sorrow permeates the whole Jewish year. Because the Temple was destroyed, the traditional synagogue still excludes instrumental music from its services, the *tallit* (prayer shawl) commonly incorporates black stripes, and the daily prayers always include a plea for the Temple's restoration.

Paradoxically, Judaism remains a religion of optimism. Perhaps this is because we do not see these calamities as meaninglesss disasters, but believe that they are part of God's larger purpose. The mourning of *Tish'ah Be'Av* is ancient, but not endless; history is steadily moving toward fulfillment. The reading for *Tish'ah Be'Av* is the book of Lamentations, which contains five chapters, each of which—except chapter 3—contains twenty-two verses. These chapters parallel the twenty-two letters of the Hebrew *alef-bet* (alphabet). The third chapter contains sixty-six verses (three times twenty-two). Thus Jeremiah invokes the entire *alef-bet* seven times in his lament over Jerusalem.

At the climax of his lament the writer reveals a message of hope, saying "For rejection by *ADONAI* does not last forever. He may cause grief, but he will take pity, in keeping with the greatness of his grace" (Lam. 3:31–32). Scripture recognizes tragedy and grief, but its final note is always hope.

Today I Will

. . . pray for the full restoration of Jerusalem and of the Jewish people. I will believe in God's unchanging mercy, even when it is not apparent.

He [Jehoshaphat] appointed those who would sing to *ADONAI* . . . as they went out ahead of the army (2 Chron. 20:21).

Praise is a powerful weapon in our battle against the forces of evil. The first thing the Adversary seeks to rob from us is our joy, because he knows he will always win over the Messianic Jew who does not "rejoice in union with the Lord always!" (Phil. 4:4)

When Leah named her fourth son Yehudah (Judah; literally, "praise"), she had no idea that Jacob's many descendants would one day identify themselves by a similar name—"Jew." But the name is prophetically fitting. The time will come when the ransomed among the Jewish people will return with the same praise that Jehoshaphat's front-line warriors expressed, a praise that overcomes all things through the strength of God's enduring love.

Throughout Jewish history, the Adversary has sought to destroy the praise of Israel. The Holocaust was an extreme example. Survivors recount that they were forbidden to sing in the camps while walking or performing duties. Those caught doing so could be shot on sight. During those dark days, the Adversary didn't just rob our people's joy. He sought to kill it forever, along with the word "Jew." But he failed.

When Messianic Jews praise God always and in all things, we are declaring to all that the Jewish people live! And each of us begins to truly live as well.

Today I Will

. . . place praise at the head of my life because God loves me and enables me to conquer all evil.

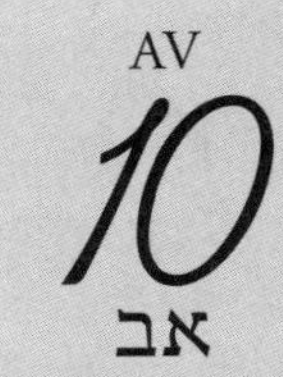

July 23, 1999
Aug. 11, 2000
July 30, 2001
July 19, 2002
Aug. 8, 2003
July 28, 2004

Biblical
On this day, Jerusalem burned to the ground (Jer. 52:12–13); Ezekiel received a prophecy for the elders of Israel (Ezek. 20:1).

Prayer Focus

MW

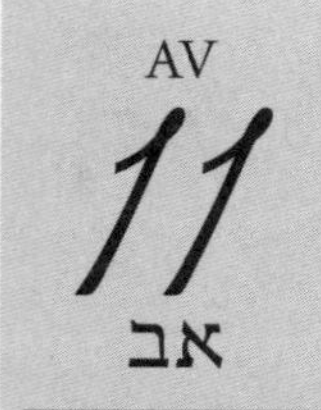

AV

11

אב

July 24, 1999 (45)
Aug. 12, 2000 (45)
July 31, 2001
July 20, 2002 (45)
Aug. 9, 2003 (45)
July 29, 2004

I, even I, am He who comforts you (Isa. 51:12 NKJV).

These words open the fourth of seven *Haftarot* (portions from the Prophets) of consolation—passages from Isaiah that accompany the weekly *Torah* readings following *Tish'ah Be'Av* (the 9th of Av). *Tish'ah Be'Av* symbolizes Israel's exile in all its bitterness and loss. Now it is time to restore hope and receive encouragement from God.

The Lord says *anochi, anochi* (I, even I) to underline the fact that he will *personally* comfort his people. This exact Hebrew phrase is unusual in Scripture, appearing only here and in two other passages where such strong emphasis is required: "I, even I, am the Lord, and besides Me there is no savior" (Isa. 43:11 NKJV), and "I, even I, am He Who blots out your transgressions for My own sake; and I will not remember your sins" (Isa. 43:25 NKJV). All three of these encouraging and consoling passages speak of God's personal comfort, expressed through mercy, salvation, and forgiveness.

The Lord has many concerns, but here is one area in which he deeply invests himself—saving and comforting his people.

Prayer Focus

Today I Will

. . . not look to impersonal things or theories to comfort me in my trials, but to Messiah himself.

RR

Look! God's lamb! The one who is taking away the sin of the world! (John 1:29)

You're going to have to sit down for this one because it's going to be tough. I have to have a word with you about the life of crime you've been leading. You've been pulling off some big heists lately. And you have to stop! The jig is up! It's time to come clean. "But I'm not a thief!"—you protest. The truth is you are. We are all thieves. You see, a thief is someone who takes what doesn't belong to him, but belongs to someone else.

So what is this big heist you've been pulling off? When Messiah died, he took all your sins, guilt, and burdens. But you're still carrying around your sins, your past, your guilt, worries, and the burdens of your life! Do you see now why you're a thief? In taking them back, you're stealing from Messiah!

Messiah took your sins and the burdens of your life. They are his. They don't belong to you anymore. If you are in possession of them, you're in possession of stolen property. So my fellow thieves, burglars, and criminals, remember Gulgolta (Golgotha)—the place where Yeshua died—and give back all you have stolen. Hand over your failures, worries, guilt, sins, and regrets to their rightful owner. The jig is up! It's time to renounce your life of crime and come clean!

Today I Will

. . . write down one worry, one burden, and one sin that I've stolen back from Messiah. I'll give these to the Lord in prayer and destroy the paper, allowing them to remain forever in his hands.

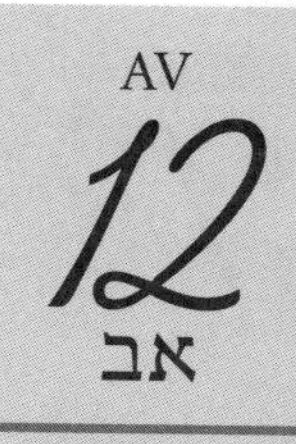

July 25, 1999
Aug. 13, 2000
Aug. 1, 2001
July 21, 2002
Aug. 10, 2003
July 30, 2004

Prayer Focus

JC

July 26, 1999
Aug. 14, 2000
Aug. 2, 2001
July 22, 2002
Aug. 11, 2003
July 31, 2004 (45)

Stripping off falsehood, let everyone speak truth with his neighbor (Eph. 4:25).

I have been amazed at how easy it is for people to lie to one another. We've gotten so used to it that we don't even consider it lying! We lie to avoid inconvenience and we lie because we don't want to hurt others with the truth. Have you ever been in a situation where someone called to speak to you and you told the person answering the phone, "Tell them I'm not in"? It's a lie, but people do it all the time.

An old Yiddish proverb says, "*Mit lign kumt men veyt ober nit tsurik*" (with lies you will go far, but not [be able to come] back again). When we allow ourselves even the most "innocent" kinds of "white lies," we lose a great deal. Small lies invariably lead to big ones. A habit of fudging leads to a pattern of falsehood. God wants our lives to be characterized by the truth, for truth is what characterizes God. He cannot lie and neither should we, under *any* circumstance. If a little lie has led you astray, only the truth will bring you back to stay.

No matter how uncomfortable or how inconvienient it is, telling the truth is the only option for the child of God.

Prayer Focus

Today I Will

. . . commit myself to telling the truth in all circumstances, no matter what the consequences.

DB

The thoughts of fools are in the house of pleasure (Eccles. 7:4).

It would seem at first glance that Shlomo (Solomon) is speaking against pleasure. But a more careful reading of the Scripture above reveals that Shlomo speaks not against pleasure, but against the house of pleasure; that is, the house of ill-repute.

Shlomo speaks much on the subject of pleasure in the book of Ecclesiastes, emphasizing the futility of seeking it: "I said to myself, 'Come now, I will test myself with pleasure and enjoying good things'; but this too was pointless. Of laughter I said, 'This is stupid,' and of pleasure, 'What's the use of it?'" (Eccles. 2:1–2)

Shlomo is not focusing on spiritual pleasures but on "pleasures of the flesh." For Shlomo, "pleasure" describes all the things man tries to use to satisfy and fulfill himself. However, his conclusion is that nothing this world can offer will fulfill the longing of man's soul except service to the God who created man.

I enjoy good food and nice clothes, a fast car and some cash in my wallet. But none of these things is a lasting source of pleasure for me. A close relationship with a dear brother in our common faith, a discovery of a new truth from God's Word, a soul that receives Yeshua—each of these provides immeasurable, satisfying pleasure that has value both now and for all eternity.

Today I Will

. . . seek after the pleasure of knowing God and enjoying the fellowship of Messiah Yeshua.

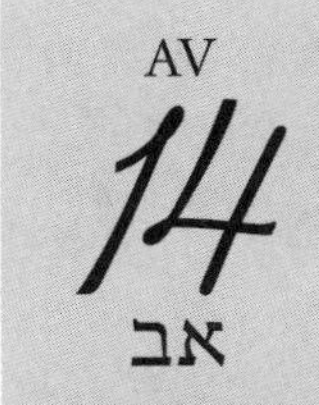

July 27, 1999
Aug. 15, 2000
Aug. 3, 2001
July 23, 2002
Aug. 12, 2003
Aug. 1, 2004

Prayer Focus

JS

July 28, 1999
Aug. 16, 2000
Aug. 4, 2001 (45)
July 24, 2002
Aug. 13, 2003
Aug. 2, 2004

Traditional
Tu Be'Av
(the 15th of Av)

Prayer Focus

ADONAI, God, prepared a castor-bean plant and made it grow up over Yonah [Jonah] to shade his head and relieve his discomfort (Jon. 4:6).

The day had finally arrived; I was driving to the jeweler's to make my last payment on a necklace for the girl of my dreams. On the front side of the necklace, the silversmith had designed the symbols of the everlasting *Brit Chadashah* (New Covenant): *matzah* (unleavened bread) and a cup of wine. On the back, I had him engrave the words, "Harumi, will you marry me?"

I was entering the mall parking lot when I realized I had miscalculated the tax. I was twenty dollars short. "No problem," I thought, "I'll go to the ATM and then to the jeweler." Stepping out of the car, I started toward the mall entrance when I noticed in the distance a piece of paper being carried along by the wind.

It captured my attention and I stopped to watch it. Just like in the movies, it sailed closer and closer until it passed right in front of me. I grabbed it, then opened my hand. It was a twenty dollar bill! I couldn't help but laugh with joy and thankfulness. *Adonai Yir'eh* (the Lord who will provide) is a living God who wanted to be part of purchasing this most special necklace.

The Lord is concerned with the little things in our lives, not just the big things. The same God who provided a way through the Red Sea also provided a vine as shade for one of his precious prophets (Jon. 4:6).

Today I Will

. . . keep my eyes open for the little ways in which the Lord expresses his love for me.

DR

Hagar! Sarai's slave-girl! Where have you come from, and where are you going? (Gen. 16:8)

July 29, 1999
Aug. 17, 2000
Aug. 5, 2001
July 25, 2002
Aug. 14, 2003
Aug. 3, 2004

When God came to Hagar with this important question, she was standing at a crossroads in her life. Her mistress Sarai had sent her away and she was facing an uncertain future. What would she do? Where would she go?

God had a plan for Hagar, as he does for each of us. But for Hagar to discover it, she would first need to understand where she had come from and where the Lord was calling her to go.

Where did *you* come from? Where were you when Messiah called out to you and came into your life? From what circumstances did he deliver you? Remembering who we were before we met him helps us guard against attitudes of self-righteousness, ingratitude and pride, and reminds us to stay close to Yeshua.

Where are you going? God has a purpose for your life that only you can fulfill. Understanding that purpose can give us meaning and direction. Not knowing it can result in idleness, spiritual lethargy and indifference. Ask the *Ruach HaKodesh* (Holy Spirit) and he will reveal the destiny Messiah has for you. Salvation is only the beginning of the journey!

Prayer Focus

Today I Will

. . . remember where I came from and ask the Lord to show me where I am going.

JB

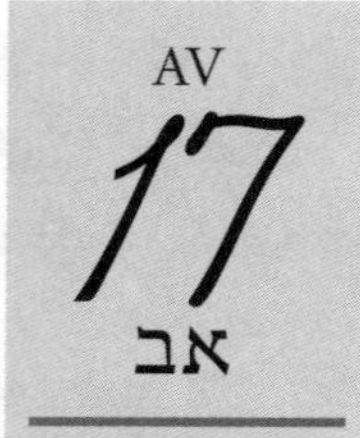

July 30, 1999
Aug. 18, 2000
Aug. 6, 2001
July 26, 2002
Aug. 15, 2003
Aug. 4, 2004

Marta, Marta, you are fretting and worrying about so many things! (Luke 10:41)

Have you noticed that there are always too many things to do, and they never seem to get completed? We live in a fast-paced, high-tech world that demands virtually all of our time. If we had twenty-eight hours in the day, we would soon need thirty-two. On top of that, our priorities become confused and the things that are most important, such as God and family, often get pushed out of the way.

One day, Yeshua came to visit a beloved Messianic family. Apparently, the parents were deceased and Marta (Martha), the oldest, was in charge. She had two younger siblings: Miryam (Mary) and El'azar (Lazarus—of resurrection fame). Marta was busy playing the part of the good *yiddishe mama* (Jewish mother), preparing the meal for Yeshua. Miryam was not helping but was sitting at Messiah's feet, receiving personal teaching. Finally, Marta blew up and demanded that Yeshua make Miryam come in and help her.

We need godly women like Marta who are hard laborers for the Kingdom of God and who are gifted in hospitality. But, sometimes, even the most dedicated of God's people can become too busy and miss out on what God has for them. Do you get so busy that it is hard to spend time with the Lord, get out to services, go to a prayer meeting, or have any family time at all? Then you are too busy! Change your life. "Re-prioritize" your activities by putting spiritual matters first. Take the time to sit at Yeshua's feet and learn from him.

Prayer Focus

Today I Will

. . . choose to "re-prioritize" my life. I will not be too busy to spend time with God, but put him first in my life.

DC

The light has come into the world, but people loved the darkness rather than the light (John 3:19).

Walking through the Museum of Natural History in the Upper West Side of Manhattan, I spotted a curious display: the official New York City bird. It was a cockroach! If you live in New York City like I do, you have to laugh and admit that this is a most appropriate choice. Most New Yorkers have experienced that middle-of-the-night trip to the kitchen, when the cockroaches, surprised by the sudden light, scurry to safety under the refrigerator.

Cockroaches naturally avoid light. I suppose they sense the danger to their continued existence. Perhaps they are haunted by a primordial memory of a giant human foot crushing their distant ancestors.

Moths, on the other hand, are attracted to light. Without it, moths lose their sense of direction. Disoriented, they have no focal point by which to fly. When they see light, they are immediately attracted.

What is your response to God's light? Do you shrink from it and run for cover, not wanting to be exposed? Or are you attracted to his light and long to approach it at all costs? Yeshua, the light of the world, came to bring light and orientation to a darkened planet, yet some continue to choose the darkness. They stumble and hurt themselves, fearing the exposure of their deeds of darkness.

What are you: a cockroach or a moth?

. . . be conscious of my response to God's light of conviction shining on me, and strive to move toward that light, not away from it.

July 31, 1999 (46)
Aug. 19, 2000 (46)
Aug. 7, 2001
July 27, 2002 (46)
Aug. 16, 2003 (46)
Aug. 5, 2004

Prayer Focus

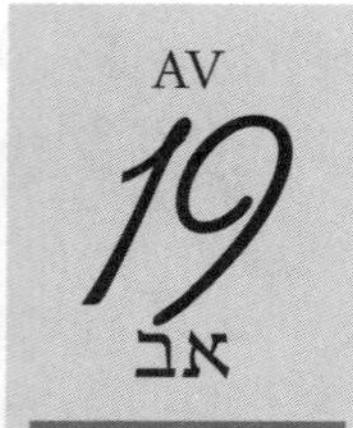

Aug. 1, 1999
Aug. 20, 2000
Aug. 8, 2001
July 28, 2002
Aug. 17, 2003
Aug. 6, 2004

I keep pursuing the goal in order to win the prize offered by God's upward calling in the Messiah Yeshua (Phil. 3:14).

A man who was interested in learning to shoot well visited a practice range. There, as he surveyed each of the bays where the targets were located, he noticed one that had all perfect bulls-eyes. Intent on finding the one responsible for such sharpshooting, he was told that Simon Greenstein was his man. He went out in search of him.

When he found Mr. Greenstein, he was shocked that this man of small stature had such enormous shooting prowess. He asked the little man, "How are you able to hit the center of the target each time?" Mr. Greenstein replied, "It's simple. First I shoot and then I draw a circle around the bullet hole so that the bullet is in the exact center of the target."

Unfortunately, too many people live their lives like the "sharpshooting" Mr. Greenstein. We act first and then justify the act by rationalization. Instead, we need to get acquainted with the target and shoot to hit the mark.

One of the Bible's words for sin is *chet. Chet* describes an archer whose arrow has fallen short of the target. The Lord's guidebook, the Scriptures, clearly circumscribes our target—God's will for our lives. We need to make sure our acts aim to hit it!

Prayer Focus

Today I Will

. . . consult the Word of God and aim my actions to fall within the target.

EK

In the same way as you judge others, you will be judged (Matt. 7:2).

Aug. 2, 1999
Aug. 21, 2000
Aug. 9, 2001
July 29, 2002
Aug. 18, 2003
Aug. 7, 2004 (46)

The word "perception" has been very helpful to me over the last few years. I have learned to preface very strong opinions that I hold, or occasions of correcting my co-workers, with the words, "I perceive." Before I learned the word "perception," it was easy for people to think of me as a "bull in a china shop." My reputation as an opinionated and harsh person preceded me wherever I went. Then I learned the words, "It is my perception that . . . " Such wording softens the strong opinions or feelings I hold and gives opportunity for the other side to evaluate the matter without having their feelings hurt.

The prophet Jeremiah said, "The heart is more deceitful than anything else" (Jer. 17:9). When it comes to making judgments concerning people, we must be very careful. We cannot see into another person's heart. Only God can do that. The best that we can do is have a perception. Even when we are forced to make an evaluation, we ought to check twice and even three times with honorable witnesses, and always judge according to the measure of God's grace toward us.

Let us devote time and effort to expressing our perceptions with love and understanding toward our brothers.

Prayer Focus

Today I Will

. . . be careful in the way that I communicate my perceptions to others.

JS

Aug. 3, 1999
Aug. 22, 2000
Aug. 10, 2001
July 30, 2002
Aug. 19, 2003
Aug. 8, 2004

It is better to take refuge in the Lord than to trust in mortals (Ps. 118:8).

The Titanic was the largest ship of its day. It was almost three football fields long and weighed over 46,000 tons. Its nickname was "unsinkable." Many aboard were drinking and dining and dancing. The band was playing. It was on its maiden voyage from England to New York City when it struck an iceberg 1600 miles northeast of its destination. In two and a half hours the unsinkable sank. There were not enough life boats. Only 705 out of the 2200 passengers were rescued.

The Hindenburg was an airship, a German-built blimp, 800 feet long and 135 feet in diameter. It was one of the premier commercial transcontinental airships in the days before jets. On its final voyage from Germany, it burst into flames while approaching a landing in New Jersey. Thirty-six passengers perished.

The space shuttle Challenger blew up in the air and was destroyed only 73 seconds after lift-off. All seven crew members were killed. The cause of the worst space disaster in the history of NASA was a defective rubber seal on one of the Challenger's two booster rockets.

Some of the most advanced man-made vehicles of their times have been involved in some of the worst tragedies of the 20th century. Man's achievements may, at times, seem impressive, but putting our faith in man's best efforts cannot compare to trusting in God.

Prayer Focus

Today I Will

. . . put my confidence in God.

EK

I will put my trust in him [Yeshua] (Heb. 2:13).

Aug. 4, 1999
Aug. 23, 2000
Aug. 11, 2001 (46)
July 31, 2002
Aug. 20, 2003
Aug. 9, 2004

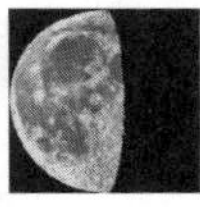

A recent survey asked professing followers of Yeshua if they believed in absolutes of right and wrong. The majority said they did not. Some years back, Joseph Fletcher, a liberal Episcopalian priest considered to be the father of situational ethics, argued that morality was simply a matter of what is "right" at any given moment. Take, for example, Mrs. Throckmorton, who is told that unless she commits adultery, the guards at the political prison will kill her husband. What is the correct thing to do? According to Fletcher, it is to commit adultery, for the *Torah*, in his opinion, only provides *guidelines* for what is right in ordinary situations. Our society has come to agree with Fletcher. Thus, without the *Torah* in absolute terms, love has devolved into mere humanistic sentiment.

The ends *never* justify the means. Human calculations of ends and probabilities may be considered, but are only legitimate within the boundaries of the *Torah*. The prison official who asked Mrs. Throckmorton to commit adultery is certainly untrustworthy. He may kill her husband anyway. There is only safety in trusting God and obeying his *Torah*. Then we will have God's promised supernatural backing and we maximize the potential for good. Our confession should be, "Even unto death, I will not deny my faith or God's *Torah*." Perhaps God will intervene as he did with Daniel, Shadrach, Meshach, Abednego, and Joseph. There is a God in heaven and in Israel who is capable of delivering us.

Prayer Focus

Today I Will

. . . commit to fully obeying God.

DJ

Aug. 5, 1999
Aug. 24, 2000
Aug. 12, 2001
Aug. 1, 2002
Aug. 21, 2003
Aug. 10, 2004

Eli! Eli! L'mah sh'vaktani? (My God! My God! Why have you deserted me?) (Matt. 27:46)

Have you ever felt deserted by God? Is any feeling worse than that? Yeshua had enjoyed unbroken fellowship with God from before the beginning of eternity. His own words on the matter reflect the greatest intimacy: "My Father has handed over everything to me. Indeed no one fully knows the Son except the Father, and no one fully knows the Father except the Son" (Matt. 11:27). How painful, then, was his cry, "*Eli! Eli! L'mah sh'vaktani?*"

What can be more of a nightmare than staring into the abyss of our Father's abandonment? Yet we must be willing to walk even into the darkest places if we are to emerge in the light of resurrection. That is where God's love shines.

Yeshua has faced down the horror of sin. The prophet Yesha'yahu (Isaiah) wrote that God was pleased to crush him (Isa. 53:10) because his stripes healed us (Isa. 53:5). Yeshua paid the price to redeem us. We enjoy everlasting fellowship with our Father because Yeshua faced the abandonment we deserved.

The second blessing of the *Amidah* (Standing Prayer) states, "You are eternally Mighty, O God, You bring the dead back to life. . . ." *Techiyat HaMeytim* (the resurrection of the dead) makes permanent the meaning of life. In Yeshua, we can enjoy the fruits of fellowship with God—forever.

Prayer Focus

Today I Will

. . . draw close to God and taste the fruits of everlasting fellowship.

JEF

While continuing to expect the blessed fulfillment of our certain hope (Titus 2:13).

God has given us a great promise: the return of the Messiah Yeshua. Yeshua and his coming are our "certain hope." Some believe that through our own efforts we can bring Messiah to earth. The Jerusalem *Talmud* records Rabbi Levi saying, "If Israel would keep a single Sabbath in the proper way, forthwith the Son of David will come" (Ta'anit 1:1). Sadder still is the fact that the majority of our people have altogether given up believing in Messiah's coming. We who know Yeshua confidently await his return!

There was a large fishing boat returning to port after several weeks at sea. The men in the boat gazed eagerly toward the dock where their loved ones were waiting. One of the fishermen became anxious when his wife wasn't there to meet him. He left the dock and walked to his home where he could see the front porch light on. As he opened the door, his wife ran to him, saying, "I've been waiting for you." The fisherman replied, "Yes, but the other men's wives were *watching* for them."

It is not enough for us to leave the front porch light on. We need to be diligent and watch expectantly every day for our Lord. He could come at any time. Let's strive to seek the Lord and to long for his appearance.

Aug. 6, 1999
Aug. 25, 2000
Aug. 13, 2001
Aug. 2, 2002
Aug. 22, 2003
Aug. 11, 2004

Prayer Focus

Today I Will

. . . renew my hope in the coming of Messiah, and though he tarries, I will wait for him. *Maranatha*! (Come, Oh Lord!)

DB

Aug. 7, 1999 (47)*
Aug. 26, 2000 (47)*
Aug. 14, 2001
Aug. 3, 2002 (47)*
Aug. 23, 2003 (47)*
Aug. 12, 2004

Remember the day, *Shabbat*, to set it apart for God (Exod. 20:8).

The fourth *mitzvah* (commandment) of the Ten Commandments concerns the remembrance of the *Shabbat* (Sabbath). *Shabbat* literally means "rest . . . to desist from work." Unfortunately, through the years, the *Shabbat* has been misunderstood by both Jews and Christians.

Shabbat was never meant to be an "intolerable burden" laced with hundreds of additional man-made expectations. God's guidelines for *Shabbat* in the *Torah* are quite simple: rest, don't work, and hold a holy convocation to the Lord.

In addition, God did not intend for *Shabbat* to be replaced by Sunday (which was ordained at a Church council only a few centuries after Yeshua). The *mitzvah* to rest on the *seventh day* did not, in fact, originate in the Ten Commandments but was sanctified by God at the end of the creation! (Gen. 2:1–3)

The purpose of this special day is to rest, be with family, gather at God's house for worship, and get refocused and refreshed for the coming week. *Shabbat* is a time of rest for our souls as well as our bodies.

The writer of the book of Hebrews says, "So there remains a *Shabbat*-keeping for God's people" (Heb. 4:9). Enjoy the *Shabbat*! Rest in the Lord.

Prayer Focus

Today I Will

. . . seek to take seriously the commandment concerning *Shabbat* and dedicate this day to the Lord. "Lord, help me to live *every* day resting in you."

DC

The measure with which you measure out will be used to measure you (Matt. 7:2).

Measure with exacting justice, and you will be measured that way, too. As Shlomo *HaMelech* (King Solomon) put it, "So don't be overly righteous or overly wise; why should you disappoint yourself?" (Eccles. 7:16)

There was once a ruler who believed in justice and the need for absolute adherence to the law. A certain beggar, caught stealing cheese and bread from the royal kitchen, was ordered to be hanged, according to the law. The facts that he was hungry, destitute, and tempted by the food made no difference to the king.

On the way to the gallows, the convicted thief moaned, "Now my father's secret will die with me." Pressed for the secret, he revealed that a pomegranate seed could be planted in such a way that it would grow and bear fruit overnight. The king was told, and a pomegranate seed was presented to the thief. He dug a hole in the ground, then explained that the seed could be planted only by someone who had never taken anything that didn't belong to him.

A search was made, but no one could be found to plant the seed. Even the accountant backed off, saying that he may have subtracted wrong and overcharged someone on taxes. The king alone remained, but he too had hidden a royal necklace when he was a young child, fascinated by the color of the gems. From that day on, the king amended the laws so that they would be enforced with compassion as well as justice.

Aug. 8, 1999
Aug. 27, 2000
Aug. 15, 2001
Aug. 4, 2002
Aug. 24, 2003
Aug. 13, 2004

Prayer Focus

Today I Will

. . . show compassion to someone I have already judged.

JEF

Aug. 9, 1999
Aug. 28, 2000
Aug. 16, 2001
Aug. 5, 2002
Aug. 25, 2003
Aug. 14, 2004 (47)*

Prayer Focus

We are now going up to Yerushalayim (Mark 10:33).

Have you ever noticed that Yeshua always goes "up" to Yerushalayim (Jerusalem)? Even when he is going south, he goes "up" to Yerushalayim. Why? Yerushalayim is high up on the Judean hills. But more than that, it's the city of God. You never go down to God. You always go up, so the journey to Yerushalayim was given a special name—*aliyah* (going up). Thus, whenever Jewish people return to live in Israel it is said they are making *aliyah.* They're going up.

In the same way, if you're born again, you're a child of Abraham and that means your life is to be an *aliyah.* The direction of your life is not to the east or west or toward money or success. The direction of your life is *aliyah*—going up to God. He calls you not to the most comfortable life, but to the life of highest good.

Going up may require more effort and determination, but it's a glorious journey and the view at the top is breathtaking! Every day we're given choices as to where we will place our next step. Don't compromise. Always choose to step *up*, for that's the direction of *aliyah.* Don't be afraid of heights. If you go for the top, you'll be amazed at what happens to your life. You're going up. You're making *aliyah.*

Today I Will

. . . take the higher step, for my life is now an *aliyah.*

JC

Even the dogs eat the leftovers that fall from their master's table (Matt. 15:27).

Aug. 10, 1999
Aug. 29, 2000
Aug. 17, 2001
Aug. 6, 2002
Aug. 26, 2003
Aug. 15, 2004

Humility is spiritual strength, not weakness. In the above Scripture, the Syrophoenician woman humbly acknowledges her social position. She is a Gentile woman who must wait in line behind the Jewish children to be fed. Rather than protest the unfairness of her situation, or become indignant that Yeshua doesn't bother to answer her the first time, the woman again cries out for help. This time, Yeshua responds by saying that he was sent to the house of Israel. Would she have him feed the children's food to a dog? Her humility is tested. She answers that even a dog feeds on the crumbs that fall to the floor! Could you continue to plead your case after being compared to a dog? Touched by her humility, Yeshua immediately grants her request to heal her daughter.

Our dog is a husky boxer who loves to go for car rides. Long ago, he gave up insisting on accompanying us into restaurants. Our dog is content with his car ride. He is happy with his lot. Are you content with your own lot in life?

Prayer Focus

Today I Will

. . . be happy about my position in life and stop comparing myself to others.

JEF

Aug. 11, 1999
Aug. 30, 2000
Aug. 18, 2001
(47/D)*
Aug. 7, 2002
Aug. 27, 2003
Aug. 16, 2004

Prayer Focus

He was given a grave among the wicked; in his death he was with a rich man (Isa. 53:9).

Isaiah 53 contains a most amazing description of the Messiah suffering and dying for our sins. Hidden inside this prophecy is something most unusual. Is it a mistake or an ancient mystery? You won't read it in English translations. Verse nine in Hebrew states, "*Ve'et-ashir bemotav,*" which literally means "with a rich man in his deaths."

How can one man die many deaths? How can many deaths be linked to just one man? The answer is clear. When Yeshua died on the *tzlav* (cross), he died all our deaths, taking them on as his own.

Therefore, Isaiah 53 is not just a prophecy of Yeshua's death, but our deaths too. When it says "in his deaths," one of those deaths is the death of your old life. You died with Yeshua. Therefore, you have the power to be completely free and to walk in the newness of life. Be free of what is old and gone; the old you is truly dead. Do you want proof? It's right there in Isaiah 53, in a Hebrew mystery—"in his deaths."

Today I Will

. . . do one new thing that I've never done before to celebrate my new identity and life with Messiah.

JC

I will live in the house of *ADONAI* for years and years to come (Ps. 23:6).

Even as a small child, I wondered whether there was life after death. When I asked my parents, they always answered, "You will live on as a good memory in the lives of those you leave behind." Though their response disturbed me, over time I grew to accept it. What in childhood began as a curiosity became, in later years, a crisis. At times a "death anxiety" would overcome me as I pondered the eternal nothingness which lay ahead.

My parents' generation of Jewish people was not the first to doubt the continuation of life after death. We know that as far back as the first century, the *Tzedukim* (Sadducees) rejected the thought as well. Acts 23:8 states, "For the *Tzedukim* deny the resurrection and the existence of angels and spirits; whereas the *Perushim* [Pharisees] acknowledge both." Arguments on this subject between *Perushim* and *Tzedukim* are also recorded among the discussions in the *Talmud.*

As a child, I certainly was not aware of this first-century controversy, but I *was* aware of Scripture verses like the one from Psalm 23 quoted above. However, my *Tzeduki* (Sadducean) leanings and the accompanying emptiness did not leave me until one January night in 1971 when I invited Yeshua into my life as Messiah and Savior. As I clearly sensed God's presence in my heart, I knew for the first time that I had an eternal spirit! With his incredible love, God destroyed my anxiety over death.

Today I Will

. . . rejoice that, after this life, I will continue to enjoy an abundant life with the Lord forever.

Aug. 12, 1999
Aug. 31, 2000
Aug. 19, 2001
Aug. 8, 2002
Aug. 28, 2003
Aug. 17, 2004

Traditional
Rosh Chodesh
(the New Moon)
Day 1

Prayer Focus

MW

Aug. 13, 1999
Sept. 1, 2000
Aug. 20, 2001
Aug. 9, 2002
Aug. 29, 2003
Aug. 18, 2004

Biblical
Rosh Chodesh
(the New Moon)

On this day, Haggai received a prophecy for Zerubbabel to rebuild the Temple (Hag. 1:1).

Traditional
Rosh Chodesh
Day 2

Prayer and fasting is encouraged as much as possible during the month of Elul in preparation for the *Yamim Nora'im* (Days of Awe).

Prayer Focus

He will hide me in the folds of his tent [*sukkah*], he will set me high on a rock (Ps. 27:5).

The final month of the Jewish year, Elul is a time to prepare spiritually for the High Holy Days. Tradition recommends reciting the psalms throughout Elul, especially Psalm 27. Why this particular psalm? It opens, "*ADONAI* is my light and salvation." A *Midrash* (traditional commentary) states that "my light" refers to *Rosh HaShanah* (the traditional New Year), the Day of Judgment. Likewise, "my salvation" refers to *Yom Kippur* (the Day of Atonement), when God provides salvation through atonement for sins. Finally, Psalm 27 hints at *Sukkot* (the Feast of Tabernacles) in the words, "He will hide me in the folds of his tent [*sukkah*]."

This last reference is surprising. A *sukkah* is a temporary and even flimsy structure, yet the psalmist uses it as a synonym for God's house. A *sukkah* is a place to celebrate God's deliverance of our people from Egypt, yet the psalmist calls it a place to hide from trouble. This provides a lesson for us. Elul is a time of spiritual preparation. The most essential preparation may be learning to hide in the Lord. We need to examine ourselves, confess wrong, and make amends; however, we are not fully prepared until we seek refuge in God's mercy. This may seem like a flimsy response to our trials, but God's refuge is secure.

Today I Will

. . . seek restoration by drawing close to the Lord and depending on his mercy.

RR

My soul, why are you so downcast? Why are you groaning inside me? Hope in God (Ps. 42:11[12]).

Depression is a common malady in modern life, afflicting unbelievers and believers alike. The depressed person often endures an endless stream of words within his mind, words of helplessness and failure that only deepen his depression. Cognitive therapy has proven to be among the most effective responses to this condition. This treatment does not seek to analyze or reason with the negative words of depression, but simply to replace them with words of hope and encouragement.

The psalmist instinctively does something similar. In his exile, he longs to return to the holy Temple and the true worship of God. He feels downcast and forsaken. To cheer himself up, he speaks to his *nefesh* (soul), the breath of life within himself, challenging its depression. As a man of faith, he takes charge over his own mental state and resolves to praise God despite circumstances. He speaks to his *nefesh*, not of the loneliness that he feels, but of the praise that he knows God deserves. As a result, his hope is renewed and he can speak of "God, my exceeding joy" (Ps. 43:4). We also can speak to our *nafshim* (souls) when we feel downcast, choosing words of Scripture over our own words of discouragement and fear.

Today I Will

. . . not yield to depression if it arises, but will speak words of Scripture to my soul.

Aug. 14, 1999 (48)
Sept. 2, 2000 (48)
Aug. 21, 2001
Aug. 10, 2002 (48)
Aug. 30, 2003 (48)
Aug. 19, 2004

Prayer Focus

RR

ELUL

3

אלול

Aug. 15, 1999
Sept. 3, 2000
Aug. 22, 2001
Aug. 11, 2002
Aug. 31, 2003
Aug. 20, 2004

Prayer Focus

An argument arose among the *talmidim* [disciples] as to which of them might be the greatest (Luke 9:46).

This argument involving Yeshua's *talmidim* (disciples) embarrasses us. How can men who intimately knew Yeshua—the one who embodies humility—argue about who is the greatest among them? The disciples seem hopelessly unspiritual, yet perhaps they are simply more transparent than the rest of us. We too wonder how we might rank if the *Malchut HaShem* (Kingdom of God) had a rating system. Perhaps such thoughts are not altogether wrong. If we are serving the Lord, it may be good at times to evaluate our performance.

The disciples' problem was that they had not resolved a more basic question: What is true greatness? Surely the criteria we use today—wealth, recognition, and power—are skewed. A woman once asked some sages what God had been doing since creation. Rabbi Yoseph ben Halafta replied, "Building ladders for some to ascend and for others to descend." God often humbles the "great" and makes great the humble. The disciples were climbing after the wrong sort of greatness, ignoring their master's definition: "Whoever wants to be first must be your slave! For the Son of Man did not come to be served, but to serve—and to give his life as a ransom for many" (Matt. 20:27–28). Surely this example—in contrast to wealth, recognition, and power—defines true greatness.

Today I Will

. . . descend the ladder to serve others, rather than making personal comfort, prestige, and influence my priorities.

RR

We will boast in our God all day and give thanks to your name forever (*Selah*) (Ps. 44:8[9]).

When I first started reading the Bible, I was puzzled when I got to the Book of Psalms and read the word *selah*. Now I know that its meaning is actually very deep. The Hebrew word *selah* comes from the root that means "hang up," as in "hanging up your harp." It means "pause, give it a rest." You just can't keep going and going. You have to *selah*—stop, take a break.

If songs sung to God need *selah*s, holy pauses, how much more do our lives need them? If psalms of distress and trouble have *selah*s, then we also need *selah*s in our times of stress and trouble. If psalms of praise have *selah*s, then we also need to have *selah*s in our praise, worship, and service to God. We need time to be still and to receive what God has for us.

A life of beauty is to be like a psalm, and a psalm needs many *selah*s. Our *selah*s will allow us to consider and reconsider what is most important. Our *selah*s will allow us to be refreshed, to receive and take God to heart, soaking in his love.

Selah: it's the holy pause, the holy ceasing, the holy act of getting "hung up" on the wonders of God's love. Learn to do it. *Selah.*

Today I Will

. . . take a holy pause, drop the heavy load, and soak up God's Word.

ELUL

4

אלול

Aug. 16, 1999
Sept. 4, 2000
Aug. 23, 2001
Aug. 12, 2002
Sept. 1, 2003
Aug. 21, 2004 (48)

Prayer Focus

JC

ELUL

5

אלול

Aug. 17, 1999
Sept. 5, 2000
Aug. 24, 2001
Aug. 13, 2002
Sept. 2, 2003
Aug. 22, 2004

Biblical
On this day, Ezekiel was translated in the Spirit and shown idolatry in the Temple (Ezek. 8:1).

Prayer Focus

Bear one another's burdens (Gal. 6:2).

A *geshvir iz a guteh zach bey yenem untern orem* is Yiddish for "A boil is fine as long as it's under someone else's arm." I visit Mexico each year for a Messianic conference. The first time I arrived, I was introduced to the leader of a Mexican Messianic congregation. We hit it off right away. I remember starting to get my bags to go to the conference when this man, with a beautiful example of a servant's heart, absolutely would not let me carry them. I wanted to say, "Give me my bag!"—but I knew he would insist.

Something happened there that joined my heart to this man's. Here was someone who was taking care of his own flock and much of the conference, and was still able and willing to take care of me. Day after day, I saw this *chasid* (righteous one) of God pouring out his life for the people around him.

Yeshua came to serve. If someone has a boil, Yeshua is concerned about it, and he is not just glad that it is not his boil. I want to see in my own life the servant attitude I saw in Mexico. Bearing each other up is part of Messianic Jewish *halakhah* (law) and is part of the *Torah* (Law) of Messiah.

Today I Will

. . . be aware of the gentle prodding of the *Ruach* (Spirit), encouraging me to help others.

JR

The lazy person's way seems overgrown by thorns (Prov. 15:19).

A *z mi iz foiyl, hot men nit in moiyl* is Yiddish for "The lazy person acquires no food." A man called my office, complaining that he had a flat tire. "Rabbi, what can I do? Can you pray with me about this? The devil is attacking me!" I asked if he had a spare tire. He responded by saying that he had a good one. I asked why he had called the office before trying to change the tire himself. He said that he was too tired. I prayed with him and promptly suggested that changing the tire would solve his dilemma and that in the future he should regularly check his pressure and the general condition of the car.

People will call for similar reasons after having neglected their devotional lives, fellowship during the week, congregational Bible studies, worship services, etc. Band-aids are proper for their purpose, but laziness is laziness. If we gave one thousand dollars to each person who came to our congregational services, there would be standing room only. We must ask the Lord to reprioritize what we value.

Do we share God's values? What are we willing to invest our time and effort in? Spiritual laziness leads to a dry *neshamah* (soul). We need to *invest* in our spiritual lives.

Today I Will

. . . not give in to a lazy mindset. I will work while it is today.

ELUL

6

אלול

Aug. 18, 1999
Sept. 6, 2000
Aug. 25, 2001 (48)
Aug. 14, 2002
Sept. 3, 2003
Aug. 23, 2004

Prayer Focus

JR

ELUL

7

אלול

Aug. 19, 1999
Sept. 7, 2000
Aug. 26, 2001
Aug. 15, 2002
Sept. 4, 2003
Aug. 24, 2004

We've heard about all the things that have been going on in K'far-Nachum (Luke 4:23).

In Hebrew, *kefar* means "village" and *nachum* (like the prophet Nahum) means "repentance" or "comfort." Put the two Hebrew words together and you get Kefar-Nachum, which in Hebrew means "village of repentance" or "village of comfort." It's a real place; it was the village where Messiah lived and ministered. Kefar-Nachum (Capernaum) was the village where Messiah chose to heal, to comfort, to bring the good news, and to perform miracles.

To dwell with the Lord is to live inside Kefar-Nachum, the village of comfort. But *Nachum* also means "repentance." If you want to dwell in the Lord's town, you must dwell in Kefar-Nachum, the "village of repentance." Where do we find Messiah? In a place of repentance. When you come to a real place of repentance, that's when you'll also come to a real place of comfort.

So come today to the place of repentance in your life. Come to the village of the Lord, a beautiful town in which you'll find his presence, his healing touch, and his miracles. It's Kefar-Nachum, the village of his comfort.

Prayer Focus

Today I Will

. . . put aside all distractions and meditate on Psalm 91, comforted by God's presence.

JC

Don't take vengeance on or bear a grudge against any of your people (Lev. 19:18).

When we read the Scriptures, we find that forgiving others is a commandment, not an option. There are no exceptions. The above verse implies that a wrong was committed which might lead to grudge-bearing. The transgressor's attitude is not mentioned. Likewise, verse 17 (the verse before the one quoted) emphasizes the necessity of rebuking while not hating—but doesn't mention the offender's response. No matter *what* the response, the commandment to forgive stands.

How, then, should we act toward unrepentant offenders after we forgive them? Rabbi Sha'ul (Saul; i.e., Paul) tells us in 2 Thess. 3:14–15 that it is possible to forgive someone, and yet choose not to spend time with him. In other words, there is a world of difference between unforgiveness, which is a sin, and tough love which is sometimes a necessity.

Grudge-holding takes a terrible physical, emotional and spiritual toll. Man was never meant to carry bitterness. Yeshua's words about these "torments" in Matt. 18:34–35 are echoed by the rabbis, who say in the *Talmud*, "The man who declines to forgive . . . becomes the guilty party, and God's anger is turned away from the other and directed toward him." Certainly, many lack peace and wholeness today because they fail to obey the crucial *Torah* commandment, "Don't take vengeance on or bear a grudge against any of your people."

ELUL

8

אלול

Aug. 20, 1999
Sept. 8, 2000
Aug. 27, 2001
Aug. 16, 2002
Sept. 5, 2003
Aug. 25, 2004

Prayer Focus

Today I Will

. . . choose to forgive all who have offended me.

MW

ELUL

9

אלול

Aug. 21, 1999 (49)
Sept. 9, 2000 (49)
Aug. 28, 2001
Aug. 17, 2002 (49)
Sept. 6, 2003 (49)
Aug. 26, 2004

Prayer Focus

Everything in me waits for *Adonai* more than guards on watch wait for morning (Ps. 130:6).

An old Jewish story tells of a mute shepherd boy who slips into the back of a synagogue toward the end of the *Yom Kippur* (Day of Atonement) service. He is frustrated that he cannot join in with the fervent prayers of the Holy Day. The service approaches its climax as the entire congregation cries out seven times , "*ADONAI Hu HaElohim*!" (the LORD he is God!) The shepherd boy pulls from his pocket a little whistle that he has carved from a peach pit to call his sheep. At the final repetition of the mighty declaration, he lets out a shrill blast that lingers long after the words end. The congregation gasps in unison and gazes at him in horror. He has desecrated this holy moment! But the wise old rabbi smiles at the lad. "Finally," he says, "we are ready to end the service, because we have prayed with all our hearts."

The form of prayer is important, but *kavvanah*—the heart's intention to worship God—is indispensable. We are involved in a constant struggle to maintain *kavvanah* in the midst of our busy routines. Sometimes even religious routine can inhibit *kavvanah*. But like the old rabbi, we must recognize that some "distractions" may actually serve to draw us closer to God.

Today I Will

. . . be open to the unexpected people or events that may come to shake up my routine and restore my focus on God.

RR

The ones standing highest are chopped down, the lofty are laid low (Isa. 10:33).

Pride is a tricky thing. It creeps in, unexpected, seeking to take us hostage. Its goal is to keep us from the blessing of God and to put God in a position where he must resist us when he longs to embrace us. Pride loves to wear a spiritual cloak, causing God to appear conceited to the world.

Many years ago, when I began in ministry, I had a meeting with an Orthodox rabbi. We both had spiritual concerns about a new Jewish believer in my synagogue (his concerns, of course, were different from mine). In the process of a very frank discussion, this rabbi told me sincerely that he kept all 613 *mitzvot* (commandments) in the *Torah.* I had never heard a rabbi say that before, and it surprised me. When I got home, it occurred to me that there was one commandment this rabbi could not be keeping—to walk humbly with God (Mic. 6:8). Like Benjamin Franklin, who always kept twelve of his personal thirteen commandments and always failed number thirteen, the rabbi was failing even as he declared his success. Of course, Franklin's number thirteen was "avoid pride."

Is pride holding you hostage? There is a way out, and it begins with embracing God's undeserved love.

Today I Will

. . . acknowledge my pride and choose to humbly depend on God's grace for my confidence.

Aug. 22, 1999
Sept. 10, 2000
Aug. 29, 2001
Aug. 18, 2002
Sept. 7, 2003
Aug. 27, 2004

Prayer Focus

MW

Aug. 23, 1999
Sept. 11, 2000
Aug. 30, 2001
Aug. 19, 2002
Sept. 8, 2003
Aug. 28, 2004 (49)

Those who hope in *ADONAI* will renew their strength (Isa. 40:31).

If you're like me, you hate to wait. I become impatient standing in line. I get exasperated when I'm stuck behind someone who's driving too slowly. So for me, one of the most difficult commands to obey is the command to wait on the Lord.

There is an old Jewish proverb that says, "Patience is half of wisdom." If we have enough wisdom to wait for God, he will provide us with the other half of the wisdom we need. God wants us to slow down enough so that we can hear the sound of his still, small voice, so that we can be fed and built up through spending time with him. Only then can we have the strength to run with God and not grow weary.

But some people think that waiting on the Lord is a passive behavior rather than an active one. They use the command to wait as an excuse for their own indolence: "I don't want to do this or that because I'm waiting on the Lord." Waiting on God is active, not passive. We wait on God through actions like prayer, fasting, worship, and meditation on God's Word. It requires devotion, concentration, thought, and it has a goal. The goal for those who wait on God is to have strength renewed, to soar like eagles, and run the race God has set before them.

Prayer Focus

Today I Will

. . . renew my strength through actively waiting on the Lord.

DB

Have no fear, Ya'akov, you worm, you men of Isra'el! I will help you (Isa. 41:14).

Once I was reading Isa. 41:10–16, in which God told Israel how he would utterly defeat all of her enemies. When I came to this verse about the "worm," I thought, "How insulting! Why would God call Israel a worm in the middle of this wonderful promise of deliverance?" Then I understood. It is because we are! Rabbi Sha'ul (Saul; i.e., Paul) said it a little differently in the *Brit Chadashah* (New Covenant Scriptures), "My power is brought to perfection in weakness" (2 Cor. 12:9).

It was during a time of great stress, trial, and tribulation in my ministry when I received this revelation. I suddenly understood that I needed to become weak—a worm—in order for God to be strong within me. The victory eventually came, not through my abilities, but by God's mighty hand. Interestingly, later in that same passage, God said he would transform this worm into a "threshing-sledge" (Isa. 41:15) that would pulverize mountains! When we yield to him totally, he will transform us into mighty instruments of righteousness.

Do you have any mountains today that need pulverizing? Trust the Lord completely, and he will become strong in you. Recognize that your strength for this spiritual walk comes from him alone. Let God perfect his strength in you.

Today I Will

. . . recognize that I cannot live a victorious life in the Messiah through my flesh. It can only be done in the Spirit.

ELUL

12

אלול

Aug. 24, 1999
Sept. 12, 2000
Aug. 31, 2001
Aug. 20, 2002
Sept. 9, 2003
Aug. 29, 2004

Prayer Focus

DC

ELUL

13

אלול

Aug. 25, 1999
Sept. 13, 2000
Sept. 1, 2001 (49)
Aug. 21, 2002
Sept. 10, 2003
Aug. 30, 2004

Praised be God, Father of our Lord Yeshua the Messiah, compassionate Father (2 Cor. 1:3).

Rabbi Sha'ul's (Saul's; i.e., Paul's) description of God as the "compassionate Father" recalls in my mind the words of *Yedid Nefesh*, the beautiful prayer recited just before the arrival of *Shabbat* (the Sabbath): "Beloved of the soul, compassionate Father, your servant will run like the deer, he will bow down before your splendor."

We are drawn to God because he is the "compassionate Father," but how well do we really understand compassion? We define God's compassion as guarding us from all trouble, but Scripture defines it as God's drawing near to us during trouble. If we respond to our trials by running toward God, as the prayer says, we learn that he is indeed the "beloved of our souls," there to sustain us in difficult times.

Likewise, the Lord is the "God of all encouragement and comfort" (2 Cor. 1:3b). The original Greek wording here suggests that he comes alongside us to strengthen us, to be our advocate in the midst of trial. God does not shield us from all trouble, but draws near to us through trouble, so that we learn to depend more fully upon him. Then we are able to comfort others with God's comfort, not by trying to smooth over their pain, but by doing what God does: drawing alongside, staying close, and listening carefully.

Prayer Focus

Today I Will

. . . respond to trouble not by questioning God's goodness, but by turning toward him as he draws close to me.

RR

Give to a wise man, and he grows still wiser; teach a righteous man, and he will learn still more (Prov. 9:9).

Aug. 26, 1999
Sept. 14, 2000
Sept. 2, 2001
Aug. 22, 2002
Sept. 11, 2003
Aug. 31, 2004

Over several years in the ministry, I've encountered two different kinds of people. The first respond like the disciples did when Yeshua told them that one of them would betray him. Each of them humbly asked, "Is it I?" The second type of person would give a different response, something like "How dare you suggest I'm capable of that?" I have found that the first kind make good disciples; the second do not.

There are many reasons why some of us respond more defensively than others to loving instruction and correction. Explanations can range from childhood extreme overcorrection to extreme undercorrection, from a distorted sense of being unjustly persecuted to a distorted sense of superiority. Whatever the reasons, the Scripture tells us that such people lack wisdom.

How does one change in this area? After all, habits don't die easily. Some sincere believers have spent a lifetime closing their ears to correction whenever it was directed at them. I believe the answer starts with the biblical definition of wisdom: "The fear of *ADONAI*" (Prov. 9:10). When we respond to God as David did in Ps. 139:24, asking him who sees all to search us and reveal anything hurtful within us, then we will be more open when the answer comes through one of God's servants. In this way, we can cultivate teachableness in our lives.

Prayer Focus

Today I Will

. . . open my ears as someone well taught (Isa. 50:4) when a fellow believer has a loving word of instruction or correction for me.

MW

ELUL

15

אלול

Aug. 27, 1999
Sept. 15, 2000
Sept. 3, 2001
Aug. 23, 2002
Sept. 12, 2003
Sept. 1, 2004

Prayer Focus

ADONAI is my light and salvation; whom do I need to fear? (Ps. 27:1)

I was visiting a local conservative synagogue with my family. At the break, I met some longtime friends, including my former *chazzan* (cantor, worship leader), who had recently moved to Israel. The *chazzan* was now working for an organization that promoted Orthodox Judaism among secular Israeli Jews. He was glad to see me . . . until I told him I was a Messianic Jew. The rabbi motioned for everyone to be seated, but the *chazzan*, outraged at my confession, kept turning in his seat to accuse me of betraying my people. I tried answering his accusations, but he grew only more furious—and meanwhile, the service was starting. People seated in front of us were looking back. I felt very embarrassed. I also felt afraid. I had never encountered such hostility in a synagogue.

I didn't know what to do, so I silently prayed for the Lord's help. Just then, I heard the rabbi say, "Please turn to Psalm 27." The Scripture served as an anchor for my soul. As I repeated the words, along with the rest of the congregation, my embarrassment left and my fear disappeared. Strength filled my soul. After the service, the *chazzan* argued even more intensely with me for several hours. He pushed me, spat on me and insulted me in front of my family, but I was able to maintain peace in my heart and respond to him with gentleness and self-control.

Are you ever afraid? The Word of God is a hammer that breaks fear into pieces.

Today I Will

. . . memorize Ps. 27:1–2 so that I will be able to recall it in times of fear.

DR

The woman you gave to be with me—she gave me fruit from the tree, and I ate (Gen. 3:12).

In this record of Adam's words, we have history's first blame-shift. Not coincidentally, we also have history's first case of marital strife. Blame-shifting and strife are like Siamese twins; they're inseparable. That's because all sin leads to blame-shifting, which leads to strife. Though we may give blame-shifting other names, like "denial" or "rationalization," it remains what it was in Adam's day—part of the sin cycle. It now enslaves people everywhere. The only remedy is full repentance, which includes taking full responsibility for our actions.

The lie at the root of what is called "Christian anti-Semitism" is the most grievous example of blame-shifting. Central to this form of blame-shifting is the accusation that the Jewish people are singularly responsible for the death of Messiah Yeshua. The fruits of this blame-shift have included darkness in the Church and death to millions. Kefa (Peter) lays the blame for Yeshua's death where it truly belongs—on *all* of us. "This has come true in this city, since Herod and Pontius Pilate, with the *Goyim* [Gentiles] and the peoples of Israel, all assembled against your holy servant Yeshua" (Acts 4:27). The truth contained in this passage has brought true repentance to many believers in Yeshua. Ultimately, blame-shifting has no place in the discussion of Yeshua's death, because every one of us is to blame.

Today I Will

. . . face responsibility for my own sin, instead of shifting blame.

ELUL

16

אלול

Aug. 28, 1999 (50)
Sept. 16, 2000 (50)
Sept. 4, 2001
Aug. 24, 2002 (50)
Sept. 13, 2003 (50)
Sept. 2, 2004

Prayer Focus

MW

Aug. 29, 1999
Sept. 17, 2000
Sept. 5, 2001
Aug. 25, 2002
Sept. 14, 2003
Sept. 3, 2004

My servant Kalev [Caleb], because he had a different Spirit with him and has fully followed me (Num. 14:24).

In Num. 13:4–16, God lists the twelve tribal leaders who were sent out to spy on the Land. It is just a list of names. Other than Yehoshu'a (Joshua), they are all unknown. We are told their tribes and the names of their fathers, but nothing is given that distinguishes one from another.

Yet forty days later, there are two names that stand out from the rest. Two are honored while ten go down in infamy as the wicked congregation that turned the hearts of Israel away from God. What's the difference? They all had the same opportunity, they all saw the same things, they all had heard the same promises. Kalev and Yehoshu'a were motivated and animated by a different spirit.

Our names are on the list of all humanity. When the list is read at the end of days, what will be known about each of us? We can choose which spirit we will follow.

Prayer Focus

Today I Will

. . . sow to the *Ruach* (Spirit), so that I might reap abundant life in Yeshua.

MM

With everlasting grace I will have compassion on you (Isa. 54:8).

Aug. 30, 1999
Sept. 18, 2000
Sept. 6, 2001
Aug. 26, 2002
Sept. 15, 2003
Sept. 4, 2004 (50)

Our view of God's character shapes every attitude and relationship in our lives. Is God harsh and aloof, watching from a distance for us to stumble, or is he unshakably loyal, always there for us, no matter what we may encounter?

Isaiah grapples with this question as he considers Israel in exile, seemingly forsaken by God. Has God given up on Israel? No, Isaiah reminds them, "For your husband is your Maker, *ADONAI-Tzva'ot* [LORD of Hosts] is his name" (Isa. 54:5). God's character reflects *chesed* (unwavering favor and loyalty) such as underlies any healthy marriage. This favor depends not on Israel's performance, but on God's faithfulness to his own covenant promises. God, moreover, shows Israel not only *chesed*, but *chesed olam* (everlasting kindness).

Some theologians claim that God has divorced Israel, but the Lord says that the separation is only temporary; his favor and kindness are permanent. Messiah came to bring repentance, forgiveness, and atonement to Israel, so that the marriage between God and his people can be restored. In Messiah, God offers his *chesed* to all who believe. As we understand this *chesed*, we begin to practice it toward others, not treating them according to their performance or our prejudices, but giving favor freely—as God himself does.

Prayer Focus

Today I Will

. . . treat those around me with *chesed*, even if they don't deserve it, because God has shown me favor and kindness that I do not deserve.

RR

Aug. 31, 1999
Sept. 19, 2000
Sept. 7, 2001
Aug. 27, 2002
Sept. 16, 2003
Sept. 5, 2004

One day you will see the Son of Man sitting at the right hand of *HaG'vurah* and coming on the clouds of heaven (Matt. 26:64).

Jacob's son Joseph had a dream. His eleven brothers, mother, and father, represented by eleven stars, the moon and the sun, all bowed before him. This dream aroused the brothers' jealousy and inspired them to sell Joseph into bondage in Egypt. Yet years later, when Joseph had become viceroy over all Egypt, and his brothers were brought before him, they did indeed bow before him. The sages say that the brothers bowed before Joseph a total of five times throughout the story. The one whom they had rejected became their ruler and judge, as well as their savior.

Centuries later, the *Cohen HaGadol* (High Priest) of Israel sat in judgment over an itinerant Galilean rabbi named Yeshua, who was making outrageous claims about himself. Yeshua told the *Cohen HaGadol* that "one day" he would see him sitting in the place of judgment at the right hand of *HaGevurah* (God; literally, the Power). Yeshua knew he was about to die, yet he spoke of the resurrection, a day when the *Cohen HaGadol* would be summoned before the throne of God to receive his eternal reward. He would then look up toward the throne of God, and would see this same Yeshua, whom he had turned over to the Gentiles for execution, sitting as ruler, judge and savior of those who had acknowledged him.

Prayer Focus

Today I Will

. . . bow before Yeshua, recognizing him as Messiah and Lord in all aspects of my life.

RR

Praised be God, Father of our Lord Yeshua the Messiah, who, in keeping with his great mercy (1 Pet. 1:3).

Sept. 1, 1999
Sept. 20, 2000
Sept. 8, 2001 (50)
Aug. 28, 2002
Sept. 17, 2003
Sept. 6, 2004

The Hebrew word for "mercy" is *rachamim.* It's plural. In Hebrew, you can't say "mercy" (singular). You can only say "mercies" (plural). This is good news! It means that God has loads and loads of mercy—not just one mercy, but mercy upon mercy upon mercy. It's enough not just for one time, but for every time we need it. It's enough not just for bad sins, but also for the very, very bad sins.

In Hebrew, the word for "sin" can be in the singular, but "mercy" is always in the plural. What is the lesson? Your sins may be great, but rest assured, his *rachamim* are greater. We ask for mercy and God gives us *rachamim.* He gives us mercies overflowing and able to fill up and cleanse every sin and failure, with mercies to spare. So open your heart wide. He doesn't just have mercy for you. He has mercies—and more than enough for you to live a life of abundant joy and victory.

Prayer Focus

Today I Will

. . . let the failures, the sin, the pain, and the guilt of the past be healed by God's *rachamim.*

JC

Sept. 2, 1999
Sept. 21, 2000
Sept. 9, 2001
Aug. 29, 2002
Sept. 18, 2003
Sept. 7, 2004

What is revealed is God's anger from heaven against all the godliness and wickedness (Rom. 1:18).

Most people have a hard time believing in the wrath of God. We are more comfortable envisioning God as a benevolent grandfather-type who pats his erring children on the head, smiles beneficently and encourages us to run along and do better. When we have a low or diminished view of sin, we have a low or diminished view of God.

One day when I was witnessing in downtown Chicago, a woman approached and declared defiantly, "I am a good person. I can't believe in a God who would judge someone for making a few mistakes." God doesn't change to suit our opinions. He wasn't created in our image; we were created in his. Some people have a "check-out counter" theology; they think that they can choose the items they like and leave behind the ones they don't.

Moshe *Rabeynu* (Moses our Teacher) didn't come down from the mountain carrying the Ten Suggestions. The standard that God set forth in his Word is non-negotiable. "Thou shalt not." There's not a lot of gray area there. Micah declares, "Human being, you have already been told what is good, what *ADONAI* demands of you. . . . " (Mic. 6:8) There's no mystery here. Instead of minimizing sin, we must remember God's wrath. Only then can we truly understand and rejoice in the salvation he provides through Yeshua.

Prayer Focus

Today I Will

. . . refuse to minimize the power of sin or the wrath of God. I will hold my life up to the standard of righteousness revealed in his Word and seek to turn from sin through faith in Yeshua the Messiah.

DB

Don't condemn, and you won't be condemned (Luke 6:37).

We live in a world where most people are quick to condemn others for the faults they see. Cynicism and suspicion are the order of the day. Instead of looking for the good in others, we look for evil, and we're usually not disappointed. An old Yiddish proverb says, "*Az me vil a hunt a zets geben, gefint men a shteken.*" (When you want to beat a dog, you're sure to find a stick.) We're good at finding fault. This is particularly true among believers, I'm sad to say.

It takes special grace from the Lord not to judge others quickly. It takes a willingness to listen and really hear before we speak. God gave us two ears and one mouth. There's a lesson in anatomy. Can you imagine what we would be like if it were the other way around? It takes a conscious effort to resist our natural propensity to judge and condemn. If we listen before we speak and hear the other side before we draw conclusions, we will find more understanding and less cause for offense. It is only through the grace of God that we can find it in our hearts to forgive others.

Sept. 3, 1999
Sept. 22, 2000
Sept. 10, 2001
Aug. 30, 2002
Sept. 19, 2003
Sept. 8, 2004

Prayer Focus

Today I Will

. . . resist the temptation to judge others. Instead, I will listen before speaking and extend forgiveness as Messiah has forgiven me.

DB

Sept. 4, 1999
(51, 52)
Sept. 23, 2000
(51, 52)
Sept. 11, 2001
Aug. 31, 2002
(51, 52)
Sept. 20, 2003
(51, 52)
Sept. 9, 2004

Prayer Focus

On the Day of Judgment people will have to give account for every careless word they have spoken (Matt. 12:36).

Before *Rosh HaShanah* (the traditional New Year), Orthodox Jews will sometimes ask a panel of judges to annul any vows they have taken carelessly and become unable to fulfill, so the vows will not be held against them on the Holy Day. Under rabbinic law, a vow, although accepted voluntarily, becomes a compulsory commandment of *Torah*: "[He] is to do everything he said he would do." The one who fails to carry out his vow violates a negative command of *Torah*: "He is not to break his word" (Num. 30:2[3]).

This legal principle demonstrates the great power of every word that we speak. No wonder Messiah warns us against using words idly! Every word has a potential impact we can hardly imagine. The *right* word can brighten the day for a discouraged child or give a young person direction for the rest of his or her life. The power of words should not be wasted.

Our age of cheap and abundant talk tempts us to scatter our words carelessly. It encourages us to say something untrue just to keep the peace or to satisfy someone else's expectation. But Yeshua reminds us, "Just let your 'Yes' be a simple 'Yes,' and your 'No' a simple 'No'; anything more than this has its origin in evil" (Matt. 5:37).

Today I Will

. . . limit myself to words that are true, positive, and a good investment of the power that God has placed in them.

RR

As you have received Messiah Yeshua the Lord, so walk in Him, rooted and built up in Him and established in the faith, as you have been taught, abounding in it with thanksgiving (Col. 2:6–7 NKJV).

Sept. 5, 1999
Sept. 24, 2000
Sept. 12, 2001
Sept. 1, 2002
Sept. 21, 2003
Sept. 10, 2004

Biblical
On this day, the Israelites resumed building the second Temple after a sixteen year suspension (Hag. 1:14–15).

Prayer Focus

In the above passage, we are exhorted both to be "established" and to "abound" in faith. What does it mean to be established in the faith? Is there a difference between being established and abounding in the same faith? I believe there is.

Being established in the faith involves becoming solid and secure in one's doctrine, character and lifestyle. It means we have developed a consistent devotional life, are regularly tithing to our local congregation, and are living out the tenets of our faith in our daily lives.

Abounding in the faith, on the other hand, has to do with fruitfulness—a daily fellowship with God that carries us beyond merely being consistent in our walk with Messiah to a place of responding generously to the daily promptings of the *Ruach* (Spirit). A person abounding in the faith will actively and wholeheartedly pursue God on a daily basis, listening for his voice and obeying his leading. He will hear and respond when God says, "Go over and speak to that person now" or "Give such and such an amount in the offering today."

What about you? Are you established in the faith? Are you experiencing that abounding fruitfulness the above passage exhorts us to pursue? In order to be well-rounded and mature believers, we need to do both!

Today I Will

. . . choose to become better established in the faith and also to abound in fruitfulness in my daily life.

JB

Sept. 6, 1999
Sept. 25, 2000
Sept. 13, 2001
Sept. 2, 2002
Sept. 22, 2003
Sept. 11, 2004
(51, 52)

Traditional
Esrim VeChamishah Be'Elul
(the 25th of Elul)

Prayer Focus

The fame of your majesty spreads even above the heavens! (Ps. 8:2)

Look up in the sky. The heavens do indeed declare God's glory. We are an infinitesimal part of the universe. We live in a solar system comprised of one star—known to us as the sun. This solar system is in the galaxy called the Milky Way. The Milky Way contains 300 billion stars. There are at least 200 billion galaxies, all of which contain at least 100 billion stars. That is what we know. There is much more we do not know. The vastness of the universe is awesome.

Some believe there is no end to the universe. That seems impossible. Others believe there is an end. Then what lies beyond? These are questions to which we may never know the answer.

The distances across the galaxies are immense. The Hubble Telescope is purportedly looking at stars that approach 15 billion light years away. We look up in the sky knowing that we will never get to those far-off bodies.

The heavens are a testimony of the great artist who painted them and the physical principles that keep them intact. From the smallest grain of sand to the great expanse above, from the single-celled animal to the intricacy of the human brain, there is a similarity in the stroke of the brush of our Creator.

Today I Will

EK

. . . praise God for that which he has created.

Those who sow in tears will reap with cries of joy (Ps. 126:5).

Sept. 7, 1999
Sept. 26, 2000
Sept. 14, 2001
Sept. 3, 2002
Sept. 23, 2003
Sept. 12, 2004

Each of the High Holy Days contains a prophetic mystery. The first is *Yom Teru'ah* (the Day of Blowing Trumpets), when the *shofar* (ram's horn) is blasted, calling God's people to stop what they're doing and get ready to meet the Lord. Next is *Yom Kippur* (the Day of Atonement), which calls God's people to repent and come into his presence to be washed and forgiven. The last is *Sukkot* (the Feast of Tabernacles), the great day of celebration, which calls God's people to be thankful and rejoice in his blessings.

Each feast can be described in one word: *Yom Teru'ah*: Stop! *Yom Kippu*r: Repent! *Sukkot*: Rejoice! Now put them all together and you have a powerful message straight from God: Stop! Repent! Rejoice!

God wants us to rejoice, but we can only really rejoice inasmuch as we repent. We can only really repent inasmuch as we really stop. Do you want real joy? You need to really repent. Do you want to really repent? Then you need to really stop.

You can't change if you don't stop. God wants you to have real joy, but it all starts by stopping.

Prayer Focus

Today I Will

. . . stop watching TV or reading, and invest one hour in being close with the Lord.

JC

Sept. 8, 1999
Sept. 27, 2000
Sept. 15, 2001 (51)
Sept. 4, 2002
Sept. 24, 2003
Sept. 13, 2004

Prayer Focus

I thank you because I am awesomely made, wonderfully; your works are wonders—I know this very well (Ps. 139:14).

The eye measures only one inch in diameter. Yet it can see objects as far away as the distant stars and as small as a grain of sand. It can adapt to various shades of light and dark. The eye can distinguish among more than 150 different colors. It can judge distances and discern the thickness of objects. The eye can focus even when the head is moving. It is a wonderful creation that gives us the ability to perceive our environment better.

The heart weighs less than one pound. It beats 10,000 times every day and pumps over 75 gallons of blood through its chambers every *hour* of every day. It is responsible for circulating the blood supply through 100,000 miles of blood vessels throughout the body.

The brain weighs three pounds. It is the master control center of the body. There are 100 billion neurons in the brain that control all of the systems of the body, enabling us to think and move.

These organs are wonderfully made. They are so intricate and yet so simple. They defy man's ability to totally comprehend their workings, and yet they have inspired such inventions as the telescope, the artificial heart and the computer. These organs attest to the awesomeness of their Creator.

Today I Will

. . . praise God for his wonderful creation—me.

EK

When I look at your heavens, the work of your fingers . . . what are mere mortals . . . that you watch over them with such care? (Ps. 8:3[4]–4[5])

When God created "lights in the dome of the sky to divide the day from the night," he said, "Let them be for signs, seasons [*mo'adim*], days and years" (Gen. 1:14). Later, these *mo'adim* became known as *mo'adey Adonai* (the appointed times of the Lord)—the yearly cycle of festivals ordained for Israel (Lev. 23:1–2, 44). Before Israel or even mankind had been created, God anticipated Israel's life of worship and made detailed provision for it.

Science may describe the "heavenly lights" as distant planets, stars, and galaxies hurling through empty space. Humankind, in this view, often seems dwarfed and insignificant against the vastness of the cosmos. To the eye of faith, however, these same planets and stars are reminders of a loving Creator. He is not a nameless force, but a Father who made plans for his children from the very beginning. Here is an aspect of love that we do not always speak of, but that parents understand instinctively. Love anticipates the needs of the beloved and seeks to meet them before they even arrive. The Lord who created the boundless expanse of space "is mindful of us." Such is the Father's love!

Today I Will

. . . think in advance of the needs of my loved ones, even as the Lord is ever mindful of me.

Sept. 9, 1999
Sept. 28, 2000
Sept. 16, 2001
Sept. 5, 2002
Sept. 25, 2003
Sept. 14, 2004

Prayer Focus

RR

Sept. 10, 1999
Sept. 29, 2000
Sept. 17, 2001
Sept. 6, 2002
Sept. 26, 2003
Sept. 15, 2004

Biblical
Erev Yom Teru'ah
(the Eve of the Day of Blowing [the *Shofar*])

Traditional
Erev Rosh HaShanah
(the Eve of the New Year)

Prayer Focus

Then the sign of the Son of Man will appear in the sky. . . . He will send out his angels with a great *shofar* (Matt. 24:30–31).

In ancient Israel, the *shofar* (ram's horn) was sounded to announce the visit of a king, to call the people to prepare their town for his entry, and to escort him into their walls. *Yom Teru'ah* (the day of the *shofar*-blast; see Num. 29:1), recalls the *shofar*-blast at Mount Sinai that announced the presence of the Lord and called Israel to welcome him.

Yom Teru'ah also looks forward to a *shofar*-blast to come. One of the prayers recited on this day says, "Our God and God of our fathers, sound the great *Shofar* for our freedom, lift up the banner to gather our exiles." What is the banner? Yeshua revealed that "the great *Shofar*" would sound at his return, and that a "banner" would accompany it—the sign of the Son of Man. This mysterious phrase may be simply another way of saying, "They will see the Son of Man coming on the clouds of heaven" (Matt. 24:30) as visible as "lightning that flashes out of the east and fills the sky to the west horizon" (Matt. 24:27). The returning Messiah himself will be the banner, the sign that the promised kingdom will be established at last. Yeshua told his followers to "stay alert" and "be ready" (Matt. 24:42, 44) to hear the *shofar*, to see the banner, and to welcome him at his coming.

Today I Will

. . . be alert to listen for the sound of the *shofar* announcing Messiah's return.

RR

Appendix A

Biblical Festivals

God was already designing his calendar as early as the fourth day of Creation. He thought about time and the various ways in which his children would count time, including days, lunar months, festival times,[1] and years. This is one of the reasons why he created the moon and sun (Gen. 1:14; Ps. 104:19).[2]

In ancient times, the prophets and apostles looked to the moon to determine the time of month. They understood that a new moon marked the beginning of a month and a full moon marked the middle of a month. In keeping with this ancient and God-inspired method of counting months, this devotional includes a pictorial tracing of the lunar cycle.[3]

The Appointed Times of the Lord

All the festivals of the Lord are noted in this devotional and are designated in the side margins under the "Biblical" heading. At the heart of their devotional meaning is the way in which each one points to Yeshua and magnifies him. *Rosh Chodesh* (the New Moon) remembers his birth, *Pesach* (Passover) his death, *Matzot* (the Feast of Unleavened Bread) his purity, *Bikkurim* (the Feast of First Fruits) his resurrection, *Shavu'ot* (the Feast of Weeks) the pouring out of his Spirit, *Yom Teru'ah* (the Day of Blowing the *Shofar*, Trumpet) his return, *Yom Kippur* (the Day of Atonement) his priestly ministry, and *Sukkot* (the Feast of Tabernacles) the establishment of his kingship over all the nations of the earth.[4]

Though *Chanukkah* (the Feast of Dedication) is often included among the biblical festivals because of its mention in the Scriptures (John 10:22), we have chosen to classify it under the "Traditional" heading since it is not commanded by God. Likewise, *Purim*, though mentioned in the Book of Esther, it is not commanded by God, but by man (Es. 9:27–32). See Appendix B for more information on the meanings of *Chanukkah* and *Purim*.

God's calendar also serves as a devotional tool in prioritizing time with God. Living by God's calendar leads to spending consistent time with *Avinu* (our Father) on special weekly, monthly and annual occasions. Think of it in this way. The Lord has his own appointment book in heaven in which he schedules appointments to meet with his children. These are his "appointed times" and Leviticus 23 is a copy of his heavenly schedule. If we approach these times of sacred assembly in the right way, with humble and thankful hearts, we will experience especially anointed times of praise, worship and fellowship with God. His presence will be especially revealed to us on these occasions.

The festival dates below are provided that you may plan your schedule for celebrating God's appointed times several years in advance.

JEWISH YEAR	5759	5760	5761*	5762	5763	5764	
WESTERN YEAR	1998	1999	2000	2001	2002	2003	2004
FESTIVAL							
Purim	3/12–13	3/2–3	3/21–22	3/9–10	2/26–27	3/18–19	3/7–8
Pesach	4/10	3/31	4/19	4/7	3/27	4/16	4/5
Matzot	4/11–17	4/1–7	4/20–26	4/8–14	3/28–4/3	4/17–23	4/6–12
Bikkurim (biblical)**	4/12	4/4	4/23	4/15	3/31	4/20	4/11
Shavu'ot (biblical)**	5/31	5/23	6/11	6/3	5/19	6/8	5/30
Yom Teru'ah	9/21	9/11	9/30	9/18	9/7	9/27	9/16
Yom Kippur	9/30	9/20	10/9*	9/27	9/16	10/6	9/25
Sukkot	10/5–12	9/25–10/2	10/14–21	10/2–9	9/21–28	10/11–18	9/30–10/7

*The year 2000–2001 (5761) is a Sabbatical year[5]

**See Appendix B, endnote 6.

The following chart details the original, New Covenant and last days meanings of each of these festivals. [6]

Festival	Original Meaning	New Covenant Meaning	Last Days Meaning
ROSH CHODESH The New Moon (1st day of each month)	The moon was created, in part, to be the building block of the biblical calendar. *Rosh Chodesh* (the New Moon) refers to the phase of the lunar cycle when no part (or only a thin crescent) of the moon is visible. *Rosh Chodesh*, then, is a time to announce the beginning of new months and festival seasons (Gen. 1:14; Num. 10:10).	*Rosh Chodesh* points to Yeshua, whose light shines in the darkness. At first, he was not visible to men. Then, he was born into this world and became a source of light to men who walked in darkness. The birth of *Rosh Chodesh*, then, is a time to remember Yeshua's birth and give honor and glory to the Light of the World (Gen. 1:16; Matt. 4:16; John 8:12; 12:46; Col. 2:16–17).	*Rosh Chodesh* is a symbol of the eternity we will spend in fellowship with God in the new heavens and new earth (Isa. 66:22–23).
PESACH Passover (Nisan 14 at twilight)	*Pesach* (Passover) is a commemoration of the evening on which God redeemed his people from Egypt. God passed over the Israelites who had lamb's blood applied to the doorposts of their houses, while the firstborn of all the Egyptians perished. Pharaoh was humbled by the signs and wonders of the God of Israel, who showed himself to be more powerful than all the Egyptian deities. Consequently, Pharaoh begged the Israelites, who had been his slaves, to leave (Exod. 12; Lev. 23:4–5).	Yeshua is the *Pesach* lamb. His blood covers our sins so that we escape the coming judgment. By his shed blood, we have been set free from the bondage of sin and the power of the Adversary. As a result, we sing with all the angels in heaven, "Worthy is the Lamb, who was slain . . . " *Pesach* is a time to rejoice in our salvation as spiritual slaves set free (Rom. 4:7; 6:16–22; 1 Cor. 5:7; Col. 1:13–14; 1 Pet. 1:18–20; Rev. 5:11–12).	*Pesach* reminds us that a day will come when the Lord will break the yoke of the antiMessiah (antiChrist)—an oppressor of God's people—and the Lord will once again triumph by signs and wonders over the demonic forces in which the nations of the earth will put their trust. When Yeshua returns, he will celebrate *Pesach* with us. The feast will be a time of wonderful reunion (Luke 22:15–16; Rev. 11:3–6; 15–16; 19:19–20:10).

Festival	Original Meaning	New Covenant Meaning	Last Days Meaning
MATZOT The Feast of Unleavened Bread (Nisan 15–21)	When Pharaoh let the Israelites go, they left Egypt in such a hurry that they did not have time to let their bread rise. Consequently, they ate unleavened bread on their journey into the desert to meet with God. *Matzot* (the Feast of Unleavened Bread) reminds us of their hurried exodus (Exod. 12:31–34; Lev. 23:6–8).	Leaven is a symbol of sin. As leaven must be removed from our houses during this time, so must sin be removed from our lives. *Matzot* is, therefore, a time of spiritual spring cleaning. Each day we are dedicated to putting off the old self (i.e., the flesh; symbolized by leavened bread) and putting on the new self (unleavened bread) to be transformed into the image of Messiah (Exod. 12:14–20; 13:3–10; 1 Cor. 5:6–8; Eph. 4:22–24).	*Matzot* reminds us of a day to come when the world will be full of the glory of God. We will have resurrected bodies and sin will be but a memory (Matt. 13:41; Rev. 21:4, 27).
BIKKURIM The Feast of First Fruits (The day after the Sabbath during *Matzot**)	When the Israelites entered the Promised Land which flowed with milk and honey, they were to present an offering of the first fruits of the Land to the Lord God. *Bikkurim* (the Feast of First Fruits) is a time of thanksgiving to the Lord for fulfilling his promise and providing abundant provision. It is also a time to beseech God for his continued blessing (Lev. 23:9–14; Deut. 26:1–15).	As we thank God for his fulfilled promises, provision and blessing, we are to remember that Yeshua rose from the dead on the Feast of First Fruits. Through his death and resurrection we have entered into God's kingdom, a Land flowing with spiritual milk and honey (Mark 16:1, 9; 1 Cor. 15:20).	Yeshua was resurrected, the first fruit of those who sleep in their graves. The feast is, therefore, a wonderful reminder of our resurrection at his second coming (1 Cor. 15:20–23).
*SHAVU'OT*** The Feast of Weeks (50 days after *Bikkurim*)	The climactic spring harvest festival. A time to rejoice in the fullness of God's provision (Exod. 34:22;	The Holy Spirit (*Ruach HaKodesh*) was poured out on *Shavu'ot*, which resulted in a great harvest of Jewish souls. The feast	*Shavu'ot* is a reminder that, in the last days, the Lord will pour out his Spirit on the whole house of Israel. Israel will

FESTIVAL	ORIGINAL MEANING	NEW COVENANT MEANING	LAST DAYS MEANING
SHAVU'OT, Continued	Lev. 23:15–22; Deut. 16:9–12).	is, therefore, a time to renew our passion for outreach and to pray that the Lord of the Harvest would send a fresh outpouring of his *Ruach* (Spirit), even revival, with anointed workers to labor in the harvest field (Matt. 9:37–38; Acts 2:1–5, 41).	become an anointed priestly nation that ministers worldwide revival (Ezek. 36:24–27; 37:1–14; Joel 2:27–32).
*YOM TERU'AH**** The Day of Blowing (Tishri 1)	*Yom Teru'ah* (the Day of Blowing the *shofar*—ram's horn) called the people of Israel to prepare themselves for *Yom Kippur*, which took place ten days later. *Yom Teru'ah* was a time to begin humbling oneself before the Lord and repenting of one's sins (Lev. 23:23–27; 2 Chron. 7:14–16).	The feast is an opportunity to begin a ten day period of sincere humbling and asking the Lord to examine one's heart. It is also an appropriate time to intercede for the salvation of one's family, friends and nation (Ps. 26:2; 139:23–24; Dan. 9:4–23; Rom. 9:1–4; 10:1).	*Yom Teru'ah* points to the heavenly *shofar* (ram's horn) that will be blown at the second coming of Yeshua. When the *shofar* sounds, the Lord will fight against all the nations of the earth who have attacked Israel. The dead in Messiah will rise, the righteous who are alive will meet Yeshua in the clouds, and all of heaven will rejoice (Zech. 9:14–16; Matt. 24:30–31; 1 Cor. 15:51–52; 1 Thess. 4:13–18; Rev. 11:15–19).
YOM KIPPUR The Day of Atonement (Tishri 10)	*Yom Kippur* (the Day of Atonement) was a time to be forgiven for sins the Israelites had committed during the previous year. This forgiveness was received through repentance and believing that the High Priest's intercessory ministry was acceptable to God (Lev. 16; 23:26–32; Heb. 9:7).	*Yom Kippur* points to Yeshua, the great High Priest, in the order of Melchizedek, who entered the heavenly Tabernacle with his own blood to make atonement for all the sins of *all* men, for all time (including the sin of Adam). *Yom Kippur* is, therefore, a time to glorify Yeshua and reflect	*Yom Kippur* points to the fountain of cleansing that will be opened up after the return of Yeshua, causing the spiritual transformation of Israel and consequently all the nations of the earth (Ezek. 47:8–12; Zech. 12:10; 13:1; 14:8; Rev. 22:1–2).

Festival	Original Meaning	New Covenant Meaning	Last Days Meaning
YOM KIPPUR, Continued		on his priestly ministry in heaven. Consequently, this day is an appropriate time to deal with areas of sin in our lives that have resulted in a breach of relationship with God or man (Heb. 4:14–16; 5:1–10; 6:19–20; 7:11–28; 8:1–5; 9:11–28; 10:1–14, 19–22).	
SUKKOT & *SHEMINI ATZERET* The Feast of Tabernacles & 8th Day Assembly (Tishri 15–22)	*Sukkot* is the end-of-the-year harvest festival. It is a time to remember God's provision for the Israelites during their forty years of wandering in the desert, when they dwelt in huts or tabernacles. The feast is a time to renew our faith in *Adonai Yir'eh,* the Lord who will provide (Exod. 23:16; Lev. 23:33–43; Deut. 8; 16:13–17).	Yeshua was the Word made flesh, who tabernacled among us. *Sukkot* is a time to rejoice in the birth and earthly ministry of the Messiah (John 1:14).	As a harvest festival, *Sukkot* points to the great harvest of souls from among the nations in the last days. After the second coming of Yeshua, all the nations of the earth will celebrate *Sukkot* and send representatives to Jerusalem to worship Yeshua the King (Zech. 14:16–19).

* see Appendix B, endnote 6

** Referred to as Pentecost in the Greek New Testament

*** Traditionally referred to as *Rosh HaShanah*

Endnotes

1. The Hebrew word *mo'adim* in Gen. 1:14 is commonly translated "seasons." The same word appears throughout Leviticus 23 and is commonly translated "festivals" (see 23:4). Why the difference in translation? If *mo'adim* in Gen. 1:14 was translated "festivals," it would clearly imply to the reader that the biblical calendar had been in the mind of God when he created the heavenly bodies, and that the Lord's festivals were created for mankind in general, and not Israel alone. Christian translators, therefore, render the word "seasons" to rule out this universal application. Nevertheless, "festivals" is a more accurate translation on the basis of Ps. 104:19. The psalmist makes it clear that the *mo'adim* in Gen. 1:14 are the Lord's festivals because they are "marked off by the moon." The word "seasons" is an incorrect translation since the four seasons are "marked off by the sun." Thus, *The Stone Edition Tanach* translates Gen. 1:14, ". . . and they shall serve as signs, and for festivals, and for days and years" (Rabbi Nosson Scherman, editor, *The Stone Edition Tanach*, p. 3. See also Rabbi Aryeh Kaplan, *The Living Torah* (New York: Moznaim Publishing Corporation, 1981), p. 3. Scherman and Kaplan's translation of *mo'adim* in Gen. 1:14 agrees with the conclusion of Brown, Driver and Briggs, "It is most probable that in Gen. 1:14 the reference is to the sacred seasons as fixed by the moon's appearance; and so also Ps. 104:19, although many lexicons and commentaries refer these to the seasons of the year" (*The New Brown-Driver-Briggs-Gesenius Hebrew and English Lexicon*, p. 417). Holladay concurs that *mo'adim* in Genesis 1:14 refers to a "(time of) feast" (*A Concise Hebrew & Aramaic Lexicon*, p. 186); compare with Kittel, *Theological Dictionary of the New Testament*, vol. 3, p. 459.
2. God's calendar is based on the cycles of the moon and sun. Lunar months must correspond to the four seasons of the year, which are determined by the sun. The first month, for example, must coincide with the spring harvest festivals, First Fruits and Weeks (*Bikkurim* and *Shavu'ot*), and the seventh lunar month must coincide with the fall harvest festival, Tabernacles (*Sukkot*). This raises an interesting problem: The solar year (365 days) is approximately 11 days longer than 12 lunar months. Therefore, every 3 years, the calendar is unbalanced by approximately one month. Consequently, the spring harvest festivals (*Bikkurim* and *Shavu'ot*), without correction, will naturally retrogress toward winter and the fall harvest festival (*Sukkot*), without correction, will naturally retrogress toward summer. The historical solution to this problem, from as far back as the days of Yeshua, has been to add an extra month to the calendar approximately every three years called "second Adar." Though this method is nowhere prescribed in the Scriptures, it is clearly a practical necessity and there is little alternative. Yeshua upheld this approach to

maintaining God's calendar by virtue of his conformity to the dating of first century festivals. For a thorough discussion of the elements and design of the Jewish calendar, see Arthur Spier, *The Comprehensive Hebrew Calendar* (New York: Feldheim Publishers, 1986).

3. Pictures of the lunar cycle in this devotional are approximations and relative to the time of day and year.
4. See Barney Kasdan, *God's Appointed Times* (Baltimore: Lederer Publications, 1993); Kevin Howard, *The Feasts of the Lord* (Orlando: Zion's Hope, 1997); Samuele Bacchiocchi, *God's Festivals in Scripture and History* (Berrien Springs: Biblical Perspectives, 1995); Mitch and Zhava Glaser, *The Fall Feasts of Israel* (Chicago: Moody Press, 1987); Ceil and Moishe Rosen, *Christ in the Passover* (Chicago: Moody Press, 1978).
5. B. Zuckerman, *A Treatise on the Sabbatical Cycle and the Jubilee* (New York: Hermon Press, 1974; first published in London, 1866), p. 64.
6. David J. Rudolph, *The Back to the Torah Calendar Supplement*, 1996.

Appendix B

Traditional Jewish Observances

Every nation has its own culture and tradition. In this regard, every nation has its own calendar customs. The United States has the 4th of July and Thanksgiving. Japan has Girls' Day, Children's Day and Older Person's Day. Jewish tradition includes observing special days. Over thirty of them are designated in this devotional.

Jewish tradition is unique in that it draws heavily from biblical themes, which has both a positive and negative side. On the positive, much of Jewish culture is devotionally rich. For example, on *Simchat Torah* (the Joy of the *Torah*), our people come together to sing and dance with the *Torah* scroll in celebration of the preciousness of God's Word. All traditional Jewish commemorations can be creatively applied for devotional purposes.

On the negative side, because Jewish tradition often draws from biblical themes, many people lose clarity over what is biblical and what is traditional. Messianic Jews and Gentiles must discern the difference between *Torah* and tradition, what is God inspired and what is man inspired. Only then is it possible to establish correct priorities and choose which practices to follow as part of one's family tradition. In the margins of this devotional, the term "Biblical" is used to refer to practices that are "inspired by God." The term "Traditional" is used to designate practices that are "inspired by men."[1] Those who are new to the Jewish calendar will find these categories very helpful.

However, it is true that in some cases it is difficult to know where the line between "Biblical" and "Traditional" should be drawn. The division between *Torah* and tradition is sometimes like the division between spirit and soul. In such instances, culture can dovetail with the spirit of God's commandments and function as a kind of *halakhah* (law; i.e., the application of God's commandment to a specific time, place and circumstance). [2]

Another problem associated with the traditional calendar is that, over the centuries, some biblical calendar commandments have been changed or displaced by tradition. Here are a few examples that Messianic Jews and Gentiles need to be aware of:

Festival	Biblical	Traditional
Rosh Chodesh (the New Moon)	One day [3]	Sometimes 2 days
The New Year	Nisan 1[4]	Tishri 1[5]
Matzot (the Feast of Unleavened Bread)	7 days Days 1 & 7 are annual sabbaths	Called "8 days of Passover" Days 1, 2, 7 & 8 are annual sabbaths in the diaspora
Bikkurim (the Feast of First Fruits)	Day after the Sabbath after *Pesach* (Passover)[6]	Nisan 16, day of week varies
Sefirat Ha'Omer (Counting the Omer)	Begins on the day after the Sabbath after *Pesach*	Begins on Nisan 16
Shavu'ot (the Feast of Weeks)	Sunday, 7 weeks after *Bikkurim* One day	Sivan 6, day of week varies Two days in the diaspora
Yom Teru'ah (the Day of Blowing the *shofar*)	One day	Two days Called "*Rosh HaShanah*" (New Year)
Sukkot (the Feast of Tabernacles) & *Shemini Atzeret* (the 8th Day Assembly)	Day 1 & Day 8 (*Shemini Atzeret*) are annual sabbaths	Days 1, 2, 8 (*Shemini Atzeret*) and 9 (*Simchat Torah*) are annual sabbaths in the diaspora

The Messianic Jewish community teaches that Scripture alone is the authoritative instruction of God and takes precedence over the traditions of men.[7] In this regard, when tradition conflicts with *Torah*, Messianic Jews and Gentiles ought to uphold *Torah*. This is the clear teaching of Yeshua (Mark 7:6–13).

On a practical note, Messianic Jews and Gentiles need to maintain proper priorities with regard to tradition. Whereas it is wrong to pick and choose from God's commandments, it may be appropriate to chooose only those traditions commonly observed within the Jewish comunity.

All traditional commemorations are noted in the side margins of the devotional and keyed to the following chart.[8]

Date	Observance	Translation	Purpose
TISHRI			
1	*Rosh HaShanah*	The New Year	Regarded as the New Year because of its association with God's judgment and the righteous having their names inscribed in the Book of Life on this day. Also, it is the anniversary of the creation of Adam, the completion of Creation. See endnote 5.
1–10	*Yamim Nora'im*	The Days of Awe	Ten-day period to seek the Lord and to return to his paths of righteousness in order to be inscribed in the Book of Life. Messianic Jews and Gentiles believe that only through repentance and trusting in the atonement of Yeshua can one be written in the Book of Life.
2	*Rosh HaShanah* (Day 2)	The New Year (Day 2)	One-day extension of *Rosh HaShanah* is observed to ensure that the traditional New Year conforms with the appearance of the New Moon. Observed in the diaspora only.
3	*Tzom Gedaliah*	The Fast of Gedaliah	Public fast in memory of the assassination of Gedaliah, the last governor of Judah (Jer. 41:1–2; 2 Kings 25:25). After the destruction of the First Temple in 586 B.C.E., he was appointed by Nebuchadnezzar, the King of Babylon, to oversee the Jewish remnant who remained in the Land.
16	*Sukkot* (Day 2) (in diaspora only)	The Feast of Tabernacles (Day 2)	Additional day of *Sukkot*—considered an annual Sabbath—is observed in the diaspora to ensure that the celebration is in conformity with the appearance of the New Moon.

Date	Observance	Translation	Purpose
TISHRI, Continued			
21	*Hosha'na Rabbah*	The Great *Hosanna*	Concluding day of the judgment period that commenced with *Rosh HaShanah.*
22	*Simchat Torah* (in Israel only)	The Joy of the *Torah*	Celebration of the completion of reading the *Torah.* Also, a time to remember Moses's death and the appointment of Joshua to be his successor (Deut. 34). Moses was informed of his impending death on *Shemini Atzeret* (the closing assembly of *Sukkot*) and he waged his last war on *Simchat Torah.*
23	*Simchat Torah* (diaspora only)	The Joy of the *Torah* (See above)	Additional day of *Shemini Atzeret* (the closing assembly of *Sukkot*) is observed in the diaspora to ensure that the celebration is in conformity with the appearance of the New Moon. The day doubles as *Simchat Torah* in the diaspora.
KISLEV			
25–TEVET 2/3	*Chanukkah*	The Feast of Dedication	Time to remember the Maccabean victory over the armies of Antiochus Epiphanes and the rededication of the Temple which had been desecrated (John 10:22–23).
TEVET			
10	*Asarah BeTevet*	The 10th of Tevet	Public fast in memory of the siege of Jerusalem by Nebuchadnezzar in 588–586 B.C.E. (2 Kings 25:1; Zech. 8:19) and Titus in 70 C.E.
SHEVAT			
1	*Echad BeShevat*	The 1st of Shevat	Day to remember that Moses began delivering Deuteronomy on Shevat 1 and continued for thirty seven days until his death on Adar 7.

Date	Observance	Translation	Purpose
SHEVAT, Continued			
15	*Tu BeShevat*	The 15th of Shevat	In the Land of Israel, the annual rains come to an end by this time and a new cycle of tree growth begins. Historically, the day marked the beginning of the separation of the tithes of fruit. Today it commemorates the transformation of the Land of Israel from barren desert to blooming valleys and forests. Israelis regard it as Arbor (Tree) Day.
ADAR			
13	*Ta'anit Ester*	The Fast of Esther	Public fast in memory of Esther's fast before the Lord, that God would soften the heart of King Ahasuerus and spare his people Israel from Haman's evil plan of annihilation (Esther 4:9–16).
14–15	*Purim*	The Feast of Lots	Commemoration of God's deliverance of the Jews from Haman's evil plan of annihilation. Instead of allowing Haman to succeed in annihilating the Jews, the Lord turned the tables on Haman so that *he* and *his family* were killed instead. As a result, many pagans became Jews. *Purim* is a reminder that, throughout history, the Adversary will seek to destroy God's people, yet God is faithful to his covenant and will not allow this to happen.
15	*Shushan Purim*	Susa Lots	Day of *Purim* for Jews who live in walled cities, such as Jerusalem. Many Jews outside of these cities also celebrate it as a semi-holiday (Esther 9:18).

Date	Observance	Translation	Purpose
NISAN			
14	*Ta'anit Bekhorim*	The Fast of the Firstborn	Day to remember the Jewish firstborn who were saved during the last plague that fell upon Egypt (Exod. 11:1-7). A time for firstborn males to fast in gratitude.
16	*Pesach* (Day 2) (in diaspora only)	Passover (Day 2)	Additional day of *Pesach*—considered an annual Sabbath—is observed in the diaspora to ensure that the celebration is in conformity with the appearance of the New Moon.
16–Sivan 6	*Sefirat Ha'Omer* (traditional dates)	Counting the Omer	Counting of fifty days from *Pesach* to *Shavu'ot* (see endnote 6). Also, a period of semi-mourning in commemoration of the plague that killed 12,000 disciples of Rabbi Akiva.
22	*Pesach* (Day 8) (diaspora only)	Passover (Day 8)	Additional day of *Pesach*—considered an annual Sabbath—is observed in the disapora to ensure that the celebration is in conformity with the appearance of the New Moon.
27	*Yom HaSho'ah*	Holocaust Day	In memory of the six million who perished in the Holocaust and the many who gave their lives in the Warsaw Ghetto uprising.
IYYAR			
4	*Yom HaZikkaron*	Remembrance Day	In memory of those who gave their lives in defense of Israel's independence and security.
5	*Yom Ha'Atzma'ut*	Israel Independence Day	Anniversary of the day in 1948 when Israel's Declaration of Independence was signed and Israel became a modern-day nation.
18	*Lag Be'Omer*	The 33rd Day of the *Omer*	Day marking the suspension of semi-mourning during *Sefirat Ha'Omer*, and a time for joy.

Date	Observance	Translation	Purpose
IYYAR, Continued			
18	*Lag Be'Omer,* Continued		Day to commemorate the First Jewish Revolt against Rome in 66 C.E. This day also commemorates the survival of the Jewish people despite Roman persecution. Also known as Scholar's Day, because a plague that struck down 12,000 students of Rabbi Akiva ended on this day. Finally, Hitler died on this day, marking the end of Nazi tyranny.
28	*Yom Yerushalayim*	Jerusalem Day	Day to remember Israel's victory over Arab armies in the 1967 Six Day War. For the first time since 70 C.E., the Temple Mount and the Western Wall came under Jewish control.
SIVAN			
6	*Shavu'ot* (traditional)	The Feast of Weeks	Anniversary of the giving of the *Torah* — Exod. 20–31.See endnote 6.
7	*Shavu'ot* (Day 2) (in diaspora only)	The Feast of Weeks (Day 2)	Additional day of *Shavu'ot* is observed in the diaspora to ensure that the celebration conforms with the appearance of the New Moon.
TAMMUZ			
17	*Shiv'ah Asar BeTammuz*	The 17th of Tammuz	Public fast to remember that on this day: the tablets of the Ten Commandments were broken, the wall of the First Temple was breached, the heathen Apostomos burned the sanctuary *Torah* scrolls, an idol was erected, the daily offering was suspended, and Jerusalem was captured by the Romans.
18–Av 8	*Beyn HaMeytzarim*	Between the Straits	Three-week mourning period between public fast days *Shiv'ah Asar BeTammuz* and *Tish'ah Be'Av.* Motivated by profound sadness over the destruction of Jerusalem and the Temple.

Date	Observance	Translation	Purpose
AV			
9	*Tish'ah Be'Av*	The 9th of Av	Public fast in memory of the following events: the Israelites were forbidden from entering the Promised Land, both Temples were destroyed, the Bar Kochba revolt ended, Hadrian plowed Jerusalem, and all Jews were expelled from Spain in 1492.
15	*Tu Be'Av*	The 15th of Av	Day to remember the Israelites who perished in the desert because of their sins (Num. 14:26–35). During the First Temple period, the annual dance of the maidens (Judg. 21:19–21) occurred on this day. It also marked the end of the wood-cutting season and a time when Jews donated wood for the service of the Temple. In more recent history, the day commemorated the end of the Hadrianic persecutions. Overall, it is a day of joy to counterbalance the three weeks of mourning that led up to *Tish'ah Be'Av*.
ELUL			
25	*Esrim VeChamishah Be'Elul*	The 25th of Elul	Day on which Creation began. From this day until *Rosh HaShanah*, the day on which Creation was completed, (with the creation of Adam), it is customary to read the corresponding Scripture passages from Genesis 1.

Endnotes

1. The reader may wonder how we handled *Purim* (Feast of Lots) and *Chanukkah* (Feast of Dedication). *Chanukkah* is mentioned in the Scriptures (John 10:22), but not explicitly commanded. *Purim*, on the other hand, is not explicitly commanded by God, but it is commanded by a servant of God to be "observed in every generation" (Esther 9:28). This pronouncement was then recorded in God's Word for all future generations to see. Since the observance of neither *Purim* nor *Chanukkah* are commanded by God, we put both festivals in the "Traditional" category.
2. Eliezer Berkovits, *Not in Heaven: The Nature and Function of Halakha* (New York: KTAV Publishing House, 1983), pp. 1–2.
3. See Num. 28:11. Even traditional Jewish scholars concur that the Lord commanded only one day of *Rosh Chodesh* to be observed: "In the Torah only one *Rosh Chodesh* is prescribed—the first day of the new month" (Eliyahu Kitov, *The Book of Our Heritage: The Jewish Year and Its Days of Significance* [New York: Feldheim Publishers, 1978], vol. 1, p. 241).
4. See Exod. 12:2.
5. The historical origin of the Tishri 1 new year is found in the return of the Jewish people from Babylonian exile. Tishri 1 was the new year of the Babylonian calendar. The following table details the correlation between the biblical and traditional month orders:

Month	Biblical Order	Traditional Order
Nisan	1	7
Iyyar	2	8
Sivan	3	9
Tammuz	4	10
Av	5	11
Elul	6	12
Tishri	7	1
Cheshvan	8	2
Kislev	9	3
Tevet	10	4
Shevat	11	5
Adar (I/II)	12	6

The rabbinical view that Tishri 1 was Noah's new year is not based on Scripture, but on a mystical interpretation of the first Hebrew word of Genesis (*Berey'shit* inverted reads Tishri 1).

6. When Lev. 23:11 is read in the context of 23:15–16, it is clear that *Bikkurim* (Feast of First Fruits) and *Shavu'ot* (Feast of Weeks) occur on the same day of the week but 49 days apart. *Shavu'ot* falls on "the day after the seventh sabbath" (v.16). That the weekly Sabbath is meant here is self-evident since one cannot find seven festival sabbaths leading up to the month of Sivan. Thus, *Shavu'ot* must occur on the day after Saturday (i.e. Sunday; beginning Saturday evening). If *Shavu'ot* always falls on a Sunday, then counting backwards 49 days, *Bikkurim* must also fall on a Sunday, and in the middle of *Matzot* (Feast of Unleavened Bread) week. The Messianic Jewish community seeks to uphold the plain meaning of Scripture whenever possible and does not recognize the authority of Oral Law interpretation (see endnote 7). Such are the principles that must govern the determination of the dating of *Bikkurim.* The traditional practice of dating *Bikkurim* on Nissan 16 is Pharisaic in origin and based on the Oral Law. In contrast, the early believers observed *Bikkurim* and the period of *Sefirat Ha'Omer* (Counting the Omer) from the Sunday after Passover (J. Van Goudoever, *Biblical Calendars,* Leiden: E. J. Brill, 1961, pp. 164–175). This was also the practice of the Sadducees (who oversaw the Temple service), the Boethusians, the Samaritans and the Karaites (Norman Snaith, *The Jewish New Year Festival: Its Origins and Development,* London: Society for Promoting Christian Knowledge, pp. 125–127). A final argument in support of the Nazarene position is that Leviticus 23 provides exact dates for all of God's appointed times except *Bikkurim* and *Shavu'ot.* If Nisan 16 and Sivan 6 were the correct dates for celebrating these festivals, surely the Lord would have made this explicit in the Scriptures, but he did not. Rather, the Lord taught Israel how to calculate the times of these festivals, implying that the festival dates changed each year. Notable Jewish scholars support the above conclusion. See Baruch Levine, *Leviticus, The JPS Torah Commentary* (New York: The Jewish Publication Society, 1989), p. 159; and Harold Louis Ginsberg, "The Grain Harvest Laws of Leviticus 23:9–22 and Numbers 28:26–31," ed. S.W. Baron and I.E. Barzilay, *American Academy for Jewish Research* (Jerusalem: AAJR, 1980), Jubilee Volume, p. 146.
7. "Traditional Judaism teaches that the *Tanakh* (Hebrew Scriptures) *and* the *Talmud* are God's Eternal Word, that the New Testament lacks this authority, and that Yeshua is not the Messiah. Messianic Judaism, in contrast, teaches that the *Tanakh* and the New Testament Scriptures together are God's Eternal Word, that the *Talmud* lacks this authority, and that Yeshua is the Messiah"
8. David J. Rudolph, *The Back to the Torah Calendar Supplement,* 1996.

Appendix C

Synagogue Reading Cycle

Each week, in synagogues throughout the world, a portion of the Scriptures is read from the *Torah* and the *Nevi'im* (the Law and the Prophets).[1] These readings serve as Israel's primary source for hearing the Word of God. Two-thirds of the *Torah* and *Haftarah* (prophetic) readings are thematically related. The other one third can often be linked to upcoming festivals or commemorations. [2] Relevant portions from the *Ketuvim* (Writings) [3] are also read during special holiday occasions.

Because of its devotional significance to our people, the synagogue reading cycle has been included in this book. To help the reader identify a given week's *sidra* (section), all *sidrot* (sections) have been coded and keyed to the following charts. You will notice these codes if you look next to the Gregorian date of each Sabbath. The numbers identify the *Torah* and *Haftarah* readings. Capital letters identify any additional or replacement readings. Festival readings are noted by a *mem* (מ) which is the first Hebrew letter of the word for "appointed times" (*mo'adim*).

In addition to the traditional readings, *Brit Chadashah* (New Covenant) readings for Sabbaths and festivals are also included.[4]

A Schedule for Intercession!

Do you intercede for Israel's salvation? If not, the synagogue reading cycle, like an alarm clock, can wake you up to this most important responsibility. It will remind you of the seasons when many of our people around the world are turning their hearts to God in prayer, repentance and meditation on his Word. These are the ideal times to pray for our people—marvelous windows of opportunity to send our prayers heavenward. Let us remember that the best time to pray for Israel is when Israel is praying.

When we see the synagogue readings for the Sabbath noted in this devotional, let us intercede that Yeshua would be revealed to our people through Moses and the Prophets.

When we see the synagogue readings for the New Moon noted in this devotional, let us intercede that Yeshua would be revealed to our people on this day of new beginnings.

When we see the synagogue readings for God's appointed times noted in this devotional, let us intercede that Yeshua would be revealed to our people on these days of meeting with the Lord.

When we see the synagogue readings for traditional fasts noted in this devotional, let us intercede that Yeshua would be revealed to our people on these days of repentance.

By viewing the synagogue reading cycle as a schedule for intercession, the Messianic Jewish community and the worldwide body of believers can together, in one accord, pray for the spiritual *shalom* (peace) of Jerusalem. If we pray for Israel when Israel is praying, the Lord will most certainly hear our cries, and pour out his Spirit of grace and supplication on our people. Let us devote ourselves wholeheartedly to this endeavor, that Yeshua would return soon and establish Jerusalem as a *beyt tefillah* (house of prayer) for all nations (Isa. 56:7).

Chart 1—Weekly Scripture Readings

***Torah* (Law), *Haftarah* (Prophets) and *Brit Chadashah* (New Covenant) readings for the Sabbath & New Moon**

#	Section	Translation	Torah	Haftarah	Brit Chadashah
1	*Berey'shit*[1]	In the beginning	Gen. 1:1–6:8	Isa. 42:5–43:10	John 1:1–5
2	*Noach*	Noah	Gen. 6:9–11:32	Isa. 54:1–55:5	1 Pet. 3:18–22
3	*Lekh lekha*	Go forth, yourself!	Gen. 12:1–17:27	Isa. 40:27–41:16	Rom. 4:1–25
4	*Vayyera*	And he appeared	Gen. 18:1–22:24	2 Kings 4:1–37	2 Pet. 2:4–11
5	*Chayyey Sarah*	Life of Sarah	Gen. 23:1–25:18	1 Kings 1:1–31	1 Cor. 15:50–57
6	*Toledot*	Generations	Gen. 25:19–28:9	Mal. 1:1–2:7	Rom. 9:6–13
7	*Vayyetze*	And he went out	Gen. 28:10–32:2(3)[2]	Hos. 11:7–14:9(10)	John 1:43–51
8	*Vayyishlach*	And he sent	Gen. 32:3(4)–36:43	Obad. 1–21; Hos. 11:7–12:12	Matt. 26:36–46
9	*Vayyeshev*	And he settled	Gen. 37:1–40:23	Amos 2:6–3:8	Acts 7:9–16
10	*Mikketz*	At the end of	Gen. 41:1–44:17	1 Kings 3:15–4:1	1 Cor. 2:1–5
11	*Vayyiggash*	And he drew near	Gen. 44:18–47:27	Ezek. 37:15–28	Luke 6:9–16
12	*Vayyechi*	And he lived	Gen. 47:28–50:26	1 Kings 2:1–12	1 Pet. 1:3–9
13	*Shemot*	Names	Exod. 1:1–6:1	Isa. 27:6–28:13; 29:22–23; Jer. 1:1–2:3	Acts 7:17–29
14	*Va'eyra*	And I appeared	Exod. 6:2–9:35	Ezek. 28:25–29:21	Rom. 9:14–24
15	*Bo*	Enter!	Exod. 10:1–13:16	Jer. 46:13–28	1 Cor. 11:20–34
16	*Beshallach*	When he let go	Exod. 13:17–17:16	Judg. 4:4–5:31	John 6:22–40
17	*Yitro*	Jethro	Exod. 18:1–20:23	Isa. 6:1–7:6; 9:5–6	Matt. 5:17–32
18	*Mishpatim*	Judgments	Exod. 21:1–24:18	Jer. 34:8–22; 33:25–26	Matt. 5:38–42
19	*Terumah*	Offering	Exod. 25:1–27:19	1 Kings 5:12(26) –6:13	Matt. 5:33–37
20	*Tetzaveh*	You shall command	Exod. 27:20–30:10	Ezek. 43:10–27	Heb. 13:10–17
21	*Ki tissa*	When you elevate	Exod. 30:11–34:35	1 Kings 18:1–39	1 Cor. 8:4–13
22	*Vayyakheyl*	And he assembled	Exod. 35:1–38:20	1 Kings 7:13–26, 40–50	2 Cor. 9:6–11
23	*Pekudey*	Accountings of	Exod. 38:21–40:38	1 Kings 7:40–8:21	2 Cor. 3:7–18
24	*Vayyikra*	And he called	Lev. 1:1–6:7(5:26)	Isa. 43:21–44:23	Heb. 10:1–18
25	*Tzav*	Command!	Lev. 6:8(1)–8:36	Jer. 7:21–8:3; 9:22–23	Heb. 8:1–6
26	*Shemini*	Eighth	Lev. 9:1–11:47	2 Sam. 6:1–7:17	Acts 10:9–22, 34–35
27	*Tazria*	She bears seed	Lev. 12:1–13:59	2 Kings 4:42–5:19	Matt. 8:1–4
28	*Metzora*	Infected one	Lev. 14:1–15:33	2 Kings 7:3–20	Rom. 6:19–23
29	*Acharey mot*	After the death	Lev. 16:1–18:30	Ezek. 22:1–19	Heb. 9:11–28

#	Section	Translation	Torah	Haftarah	Brit Chadashah[4]
30	*Kedoshim*	Holy ones	Lev. 19:1–20:27	Ezek. 20:2–20; Amos 9:7–15	1 Pet. 1:13–16
31	*Emor*	Say!	Lev. 21:1–24:23	Ezek. 44:15–31	1 Pet. 2:4–10
32	*Behar*	On the Mount	Lev. 25:1–26:2	Jer. 32:6–27	Luke 4:16–21
33	*Bechukkotai*	In my statutes	Lev. 26:3–27:34	Jer. 16:19–17:14	2 Cor. 6:14–18
34	*Bemidbar*	In the wilderness	Num. 1:1–4:20	Hos. 2:1–22	1 Cor. 12:12–20
35	*Naso*	Elevate!	Num. 4:21–7:89	Judg. 13:2–25	Acts 21:17–26
36	*Beha'alotkha*	In your setting up	Num. 8:1–12:16	Zech. 2:14–4:7	1 Cor. 10:6–13
37	*Shelach lekha*	Send for yourself!	Num. 13:1–15:41	Josh. 2:1–24	Heb. 3:7–19
38	*Korach*	Korah	Num. 16:1–18:32	1 Sam. 11:14–12:22	Rom. 13:1–7
39	*Chukkat*	Ordinance of	Num. 19:1–22:1	Judg. 11:1–33	John 3:10–21
40	*Balak*	Balak	Num. 22:2–25:9	Mic. 5:6–6:8	1 Cor. 1:20–31
41	*Pinchas*	Phinehas	Num. 25:10–29:40 (30:1)	1 Kings 18:46–19:21	John 2:13–22
42	*Mattot*	Tribes	Num. 30:1(2)–32:42	Jer. 1:1–2:3	Phil. 3:12–16
43	*Mass'ey*	Journeys of	Num. 33:1–36:13	Jer. 2:4–28; 3:4; 4:1–2	James 4:1–12
44	*Devarim*	Words	Deut. 1:1–3:22	Isa. 1:1–27	1 Tim. 3:1–7
45	*Va'etchanan*	And I pleaded	Deut. 3:23–7:11	Isa. 40:1–26	Mark 12:28–34
46	*Ekev*	As a result	Deut. 7:12–11:25	Isa. 49:14–51:3	Rom. 8:31–39
47	*Re'eh*	See!	Deut. 11:26–16:17	Isa. 54:11–55:5	1 John 4:1–6
48	*Shof'tim*	Judges	Deut. 16:18–21:9	Isa. 51:12–52:12	John 1:19–27
49	*Ki tetze*	When you go out	Deut. 21:10–25:19	Isa. 54:1–10	1 Cor. 5:1–5
50	*Ki tavo*	When you enter in	Deut. 26:1–29:9(8)	Isa. 60:1–22	Acts 7:30–36
51	*Nitzavim*	You are standing	Deut. 29:10(9)–30:20	Isa. 61:10–63:9	Rom. 10:1–13
52	*Vayyelekh*	And he went	Deut. 31:1–30	Isa. 55:6–56:8	Rom. 7:7–12
53	*Ha'azinu*	Give ear!	Deut. 32:1–52	2 Sam. 22:1–51	Rom. 10:14–11:12
54	*Vezo't haberakhah*	And this the blessing	Deut. 33:1–34:12	Josh. 1:1–18	1 Thess. 5:1–11
*	*Mevarchim HaChodesh*	(Proclamation of the New Moon)		Num. 28:1–15 (weekdays and Sunday); Num. 28:9–15 (Sabbaths)	

Note: This chart combines *Ashkenazi* (French, German, Eastern European) and *Sephardi* (Hispanic, Mediterranean, Middle Eastern) readings.

1 *Sidra* (Section) names correspond to the first Hebrew word of the *Torah* portions.

2 Numbers in parentheses refer to the chapter/verse divisions as they appear in the Jewish Bible (*Tanakh*).

Chart 2—Special Sabbath Readings

Special *Torah* readings that are *added* to the regular ones noted in Chart 1 plus special *Haftarah* readings that *replace* the regular ones noted in Chart 1

	Occasion	Additional *Torah*/Replacement *Haftarah*
A	Sabbath & New Moon	Isa. 66:1–24[2]
B	Sabbath preceding New Moon	1 Sam. 20:18–42
C	Sabbath & New Moon (specific months)[1]	Isa. 66:1, 24[2]
D	Sabbath preceding New Moon (specific months)	1 Sam. 20:18, 42
E	First Sabbath of *Chanukkah*	Zech. 2:10(14)[3]–4:7
F	Second Sabbath of *Chanukkah*	1 Kings 7:13–26, 40–50
	Sabbath of Vayya'khel (#22) or Pekudey (#23)	1 Kings 7:13–26 (#22); 1 Kings 7:40–50 (#23)
G	Sabbath of *Acharey mot* (#29)	Amos 9:7–15; Ezek. 22:1–16
H	Sabbath of *Kedoshim* (#30)	Amos 9:7–15; Ezek. 20:2–20
I	Sabbath after the Fast of Tammuz	Jer. 1:1–2:3
J	Second Sabbath after the Fast of Tammuz	Jer. 2:4–28; 3:4; 4:1–2
K	*Shabbat Shuvah* (Sabbath during the Days of Awe)	Hos. 14:2–9(10); Mic. 7:18–20; Joel 2:15–27
L	*Shabbat Shekalim* (Sabbath preceding Adar 1)	Exod. 30:11–16; 2 Kings 11:17–12:16 (17)
M	*Shabbat Zachor* (Sabbath preceding *Purim*)	Deut. 25:17–19; 1 Sam. 15:1–34
N	*Shabbat Parah* (Sabbath preceding *Shabbat HaChodesh*)	Num. 19:1–22; Ezek. 36:16–38
O	*Shabbat HaChodesh* (Sabbath preceding Nisan 1)	Exod. 12:1–20; Ezek. 45:16–46:18
P	*Shabbat HaGadol* (Sabbath preceding Passover)	Mal. 3:4–4:6(3:24)
*	*Mevarchim HaChodesh* (proclamation of the New Moon)	Num. 28:1–15 (weekdays and Sundays); Num. 28:9–15 (Sabbaths)

Note: This chart combines *Ashkenazi* (French, German, Eastern European) and *Sephardi* (Hispanic, Mediterranean, Middle Eastern) readings.

1 When the New Moon occurs on *Re'eh* (#47), many congregations recite *Haftarah* A instead of C. The regular *Haftarah* for *Re'eh* is then added to the *Haftarah* of *Ki Tetze* (#49) two weeks later.

2 Num. 28:9–15 is also read in addition to the regular *Torah* portion.

3 Numbers in parentheses refer to the chapter/verse divisions as they appear in the Jewish Bible (*Tanakh*).

Chart 3—Festival Scripture Readings (מ: "*mo'adim*" or festival)

Torah **(Law),** ***Haftarah*** **(Prophets), Five** ***Megillot*** **(Scrolls) and** ***Brit Chadashah*** **(New Covenant) Readings for Festivals and Minor Fast Days**

DATE	FESTIVAL	TORAH	HAFTARAH	BRIT CHADASHAH
TISHRI				
1–2	***Rosh HaShanah*** (the New Year)			
	Day 1	Gen. 21:1–34; Num. 29:1–6	1 Sam. 1:1–2:10	1 Thess. 4:13–18
	Day 2	Gen. 22:1–24; Num. 29:1–6	Jer. 31:1–19	Heb. 11:17–19
10	***Yom Kippur*** (the Day of Atonement)			
	Morning	Lev. 16:1–34; Num. 29:7–11	Isa. 57:14–58:14	Rom. 3:21–26
	Afternoon	Lev. 18:1–30	Jonah; Mic. 7:18–20	Heb. 10:1–12
15–21	***Sukkot*** (the Feast of Tabernacles)			
	Day 1	Lev. 22:26–23:44; Num. 29:12–16	Zech. 14:1–21	Rev. 21:1–4
	Day 2	Lev. 22:26–23:44; Num. 29:12–19	1 Kings 8:2–21	John 1:10–14
	Day 3	Num. 29:17–25		
	Day 4	Num. 29:20–28		
	Day 5	Num. 29:23–31		
	Day 6	Num. 29:26–34		
	Day 7 (***Hosha'na Rabbah***)	Num. 29:26–34		John 7:37–44
	Intermediate Day Sabbath	Exod. 33:12–34:26 (+ daily reading)[1,2]	Ezek. 38:18–39:16	1 Thess. 5:1–11
22	***Shemini Atzeret*** (the 8th Day Assembly)	Deut. 14:22–16:17; Num. 29:35–30:1	1 Kings 8:54–66	Mark 12:28–33

DATE	FESTIVAL	TORAH	HAFTARAH	BRIT CHADASHAH
TISHRI, Continued				
22/23	***Simchat Torah*** (the Joy of the *Torah*)	Deut. 33:1–34:12; Gen. 1:1–2:3; Num. 29:35–30:1	Josh. 1:1–18	Rom. 7:21–25
KISLEV				
25–TEVET 2/3	***Chanukkah*** (the Feast of Dedication)			
	Day 1	Num. 7:1–17		John 10:22–24
	Day 2	Num. 7:18–29		
	Day 3	Num. 7:24–35		
	Day 4	Num. 7:30–41		
	Day 5	Num. 7:36–47		
	Day 6	Num. 7:42–53 + (New Moon readings*)		
	Day 7	Num. 7:48–59 (if a New Moon, read Num. 7:48–53 + see below*)		
	Day 8	Num. 7:54–8:4		
	First Sabbath	Weekly *Torah* Readings (Chart 1) +(daily reading)[3]	Zech. 2:10(14)[4]–4:7	
	Second Sabbath	Weekly *Torah* Readings (Chart 1) +Num. 7:54–8:4	1 Kings 7:13–26, 40–50	
ADAR				
14–15	***Purim*** (the Feast of Lots)	Exod. 17:8–16[2]		
NISAN				
15–22	***Pesach*** (Passover)			
	Day 1	Exod. 12:21–51; Num. 28:16–25	Josh. 3:5–7; 5:2–6:1, 27	Luke 22:7–20
	Day 2	Lev. 22:26–23:44; Num. 28:16–25	2 Ki. 23:1–9, 21–25	

DATE	FESTIVAL	TORAH	HAFTARAH	BRIT CHADASHAH
NISAN, Continued				
15–22	***Pesach*** (Passover), Continued			
	Day 3	Exod. 13:1–16; Num. 28:19–25		
	Day 4	Exod. 22:24(25)–23:19; Num. 28:19–25		
	Day 5	Exod. 34:1–26; Num. 28:19–25		
	Day 6	Num. 9:1–14; 28:19–25		
	Day 7	Exod. 13:17–15:26; Num. 28:19–25	2 Sam. 22:1–51	Rev. 15:1–4
	Day 8	Deut. 15:19–16:17 (on Sabbath—Deut. 14:22–16:17); Num. 28:19–25	Isa. 10:32–12:6	
	Intermediate Day Sabbath	Exod. 33:12–34:26; Num. 28:19–25[2]	Ezek. 36:37–37:14	1 Cor. 5:6–8
SIVAN				
6–7	***Shavu'ot*** (the Feast of Weeks)			
	Day 1	Exod. 19:1–20:26 (23); Num. 28:26–31[2]	Ezek. 1:1–28; 3:12	Acts 2:1–21, 37–41
	Day 2	Deut. 15:19–16:17 (on Sabbath—Deut. 14:22–16:17); Num. 28:26–31	Hab. 2:20–3:19	
NEW MOON				
*	***Mevarchim HaChodesh*** (Proclamation of the New Moon)	Num. 28:1–15 (weekdays and Sundays); Num. 28:9–15 (Sabbaths)		

Minor Fast Days

Date	Fast	Torah	Haftarah	Brit Chadashah
Tishri 3[5]	***Tzom Gedaliah*** (the Fast of Gedaliah)	Exod. 32:11–14; 34:1–10	Isa. 55:6–56:8	Matt. 6:16–18; Luke 2:36–37
Tevet 10	***Asarah BeTevet*** (10th of Tevet)	Exod. 32:11–14; 34:1–10	Isa. 55:6–56:8	Matt. 6:16–18; Luke 2:36–37
Adar 13	***Ta'anit Ester*** (the Fast of Esther)	Exod. 32:11–14; 34:1–10	Isa. 55:6–56:8	Matt. 6:16–18; Luke 2:36–37
Tammuz 17	***Shivah Asar BeTammuz*** (the 17th of Tammuz)	Exod. 32:11–14; 34:1–10	Isa. 55:6–56:8	Matt. 6:16–18; Luke 2:36–37
Av 9	***Tishah Be'Av*** (the 9th of Av)			
	Morning	Deut. 4:25–40	Jer. 8:13–9:24(23)	Matt. 23:16–23; 24:1–2
	Afternoon	Exod. 32:11–14; 34:1–10[2]	Isa. 55:6–56:8; Hos. 14:2–9(10); Mic. 7:18–20	

Note: This chart combines *Ashkenazi* (French, German, Eastern European) and *Sephardi* (Hispanic, Mediterranean, Middle Eastern) readings.

1 Day 1 (Num. 29:17–22); Day 2 (Num. 29:20–25); Day 4 (Num. 29:26–31).

2 The Five *Megillot* (Scrolls) are read on the following festivals: *Sukkot* (Ecclesiastes); *Purim* (Esther); *Pesach* (Song of Solomon); *Shavu'ot* (Ruth); *Tish'ah Be'Av* (Lamentations).

3 Day 1 (Num. 7:1–17); Day 2 (Num. 7:18–23); Day 3 (Num. 7:24–29); Day 4 (Num. 7:30–35); Day 5 (Num. 7:36–41); Day 6 (Num. 28:9–15; 7:42–47); Day 7 (Num. 7:48–53; on a New Moon, add Num. 28:9–15).

4 Numbers in parentheses refer to the chapter/verse divisions as they appear in the Jewish Bible (*Tanakh*).

5 When a minor fast day falls on the Sabbath (a day of celebration), it is moved to the following Sunday, with the exception of *Ta'anit Ester* (Fast of Esther) and *Ta'anit Bekhorim* (Fast of the Firstborn) which are moved to the preceding Thursday.

Endnotes

1. The present day synagogue reading cycle is annual and of Babylonian Jewish origin. The more ancient reading cycle was probably triennial and of Jerusalem origin (Megillah 29b; 23a; iv.2, 4). See Aileen Guilding, *The Fourth Gospel and Jewish Worship: A Study of the Relation of St. John's Gospel to the Ancient Jewish Lectionary System* (Oxford: At the Clarendon Press, 1960), pp. 8–10. In response to Guilding, see J. R. Porter, "The Pentateuch and the Triennial Lectionary Cycle," *Promise and Fulfillment* (Essays presented to S. H. Hooke, ed. F. F. Bruce, Edinburgh, 1963); L. Morris, *The New Testament and the Jewish Lectionaries* (London, 1964); L. Crockett, "Luke 4:16–30 and the Jewish Lectionary Cycle," JJS xvii (1966), pp. 13ff; and J. Heinemann, "The Triennial Lectionary Cycle," JJS xviii (1968), pp. 41ff; David Rosenberg, *The Mystery of the Torah/Haftarah Cycle: The Babylonian Torah Cycle in the Open Text of Luke 3 & 4* (Baldwin: Congregation Shuva Israel, 1997).
2. Alfred J. Kolatch, *This is the Torah* (Middle Village: Jonathan David Publishers, 1994), p. 250. Kolatch's book answers many questions about the synagogue reading cycle.
3. The *Ketuvim* (Writings) include the following books: Psalms, Proverbs, Job, Song of Solomon, Ruth, Lamentations, Ecclesiastes, Esther, Daniel, Ezra, Nehemiah and 1 & 2 Chronicles.
4. The *Brit Chadashah* (New Covenant Scripture) readings were taken from the *Messianic Jewish Art Calendar 1998–1999 (5759)* Baltimore: Messianic Jewish Publishers, ©1998.

Index